Truly
Wilde

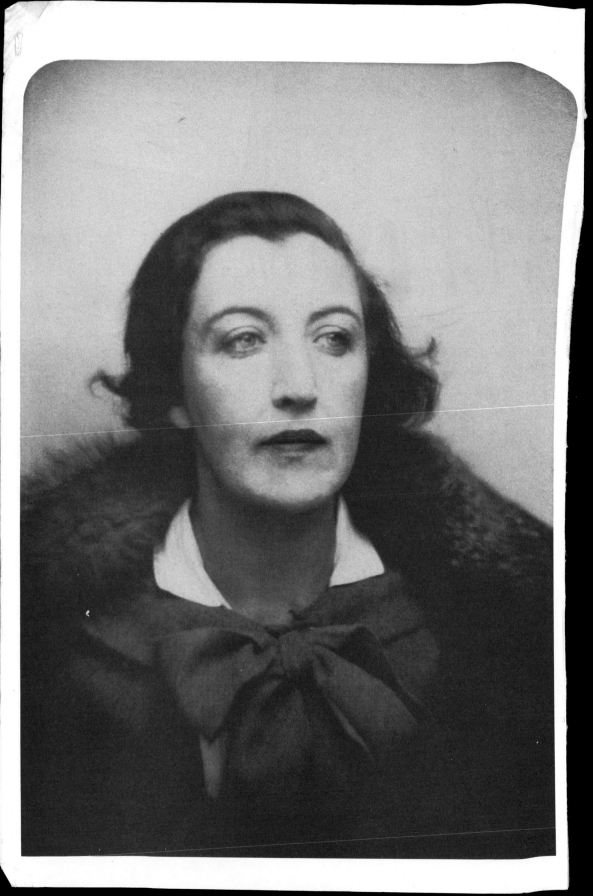

Truly Wilde

The Unsettling Story
of Dolly Wilde,
Oscar's Unusual Niece

JOAN SCHENKAR

DA CAPO PRESS

All photographs and drawings in this book © JM Schenkar, except for the following:
Eugene and Angela Power © photo page 1 of plate section, top right
Cara Lancaster © photos page 2 top left; all on page 3 and 4, page 10 bottom
George Wickes © photos page 2 bottom left; page 5 bottom right; page 7 top
Cecil Beaton Archives, Sotheby's © photos page 2 top right, bottom right
Topham Picturepoint © photo page 9 center right
Hervé Fauchier Delavigne © photo page 9 top right
Camera Press Ltd © bottom page 13

Cataloging-in-Publication data for this book is available from the Library of Congress.

First Da Capo Press edition 2001
Reprinted by arrangement with Basic Books.
First published in Great Britain by Virago Press 2000.
ISBN: 0-306-81079-4

Typeset in Centaur by M Rules

Da Capo Press books are available at special discounts for bulk purchases in the U.S. by corporations, institutions, and other organizations. For more information, please contact the Special Markets Department at the Perseus Books Group, 11 Cambridge Center, Cambridge, MA 02142, or call (617) 252-5298.

1 2 3 4 5 6 7 8 9 10—05 04 03 02 01

With love and gratitude,
for Berthe Cleyrergue
(1904-1998)

I believe life could be one delightful sensation after another – I really do!

Dolly Wilde

Your life has hurt me more than all the lives
That living long with love has gathered
round my hearth . . .

Natalie Clifford Barney

ERNEST: *Life then is a failure?*
GILBERT: *From the artistic point of view, certainly.*

Oscar Wilde

Contents

A Few of the Principal Players

Natalie Clifford Barney (1876–1972): She could have been the heroine of a Henry James novel: a ruling-class American millionaire with compelling, blonde good looks, perfected French grammar and style, incredible self-assurance, and the will to sustain a subversive Modernist salon in the heart of literary Paris for most of the twentieth century. She was a notoriously successful seducer of women and the friend of every interesting male writer in Paris. And she was deeply involved with Dolly Wilde.

Oscar Wilde (1854–1900): The Lord of Language and the Pied Piper of Literature. He belonged to the 'first' Wilde family and came to disdain his dissolute brother Willie, Dolly's father. His three trials for 'gross indecency' in 1895 ended the most interesting literary career of the 1890s. His life, his looks, and some of his times were strangely recapitulated in the salon performances of his niece Dorothy.

Willie Wilde (1852–1899): Oscar's improvident elder brother and Dolly's father. He was the leader writer for the *Daily Telegraph*; his habits of working in the *Telegraph* newsroom stripped to the waist and of turning in his copy at the last probable moment after the most possible consumption of alcohol did not seem to affect his prose style. His motto when in New York: 'What America needs is a leisure class and I am determined to introduce one.'

Sophia 'Lily' Lees Wilde (1859–1922): Dolly's mysterious Irish mother. Her chief passion was for literary gentlemen – and she seemed to be fonder of Oscar Wilde, who had paid for her daughter's birth, than she was of Oscar's brother Willie, who was her husband. She had a happy second marriage with Alexander Teixeira de Mattos, the distinguished translator of Maeterlinck, but left no records – and no mention – of Dolly's childhood.

Lady Jane Wilde (1821–1896): Oscar's and Willie's mother, and Dolly's paternal grandmother, she was known as 'Speranza', the fiery feminist and famously outspoken Irish nationalist poet and writer. After her marriage, she kept the best literary salon at the best address in Dublin. She was the real originator of the 'Wilde style' and her tastes for outlandish costumes and extreme statements were inherited by both her sons and by her granddaughter.

Tancred Borenius (1885–1946): 'As adroit as a seal' and just as slippery, Tancred Borenius sold paintings to the very rich and held court in the cafés of Bohemia. He was the editor of the *Burlington Magazine* and a witty polymath. Sometimes reluctantly and not at all consistently, he acted as Dolly's 'guardian'. It was through Tancred Borenius that Dolly gained entry to the Stately Homes of England.

The Harris Family: Lady Cara Harris, married to the banker Sir Austin Harris, was the daughter of the only woman to have slept with both Edward VII *and* Radclyffe Hall – and she was a Surrealist prankster, painter and film maker. Her eldest daughter, Pamela 'Honey' Harris, 'born of a Prince and a spinster,' said Dolly, was Dolly's dearest friend; the distinguished cartoonist and set designer Osbert Lancaster, who also adored Dolly, was a son-in-law; and Dolly spent much time in the Harris households. The Harris family had a long, fated association with all the Wildes.

20 Rue Jacob: The legendary, dimly lit *pavillon*, at the back of a cobbled courtyard on the Left Bank, where Natalie Barney entertained most of literary Paris for more than six decades. The *pavillon* was bounded on three sides by an unusually large, unusually neglected, wild garden, where Racine was supposed to have strolled with his mistress *La Champsmesle* and where Natalie staged *tableaux vivants*, pacifist meetings, and personal dramas. Dolly spent much of her time in Paris at 20 rue Jacob, charming the literate and the luxurious in the salon — and working out her complicated relations with Natalie in other rooms.

Some of the Witnesses

Djuna Barnes (1892–1982): The brilliant journalist/painter/poet/author of *Nightwood* — and the Emily Brontë of Modernism. Djuna maintained a lifelong connection with Natalie Barney and an unremitting rivalry with Dolly. In 1928 she wrote the *Ladies Almanack*, an elaborate, encoded satire of Barney's Sapphic circle in which Dolly Wilde was portrayed as the sexually enslaved teller of tales, 'Doll Furious'.

Bettina Bergery (1902-1993): One of the three beautiful American Jones girls for whom the phrase 'keeping up with the Joneses' was actually invented, she worked for the fashion house of Schiaparelli and married Gaston Bergery. Bettina was an habitué of Natalie Barney's salon and one of the best raconteuses in Paris. Her descriptions of Dolly Wilde and Natalie Barney are as sharp as cut glass.

Cecil Beaton (1904–1980): The premier photographer and social alpinist of his time. His waspish stories and sympathetic photographs provide a double exposure of Dolly's possibilities. Beaton appeared in one of Lady Cara Harris's films, the one in which Dolly played a 'Venal Ballroom Agent' and he enacted the roles of frumpy dowager and earnest Girl Guide.

Truman Capote (1924–1984): The twenty-three-year-old 'literary lion' of the Paris winter season of 1948 and a frequenter of Natalie Barney's salon. His description of what he heard and saw in Barney's inner circle summed up all that was left of the seductive circle of wit, beauty, and intrigue that enveloped Dolly Wilde when she first joined the 'Knights of Natalie's Round Table'. Barney thought Capote was 'a one-book boy'.

Berthe Cleyrergue (1904–1998): *Gouvernante* of the Barney salon for forty years, famous cook, confidante, and source of emotional support to Natalie Barney, Dolly Wilde, Colette, Janet Flanner, Djuna Barnes et al., she kept many of the secrets of the salon in her head and all of its pictures in her photograph albums. Berthe always said that Dolly Wilde was the most wonderful and charming of all the charming, wonderful women who came to 20 rue Jacob.

Victor Cunard (1898-1960): Writer Nancy Cunard's witty cousin, he was the London *Times* correspondent in Venice, and one of Dolly's best friends. At twenty he had an affair with Vita Sackville-West's husband, Harold Nicolson. Cunard was one of many men who proposed marriage to Dolly; he had a lunch date with her on the day of her death, and wrote her obituary for the London *Times*. His humour, said Sir Harold Acton, was 'fraught with infectious malice'.

Elisabeth Eyre de Lanux (1894–1996): An American painter, sculptor, writer, furniture maker and photographer of decided talent and legendary beauty, she married a French diplomat, moved to 20 rue Jacob and was early on drawn into the doings in the *pavillon* at the back of her courtyard. Louis Aragon and Pierre Drieu La Rochelle were both in love with her and, at 102, she was the last survivor of the Barney salons and Dolly's last, 'living' rival.

Janet Flanner (1892–1978): Author of the *New Yorker* magazine's bi-monthly 'Letter From Paris' column for fifty years under the *nom de plume* of Gênet, Janet Flanner was a member of Barney's circle, and an extraordinarily acute observer of the French artistic and social *mise en scène*. But her interest in Dolly Wilde was not strictly artistic and she wrote about Dolly with the astuteness of an essayist and the authority of a lover.

The Company

Mercedes de Acosta, Sylvia Beach, Germaine Beaumont, Jean Bourgoint, Romaine Brooks, Lady Carnarvon, Joe Carstairs, the duchesse de Clermont-Tonnerre, Jean Cocteau, Arthur Cravan, Nancy Cunard, Adrian Daintrey, Lucie Delarue-Mardrus, 'Emily', Gwen Farrar, Marcelle Fauchier Delavigne, Antoinette Gentien, Rémy de Gourmont, Radclyffe Hall, Rosamond Harcourt-Smith, Allanah Harper, Vyvyan Holland, Nadine Hwang, Edmond Jaloux, Zita Jungman, Viva King, Osbert Lancaster, Mina Loy, Toupie Lowther, Dan Mahoney, Elsa Maxwell, Esther Murphy, Alla Nazimova, Liane de Pougy, Jacques Rigaut, Osbert Sitwell, Ethel Smyth, Gertrude Stein, Stephen Tennant, Alice B. Toklas, Paul Valéry, Renée Vivien, Dr Charlotte Wolff, Virginia Woolf.

1

Exits
And
Entrances

I

Atlantis Rising:
an Introduction

*I am a darting trout; shifting, glancing & flashing my
iridescent tail in a hundred pleasant pools! . . .*

*How long I shall keep in the path of virtue I can't say but
virtue with an object is so much more salutary than virtue
with its own reward!*

Dolly Wilde, Letters to Natalie Barney

She looked, said everyone who knew them both, remarkably
like her uncle Oscar. She had the same artfully posed, soft,
white hands, the same elongated face, and the same air of indolent
melancholy which Aristotle insisted was always the natural accom-
paniment of wit.

She spoke remarkably like her uncle too or, rather, like a brilliantly *female* version of Oscar — for there was nothing parodically
male about Dolly Wilde. And although she would occasionally dress
up as her uncle in borrowed, too-tight pants, a great flowing tie and
a famously ratty fur coat (perhaps it was Oscar's favourite coat after
all, the one Dolly's father Willie was supposed to have pawned when

Oscar was imprisoned), she looked most like Oscar Wilde when she was dressed up as herself: a beautiful, dreamy-eyed, paradoxical woman — wonderfully stylish and intermittently unkempt, spiritually illuminated and clearly *mondaine*. She stares out at us from her few significant photographs with a distinctly contemporary gaze; conscious of the camera, casual about her audience.

For sixty years she was a delicious rumour: Oscar Wilde's enchanting niece Dorothy, born in 1895, a scant three months after her uncle's notorious trials and shameful imprisonment. In titled, artistic, and carefully closeted circles in Paris and London and Hollywood, stories of the outrageous things Dorothy Ierne Wilde said and did were passed around like canapés at a book launch. Photographed by Cecil Beaton and the Baron de Meyer, adored by the Sitwells, the Cunards, and French Academicians such as Edmond Jaloux, attracting people of taste and talent wherever she went, Dolly Wilde was almost, as her friend Janet Flanner wrote, 'like a character out of a book . . . like someone one had become familiar with by reading, rather than by knowing' — too literary, in short, to be believed.[1]

Although she could only have been produced by the follies and grandeurs of the 1920s and the 1930s, Dolly Wilde seems sensationally contemporary. Her tastes for cutting-edge conversation and 'emergency seductions' (as she called the sexual adventures which she applied like unguent to her emotional wounds), for fast cars and foreign films, for experimental literature and alcoholic actresses, are still right up to the minute, and it is too easy to forget that she has been dead — and deader still for being unnoticed — these sixty years.

Stories of Dolly's life usually start out with stories about other people's lives — her uncle Oscar's fabled conversation, the duchesse de Clermont-Tonnerre's *bal masqué*, Natalie Clifford Barney's famous salon — because Dolly Wilde always did.[2] She adored listening to people, a trait which everyone said came from her fatal *paresse*, her indolence. And while it flattered her friends to have such a brilliant speaker listening so brilliantly to them — for Dolly was surely the world's most active audience — this tendency of hers to delay things was the first drug that imprisoned her early on. Like many fascinating people, Dolly was easily fascinated. Charming herself, she could be charmed into putting off anything, even the narratives she loved so much.

'Go on,' Dolly would say to her friend Victor Cunard, the London *Times* correspondent in Venice, as he hesitated between the irresistible desire to pour out his secret life to her and the fully justified fear that his secret would be instantly betrayed.[3] 'Go on,' she would say disarmingly in her 'bird-charmer's' voice to the *New Yorker* magazine writer Janet Flanner, who was telling her a particularly violent fairy tale, 'but tell it slowly, tell every word so that it will last longer.'[4] Dolly Wilde's life was full of such interesting, unfinished, delayed relationships through which she was sometimes tempted to try and fulfill herself.

Although Dolly often behaved like a luxury item let loose in a lavish era — treating even the *maisons de santé* where she was regularly disintoxicated like private suites in European spas — her family had undergone a famously public deconstruction. Her mother was left so impoverished that she could not afford to keep her at home; whatever her father possessed in the way of character had dissolved itself in alcohol by the time she was born; her uncle's dirty linen had been washed in every scandal sheet in Europe. Unlike her family, however, Dolly herself kept many secrets, telling — such was the refinement of her indiscretions — only the ones in which *she* was not involved.

For someone who loved stories as much as Dolly did — loved telling them, loved hearing them, loved their facts, their fictions, and all their complications — she was strangely silent on the subject of her own childhood. All her life, she avoided talking about her early years, and she resolutely refused to supply herself with a 'history'. Like most self-created people, she was infinitely more comfortable without the inconvenient explanations supplied by an actual, painful past.

There was only one anecdote from her childhood that Dolly Wilde ever told, and she only told it once. But with unerring instinct she told it to the best raconteuse in Paris, Bettina Bergery. And Bergery —

wife of the French diplomat Gaston Bergery and originally one of the three beautiful Jones girls for whom the phrase 'keeping up with the Joneses' had actually been invented – remembered the appalling little vignette for the rest of her life and wrote it down.

What Dolly told Bettina Bergery was this: when Dolly was very young, she used to like to take lumps of sugar, dip them in her pretty mother Lily's perfume, and eat them.[5]

Like Lord Goring, her uncle Oscar's theatrical double in *An Ideal Husband* (still playing in London without Oscar's name on it just before Dolly's birth in July 1895), and a lot like Oscar himself, Dolly Wilde appears to stand 'in immediate relation to modern life'. Her attachment to transgressive art, her talent for engaging the people who were creating it, put Dolly in the centre of whatever was exciting in Paris – where she lived around the corner from the hotel Oscar died in – and in London – where she died around the corner from the hotel Oscar stayed in.

But all the qualities which make Dolly seem so contemporary were underscored by a very characteristic exception. Dolly Wilde was one of the Beautiful Losers: a legendarily gifted speaker whose talent was large, whose expression was private, and whose friends, lovers, and enemies all ended by wringing their respective hands over her squandered gifts and lost opportunities. In our millennial world of hard-eyed achievers, the romantic prodigality Dolly came to exemplify – perfect for decades like the 1920s and the 1960s which dedicated themselves to excess, rapture, and the supervening laws of love – has been written almost entirely out of the books. A heroine of our time would never wheedle her rent, burn up her opportunities, or drench her prodigious talents in liquids and chemicals – at least not for very long. A superficial look at Dolly's life tempts us to criticise it, recommending a bracing stay at Betty Ford and a serious chat with a financial adviser.

Possessing many of the gifts that might have carried her into the Winners' Circle and displaying much of the style that would have made her journey there an elegant one, Dolly refused to keep her eyes on the prize. She presents an almost perverse counterpoint to all her grandmother Jane's and uncle Oscar's push and drive and swelling themes of self. Her Wildean talent to amuse did not guide her into the larger world; she ended by dazzling the select and the *soignés* in restaurants and drawing rooms, and by performing for famous writers in fabulous salons. And more regularly than not, Dolly would pour all her literary talents into personal communications and then drop, decoratively, into her correspondents' lives.

'Darling, wait for me with open arms & let me fall breathless into them,' is how she usually put it.[6]

What Dolly lost by dispersing her gifts in private rather than public ways, and the strange values and rewards that inhered to this 'wasting' of her talents, are well worth examining now — and not merely for the contrasts and resemblances they present to the life of her uncle. For Dolly Wilde's life offers a rare opportunity to look at what it means to live with the endowments but not the achievements of biography's usual subjects: those obliterating 'winners' — like Dolly's uncle Oscar — whose notorious stories have almost erased interesting histories like Dolly's own. And the ways in which Dolly carried the Wilde myth forward and what that blighted inheritance did to her own development leave us with yet another interesting 'Wildean' paradox: the serious sense that Oscar Wilde's every gain became his niece Dorothy's permanent and damaging loss.

The ambitious young Irishman who came down from Oxford to London in 1878 with little besides his remark about living up to his blue china to recommend him, was, by the time his niece Dolly was born, 'as well known as the Bank of England',[7] though considerably less solvent. Oscar Wilde had one play, *An Ideal Husband*, running in the West End, another one, *The Importance of Being Earnest*, in rehearsal there, and two well-shod feet in every interesting Mayfair salon. In Mayfair, his presence usually ensured an evening's success and his conversation regularly hypnotised whole drawing rooms-full of eager listeners.

And after his gorgeous drawing-room talk died down, and the last crystal glass of brandy had been drained, Oscar would step through the mirror of his brightly polished remarks into the second, 'secret' act of his social drama. Inspired by the two fundamental principles of all great *provocateurs*, (1) that the best place to hide something is in plain sight and (2) that it is both amusing and profitable to *épater la bourgeoisie*, he appeared in public looking, said his friend the actress Elizabeth Robins, 'as though he would bleed absinthe and clotted truffles', royally ensconced in the centre of a circle of youthful male admirers at the Café Royal. Late into the night, an ageing and antic Oscar — surely the Pied Piper of Literature — would conduct his army of young *poseurs* through conversations as brilliant as he had produced earlier in the evening in Park Lane.

Then, sporting his social violations as outrageously as he displayed his green carnation — and with perhaps the same intention — he would amble through the lobby of the Albemarle Hotel accompanied by a claque of rent boys to whom, generous as ever, he continued to give the benefit of his sparkling repartee, this time adding to it items Mayfair never saw: silver cigarette cases inscribed 'For Services Rendered'.

So annealing was Oscar Wilde's talk that dying friends actually requested his presence at their deathbeds and his wit consoled their mourners like no other person's could. One of his biographers[8] wrote that he was, strictly speaking, a kind of 'healer', for 'the virtue of happiness in him passed into others'. It was said that he exerted linguistic sorceries 'which transmuted the ordinary things of life' and that he lifted the level of living to 'strangeness and glamour'.

Everyone who met Dolly Wilde remarked on the disturbing ways in which she was like her famous uncle. Some people felt that in Dolly's enormous blue-grey eyes and virtuosic wit — so strangely like her uncle's — they were seeing another 'Oscar', born again in female form and playing to a smaller audience. Others discerned in her very public dissolution a woman tragically marked by Oscar's decline and fall. Every comparison between Dolly and Oscar Wilde — right and wrong — returns us to the crucial investigations of our own time.

Who decides on a failure? What determines a success? Why is a woman's fate so essentially different from a man's? 'Shall I', as Dolly Wilde said, 'ever get through life?'[9]

Dolly wrote that clichés, if you consider them 'impartially', are 'apt, concise & accurate'.[10] Oscar Wilde's remark to André Gide (the remark that became Oscar's obituary cliché), that he had put his talent into his work and reserved his genius for his life, can be applied with far greater accuracy to the salon career of Oscar's niece Dorothy — who performed with her life for so many of the artists whose work still 'performs' for us.

Dorothy Wilde was a 'born writer'. She had many of the freedoms and took all of the liberties that were possible for a woman to have and to take in the first forty years of the twentieth century. And none of these was enough to allow her to complete the creative life promised by her famous name, her electric wit and her gorgeous imagination. What happened to Dolly Wilde? And what did her uncanny resemblance to her uncle Oscar have to do with it?

Most of the questions and all of the problems provoked by Dolly Wilde's life are with us still — less certain, now, in their phrasing, and more unmanageable in their form than they were when Dolly was alive. But in her habitual addictions, in her affinity for high fashion and low behaviour, and in the outrageous performances of her myriad and fractioned selves, Dorothy Ierne Wilde sometimes seems like the most modern woman around.

More modern even than Dolly's habits were the exaggerations of her dazzling social character. Charged with charm, brilliantly witty, changeable as refracting light, and loaded with sexual allure, it served to conceal a repetition of hidden horrors. Her birth was badly shadowed by her uncle's infamy; her father drank himself to death when she was a toddler; her impoverished mother left her to an aunt's care and then to a country convent; her closest remaining relative begrudged the very blooms he sent to her funeral.[11]

Much of Dolly's adulthood was spent in the unsuccessful search for a 'home life' with Natalie Clifford Barney, the *salonnière* who was the twentieth century's least monogamous *femme de lettres*, and Dolly failed to find a final form for her brilliant talents. She was fashionably, then horribly, entangled with heroin; she came to use alcohol and every other available drug urgently and often. She never ever had enough money or what Virginia Woolf meant by a Room of Her Own. She died, chillingly, at the same age as her father and her uncle – and of the same addictions. And she died alone.

And yet the impressions Dolly Wilde left upon the people who saw her and heard her and knew her were so indelible that, ten and twenty years after her death, after a war so devastating that everyone's ideas of what it meant to be human were changed for ever, she was still mourned regularly and with real heart. The iridescent bubbles of her humour, her lightning-swift retorts, her devasting arrows of wit, her necromancer's ability to transform the Dull Waters of Daily Life into the Champagne of Real Living, so impressed themselves upon her accomplished friends that they continued to conjure her up – a fabulous fragment here, a sparkling shard there – until a coruscating portrait assembles itself before our eyes; a portrait framed by laments for the brilliant 'something' Dolly Wilde might have written, if only she'd been able to honour her magniloquent talents.

What even Dolly Wilde's closest friends didn't realise, was that she *had* written 'something'. That, in fact, she had been writing 'something' for the last thirteen or fourteen years of her life. For Dolly kept her writing in as covert and as casual a form as she kept her other, less socially acceptable, inclinations. She confined it, for the most part, to a literary genre which has sometimes made reputations (like those of Mme de Sevigné and Mme de Staël – one of Dolly's heroines) but which is more often relegated to the level of domestic employment, the level of 'woman's work'.

Despite this confinement of imagination or because of it, Dolly Wilde's 'secret' writing fulfils some of the promises her famous name makes. Five years ago, in an obscure library in Paris, at the dead end of what seemed to be an evaporating trail of evidence, I came upon a biographer's dream: a cache of more than 200 letters written by

Dorothy Ierne Wilde. The letters are mostly love letters, a genre for which Dolly had all the requisite talents. And they constitute, *faute de mieux*, a fascinating and intermittent form of autobiography. Wonderfully written in themselves, they are, because of Dolly's personal revelations and brilliant renderings of compelling figures of her time, social and personal documents of considerable significance.

The astonishing thing is that these letters — a landmark in the history of a family so notorious that even its laundry lists are set out in best-selling books — were hidden away for sixty years, secreted in a library not noted for its ease of use by the scholars who frequent its archives. Like her life, Dolly's writings have remained inaccessible: unknown, unread, and unpublished. And they are, in their very specific way, as gorgeously figured and concentratedly witty as any work of fiction her celebrated uncle ever wrote. But I am getting ahead of my story.

I think I must have come across *The Amazon of Letters*, by George Wickes, the biography of the *femme de lettres* Natalie Clifford Barney which introduced me to Dolly Wilde, in New York in about 1977. Style and Beauty were everything to me then and so, quite naturally, the beauteous Dolly Wilde, niece of the Emperor of Style, was an appealing subject. Dolly had her own short chapter in George Wickes's book and she came up so vividly on the page, in such a shimmer of charm and bas-relief of brilliance, that I wondered why she'd never been heard of before. With her swift ripostes (when asked what she would do that day, she replied: 'Probably nothing but hesitate'), her luscious hothouse looks (men, women, even children were always falling in love with her), her exotic imitations of Oscar in Parisian salons, and her suicidal gestures of love and extravagance (she was so drawn to death that she actually swallowed an entire bottle of sleeping tablets when she was *unconscious*), her life seemed to strike just the right notes of myth and literature. A real romantic heroine, I thought, but why didn't she *write* something?

I was much more interested in Romaine Brooks, the fabulously rich and enigmatic portrait painter who had been Natalie Barney's lover for fifty-two years and whose demons had at least prodded her to prodigious output. Or in the superior Djuna Barnes, the Emily Brontë of Modernism, who had written my favourite novel and to whom I had actually summoned the nerve to write a letter, in French of course, the language of Colette and Voltaire, the only language worthy of her, a letter I mailed to her publisher shortly before discovering that, despite her long tenure in Paris, Miss Barnes had been too superior even to learn French.

Both of these accomplished women were regular participants in an extraordinary literary salon presided over by its equally extraordinary founder, the American expatriate, belle-lettrist and multi-millionaire, Natalie Clifford Barney. The salon convened for more than fifty years in Paris on what Paul Valéry came to call 'perilous Fridays', until just before Barney's death in 1972. It was, quite simply, the most subversive literary salon that ever existed. Run by an unabashed lesbian who took her own and everyone else's sexual predilections for granted, the Barney salon invited and received only the people Natalie Barney thought were interesting – socially, professionally, and sexually. This was already a revolutionary idea. But Natalie Barney went much further.

In full agreement with her friend Gertrude Stein that 'fathers are depressing', Barney still regularly entertained not only all the great Modernist male writers – Joyce and Proust, Eliot and Valéry, Pound and Eluard – but also recruited, attracted, and showcased all the brilliant female subverters of the Modernist style. Among these extraordinary women were: Natalie Barney herself, Renée Vivien, Colette, the duchesse de Clermont-Tonnerre, Romaine Brooks, Isadora Duncan, Ida Rubenstein, Gertrude Stein, Alice B. Toklas, Lucie Delarue-Mardrus, Mercedes de Acosta, Allanah Harper, Janet Scudder, Sybille Bedford, Esther Murphy, Radclyffe Hall, Una, Lady Troubridge, Bettina Bergery, Djuna Barnes, Marie Laurencin, Mina Loy, Marguerite Yourcenar, Janet Flanner, Elisabeth Eyre de Lanux, and Dorothy Ierne Wilde.

All of these women merit – a few have already had – biographies of their own. Eyre de Lanux will have her own pages in this book; Natalie Barney has threaded her slippery, silvery self throughout it just as she wove herself in and out of Dolly Wilde's later life.

From 1927 onwards, Dolly Wilde remained in the midst of Barney's glittering gallimaufry and also at its margins, for Dolly had the cold eye for detail that comes only with distance. Every Friday afternoon and evening in Natalie Barney's salon, Dolly faithfully performed the brilliant social role she had set for herself and everyone remembers the 'variety of tones in which she could say, BUT DAR-LING'.[12] And every Friday afternoon and evening in that same salon, Dolly also — and endlessly — seemed to be rehearsing the life, the inclinations, the very essence of her dead, but still notorious, uncle Oscar.

Certainly, the fact that Dolly's life was so oddly shadowed by her crucial relative (imagine dressing up as your uncle at a *bal-masqué*, as Janet Flanner reported Dolly doing in a 1930 *New Yorker* magazine 'Letter From Paris') that she enhanced her own attractions by performing his, seemed tragically fascinating. But Dolly, as she did with everything, went too far with this uncle business: Oscar was the only family member she ever spoke about; she began to live and even to die like him. And she was almost as shameless as Oscar was about begging money from people, although a good deal more straightforward: she rarely promised anything in return.

In 1985, on a trip to Paris and on a whim, I took a room at what was then the Hôtel d'Isly on the rue Jacob, a scant half-block from where the Barney salon had been. By then I had read everything I could about the Barney salon and tracked down, in a lazy way, the few tantalising tidbits about Dolly Wilde that were available.

In the mid-eighties, the rue Jacob was only beginning to be overtaken by the *bon chic bon genre* boutiques and fabric stores that today have transformed it into a miniature Madison Avenue. By 1985 the street still retained a suggestion of its between-the-wars literary past. In the late twenties and thirties, the heyday of the Barney circle and of Dolly's salon career, the rue Jacob had been a tiny seventeenth-century street of charming, cheap hotels and private houses.

An inviting place, in short, for expatriates to perch and a street perfectly accustomed to the kinds of performance staged at Natalie
Barney's famous Fridays, where *le tout Paris* came to see such spectacles
as Mata Hari dance nude, Nadine Hwang whirl swords above the
heads of the spectators, Colette emote irrepressibly in home-made
theatricals, and Dolly Wilde incarnate some of her famous family's
style and substance.

I knew that Berthe Cleyrergue, the elderly Burgundian woman
who had been Natalie Barney's housekeeper and confidante since
1927 (when Djuna Barnes told Berthe – it could only have been in an
antic mood – that working for Natalie Barney would be just as interesting as travelling),[13] was, as recently as 1976, still living at 20 rue
Jacob in a tiny apartment over the carriage entrance to the courtyard.
Was it possible that Mme Cleyrergue was still living there in 1985?
She was as much a *personnage* as Proust's Céleste or Colette's Pauline.
What stories she could tell if I could find her!

Berthe Cleyrergue, as Janet Flanner once remarked, was the only
married woman around Natalie Barney. She had been the author of
the Barney salon's fabled cuisine and was privy to Barney's *affaires de
coeur*, in particular to the fourteen-year relationship with Dolly Wilde.
Gifted with almost total recall and an unusually vivid talent for
description, Berthe had become an invaluable source of original material for many books and films about literary Paris.

Berthe was much closer in age to Dolly Wilde than anyone else
around Natalie Barney, and Dolly and Berthe had entered the Barney
household in the same month: Berthe arrived on 8 June 1927 and
Dolly appeared on 28 June 1927.[14] Because Dolly made a practice of
being friendly with Natalie's long-suffering help, Berthe and Dolly
became very companionable, girlfriends almost. Dolly had given
Berthe the Vionnet dress she was married in and Berthe repeated until
she died that Dolly was the most wonderful and charming woman of
all the charming, wonderful women who visited Miss Barney.[15]

In happy times, Dolly and Berthe used to buy records like
teenagers, playing them on Dolly's Victrola when Natalie wasn't

around. In difficult periods — and there were plenty of these — Berthe saved Dolly from suicide more than once, fetching her back from solitary hotel rooms to the rue Jacob and nursing her to a fragile equilibrium.[16]

It seemed impossible that Berthe Cleyrergue could still be alive in 1985, or, if she were still alive, that she would still be in her apartment. I knew that De Gaulle's ex-Prime Minister, Michel Debré (Janet Flanner described him as 'porcine'), had moved into Barney's *pavillon* and engineered a renovation that had destroyed all traces of her fabled salon. Nonetheless, every day on the way to my café for a morning *crème*, I paused before 20 rue Jacob, thought about the wonderful writers who had walked those cobblestones to arrive at Barney's bed or board, reviewed the mysterious circumstances of Dolly Wilde's tragic death (at the same age as both her father Willie and her uncle Oscar!), considered my chances of conversing with Berthe Cleyrergue — if Mme Cleyrergue were still alive — without an introduction, and fought down the desire to press the buzzer releasing the courtyard doors. Finally, I consulted the telephone directory. And there she was. CLEYRERGUE, Philiberthe, 20 rue Jacob, and the telephone number. I could feel Atlantis rising.

And so began a long, richly rewarding relationship with Berthe Cleyrergue and, with it, the real beginnings of this book. For it was clear from our first meeting, or perhaps it was the second — I was so shocked by this encounter with living history that I forget the facts and remember only the feelings of our first meeting — that Berthe had chosen me to hear the history of Dolly Wilde, and to make something of what I had heard. I never asked why.

Perhaps Berthe had tired of talking always of 'Miss Barney' or of 'la belle Romaine' or of 'Mlle Colette'. God knows she had been speaking to these legendary women privately for forty years and about them publicly for another fifteen. Her stories of them sounded very well rehearsed to me and they *were* well rehearsed by now. Berthe had recited them again and again to the steady trickle of the curious, the scholarly, and the felonious — I heard terrible tales of 'writers' who arrived with innocent smiles, 'borrowed' priceless mementoes, and never returned — who had found their way to her door since the death of her fabled employer.

But the history of Dolly Wilde was a 'new' story — and something from the darker side of Natalie Barney's celebrated salon. Berthe told me what she knew of it — her side of the story — as completely as she could over many years. And she told it in the way that Dolly herself loved having stories told to her:

> . . . something she had never heard before and that seemed almost like a new secret, told by someone who had been involved in it and above all whose connection with it was so old that there was good reason to suppose that the teller had long since forgotten to tell it to anybody else.[17]

In the enchanted atmosphere of Berthe's crowded, low-ceilinged apartment, with its chronically overheated temperatures perpetually enhancing its hallucinatory qualities, Berthe's incredible photographs and mementoes of the Barney salon (arranged in shrine-like config-urations on every possible surface) regularly combined with her rich Burgundian accent and superb French cooking to produce a syn-aesthesia of historical experience that, I swear, hypnotised me into the subject.

> 'Yes, that is Miss Barney's bookmark which she kept always on her night-stand in the blue bedroom where Dolly Wilde stayed; see, here, the embroidered crest on the table linen which Miss Barney designed herself and which we regularly used on our "Fridays"; this is a letter Dolly wrote to me from London; here are *macarons* like the ones I used to make for Colette when she came to lunch with Miss Barney; this photograph of Dolly was taken after she slit her wrists in the Hôtel Astoria when Miss Barney ran off to St Petersburg after that faithless actress . . .' etc, etc, etc.[18]

Who could resist such monologues? Or such a cuisine? I was a goner. Like all chosen people, I had no choice.

Janet Flanner, who shared a sexual secret with Dolly, wrote that Dolly Wilde

> was so interesting to cull over and think about . . . because one wanted to locate in immediate recollection the particular version of her or vision of her which had been visible on that special day, and she had as many versions of herself, all as slightly different, as could have been seen in views of her supplied by a room lined with mirrors.[19]

Writing about Dolly Wilde's life has posed some hard questions about the form this biography should take (thematic, contradictory, and presented in several versions, like Dolly herself) and about the shape Dolly's biographer should assume (a posthumous friend, critically alert and thinking in prose about Dolly Wilde). Oscar, incidentally, referred pungently to all biographers as 'thieves of souls' and 'Judases'.

It is difficult — but very necessary — not to regard biography as an extended form of the obituary style. It is just as difficult not to approach it with the same slyly mortuarial intentions. Aside from Dolly's letters and the small commemorative volume Natalie Barney published about her in 1951, this book is the only remnant of Dolly Wilde's passage through the planet, functioning rather like Ortega y Gasset's remark about culture: that culture is what remains after we've forgotten everything we've ever read. The few people still alive who met Dolly are now too old to remember much about her. The impulse to gild the lily (or cosmeticise the corpse) has had to be firmly resisted at every turn, for Dolly herself is very persuasive in this respect, sometimes inclining — dare I suggest it? — to a self-presentation of dizzying social correctness. Like most intensely talented, inadequately expressed people, Dolly Wilde entertained a thoroughly mixed collection of bad motives, good intentions, and crossed purposes — and I have tried to give the proper weight to each.

Unlike biographies of living people, which often seem to be exercises in virtual 'reality' (a word Vladimir Nabokov said had meaning only when it was controlled by quotation marks), biographies of the dead are very much like ghost stories. They involve an almost incantatory attempt to raise the departed subject, to make her or him breathe once again for history's sake — and in the old way. Because of the intimacy created by this act of evocation, one of biography's more unsettling side effects — the dark asteroid circling its brighter planet — is the way in which the biographer begins to inhabit the subject and the way in which that subject takes up residence in the biographer and begins a kind of persistent haunting.

In a very 'real' sense, and to a sometimes shocking degree, I became involved with the life of Dolly Wilde. I was haunted by the idea of her, this deeply shadowed woman of great wit and glittering gifts who disappeared without a trace. And I developed a peculiar set of sensitivities which led me to information I could not have found, information which would not have been found, but for the intense telepathies produced by a communion with my subject. There is no rational explanation for these instincts and I present none. They exist, they are useful, and Dolly, I might add, would have been delighted by them. But nothing about their exercise has made any easier the experience of investigating the mercurial and instructive paradox that was Dolly Wilde. Writing about Dolly in terms that would not violate her has been as difficult and as interesting as trying to control quicksilver, invoke the scent of perfume, or precipitate a cloud.

Since many of Dolly's 'intimate friends' and/or their descendants have preserved a careful reticence about their attachments to her; since most people in Dolly's milieu had something to hide; and since Dolly herself obfuscated her chemical history, mythologised her social circumstances, and was not above lying in London to promote a purpose, or prevaricating in Paris to bolster a bank account, documenting Dolly Wilde became a complicated adventure in itself. I found myself vetting receipts from her numerous drug and alcohol detoxifications and beguiling emotional histories from people who adroitly denied having experienced them; scanning private collections of black-market erotica and deciphering hand-lettered documents; thumbing through autopsy reports in the Westminster Coroner's Office and opening albums of ancient photographs in French sitting rooms. I came upon a lost letter in a cupboard in Paris; and then, a whole cache of them in a tin box in London. I discovered Dolly's Will and then found — still alive in New York City — the 102-year-old artist who had been her rival in love.[20] All this, and much more, in search of a woman who never should have disappeared in the first place.

And despite my best efforts, I know too well and sadly that relevant materials still remain boxed in boudoirs, boarded in storage bins, secreted in damp cellars, locked away in libraries, and shut up — deliberately — in the failing memories of certain survivors.

Further, because Dolly's life does not lend itself to those conventional male biographical narratives involving a 'quest' or a 'redemption'[21] (the kind of 'quest' her uncle Oscar set out on, the kind of 'redemption' he is now enjoying), because her history does not regularly present a bundle of facts to hang out on the laundry line of chronology (how Dolly would have *laughed* at the idea of things happening one after another: things usually happened to Dolly Wilde all at once and over and over again), and because I wanted to avoid writing the kind of biography Roland Barthes called 'the novel that dare not speak its name', I had to develop some unusual ways of recovering the life of Dorothy Wilde — who, though evasive while alive, became positively elusive when dead.

Like the lives of too many Modernist women, Dolly's life was merely 'noticed', not 'recorded'. She managed to slip through literature's net, slide under the scan of the census, elude the long arm of the law, and die an unexplained death. Writing her life was like raising a rabbit from folded cloths; it was sorcerers' work and, occasionally, I have called upon sorcerers' apprentices for assistance. Among them: astrology, social anthropology, the panoply of psychologies, literary theory, chirology, psychometry and ambulomancy. In finding ways to tell her story, I allowed Dolly's own passionate interests to guide me: her feel for inventive imagery turned me to the vivid enlargements that metaphor permits; her contempt for time gave me the intense concentrations that thematic – rather than chronologic – treatment enables; her unalloyed romanticism lead me to the 'recreations' that make up the next chapter of this book, etc., etc. From time to time, I have used different styles of writing in different settings to suggest Dolly's own changing – and very elusive – states of being.

But none of these dim instruments illuminate Dolly Wilde as well as she could illuminate herself in those rare, private moments when she took the trouble to explain – pen in hand and always on someone else's writing paper – how she felt about who she was.

In the end, anyone who has ever assembled the collection of 'partial' truths (in both senses of the term), painstaking researches, hopeful conjectures, informed intuitions, and educated guesses which constitute a biography knows by heart how far short of the mark this Tantalus form always falls. And while I hope this particular biography introduces you in a pleasurable and even a personal way to a remarkable woman, and that it helps restore Dorothy Wilde to the company she should be keeping – the company of her unusual grandmother, her legendary uncle, and the fabulous generation of Modernist women in Paris and London whose achievements bloomed so beautifully in the first half of the twentieth century – I am all too aware of what the work crucially wants.

Dorothy Wilde was an artist of the spoken word. Lacking the sound of her voice as others heard it and the shape of her sentences as she uttered them, I have only been able to bring her to you complete with missing parts. It remains for you to do what Dolly could have done so beautifully for us all:

Imagine the rest.

2

Stormy Weather

The English are always degrading truth into facts. When a truth becomes a fact it loses all intellectual value.

Oscar Wilde

According to the archives of Metéo France, the Paris weather in the spring of 1927 must have felt like a passionate love affair: blowing intensely hot one moment, cooling the next, and producing storms as torrential and extreme as feelings. There was rain in Paris on 27 June, reprising the very wet weather at the end of May. On 28 June the skies were still fizzing and spitting.[1]

Romantically, but not inappropriately, Dolly Wilde, aged not quite thirty-two, walked into her future with the notorious *salonnière* Natalie Barney after a season of storms and in a shower of negative ions. This was to be the herald of their emotional weather. How the two women were introduced to each other in Paris or who arranged this meeting is one of the secrets of their long affair. Berthe Cleyrergue was the only witness to this first known *rencontre*, and Dolly and Natalie were conversing in a language Berthe did not understand.[2]

Perhaps because she did not know what she was hearing, what Berthe Cleyrergue saw that afternoon stayed with her all her life. From Berthe's recollections, from the weather records of the period, from anecdotes of other salon participants, and with a helping of historical imagination, here is what that first meeting between Dolly Wilde and Natalie Barney might have been like – and how a later Friday afternoon at the Barney salon could have gone for Dolly after she had come to stay at 20 rue Jacob.

28 June 1927: a Re-creation

En journée, le ciel reste très chargé et il tombe quelques gouttes par moment.[3]

This little Ste M[argherita] clouded in its season of rains, yet reminds me of our sunny & stormy beginnings.[4]

Natalie Clifford Barney to Dolly Wilde

Everyone in Paris in 1927 said the spring weather had been exceptionally unsettled. More unsettled than spring in Paris had been for a long time. Winds rolled down the boulevards and whipped up the streets of the *quartiers*, forcing the clientele inside the cafés. Rains fell in icy sheets, then in hard little drops. One minute the sky was the colour of graphite, the next minute sun flooded the Seine, lighting the stalls of the *bouquinistes* so brightly that even serious customers couldn't make out the titles on the books stacked up for sale.[5] The *garçons* at the great cafés on the Left Bank, Le Dôme, Le Select, and La Coupole in Montparnasse, and Deux Magots and the Café de Flore in St Germain, watched the green and yellow wicker chairs on their *terrasses* fill and empty with unusual regularity. Even the Pernod drinkers didn't want to wait out such temperamental weather.

Parisians, accustomed to taking the steadiness of their pearl-grey skies and clement climate for granted, complained philosophically, shrugged their shoulders, and went indoors. The serious social rituals of Paris street life – public arguments and private trysts – dropped off with the changing temperatures. Parks emptied out and squares were vacated as the citizenry stayed inside, sulking in their apartments, or smoking in the *zinc* bars. No one seemed even to aspire to a good mood; only the bears could bear to be out.

By early May, waves the size of *plats du jour* were still caroming off the sides of the broad-decked pleasure barges, the *bateaux mouches*, that plied the River Seine. Late in the month, it was still too wet for lovers or even tourists to buy many tickets for the romantic boat rides. By June the weather had begun to warm and on this particular Tuesday afternoon, the sky had brightened a little, the drizzle was occasional, and the wind rustled gently up the crooked streets of the 6th *arrondissement*.[6]

Dorothy Wilde, fresh as a *citron pressé* and lightly shielded from the uncertain weather in a summer wrap, had already decided against taking a taxi. She felt unusually buoyant this afternoon, as the memory of her brilliant 'performance' at Marie-Louise Bousquet's salon the previous Thursday and another, somewhat hazier, appearance on Sunday afternoon at Jean Cocteau's *salon chinois* still flooded her with small satisfactions. Not that Dolly remembered what she had said on either occasion, or who had laughed at it. Too much champagne at Mme Bousquet's (Dolly sometimes had too much champagne) and too much of whatever Cocteau was offering in his little pipes cast a shimmer of error over both gatherings, and 'facts', which Dolly liked to docket in her 'formidable memory',[7] were not precisely her forte this week. But the remnant feelings were marvellous and she was certain that the details had been divine. That, at least, was the message telephoned to her hotel yesterday afternoon by her provocative friend, the Surrealist writer Jacques Rigaut.

Dolly Wilde's wicked, darting wit was, like Dolly herself, completely spontaneous, with hardly a 'thought for the past and only a shudder towards the future'.[8] Her resplendent, unrehearsed phrases and swift, concentrated epigrams charmed and amused whole roomsfull of sophisticates in the salons and clubs, but left no traces on her own memory. It was up to her small, devoted audience to remember Dolly's 'quickest, lightest, most extravagant nonsense, with no bounds, no inhibitions . . .', just as it was up to them to notice that she could draw out even the most inhibited guests with real skill.⁹ Last Thursday afternoon Bettina Bergery was astonished to see the usually unhappy André Gide 'laughing helplessly' in his chair at something Dolly said.

Dolly was walking to her destination in the 6th *arrondissement* desultorily, almost without direction, as she always walked, *when* she walked, which was not often. She much preferred taking taxis or driving herself, but today the accidental encounters that come with being on one's feet appealed to her more than the cold comforts of punctuality. Dolly, anyway, never carried a watch and was always 'naturally' late for everything. Her lifelong habit of delaying pleasure so as to savour its prospects which, she averred, were so much more satisfying than its fulfilments, probably inspired her to walk in such changeable weather. The stroll would allow her to give some thought to a translation due all too soon — and not yet begun.

The wind blew up from the west as Dolly walked along the Quai des Grands Augustins. She knew that western winds were supposed to be 'favonian' — Dolly read widely in the classics — and are said to confer good fortune. The previous night had been so cold that Dolly was taking advantage of the day's relative mildness by walking out of her way to pass the home of Alice DeLamar, an acquaintance from her old ambulance-corps days during the Great War. Alice's narrow house was at the bottom of the rue Gît-le-Coeur. It had an apartment (decorated, at one point, by the writer and furniture designer Eyre de Lanux) which housed guests like the *richissime* Americans Sara and Gerald Murphy and, later on, Dolly herself. 'Leaning forward, hurrying up, by flurried uneven steps, as though to make up for lost time . . .'¹⁰, Dolly turned back to the *quai*, cupping her palms to light a Russian Black against the sudden wind. The violation of smoking in public was a pleasure she shared with her uncle Oscar.

Dolly decided on impulse — as she decided everything — to go back along the river and turn left up the rue de Seine. She wanted a look at the sneering statue of Voltaire insouciantly installed at the river end of that narrow street. The filmy air of the day was obscuring the details of her walk; the contrasts of foreground and background were softer than in any Impressionist sketch, but Dolly was alive with anticipation for this rendezvous with a woman she'd been hearing about for years, a woman whose notoriety had even reached the ears of her cousin, Vyvyan Holland, in London.

Dolly's excitement was so pronounced that she just had to delay her encounter a little more, and so, as she turned up the rue de Seine off the *quai*, she stopped to look carefully at the statue of Voltaire. Perhaps it was now that she noticed that the house towards which she was heading — a *pavillon* at the end of a courtyard on the rue Jacob — was virtually around the corner from the hotel where her uncle Oscar had died almost thirty years before.

A few hours before Dolly began her walk, Berthe Lauvernier (not yet married to Henri Cleyrergue), was making her way east along the rue Jacob. Three weeks ago, Berthe had left her job in a shop selling American products in the 6th *arrondissement* to join the household staff of the *salonnière* Natalie Clifford Barney. Berthe later said that the number 8 and the month of June were 'sacred' to her: she came to the rue Jacob on 8 June, she met her husband-to-be on 18 June, and she first saw Dolly Wilde on 28 June.[11]

This morning, Berthe was on her way to the rue de Buci's picturesque outdoor market — a scant 100 metres away from Barney's *pavillon* — to bring back delicacies for the little reception her new employer was giving this afternoon. Although Natalie Barney had been comfortably established for the last twenty years in her courtyard *pavillon*, she had terrible trouble keeping competent household staff in her employ. Her private life was a scandal and her public behaviour with servants was intensely critical. Perhaps this shopping expedition was a kind of test for the newly hired young maid.

As Berthe navigated the crowded sidewalks of the market stalls that June morning in 1927, turning the fruit for signs of bruising and comparing the colours of the various butters, she was not thinking much beyond the flowers blooming in the market stalls or the just-purchased *pâté de lapin* which was too firm, almost, to cut. Coming back from the rue de Seine, Berthe paused at the courtyard door of 20 rue Jacob to adjust the string bags she carried. She had a sudden, strange presentiment and took a moment to savour the feeling.

Late that afternoon, a little after five o'clock, Berthe, carrying a serving tray, entered the *salle à manger* — always the coolest room in Natalie Barney's dusky, dimly illuminated *pavillon* — and paused again, this time in surprise. There, in the *rotonde*, where Natalie had strictly forbidden smoking, amidst a sprinkling of other guests, sat a beautiful, dark-haired woman with violet-blue eyes, skin like the petals of a hothouse flower, and a pronounced widow's peak, decoratively arranged on a side chair and deliberately inhaling a smouldering cheroot. She was speaking swiftly and intimately, punctuating her remarks with languid displays of her lovely white hands. She had a clear, low, musical voice and her very occasional gestures scattered ashes all down the front of her fitted jacket and over the Persian carpet.

She looked as full and as delicately flushed as a bouquet of white peonies, miraculously delivered from a sweeter season and a more exotic country. She seemed to radiate, as if from some secret, personal reserve, both light and heat in that cool, dim room, and Berthe instinctively stepped closer to her to engage the warmth of her presence. In front of the visitor, apparently entranced and ignoring the smoke, the ashes, and her own household rules, was Berthe's employer, Natalie Barney, Rémy de Gourmont's 'Amazon' of letters, and the most notorious *salonnière* in Paris.

On this day, Natalie scarcely said a word as her lovely visitor continued a delightful monologue, 'scintillating with . . . so many epigrams that no one had time to remember any'.[12] Natalie never took her eyes from the young woman's floral features. She was concentrating hard, and she laughed and laughed as she looked. Nothing, usually, was ever that funny to Natalie Barney, who was used to making her own rules and watching the world abide by them. Clearly, the young woman in front of her was an 'exceptional being'. 'When I saw the beauty of that woman sitting in the *rotonde*, I was astonished,' said Berthe.[13]

The blooming beauty with the dramatic attitide whose looks Berthe so admired, was, of course, Dolly, who was making her first recorded appearance at 20 rue Jacob. Sitting in Natalie's chair that afternoon, delivering charming variations on her bons mots at Mme Bousquet's salon, Dolly was on the verge of increasing her audience. She was about to become one of the brighter stars in the firmament of Natalie Barney's salon, as incandescent and memorable as any of the remarkable personalities Barney collected at 20 rue Jacob – the place where, as Bettina Bergery said, 'Dolly shone at her brightest'.

To Natalie, Dolly must have seemed the jewel in the crown of her long, imaginative involvement with the life and legend of Oscar Wilde, begun when she was a child. To Dolly, Natalie must have appeared as the enchanted gatekeeper to her own aspirations to be a 'famous conversationalist'[14] and to have a real 'home life' and a 'true friend'. In any case, Dolly Wilde was soon to be installed in both the rue Jacob salon and in Natalie Barney's bedroom. She became Barney's second-best and most troublesome lover, finding in her thirteen-year relationship with that cool enchanter a storm system unequalled by any weather produced in the changeable Paris spring of 1927.

Given the quick affections and sexual directness of both Dolly Wilde and Natalie Barney, Dolly was probably already on her way to Natalie's bed by the time Berthe Cleyrergue first saw her. Berthe was not privy to the particulars of Dolly's and Natalie's conversation which, like all their conversations in front of servants, was conducted exclusively in English.

Berthe, in fact, knew only one phrase in English – 'Thank you very much' – and her pronunciation of it reproduced with wonderful charm the cadences of Natalie Barney's American accent; an accent, as Dolly's friend Scott Fitzgerald wrote about someone else, that was 'full of money'. Still Berthe, whose loyal identification with Natalie was almost complete, said, 'We always spoke English with Dolly.' Natalie and Dolly enclosed their love affair in English when they were together in Berthe's presence – and then confided in her separately, each in her own way and each in French, when they were apart.[15]

Although Natalie usually shut down her salon by the middle of June and left an ordinarily hot and dusty Paris for the country, she might have stayed on in the city this summer solely for the purpose of seducing Oscar Wilde's attractive niece. Natalie had certainly braved extremes of time and temperature before to seek out women who interested her. When she and the poet Renée Vivien were having their love troubles, Natalie used to wait through long nights outside Vivien's door just for the cruel pleasure of rejecting her in the morning. At another time, pierced through the heart by the beautiful actress Henrietta Roggers, Natalie dropped everything and pursued the woman the whole frozen way to St Petersburg, Russia. Only, as Natalie said later, to be cuckolded by a series of titled and articled gentlemen.

However Dolly and Natalie found each other, it is clear from the dating of their first letters that the relationship kindled very quickly and just as quickly became a deep one. 'The Nile has overflowed its banks & wet a strip of arid desert *très bare*,'[16] wrote a momentarily overcome Dolly to Natalie; and whatever their love affair's emotional weather, it brought Dolly (for a while) in out of the cold of her constant *déménagements*, her 'emergency seductions', and some of her well-founded financial terrors.

Before falling in love with Natalie Barney, Dolly had been able to forget herself whenever she wanted. She sought out her several oblivions, she evaded or encountered private love and public life at will, and she scumbled over her history, refusing to keep track of herself with the creative unconsciousness of someone who lives for the present – someone who does not want to look at where she's been for fear of knowing where she's going.

After falling in love with Natalie, Dolly had a kind of planetary home, a 'fatal moon', since Natalie's blonde paleness often elicited lunar images. 'Pale lunar enchantress', Dolly called her as she whirled around Natalie in successive orbits: 'You compel my imagination, make turmoil of my thoughts & every night I miss your lover's attentions – what else is love? (J'ai été l'amant mais personne n'a été mon amant.)'[17]

After Natalie, Dolly could never again be incognito in quite the same way. She had to give an account of herself, as she does in her letters, and that account is often a candid one. When Dolly did not send reports regularly (and Natalie complained that she did not), Dolly's next picking up of the epistolary stitch would always begin with an apology.[18]

When Dolly first entered Natalie's *pavillon* in 1927, she was a fortnight from her thirty-second birthday and at the peak of her salon form. Provocatively arranged in Natalie's dining room, 'half-androgyne and half-goddess', as Natalie described her,[19] dazzling her hostess with a flood of epigrams and a wealth of wit, scattering her ashes in forbidden places, and displaying her white hands with 'touching candour', Dolly was merely doing what she did best: performing her personality for a very appreciative and very attracted Audience of One.

At this time Dolly was probably occupying her favourite room, a front one, Room 65, in the Hôtel Montalembert, Paris's newest and smartest hotel in the 7th *arrondissement*. Room 65 was (and still is) a small, classically square room, dominated by a beautifully inlaid Louis Philippe bed, adorned with the kind of curves Dolly appreciated, and a matching armoire. The room has one of the largest balconies on the sixth floor: a view of the roofs of Paris and a generous expanse of sky were available to Dolly whenever she chose to look at them. Perhaps as pertinent to Dolly as its attractive skyscape was the fact that the Montalembert had one of the first cocktail bars in Paris.

It was widely agreed that Dolly rarely spent a night at her hotel, but where else and with whom she was spending her nights at this time were not generally known. After 28 June 1927, however, whole parts of Dolly's days and many of her Paris nights were spent chez Natalie Barney. With Natalie, Dolly began the longest, most serious instalment in the narrative of her love life. With Dolly, Natalie began an important passage in the history of the Barney salon. This new chapter, with both the salon and the *salonnière* equally involved, continued to offer Dolly a tantalisingly and completely unattainable 'family life'; a 'home life' she could never quite embrace, or keep to herself, or believe in for more than the length of a letter.

Dolly at the rue Jacob: April, 1930: a Re-creation

Here is a typical Friday afternoon at Natalie Barney's salon as it might have happened after Dolly Wilde came to illuminate it with her presence. It is spring, 1930 now. Dolly Wilde and Natalie Barney have been lovers for three years and Dolly has an official room in Natalie's *pavillon*, the 'blue room', which she uses when Natalie is on vacation with Romaine Brooks, or out of Paris in pursuit of some fresher conquest.

Berthe Cleyrergue, now married to her beloved Henri (in a grey dress designed by Mme Vionnet and given to her by Dolly)[20] and installed in the *entre-sol* over the carriage entrance to 20 rue Jacob, is in the kitchen of the *pavillon* where she is regulating the ovens and cutting dozens of cucumber sandwiches. She has been promoted up through the ranks of Natalie's servants to *gouvernante* of the Barney salon now, and she is also Natalie's personal attendant. Although the salon will see some twenty cooks come and go by 1935, Marie, the cook of 20 rue Jacob much loved by Dolly, is still there and the five other members of Natalie's staff — rather poorly trained because Natalie's outrageous amatory behaviour still encourages a rapid belowstairs turnover — are preparing the house for company. They are placing huge bouquets of white lilies, their mistress's signature flower, everywhere. Natalie is out 'visiting' with her grey-clad chauffeur, and Dolly is upstairs in 'the blue room', preparing for the afternoon's festivities by pouring a clear liquor into a cordial glass and downing it.

Dolly is thirty-five now, and drinking a little more heavily than she did when she was in her twenties. Her body has thickened somewhat and her resemblance to Oscar is even more 'hallucinating'. She has temporarily abandoned the champagne with which she used liberally to baptise most public and private occasions. She drinks red wine and gin now and she drinks too much of them. Drinking is a poisonous activity for someone with her heredity, but she has yet to become alcoholic. Drinking just a little too much allows her to sustain that semblance of 'romance' without which her life is beginning to feel like a badly mortgaged house whose beautiful furnishings are slowly being repossessed.

Romantic ideas or no, Dolly is smuggling bottles into the blue room at rue Jacob or hiding them in her closet at the Hôtel Montalembert.[21] She is suffering terribly from being Natalie Barney's second-best lover, just as her father Willie suffered from being the second-best Wilde. Dolly's suffering has forced her to violate her uncle Oscar's most cherished precept — that art and life are distinctions with a difference — and her violation takes the form of living out roles she used only to assume. In the last year, Dolly has come to refer to herself as 'Oscaria' and to insist, ironically: 'I am more Oscar-like than he was like himself.'[22]

Nonetheless, Dolly continues to retain much of what Janet Flanner called 'that floral quality which was the bloom of her charm', and she appears bedewed with an 'almost mythical pristine freshness . . . that, alas, later became a bit tarnished, though she never completely lost it', as Alice Toklas wrote.[23] Still, Dolly has been seen exiting numerous private bathrooms blowing white powder out of her nose and laughing her marvellous musical laugh, which her friend Katy Fenwick always insisted was the response Dolly substituted for tears.

On this particular Friday afternoon, all is running smoothly. Romaine Brooks, Natalie Barney's favourite companion for almost fifteen years now, is at the country house she and Natalie have built together in Beauvallon: the Villa Trait d'Union, the Villa Hyphen, composed of two separate living and working quarters joined by a common room for dining; it is a symbol of the independences upon which the relationship of these two extraordinary women rests. There will be no strained exchanges between Dolly and Romaine on this day, no ultimatum from Romaine to Natalie, as there has been in the past, about shaking 'the rat [Dolly] from out of your skirts'.[24]

Of course Romaine Brooks is also fond of Dolly, and sends her money and words of comfort when Natalie betrays her with other women. But periodically Romaine feels the need to assert her primacy and Dolly is packed off to London or Warsaw or Biarritz, until Romaine's emotional boil cools to a simmer. This toing and froing at the mercy of her beloved's other relationship is a 'herald of unimaginable suffering' for Dolly and does not discourage her habits of finding solace in liquids or inspiration in chemicals.

Dolly's final preparation for this Friday is a hypodermic which she keeps in her purse. She takes it out, injects herself quickly in the thigh — something she will do quite openly at dinner parties in London, but only secretly in Paris — and leans back until the initial rush of the drug subsides to a steady buzzing hum; a line of life she can build on; a vibration that erases her inhibitions, frees her flowing phrases, and quiets her anxieties. At last, she has set herself 'straight' enough to descend the staircase.[25]

In the little salon, all is waiting. The square table is set beautifully for tea with hundreds of Berthe's sandwiches, dozens of rich cakes, champagne, and the sweet wine Natalie likes. Berthe's gallicised version of fruit cup will be brought out at the end of the evening at around eight o'clock, to sweeten the discussion and speed the farewells. Moët et Chandon will be served as well, but sparingly — three bottles here, five bottles there. After Natalie's death, Berthe insisted that people got more champagne in her tiny apartment than in the whole of Miss Barney's salon. Dolly, who loved life's finest, always complained bitterly when Natalie served *vin mousseux* instead of champagne.[26] In the careful lists she made and kept for her receptions, Natalie Barney noted the price of everything and what was to be served – and re-served.[27]

The mirrored walls of the salon room reflect banks of white lilies, the four abandoned nymphs painted on the ceiling, and an oil portrait of Rémy de Gourmont in the drawing room, which Natalie commissioned when Gourmont was at the height of his infatuation with her.[28] Everything is slightly distorted by the patinations of the old reflecting glass. Although she is generally completely without physical self-consciousness, Dolly doesn't trust mirrors and avoids them now. She has remarked that 'mirrors are more lying than photographs', that most people are not 'mirror-genic', and that 'no mirror can ever show you your real appearance'.[29]

On her way to the garden, Dolly circumnavigates the drawing room which she says is so 'frowsty and damp' that if you turned the chairs up, you'd find oysters growing on their bottoms.[30] Now that Dolly has a room in Natalie's house, she abides by its rules. When Dolly wants to smoke, which is often, she walks the garden paths between the tall trees. Recollections of the 'Fridays' at the rue Jacob might begin with Dolly viewed in the garden through the salon windows. She is always smoking and walking – and she is always talking.

This Friday, as ever, Berthe Cleyrergue is at the front door, greeting the old friends as they arrive, and dispensing carefully measured doses of gossip to the journalists looking for copy. Natalie has returned from whatever rendezvous engaged her and she is pouring tea in the salon, having changed into a white Vionnet gown like any correct lady of good society. Dolly suspects Natalie has just come from an afternoon with the actress Rachel Berendt, who will be present later on. Dolly has yet to undergo the double indignity that will come when Natalie moves the Chinese lawyer-cum-cross-dressing-army officer, Nadine Hwang, into the *pavillon* – and begins to make canny use of her as both chauffeur and secretary.

Because there is no official 'entertainment' planned for this evening, no reading or theatrical presentation or musicale, and because this is not a Friday for the *Académie des Femmes*, that society which Natalie Barney loosely formed as a reproach to the Académie Française, the company is crowded into the salon room, the small dining room, which seats twenty at table and perhaps fifteen more on side chairs. The crowd swirls in and out, changing its character and its constituency every forty-five minutes. Natalie tends to the teapot and the conversation and Dolly, her cigarette finished, circulates vivaciously among the guests. The drug and the alcohol have done their work and Dolly is perfectly primed for company.

Here is the renowned, ancient classical scholar, Charles Seignobos, to whom Dolly gave a copy of *Lady Chatterley's Lover* – along with instructions for reading it. It is the only novel he has ever read through. When the American publisher Samuel Putnam wrote about his favourite afternoon at the Barney salon, he seemed to be describing one of Dolly's meetings with Professor Seignobos, as well as the social manner and sexual allure which suited Dolly like her Schiaparelli scarf.

> Among the guests was an exceptionally beautiful woman of the kind that radiates sex, and the aged Sorbonnist, whose lecture-room was a famous one, was getting more than his share of the refractions . . . He capered and cavorted, literally danced around the lady, who led him most expertly to the delight of everyone present. The conversation that accompanied all this as the professor made his whinnying exit was one whose subtle Rabelaisian quality Rémy de Gourmont himself would have appreciated.[31]

Over there in a corner of the salon is André Gide in serious conversation with the painter Jacques-Émile Blanche, but still capable of being reduced to tears of laughter by almost anything Dolly says. Janet Flanner, always on the alert for material for her *New Yorker* column, is talking to Djuna Barnes, who drinks much more than Dolly does and whose love troubles with the painter Thelma Wood are painful and legion; they will eventually inspire Barnes's extraordinary novel *Nightwood*. Djuna has already depicted Dolly as Doll Furious in her hand-illustrated satire of the Barney circle, *Ladies Almanack*. Doll Furious is enslaved by love and sex to Evangeline Musset, the Natalie Barney character. Although Barnes's grandmother was a friend of both Dolly's grandmother and her father and even attended Lady Wilde's salon (bringing Karl Marx's daughter with her), Dolly and Djuna carry on a kind of muted rivalry and each speaks sarcastically about the other behind her back.

H. G. Wells drops in suddenly and repeats the remark he recently made to Dolly at a Paris PEN meeting, that it is delightful to meet 'a feminine Wilde'.[32] Nancy Cunard and her Negro lover, the jazz musician and singer of spirituals Henry Crowder, appear, along with Nancy Cunard's cousin Victor Cunard, the London *Times* correspondent in Venice and Dolly's great friend and admirer, the man who, Berthe says, makes Dolly's eyes 'sparkle like sapphires'. Natalie Barney and Henry Crowder, both of whose mothers live in Washington, DC, understand each other perfectly and chat together comfortably.[33]

By now, the small circle of people around Dolly has quieted down to listen to her as she picks up on some casual inquiry and begins to fabricate a kind of monologue, an elaborate recounting of a wonderfully amusing country weekend she has just enjoyed. Dolly's clear, low voice wraps itself easily around 'resplendent phrases', 'adventurous adjectives', and 'Oscar-like epigrams', releasing them all in a dazzlingly rapid flow of fanciful inventions on the theme of her weekend, all done in 'perfect taste' and with a magnificent elevation of *esprit* (abetted by the drink, the drug, and the company) and a perfectly pointed sense of satire. Dolly — who is usually such a delightful guest that her hosts feel that they should be the ones proffering thank-you notes[34] — is, for entertainment's sake, perfectly willing to make use of her weekend for 'performance material'.

3

Dead Again

Death is the only tragedy – next to life . . . It's the only fear – the only punishment.

Dorothy Ierne Wilde, letter to
Natalie Clifford Barney

Are you dead, again, darling?

Dorothy Ierne Wilde to 'Emily'

*E*leven years later, at ten-fifteen on the morning of 10 April 1941, Lillian Whitehouse, a chambermaid employed in a slightly suspicious block of service flats at Twenty Chesham Place in the Belgravia district of London – then, as now, one of London's more luxurious addresses – used her pass-key to open the door of Flat 83.[1] Miss Whitehouse had just picked up two packages from the hall porter for the flat's occupant, Miss Dorothy Wilde. The chambermaid said she was accustomed to delivering mail to Miss Wilde every morning and that one of the packages she picked up was a letter and the other one was a bottle.

Dorothy Wilde, the vividly attractive, almost-forty-six-year-old occupant of Flat 83, had only just moved to the building from the Normandy Hotel the week before, on 2 April. In one of those odd coincidences which seemed to shadow the history of her family, Dorothy Wilde's new residence was just two short blocks and directly across the green from the Cadogan Hotel on Sloane Street. The Cadogan Hotel was the establishment from whose premises her notorious uncle had made his exit from public life in the arms of the law forty-six years before, in the very same quadrant of April in which his niece had just moved into Chesham Place. Dolly would have seen the Cadogan Hotel every time she left her lodgings at Twenty Chesham Place and she must have found the view wholly engaging: she had been compared to her dead uncle all her life.

When the police finally spoke to Mr Davis, the house manager of Twenty Chesham Place, he said he did not know much about Miss Wilde. Lillian Whitehouse, the chambermaid, was more familiar with the new tenant than the house manager was. Dorothy Wilde had always been charming and extremely sympathetic to her maids – she had been at the mercy of too many society hostesses herself not to empathise with a chambermaid's position – and it appears that she had already inveigled this one into hand-delivering her mail. When the chambermaid was questioned later she said she had last seen Miss Wilde on 9 April and that Miss Wilde appeared to be 'her usual self'.

Dr Graff, the Divisional Surgeon who was called to Flat 83 by the housekeeper of Twenty Chesham Place and who himself kept a room in the building, seemed to know that Miss Wilde was under the care of the Sloane Street physician Dr C. T. Cregan. He may also have known that Miss Wilde was a drug addict – doctors generally registered their addicted patients on the Home Office List – as well as a breast cancer patient whom Dr Cregan had been 'treating' with chloral hydrates, barbiturates, heroin and adalin. Dorothy Wilde's dosage for heroin was a grain a day, four times the dosage she had been given at her last nursing home, Chiswick House. Dr Cregan later testified that she was always asking him for more.

Harold West, a waiter in the restaurant at Twenty Chesham Place, was interested enough in Dolly Wilde to be able to recite exactly what her dinner had been the night before — soup, fish, and ice water: a distinctly penitential meal for a woman whose tastes usually ran to rich chocolates, fine champagnes, thick vinaigrettes, and fat Camemberts. Mr West also knew exactly how long Dorothy Wilde had spent eating dinner in the restaurant: forty-five minutes, from 8:50 p.m. to 9:35 p.m., and he remarked — perhaps because it was an aberration — that she didn't have anything sweet that night.

Although the waiter did not say so, Dolly almost certainly had this last dinner by herself. Forty-five minutes was the delicate minimum an 'independent spinster' — as she was described on her death certificate — would have spent alone at table in a restaurant, and, prodigious conversationalist and table-top wit that she was, Dolly would certainly have lingered longer, and with far more pleasure, in the company of good company. She was, anyway, expecting to lunch with her dear friend Victor Cunard, the following afternoon, 10 April, and was looking forward to it.

Dolly Wilde never got to her luncheon engagement. The details of her last day, recited above, and a small file of more precise and unpleasantly chemical data, are almost the only officially recorded 'facts' attesting to Dolly Wilde's life on earth. It is one of that life's many ironies that these 'facts' were written down and preserved because of what the chambermaid at Twenty Chesham Place found when she opened the door to Dolly's flat that April morning. Although the chambermaid's account is bare enough, her discovery must have provided her with nightmares for many weeks to come.

Lying with her legs still on the divan bed and her head and chest launched face down over the front end of the bed and on to the floor, was the body of Dorothy Wilde. Her robe and slippers were in a chest of drawers near the bed, she was dressed in 'night time attire' (pyjamas, most likely — she adored pyjamas), and her legs were covered by the bedclothes. She was not moving. If her personal physician Dr Cregan is correct — and he was the sole person to attempt to determine the time of her death — she had only just died within the hour. The right side of her face was abraded and livid marks were upon it.

On the dressing table by her bed were a glass and an empty bottle that had recently contained paraldehyde, an over-the-counter sleeping draught she began taking under doctor's orders during a heroin cure in January 1939. Sometime in the past year she started using it to combat the chronic insomnia which martyred her every night and made a hollow echo of her days. Somewhere in the room was a hypodermic syringe with a trace of 'whitish substance' – either heroin or morphine – still lodged in the barrel. The hypodermic's plunger was 'firmly wedged' down and stuck into the barrel, most likely glued to it by the remnant of dried sediment.

There were five other bottles of paraldehyde in the flat, in various stages of emptiness. Dr C. T. Cregan, Dolly's regular doctor, who finally arrived at two o'clock that afternoon to conduct the examination of her that would determine the time of her demise, refused to issue a death certificate without an inquest. And so the mortal remains of Dorothy Wilde were removed to the Hammersmith Mortuary to await an autopsy – her last exit in a long line of disorganised withdrawals from hotels.

The following day, 11 April, after Dolly had been dead perhaps some thirty odd hours, Dr Cedric Keith Simpson, a celebrated pathologist who was later to write the memoir, *Forty Years of Murder* (even in death Dolly managed to attract a *literary* pathologist), performed an autopsy on her body. Dolly Wilde, who had passed the last three years of her life frantically seeking alternatives to 'a surgical cure' for the cancer in her left breast because she could not bear the idea of having her flesh sliced open, now went under Dr Simpson's knife in the most complete and horrible way. Under legal order from HM Coroner, Harry Neville Stafford, Dr Simpson cut into every part of Dolly's once beautiful body, and his grim medical conclusions bear witness to the many mysteries she lived and died with.

Simpson noted the bruising on the right side of her face, which he attributed to 'terminal collapse on to the side', though neither the chambermaid, who had actually described Dolly as being completely on the floor near the bed, nor the police constable, who said he found her half in and half out of the bed, mentioned anything about her having fallen on her right side. Simpson also found a 'small cancer of the left breast', demonstrating, perhaps, the efficacy of the alternative cures Dolly sought out, for she had begun with several breast tumours and dallied so long with 'sorcières', 'serums', and holy waters, that her doctors had pronounced her tumours inoperable.

Her heart was without 'organic disease', though there was a 'marked dilation of the right side with a deeply cyanotic blood clot', consistent with a possible drug overdose. Her lungs were 'intensely congested and cyanosed in keeping with prolonged narcosis' and there was mucus in her air passages. Shockingly, there were 'occasional small deposits of cancer throughout the lungs'; her carcinoma had metastasised. Mercifully she did not know this, for she had already been climbing a wall of worry over the breast cancer, and her problems with drugs and alcohol were much intensified by her horror at what was happening to her body. She had a small uterine fibroid tumour that was 'causing slight bleeding'. Simpson found the 'strong smell of paraldehyde' about Dolly's body so significant that he typed it in red on his report.

If, in fact, Dolly Wilde did die in the morning of 10 April as recorded, it is not necessarily credible that her death was the result of a sleeping draught alone. Sleeping draughts were something she was accustomed to taking during the night to trump her tortuous insomnia or, in earlier, more dramatic days, to try to kill herself. But the *mise en scène* of her death lacks the crucial act of wrist-slitting, which was present in every previous, serious staging of her attempts at suicide.

Further, it is hardly likely that Dolly would have deliberately swallowed too much paraldehyde in a search for sleep on the very morning of a longed-for luncheon engagement with her friend Victor Cunard. She had an addict's knowledge — always considerable — of what drugs could and could not do. But it was not Dr Simpson's job to weigh the psychological circumstances of Dolly's mortality; he was only responsible for its physical causes.

Dr Cedric Keith Simpson concluded that there was no natural cause for the death of Miss Wilde and that his findings were in keeping with the effects of an overdose of a narcotic drug. As both paraldehyde and heroin were under suspicion, he 'removed suitable materials' — i.e. parts of her liver, brain, kidneys, intestines, and the contents of her stomach and bladder — for chemical analysis at a laboratory. These 'suitable materials' were sent to the pathologist along with the hypodermic syringe and the drug bottles found in Dolly's flat.

Dolly's examining pathologist, Dr G. Roche Lynch, of St Mary's Hospital in Paddington, was as highly regarded in his profession as Dr Simpson. Dolly, in fact, was to have a celebrity trio of final examiners (a circumstance which would have flattered her *amour propre* almost as much as it would have amused her intelligence) including HM's famously flamboyant Coroner, Harry Neville Stafford, for her inquest. Dr Roche Lynch reported that he could find nothing but a very small quantity of paraldehyde in the organs of the late Miss Wilde, that there was no heroin, no morphine and no barbituric acid substance, and that if any adalin were present it would only have been in a prescription dosage. He observed that the failure to detect heroin or morphine was not uncommon 'in the case of addicts to those drugs'. And he thought that the hypodermic syringe found in the flat hadn't been used recently and that five of the six bottles in the flat contained paraldehyde and the sixth smelled like paraldehyde, although the test was inconclusive.

In other words, tests conducted by the pathologist established that there was not enough paraldehyde in Dorothy Wilde's body to have killed her. And while she could have been killed by a combination of drugs — let us say paraldehyde and the heroin which might have escaped detection — the syringe found in her flat which had once contained heroin had not been used recently, and there were no other drugs or methods of delivery on the premises which could have been responsible for a self-administered overdose of anything, whether traceable by contemporary tests or not. Dr Roche Lynch concluded (without the summing up provided above), 'From the above data and from the information in my possession I do not feel that I am in a position to give a cause of death.'

At the inquisition conducted by Mr Neville Stafford, on 15 April 1941, Dr Cregan said he had never prescribed paraldehyde for Miss Wilde and that she should not have been taking it. He also said that she was suffering from pain and depression and that he 'should not be surprised if she would take her life' and yet the last time he had seen her — on 8 April two days before she died — she was 'very well and happy'.

Miss Maud Willes, otherwise known as 'Fluff', secretary to Lady Cara Harris, the mother of Dorothy Wilde's best friend Pamela 'Honey' Harris, was sent to identify Dolly's body on the day of the inquest. Dolly's only traceable relative, her uncle Oscar's son Mr Vyvyan Holland, had been notified of Dolly's death the day she was found. He had possibly declined to make an identification — he and Dolly had been estranged for some years — and he did not attend the subsequent funeral. He made his presence known later in a letter to the coroner from his solicitors, Holmes, Son & Pott, dated 1 May 1941, asking for letters of administration to Dolly's estate. The solicitor's letter mistakenly assumed that Dorothy Wilde had died intestate — which she had not done; she had a Will walled up in Paris because of the war — and many of Dolly's effects were dispersed and wrongly distributed because of this assumption. A several-years-long, unsatisfactory correspondence between the determined woman who was Dolly's beneficiary, Miss Natalie Clifford Barney, and the law firm of Holmes, Son & Pott ensued.

The burial order for Dolly's body was issued in the name of Maud Willes, who testified that she had known the deceased for ten years, that the deceased was not a healthy woman, and that Dr Cregan had been treating her for insomnia and giving her a daily sleeping draught. Miss Willes's testimony presents Dolly as a respectable invalid, an 'insomniac', as Dolly no doubt would have wanted to present herself, and carefully skirts the issue of Dolly's addictions. Miss Willes said that she telephoned to Dolly every day, that Dolly had appeared in their last conversation to be her 'usual self and happy,' and that 'I have never heard her threaten to take her life'.

How much of Miss Willes's testimony was tinctured by the decision to bury Dolly in Kensal Green Cemetery with her mother – suicide was still illegal in England – is difficult to determine. It is possible that none of it was, since Miss Willes was a famously upright woman and Victor Cunard, who found out about her death by arriving at Chesham Place to give her lunch the day of her death, told the writer Nancy Mitford that Dolly 'was quite jolly & herself to the end'.[2]

Certainly, many of Dolly's old friends assumed a suicide and could even have been notified of one. On the small piece of Hôtel Continental notepaper marking Dolly's remaining letters to her, Janet Flanner wrote: '. . . these 2 letters are from Dolly Wilde, niece of Oscar, who died (suicide) in London in 1941, after a life of turmoil in Paris.'[3] Berthe Cleyrergue, on the other hand, was certain it was the cancer that killed Dolly. Perhaps cancer was the cause of death preferred by Berthe's employer, Natalie Clifford Barney, whom many people had already blamed for the suicide of the poet Renée Vivien – and whom gossip was perhaps already allying with Dolly's death. If Dolly had in fact died of cancer or of carelessness, Natalie Barney could hardly have been held accountable for her demise.

In an uncharacteristically religious set of verses, 'Faire-Part', published ten years after Dolly's death, Natalie Barney describes an 'accidental' end for Dolly:

> The death she dared not seek
> Came to her otherwise:
> She died in Holy-Week
> – Who closed her lovely eyes?
>
> What friends, less fond than I,

Followed her as she passed
Alone – to live and die?
– I failed her first and last!

Outnumbered by the ways
Through which her death might come
'Peaceful' the wire says –
But where was Dolly's home?

Though we lie far apart
Who knocks so at my side?
And breaks into my heart
– Risen on Easter-tide?[4]

Cancer was certainly heavily hinted at in the articles which appeared on Dolly's death in the London newspapers – none of which failed to mention the presence of drug bottles in her flat. The *Daily Mail* of 12 April 1941, under the column header SENTENCE OF DEATH, quoted the woman who had been Dolly's last known lover in a statement as marked by superficiality as the findings in Dolly's autopsy report:

Miss Gwen Farrar, the revue and music-hall artist who was for many years a close friend of Miss Wilde, said, 'For the past three years Dorothy had suffered from an incurable disease. She knew she was under sentence of death. Before the illness she was a jolly and high-spirited woman, with many friends.'

Victor Cunard's notice in the obituary column of the London *Times* for 14 April 1941 overlooked the two ways Dolly had said that she'd like to be remembered – as a 'Great Lover' and as a 'lover of Nature' – but it would have delighted her all the same. It united her, in death, with the 'family life' she had spent the whole of her adulthood looking for and it was, in addition, perfectly 'true'.

She understood the joys and miseries of the human heart so well that the habit of going first to her to share happiness or find comfort in distress was quickly formed and the thought that so pleasant and profitable a habit must some day be broken was determinedly overlooked. Sympathy such as she could feel for even a discreditable weakness might have cloyed but for the wit with which it was expressed. Epigram and paradox are the weapons of the Wilde family and none of its members has used them more humanely and more effectively than Dorothy.

Whether or not, and in what strange ways, Dolly Wilde 'inherited' her reminiscent death (not to mention her reminiscent life) from her unusual uncle is an irresistible and unavoidable topic, and it presents a fibre-optic tangle of biochemical, psychological, and even literary explications. Still, the possibilities of this 'patrimony' — the ways in which Dolly seemed to embrace and reject it, and the relationship with myth, ritual, and blood weddings it implies — are so apparent to anyone even faintly acquainted with the histories of both uncle and niece that careful attention will be paid to it in this chronicle.

Dolly Wilde died at virtually the same age as her father and uncle. Her resemblance to her uncle was marked — almost, many people thought, reincarnative — and she left life flaunting most of the Wilde family's fabled weaknesses and all of her uncle's inclinations. Was her death yet another example of her failure to fulfil her undoubted gifts, a mere parody of familial possibilities? Or was it, in fact, the one promise she kept: another doubling of the inherited avuncular disaster, her *truly* Wilde end?

In one of those odd, foreshadowy series of duplications which dot the Wilde family history, Oscar Wilde's body in Paris narrowly missed a post-mortem like Dolly's in London. Oscar's loyal friend Robbie Ross was able to circumvent the horrors of the morgue by bribing the French district doctor into signing Oscar's burial order, which the French doctor, like Dolly's own personal physician, had at first refused to do, insisting that the death of Dolly's uncle must be either a murder or a suicide.[5] Murder or suicide are two of the three implied and still unresolved possibilities of Dolly's own autopsy and inquest.

When the frightened chambermaid discovered Dorothy Wilde's body and called the housekeeper of Twenty Chesham Place to her aid, she set in motion the chain of official examinations that produced Dolly Wilde's autopsy, inquisition, and inquest, and all the small contradictions and larger ironies that attended them. Dolly, whose sense of time was notoriously unlike anyone else's — Janet Flanner had called it 'lunar' — would have been greatly amused by the many different times of death (three, at least) ascribed to her mortal coil in the coroner's report alone. She would have fallen about the room laughing at the two contradictory positions fixed for her inert corpse (out of bed and in it); and the various inaccuracies regarding her age, the arrival times of the police constable, and her own emotional states during her last week of life, would have beguiled her endlessly. There is more than a faint suggestion of violence and mystery in her end (I will take this up in a later chapter) and these dark uncertainties, too, would have interested her beyond measure.

The fact that HM Coroner, Harry Neville Stafford, had what must have been his writing arm shot off in the First World War, and that, therefore, the notes he took on his cross-examination of witnesses at the inquest are virtually unreadable, would also have provided infinite amusement to the deceased Miss Wilde.

Did Dr Cregan *really* testify that he could find no 'vein holes' in Dolly Wilde's body, indicating that there had been no fatal injection of heroin possible and further deepening the mystery of her death? We will never know for certain since Coroner Neville Stafford's handwriting provides a phrase so utterly indecipherable that Dr Cregan might well have been testifying to the existence of potholes on Pont Street, and it is only by the relativity of context that Dolly's 'veins' come into play in the heroic translation of Neville Stafford's writing attempted for this book by the current Westminster Coroner's Officer, Mr Geoffrey Kirby.

I can hear Dolly's laughter at this moment.

Dolly Wilde liked things told in a 'true' way, which she understood very well was often quite different from a 'real' one, and although only she (and perhaps one other) knows the truth of her last hours, the confusions, the contradictions, and the recherché quality of the final performance of her life recorded in the coroner's report would have filled her with a horrified and condign sense of the ridiculousness of reportage and the futility of assembling 'facts'. She always said she wanted to die in bed and, if the report of PC Macdonald as to the position of her body is correct, she got half her wish.

Neville Stafford completed the inquest into the death of Dorothy Ierne Wilde on 12 May 1941 with this magisterial (and, owing to his amputated arm, practically illegible) phrase: 'She came to her Death from causes unascertainable.'

The coroner left the case marked 'Open;' it remains so to this day.

Although Dolly's death was as darkly framed as a film noir, her closest friends, the painter Pamela 'Honey' Harris and the *femme de lettres* Natalie Clifford Barney, did their best to broadcast the sentiment that flights of angels had sung her to her rest. In their letters and telegrams about Dolly, they used adverbs like 'quietly' and 'peacefully' to describe the way she died, leaving the impression that perhaps her cancer had finally done its dreadful work. Natalie Barney, in particular, sent euphemisms out into the world like soothing seraphim determined to draw a curtain of charity over the true circumstances of Dolly's departure – which were, frankly, much more like Janis Joplin's than like Beth March's.

Those who read the coroner's report, however, would have seen that Dorothy Wilde died exactly as she had lived: vividly, rather violently, and at a very good address.

2

Truly
Wilde

4

Fathers Are Depressing: the Second-Best Wildes

Willie you don't deserve my bear. Give me back my bear.

Oscar Wilde to Willie Wilde,
when they were children

As Willie never pays, he is splendid in hospitality.

Lady Jane Wilde, letter to Oscar Wilde

A single photograph of Dolly's mother, Lily Wilde, with her infant daughter has survived the dissolution of the Wilde family. It is notable both for the attractiveness of its two subjects and for the fact that Dolly's father, Willie Wilde, though 'out of the picture', signed it, dated it, labelled its contents, and dedicated it, inscribing himself for posterity on what is the only image of the 'second' Wilde family.

Lily, in a hat with a feather and her hair in a chignon, sits in a wicker chair. Some spit curls are escaping the hat and the prettiness and sensuality of her rather narrow face are apparent. The thirteen-month-old Dolly stands precociously on her lap, her little body pressed against her mother's. Their two heads are together but not quite touching and Lily's left hand is loosely hooked under Dolly's right one, balancing the child. There is no sign of a wedding ring on Lily's hand; perhaps Willie pawned it temporarily to pay for the photograph. Lily herself pawned the ring in May 1897, when she was so poor that one of her sisters was paying her rent at 9 Cheltenham Terrace; she pawned it to get food for Willie because, she said, he was 'a very sick man'.

Dolly's enormous blue eyes have been opened even wider by the photographic flash and her cupid's mouth looks rosy even through the sepia tint. Her child face is absolutely recognisable as a miniature, cherubic version of her adult face, and she has her mother's graceful, curving eyebrows. Astonished by the explosion of the flash powder, she is facing it head on and without reserve, utterly fascinated by the phenomenon. Although casually supported by Lily, she appears to be quite alone, and the mother and daughter seem isolated from each other by the circumstances of the photograph. The fact that there is no father in the picture reflects all too clearly the circumstances of Dolly's early childhood.

Willie Wilde and his younger brother looked so much alike that Willie once joked that Oscar had paid him to grow his black beard and rather straggly moustache so people could tell them apart. But where Oscar drank to excess, Willie was alcoholic; where Oscar created literature and made news, Willie, whose extensive career as a journalist – drama critic for *Vanity Fair*, leader writer for the *World* and the *Daily Telegraph*, originator of the society column – is often overlooked,[1] did odd jobs for the less important journals or did nothing by the time his daughter was born; and where Oscar occasionally gave money to his mother, Willie lived upon her. Oscar's friends clearly regarded Willie as the Wilde Family Joke. As Dolly's father, however, a joke is the very last thing Willie Wilde was.

When Willie married Dolly's mother, Sophia 'Lily' Lees, in 1894, he was a talented failure at both law and journalism, sharing an impoverished and disorderly household in London at 146 Oakley Street,

Chelsea with his theatrical and gallant mother, Lady Jane Wilde. Lady Wilde, a once notorious writer and *salonnière* of stature, had come down considerably in the world; Willie, with a much shorter distance to fall than his mother, had already fallen as far as he could.

By 1895, all three Wildes living on Oakley Street — the increasingly erratic Willie, the newly pregnant Lily, and Jane Wilde, in whose name the Oakley Street house was rented and who was responsible for keeping it — were greatly dependent on the hugely successful Oscar Wilde for the dribs and drabs of money that barely paid their household bills. And Oscar was a scant three months away from legal exposure, public shame and utter ruin. Lily Lees Wilde was in for an awful marriage, and by now she must certainly have known it.

There are two distinct versions of the character of Willie Wilde which assemble themselves through the recollections, the stories, and the pronouncements of his friends, his relatives and his detractors — some of whom occupied all three positions at once. Both of these versions coexisted in Willie's ponderous and alcoholic person in a kind of psychological disharmony. They are so persistently dissonant that printing them is the only way to achieve their reconciliation.

There is the convivial, the generous, the extravagant Willie, the Willie with the soft Irish voice and the even softer heart, a Sunday painter, a Saturday night pianist, a man who was charming to children, gallant to the ladies, a brilliant conversationalist, and a highly respected journalist. This is the version of Willie most often vaunted by his school classmates and by his newsroom peers.[2]

The other Willie — the one who drank to insensibility, refused to support his family, 'sponged', as his brother Oscar said nastily, 'on everyone one but himself', abused his spouses, yelled and stamped his foot at his seventy-two-year-old mother when she refused to give him money, and actually stole a piggy bank from the children of a woman he was hoping to marry — was the version supported by most of Oscar's literary friends and reinforced, somewhat reluctantly, by Willie's own two wives.[3]

William Charles Kingsbury Wills Wilde, as Willie was christened, had been given a very promising start. Born in Dublin on 26 September 1852, he was the first child of two of Ireland's most prominent personalities: William Wilde, an oculist and surgeon later knighted by the Queen for his medical services and noted for his books on Irish folklore and his philandering, and Jane Francesca Elgee Wilde, known as 'Speranza', the fiery feminist and famously outspoken poet of 'The Nation', who read ten languages and, after her marriage, kept the best literary salon at the best address in Dublin. Willie was idolised by his doting, highly learned, famous mother, who wrote regularly to his younger brother Oscar, recommending Willie as a reclamation project. Jane Wilde, though often describing (or concealing) the second version of Willie, never ceased to hope for the reappearance of the first one. She was perhaps the only person in the world who managed to entertain, unreconciled, both versions of Willie Wilde at the same time.

Willie's temptation to violate his mother's expectations must have been a serious one. Jane Elgee Wilde was a gloriously extravagant figure: large, tall, and wonderfully self-appreciating, she was much the most fantastic personality the Wilde family ever produced and is the true, historical originator of *le style Wildien*.[4] Jane was given to inventing grandiose ancestral connections (surely plain Jane Elgee's surname *must* be a corruption of Dante Alighieri's patronymic) and to 'metaphorising' her adored, immediate family. Her god-like references to her sons – Willie 'looked like a young Hercules' and Oscar was perpetually 'Olympian' and 'crowned with laurels' – her insistence that her husband was 'the best conversationalist' in Dublin; her dubbing of her first-born grandson, 'Prince Cyril'; all laid the foundations for Oscar's and Willie's Houses of Fiction. Jane's theatrical airs, emotional extravagances, and seasonal depressions were inherited and edited by her younger son Oscar into what we have come to think of as the 'Wilde style'. But the Wilde style also found further expression and final refinement in Jane's only granddaughter, Dolly, the last person to carry the Wilde name. Dolly, in fact, managed to refine the Wilde Family Style right out of existence.

Descriptions of Jane Wilde in her Dublin salon in dignified Merrion Square report a figure draped all over in fantastical shawls and hung with jewellery copied from ancient Celtic designs.[5] Portraits of her husband, sons, and dead daughter depended brooch-like from parts of her person, as she swayed and listed — a great, six-foot galleon in full sail — around her drawing room, dispensing outrageous comments far more liberally than her tea. '*Respectable! Never use that word here.* It is only tradespeople who are respectable. We are above respectability!' and, to a college chum of Oscar's, '. . . there is only one thing in the world worth living for and that is sin,' are among the milder of her remarks.[6]

In Dublin, Jane had been a widely known poet, as well as a political essayist and translator, with many published works to her credit. Her marriage to Dr William Wilde stopped the flow of verse. (Curiously, her son Oscar also ceased writing poetry when he married, and began again only in prison.) Although Jane strongly felt that 'genius should never wed' (referring, naturally, to herself), and mourned the fact that 'at last my great soul is prisoned within a *woman's destiny* — nothing interests me beyond the desire to make *him* [her new husband] happy — for this I could kill myself,'[7] she was besotted by her first son and delighted with her second. All Jane's poetic impulses seemed to leak into her maternity. 'Alas! the Fates are cruel/Behold Speranza making gruel!' pronounced a friend who saw her hovering over saucepans in the nursery. Her expectations for her children were never less extravagant than the ones she always entertained for herself: one of her fondest wishes was to see her elder son well married.

Jane's husband, Sir William Wilde, was the leading eye and ear specialist of his time and was responsible for medical operations so innovative that they are still being cited today. Not everyone, however, agreed about Wilde's expertise: George Bernard Shaw — always a contrarian when it came to the Wildes — insisted that the operation Sir William performed on his own father to correct a squint left Mr Shaw Senior squinting the other way around. William Wilde was also a prodigious writer and, in the best period Irish style, a convivial socialiser, an excessive drinker, and an apparently uncontrolled fornicator. He produced at least three out-of-wedlock children by two different women and he was accused of drugging and raping a young female patient, Mary Travers. The Wilde family subsequently lost the libel suit on which that accusation hung.

Sir William Wilde's personal hygiene and apparently fuliginous skin gave rise to pointed caricature and a rude riddle in Dublin: 'Question: Why are William Wilde's nails so black? Answer: Because he has scratched himself.' Allegations like this one, trailing in their roiling moral wake images of 'dirtiness' and 'disorderliness', also attached to William's sons Willie and Oscar, both of whose appearances aroused distinct revulsion in many of the people who encountered them.[8]

In his middle years, Sir William was prone to periodic depressions, enveloping himself, wrote his wife Jane, 'in a black pall and is grave, stern, mournful and silent as the grave itself', and, before her marriage, Jane Wilde herself was subject to seasonal depressions. Jane liked solitude, as she said at every opportunity, and she liked rainy days when she kept to her room, never changed out of her peignoir, and 'The writing procedes like improvisation.' She had 'very frequent depressed days'... 'black, bleak, and unutterably desolate'... 'a horrible sense of loneliness, a despairing feeling as if all the world else were standing in Sunlight, I alone condemned to darkness'. And she hated spring. 'Spring utterly takes away all power from me. It is so full of life and hope and joy and youth that I sink subdued...'[9]

Spring – in particular the month of April – was to have an awful continuing significance for the Wildes: Oscar was arrested in April and the bailiff's sale which separated his family from its physical heritage was in that same month; Dolly, like her grandmother, began many of her serious depressions during the season which that cruel month begins and it was in April that she died.

After the death of her much-desired daughter, Isola Francesca Emily, in 1867, Jane Wilde extended her generally claustral behaviour – on good days she had kept all her windows curtained, stayed indoors, and draped herself in fabrics and furbelows – and simply refused to leave her house. All her dreams of glory attached themselves even more closely to her two sons, for whom she had chosen careers like 'President of the Republic of Ireland'. From the moment he was called to the bar, Willie showed every intention of thwarting those dreams: he launched a depressing career (it certainly depressed *Willie*) of social frivolity and fiscal irresponsibility that was to last until his death.

By 1893 Willie had become, psychologically, the *revers de la médaille* of his younger brother Oscar. Outsized (perhaps six feet four inches) like Oscar and with a high laugh like Oscar's, ungainly and slow-moving like his mother, unkempt like his dead father, Willie Wilde's large features, sensual, mobile lips, brilliant blue eyes, and long, graceful hands were enough like Oscar's to invite invidious comparison. Max Beerbohm, the writer and caricaturist, wrote to Will Rothenstein on the subject of Willie: 'Quel monstre! Dark, oily, suspect yet awfully like Oscar: he has Oscar's coy, carnal smile & fatuous giggle & not a little of Oscar's esprit. But he is awful in a veritable tragedy of family likeness!'[10]

But Louis Purser, a respected don at Trinity College and Willie's former schoolmate at the Portora Royal School, remembered Willie at school as '. . . nothing but delightful . . . clever, erratic and full of vitality . . . a bit given to boastfulness . . . But he was very kind and friendly with younger boys [and] was a tolerable pianist, and I remember with gratitude many a time he played for his juniors . . .'[11]

Willie's relations with his brother Oscar when they were young men seemed to be excellent and affectionate but were almost always conducted in an odd reversal of their natal order. Willie, the elder by two years, deferred to Oscar and provided him with enthusiastic public praise, often in print. Oscar's contribution to Willie was money-on-loan and a mildly increasing resentment. The roots of their exchange apparently went deep into their early lives: Oscar told the journalist Robert Sherard that when they were boys, he gave his beloved toy bear to Willie after Willie begged him for it and then, whenever they quarrelled, he used to say, 'Willie you don't deserve my bear. Give me back my bear.'

In the specimen year of 1895, the Wilde family appeared to be balanced at the very top of a magic mountain of social acceptance and artistic success, a mountain created by Oscar's brilliant and largely self-engineered reputation. This alpine position was a grand illusion and a cruel one: it omitted the 'real' circumstances of Willie's clutch of connubial dystopia on Oakley Street and the 'secret' circumstances of Oscar's rotation of rent boys at the Albemarle Hotel. By 1894 Robert Hichens's satire of Oscar and the 'Decadents', *The Green Carnation*, had been published, and by 1895 the Marquess of Queensberry was conducting the steady chorus of public cries and private whispers that crescendoed to the five word indictment 'gross indecency with male persons' – the legal charge designed to indicate, somewhat imprecisely, just what practices Oscar Wilde had been flaunting in society's face for so long.

But Olympian visions of the Wildes had been vaunted ever since they arrived in London from Dublin in the early 1880s, principally by the major communicants in the religion of Oscar Wilde's genius: Oscar himself, his mother Jane, and, later on, Oscar's intelligent and much-tried spouse, Constance Lloyd Wilde, whose marital home in Tite Street Oscar avoided for weeks and months at a time. There is surely an argument to be made for the fact that the only trangression for which Oscar Wilde deserved prosecution was his continued emotional cruelty to his wife.

Although Oscar had all the fame and glory, Constance had all the honour of supporting it – and Lady Jane Wilde had only Oscar's present celebrity to comfort her. She was displaced in London, diminished by travail, and living in scarifying, widowed poverty with the alcoholic and shiftless Willie and the undowered and pregnant Lily. Lady Wilde's prominent position in the world of Irish politics and international letters had been reduced to the importance of being, as she once joked, the 'mother of Oscar'.

Lacking Oscar's focused ambitions, Jane Wilde's eldest son Willie had trapped himself, by the time his only child Dolly was conceived, into the pattern he had been designing since he was called to the bar (which bar? one is tempted to ask, and what did it serve?) in Dublin: an utter and unconsciously resentful dependence, both financial and emotional, upon his ruined, widowed mother. Willie Wilde's behaviour in Lady Wilde's house in Chelsea was the demotic version of his behaviour in the luxurious New York hotel suite of his first wife, the energetic newspaper publisher, Florence Miriam Leslie.

When she married Willie Wilde in 1891, Florence Leslie was a rich, forceful, highly intelligent American newspaper magnate, a feminist of (rumoured) partial Creole or Negro descent, who had known the Wildes since the early 1880s and had probably met Willie at Lady Wilde's salon in London about eight years previously. Like another American journalist, Zadel Barnes (Djuna Barnes's grandmother, also a friend of Willie Wilde), Florence Leslie frequented Lady Wilde's salon whenever she travelled to Europe. Mrs Leslie was fifty-five to Willie's thirty-nine, and before she began her career in journalism (and in marrying newspaper owners) she had been an actress.[12]

Names meant something to Mrs Leslie. She married three husbands before Willie, but Willie's surname was the only one she refused to take.[13] She was waiting, she said, until he developed some decent working habits. Willie's much-quoted remark: 'What America needs is a leisure class and I am determined to introduce one,' summed up his view of his husbandly responsibilities to his incredibly hardworking publisher-wife, and he spent his time at the Lotos Club in New York City, imitating Oscar's 'fat, potato-choked voice', drinking heavily, refusing to work, and making himself a reputation as 'the laziest man who ever wore shoe leather'.[14]

Needless to say, Mrs Leslie retained the name she married Willie with and divorced him as soon as she was able to form an opinion of his character — about six months into the marriage — reporting pithily: 'He was of no use to me either by day or by night.'[15] Although

Florence Leslie was to speak rather fondly of Willie after his death, she concluded, and said to Willie and to the press, that Oscar was the Wilde brother she ought to have married.[16]

Willie's next marriage, to Sophia 'Lily' Lees, on 11 January 1894, seems to have been a love match: certainly, the two lovers had nothing else to give each other. Willie was again destitute and living on his mother and Lily had a wholly inadequate income and no stated intention of seeking employment.

Born in 1859 at 31 Upper Pembroke Street in Dublin, Lily Lees was a lovely woman with a sensual mouth and a secretive smile. Only one thing about her is certain: she had large affinities for literary gentlemen and a particular one for her brother-in-law, Oscar Wilde. Before Willie's death and after it, Lily Lees Wilde continued fond relations with Oscar. She wrote to him admiringly, visited him in Paris just before he died, and told her daughter Dolly rather more about Oscar than she did about Willie.

Lily's father, William Armit Lees, was a Dublin man who moved his family from Ireland to the Bayswater district of London in 1882, in the same year that Willie and Jane Wilde made a similar move. William Lees's whole career was made in appointed municipal positions in Dublin[17] and in his Will – always the clearest place to look for a man's intentions – Lees provided generously for Sophia (Lily) and Georgina, his 'spinster' daughters, but left their inheritance subject to the 'life estate' of his second wife.[18] When William Lees's Will was read in 1885, Lily was not yet using the name 'Lily', although she rather looked like one. Lily's stepmother may have refused her an advance on her patrimony on the quite reasonable grounds of Willie Wilde's dubious character.

What Lily's doings were in Bohemian London and how she met the 'fantastic and irresponsible' Willie Wilde are just two of the mysteries that cloud the union of Dolly's parents. A few details emerge from their uncertain, premarital profile – and they are not pleasant ones. Lily lived, fractiously, with Willie at Malvern and Broadstairs before their wedding. During this time she thought she was pregnant and tried to get a 'powder' from Jane Wilde's housekeeper, Mrs Faithful, to terminate the condition, but Jane said that Lily had lied about having a doctor confirm her pregnancy and that she 'got up the whole thing just to try and force on the marriage . . .' Willie 'was very angry with her' and Willie and Lily almost separated over this contre-temps.[19] Meanwhile, Willie was entertaining a variety of other women at Oakley Street — and at all hours.

During this time as well, Lily is reported to have accused Willie 'of great brutality' towards her.[20] Thirty years later, Dolly indicated to Natalie Barney that Willie's brutality was not all physical: Willie Wilde engaged himself to Lily, Dolly said, then abandoned her for a year when he, perhaps, disappeared into his first marriage in New York City.[21]

Jane Wilde, Lily's new mother-in-law, found the marriage of the two middle-aged, indigent lovers, determined to move in with her, an unthinkable burden. Jane wrote forthrightly to Oscar in February 1894:

> Miss Lees has but £50 a year and this just dresses her. She can give nothing to the house and Willie is always in a state of utter poverty. So all is left *upon me* . . .

> I have an immense dislike to sharing the house with Miss Lees, with whom I have nothing in common. The idea of having her here is quite distasteful to me . . .[22]

Lily must have been an unusually winning woman, for Jane Wilde was so soon reconciled to her that less than a fortnight after the previous letter she wrote again to Oscar: 'Willie and his wife get on very well here. Mrs Willie is sensible and active in arranging the house and is very good tempered.'[23]

With both of his wives and with his mother, Willie Wilde was chaotic, destructive, alcoholic, frequently depressed, indolent to the point of paralysis, and very possibly physically threatening. In her divorce proceedings against him in 1891, Mrs Leslie's witnesses attested to his abusive behaviour towards her, and Mrs Mynors, a friend of Lady Wilde, wrote to Oscar's wife Constance of similar obstreperous behaviour in his mother's house on Oakley Street.[24]

Like some dodgy *doppelgänger* – for Oscar and Willie looked very like each other and were each, in their separate ways, linguistically brilliant – or a sad, sacrificial goat, Willie became the convenient repository for the contempt, the criticism, and the repulsed suspicions that the social world did not yet dare to voice about his brother Oscar. It is usually agreed that the brothers were so different that people had to choose between them, but it is also obvious that those who wanted or needed to embrace Oscar entirely were only too relieved to be able to cast all their abated horror of Oscar on to Willie.

The secret sexual side that Oscar was always concealing in plain sight and whose name no one dared utter; his physical rebarbativeness; his interminable self-promotion; even his shabby ways with merchants – were conveniently hung around the all-too-culpable neck of his elder brother. Except that Willie was irreproachably 'heterosexual' (*avant la lettre*, since the concept did not become current until fifteen years after his death), he had developed all of Oscar's worst traits to their highest power – and could add to the heap some interestingly awful ones of his own invention. But Willie was not so adept as Oscar at linguistic legerdemain; he could not distract you from his 'repellent physical peculiarities', as the journalist Frank Harris said that Oscar did, by persistently pulling exquisite lexical rabbits from stylish rhetorical top hats.

Willie resembled Oscar (and Oscar resembled Willie) for good and for ill much more than anyone but the mordant and incisive Max Beerbohm cared to admit; and Willie's slide into the lower depths of debt and alcoholism prefigured both Oscar's and Dolly's last years with an astonishing and hallucinatory accuracy. Someone very like Willie was what both Oscar and Dolly became before their deaths; but Willie got there first and stayed there longest.

Max Beerbohm, in particular, loved to speak ill of Willie and often managed to insert a slyly pointed reference to his dear friend Oscar into the anecdote as well. Here is Beerbohm, again, writing to Reggie Turner when he was seeing a great deal of Willie at Broadstairs, Kent, in September 1893, during the time that Willie and Lily Lees were living together:

> He is very vulgar and unwashed and inferior, but if I shut my eyes I can imagine his voice to be the voice of Oscar. Who was it that said 'Scratch Oscar and you will find Willie'? It is a very pregnant saying: if Oscar had not been such a success in life as he has been he would be the image of Willie. It was Willie, by the way, who was found by his host in the smoking-room filling his pockets with handfuls of cigars — wasn't it dreadful?[25]

Willie's journalist colleagues, however, were glad to pay tributes to Willie's convivial character and 'superlative journalism' during the 1880s and early 1890s when he was the drama critic for *Punch* and *Vanity Fair* and the correspondent and leader writer for both the *World* and the *Daily Telegraph*. During this time, Willie's coverage of the Parnell Commission for the *Daily Telegraph* was described as 'the best in England'. His habits of working in the *Telegraph* newsroom stripped to the waist, and of turning in his copy at the last probable moment after the most possible consumption of alcohol, did not seem to affect the high praise his *confrères* always gave him. Willie, said his colleagues, was a 'very brilliant writer, when he chose to take a little trouble with his work . . .'; he was 'the supreme type of cultured journalist'; and, when he talked, wrote Leonard Cresswell Inglesby in 1912, 'one always went away with the feeling that here was a real kind heart'.

Willie Wilde was what used to be called 'a ladies' man', with all the courtesies towards (and hidden resentments against) women the term implies. Willie actively sought women out; he courted them, charmed them, slept with the ones who would sleep with him, and tried in his indolent way to get himself married to a woman with a good income. When he couldn't extract an income from a woman by marrying her, he managed to do it by entertaining her. Many a well-known hostess fell before Willie's charms: one of them, Mme Gabrielli, sent him, according to Constance Wilde, 'wine, cigarettes, tonics, *and* bangles'.

Willie's urgent exchanges with women often led him into some interesting byways, of which his whirlwind courtship of Ethel Smyth is an outrageous example. Ethel Smyth was the English composer, writer, and intrepid suffragette whose 'Mass in D' performed at the Albert Hall was later to fix her as the first important woman composer in England; she was seventeen years old when she first encountered Willie Wilde on a boat trip. Miss Smyth was not at all partial to men as possible partners. She was later to have affairs with both the Princesse de Polignac (née Winaretta Singer, heir to the sewing machine fortune and an ex-lover of Romain Brooks) and Emmeline Pankhurst (the heroine of the British Suffragette Movement); and she went on in old age to a famously lengthy and publicly sexual pursuit of Virginia Woolf.

Nonetheless, such was Willie's charm that three hours after meeting him young Ethel Smyth found herself engaged to Willie Wilde and in possession of a ring. She was, at the time, beguiled by his unusual habit of making up new endings for Chopin preludes. She broke off her 'first and last engagement' three weeks later and Willie, ever the Irish gentleman, let her keep the ring. She lost it, she said, trying to break up a dogfight.[26]

Not all of Willie Wilde's engagements or amatory involvements ended so amicably and his life suffered terribly from the private excesses and public humiliations which replaced what might have been for him a concentrated career or a focused union. In a painful vignette from Willie's last years, Max Beerbohm says that he and Willie were sitting together in a restaurant, and that he had just loaned Willie ten shillings. Flush with the pleasure of being able to pay the bill, Willie, meaning no harm, whistled for the waiter, who turned on Willie in a rage: 'Don't you whistle for me,' he said to Willie, '. . . I am not a dog.' Beerbohm continues:

> You know, I will never forget it. Everything went out of Willie . . . 'But my dear fellow,' he kept mumbling, 'my dear fellow . . . I didn't mean . . . I meant nothing.' It was awful . . . that sudden capitulation. In that moment, I believe, he saw, he really saw . . . the dingy failure of his life; even behind the bulwark of that ten shillings, he saw himself face tragedy and defeat, he saw that there was nothing ahead for him . . . that he would never find a clearing in the shambles he had made for himself. He saw the end and I saw it too.[27]

Of his mother, Lady Jane Wilde, Willie Wilde wrote on her death in 1896 that 'she was his best friend'. He neglected, however, to pay for his 'best friend's' funeral or to erect a headstone for her and, like him, she languished in an unmarked grave.

She will have a fair share of the family brains.

Lily Lees Wilde, letter to Oscar Wilde

In the month before Dolly was born, June 1895, at the end of what must have been a profoundly uncomfortable pregnancy in a household driven to extremity by Oscar's incarceration in May, Lily Wilde took care to extend her relations with her disgraced brother-in-law. She wrote to the governor of Pentonville Prison asking him to give Oscar 'my fondest love' and to tell him 'how often I think of him and long to see him . . .'[28] On 17 October 1895 she visited Oscar at Wandsworth Prison, sitting with him for three-quarters of an hour. The next day she wrote that Oscar 'was altered in *every* way' and that 'The whole interview has made me more than sad'.[29] In October 1900, after Willie's death, Lily, telling Oscar of her plans for a second marriage, said she was coming to Paris on her honeymoon,

. . . and then I shall come away in the afternoon and see you. Tex [her new husband, Alexander Teixeira de Mattos] can come and fetch me as I would sooner be alone with you . . .

How are you? Sometimes I hear of your sayings and doings which amuse me . . . I shall be so glad to see you.[30]

And she wrote again to More Adey, Oscar's loyal friend, of 'Oscar who I shall always have a great affection for on account of his touching kindness to me.'[31] Lily passed this inordinate affection for Oscar on to her daughter. For Dolly, it was as indelible as a birthmark – it was, in fact, a *kind* of birthmark; and, exacerbated by Dolly's uncanny resemblance to Oscar, it was to have horrific consequences for her future.

Lily Wilde's quick affections included a sensitivity to criticism. In letters to More Adey, Lily describes her sense of injury, insisting upon the terrible effect gossip had on her relationship with Oscar – presumably gossip by the coterie of possessive men who surrounded him. One of Lily's injurers was the self-promoting journalist and professional Friend of Oscar, Frank Harris, who calumniated Lily to Willie at the Pelican Club, calling her a 'filthy woman'.[32] Dolly later made the characteristically vivid remark that Frank Harris's prose style 'reminded her of a broken ashtray full of chewed up and badly-smelling cigar ends'.[33]

Lily's surviving letters – to Oscar, to More Adey, and to Constance Wilde – are rather starkly composed, thin little packets of facts and figures and frustrations, with none of the gorgeous prose or talent for metaphor her daughter's letters display. The letters that came out of Lily's first marriage are full of accurate designations of meeting-times – '1:15 sharp' – for rendezvous with gentlemen who could help her and Willie with money, or for rendezvous with gentlemen who could help Oscar in prison or who could help her to get money *from* Oscar in prison; and these letters seem overcast by the unbearable tensions of existence in the desperately poor household at Oakley Street. Lily wrote to Oscar after Willie's death: 'After 40 one loses someway the power of being happy. At least I find it so. One has always sad memories of what Willy might have been instead of dying practically unknown & leaving his child to be supported by my sister.'[34]

Before forty, however, Lily was still able to be amused by her husband's style. Robert Harborough Sherard, Oscar's excitable and unreliable journalist friend, who visited Oakley Street when Oscar sought refuge there after his indictment, wrote a letter to Vyvyan Holland in 1928 recounting how Lily came down to breakfast one day in gales of laughter to tell Sherard that Willie, hoping to stop him from persuading Oscar to flee his coming trial, was going to sell his entire library to pay for Sherard's passage back to Paris. And a strictly third-hand story, also relayed by Sherard and therefore both interesting *and* suspect, had Edmond de Goncourt writing in his diary entry for 28 May 1895 a Grand Guignol summary of the way the Oakley Street Wildes lived their lives: 'Pitiful family, where the mother of the two brothers is always drunk, the bottles of gin filling her room, and where Oscar's sister-in-law, a poor creature whose indignation is no longer alive, said to Sherard that all the Wildes were crazy.'[35]

When not driven mad herself by money worries or exasperated out of her life by her husband's behaviour, Lily knew what to value; and what she valued was literary talent and any indication of it. She married first one, and then another literary man. She had great hopes for Willie and her very real appreciation of Oscar had much to do with his quick wit and literary reputation. And when Lily wrote to Oscar about Dolly, it was to mention a trait that mattered much more to her than her daughter's obvious prettiness: Lily told Oscar that little Dolly was going to have 'a fair share of the family brains'.[36]

On 11 July 1895, three months after the imprisonment of her uncle, Dorothy Ierne Wilde was born to Lily and Willie Wilde in her grandmother's rented house on Oakley Street, in the Chelsea district of London close to the Albert Bridge. From his prison cell, the barely solvent Oscar assumed an emblematic paternity for the baby by paying Lily's £50 lying-in fee, a fee which her husband could not muster. This characteristic act of generosity — a response, perhaps, to the fact that what monies Oscar had were given to him by the generous and high-minded banker's daughter Adela Schuster – was at once material and symbolic and it cast a long shadow over Dolly's prospects.

Dolly was the only addition to the series of subtractions (a calculation which Dolly's lover Natalie Barney said belonged to the *end* of life) which almost reduced the Wilde family to nothingness that fateful spring and summer of 1895, and she was born amidst dreadful tensions and apprehensions. Her birth was registered on 2 August 1895; on the certificate her father's profession is given as 'barrister', a trade he hadn't practised for years, and her mother's name appears as 'Lily' for the first time.[37]

Where could the name Lily have come from? Could it possibly have been conferred on Lily by the brother-in-law who had a special affection for her, the brother-in-law with whose aestheticism the lily flower was so closely associated? It is easy to imagine Oscar bestowing such a fragrant sobriquet: 'You look so like a lily, my dear, that you should be called after one. *I* shall certainly always call you Lily.' From this time forward Sophia Lees Wilde was Lily Wilde and she continued to be Lily in her letters until she died.

Lily's relationship to Dolly is difficult to precise. The affection with which she refers to 'my beloved daughter' in her Will is undeniable, but the vagaries of Dolly's infancy are very worrying. Dolly was apparently trundled in and out of her parents' house during her first few years. And on 14 March 1896, in an unexplained abandonment, Lily and Willie left the nine-month-old Dolly at their new home at Cheltenham Terrace and went away to Kent because, wrote Lily, the baby was 'very sick'.[38]

At some later point, Dolly was put out to nurse and was only returned to the household when she was three years old. And after Willie's death, when she was four, Dolly was placed 'in a country convent' – whether in England or Ireland we are not told. Lily wrote to Oscar that Dolly 'was well and happy' and was being supported by one of Lily's four sisters, Mary Doran.[39] Mary Doran, at that time

Mary Bond, had also paid Willie's and Lily's rent after Jane Wilde's death when they moved to 9 Cheltenham Terrace, a little side street not far from the old Oakley Street house. The country convent Dolly was placed in would have been the rough, religious equivalent of a temporary foster home. Lily did not express any particular regret at being separated from Dolly, at least in the rather businesslike letters she left behind her.

Even before Oscar's abasement and Dolly's birth had more or less sealed the fate of the second Wilde family, the home life on Oakley Street with Jane, Willie and Lily seemed to regular visitors much like the home life in Emily Brontë's novel *Wuthering Heights* — *after* Heathcliff took over the farmhouse. As early as September 1893, Willie was reported drunk at all hours of the day and night, and sometime in 1894 Lady Wilde's old Dublin friend Henriette Corkran came to visit, bringing with her the novelist Gertrude Atherton and a home-made cake. Before paying their respects, Corkran explained to Atherton, or so said Atherton: 'Lady Wilde is frightfully poor, her sons do little or nothing for her . . . I only hope the gas isn't turned off and you will be able to see her.'[40] Other friends were sending wine to the household with the provision that it be kept away from Willie.

After Oscar's conviction, the situation on Oakley Street worsened perceptibly and the Wildes who lived there must have felt that they were suffering an undeserved punishment. Willie's response was characteristic: 'Thank god my vices are decent ones.'[41] The seventy-three-year-old *femme de lettres*, Jane Wilde, who had done her dramatic best to get literary work and who had to beg ten-pound notes from her younger son to support her household at a time when Oscar was spending, by his own calculations, between £80 and £130 a week keeping Lord Alfred Douglas in special *cuvées* of Perrier-Jouet,[42] was now shut up in her room: old, ill, impoverished, and heartsick because of Oscar's imprisonment, she 'turned her face to the wall'.

Willie, egregiously alcoholic, was unemployable, unfaithful, and increasingly degenerate. Now he was selling his imprisoned brother's belongings for any sum he could get. Lily's misery as a pregnant woman and then as a new mother in the midst of this turmoil can only be imagined. She wrote exasperatedly to More Adey:

> Kindly understand that I take no responsibility as regards Willy and that any money from the sale of [Oscar's] clothes I had nothing to do with. Also, Willy has not earned *one* farthing for the last 10 months and I and my family have had to keep my home over my head . . .[43]

The Wilde name, of course, was anathema; it had been reviled in every newspaper in the country and was stricken from Oscar's play posters. Had Willie been looking for work he would probably not have found it.

The Oakley Street Wildes, who had so little opportunity to share in Oscar's glory, were now receiving the full, bitter measure of his disgrace. Willie, who thought he had been refused entrance to a restaurant because of Oscar's ignominy, was hauled up in court for the ensuing fracas. There he clumsily offered his fellow journalists a fiver to keep his name out of the papers and they were so insulted that they printed it forthwith. This is the atmosphere and the attitude into which Dolly was born; it is important not to forget it.

Like Dolly a generation later, all the Wildes in London in 1895 ended up trapped in forms of living for which they did not seem to be designed. Lady Wilde was consigned to a myth of the *mater dolorosa;* Oscar and Constance were sealed in high tragedy; and Willie and Lily were relegated to a dank and degrading melodrama. Utterly excommunicated from the Winners' Circle in which the three other Wildes had at least sunned themselves for a short while, Lily and Willie made up a kind of parenthesis of failure within the steady sentences of Oscar's triumphs. Although they continued to live with Jane Wilde in the painful poverty of her Oakley Street house until her death in 1896, the lives of Dolly's parents were the exception to Jane's past successes and to Oscar's recent triumphs. They were the plaintive

counterpoint to the Wilde family's victory song: a contradiction, a
worry, and an embarrassment.

Robert Sherard said — and other friends of Willie said so too —
that Willie Wilde had always been an excellent and genial host, and
there are descriptions of him as an excellent salad maker and an
expansive buyer of legs of mutton. But now, when you came to
Oakley Street for dinner, Willie would be waiting in the hallway to
dun you for the price of the food which he himself would go out to
buy, stopping along the way for a great deal of liquid refreshment.
Lily, linked by a baby with this oddly domestic mendicant, could not
have known if there would be shelter over her infant's head the month
after her birth. The Oakley Street family's only chance at solvency was
the £1000 Adela Schuster had given Oscar just before his imprisonment; the money administered by Ernest Leverson out of which
Oscar had paid Lily's lying-in costs. Both Willie and Lily may have
made random, unsuccessful assaults on the sum, angering and alien-
ating Oscar in the process.

In the terrible months after Oscar's imprisonment and Dolly's
birth, and after Jane Wilde's death in February 1896, Lily Wilde was
responsible (she is never given proper credit for this) for preserving
some of Oscar's original play manuscripts as well as some of his
favourite shirts — for which he had left clearer instructions than for
his manuscripts. These last acts of conservatory kindness on Lily's
part must have required an exile's silence and cunning. For such were
Willie's brotherly sentiments at this time that he pawned two trunk-
loads of Oscar's clothes (including, apparently, Oscar's famous fur
coat) and then drank up the profits — a gesture which must have carried for him a satisfying, symbolic pleasure.

When she was grown up and verging on her own troubles, Dolly
Wilde told Natalie Barney that when Oscar came to stay briefly at
Oakley Street after his conviction, hounded by the Marquess of
Queensbury's bully-boys out of every hotel in London, the seven-
months-pregnant Lily Wilde was instrumental in getting Willie out of
the house so that Oscar could have some repose.[44] And there is a

story that, before leaving Oakley Street, Oscar insisted on shaking hands with Lily to emphasise the special sympathies he felt for her and for her coming child.[45]

That Lily was an affectionate woman when she was relieved of some of life's grimmer realities is perfectly clear: she enjoyed a long and very loving second marriage with the translator Alexander Teixeira de Mattos. Teixeira de Mattos, a Dutch Jew by birth but an enthusiastic convert to liberal Catholicism by choice, was a prodigious worker: disciplined, humorous, cosmopolitan and uxorious – Willie's opposite in every way. Teixeira had a 'vast vocabulary' (as did Dolly – perhaps her heritage from Teixeira), and he was the official translator of Maeterlinck and many other modern writers.[46] He had been Willie's best man at his wedding to Lily, and he turned out to be the best man for Lily.

Lily and Teixeira had one son, who died a few hours after birth, and so Dolly, whenever she came into it, was the only child of their household. Teixeira seems to have admired young Dolly for her intelligence, writing to his future biographer about 'that accomplished gyurl [here he is probably imitating Lily's Irish accent], my stepdaughter, [who] had read all about [Huxley and Darwin] before she was sixteen . . .'[47] Dolly herself was unnaturally silent on the subject of Teixeira de Mattos, her mother, and on her own relations with them.

In the sense that would have mattered most to her – the immediate, physical sense – Dolly probably never had a father or a mother. Willie Wilde was absent, alcoholic and irresponsible; Lily was emotionally preoccupied by her turbulent relations with Willie and the Wilde Family Drama, and then with Teixeira de Mattos' serious heart problems. In the sense that matters most to us – the explanatory one – Dolly had two male progenitors: the father who signed her birth certificate and the uncle whose tastes, talents, and worst examples she seemed born to reprise. And then, after Lily died, Dolly had a series of close connections with older, wealthy and/or titled women who sometimes seemed to be imitating Lily's behaviour, moving Dolly (or allowing Dolly to move) in and out of their houses.

Lily ended by providing Dolly with a small inheritance after her death in 1922. That inheritance, approximately £2,000,[48] is usually ascribed to Teixeira de Mattos but it could as likely have come from the Lees family money, withheld from Lily when she married Willie. Willie's bequests to Dolly were somewhat less material: the Wilde family looks, its seriously literary intelligence, and what bio-geneticists would now call a familial disposition towards addictive and manic-depressive behaviour.

Even more than her good looks and charm, Dolly's literary intelligence and barbed wit – the 'family brains' Lily wrote to Oscar about – should have been her ticket to ride the rougher roads of her life. The persistent problem of Dolly's adulthood was to be the kind of travel to which those Wilde 'family brains' admitted her.

3

Social
Studies

5

Mädchen in Uniform

A charming voyage with Savoir in the most heavenly car which I drove with volupté! At 100 one thinks one is doing 40 – it's so smooth & quiet.

Dolly Wilde, letter to Natalie Clifford Barney

I often think of you at the wheel.

Natalie Clifford Barney, letter to Dolly Wilde

*L*ily and Willie's very intelligent daughter grew up to develop one distinctly non-intellectual taste: she became a daredevil automobile driver. Dolly drove like the wind every chance she got, always in borrowed cars. Driving was a sensual experience for her: a speeding vehicle produced the same fine, high feeling of carelessness, the same obliterating rush of blood, the same, as Dolly said, *volupté*, as her 'emergency seductions'. Controlling a beautiful machine always made her feel intensely happy and piercingly alive, as though she were outmanoeuvring her troubles. When Dolly drove, she let her spirit run the roads.

Natalie Barney often thought of Dolly 'at the wheel' of a gleaming roadster, streaking down a long country lane, the sun hot on her face, the flat fields falling away on either side of her, and 'your hair Byronicly wind-blown and colour beaten into your cheeks . . .'[1]

After her friend George Beckwith died in a flaming car crash, Dolly said:

> Think of how nice to die in what you like best, and you know what Beckwith liked best was cars and the sun. He adored driving fast in a beautiful car with the sun in his eyes. He must have felt like Apollo driving the sun itself, when his golden chariot fell over. (You know Beckwith had a new and specially shining yellow car.) Imagine the flames going up in the sun, and Beckwith going up in the flames he sprang out from. It's a hero's death in antiquity . . .[2]

Up-to-the minute as always, Dolly's own driving had an unusual history which even she couldn't entirely suppress. Dolly belonged to that first generation of young women who learned to handle a car while being shot at, shelled, and bombed. Her career as a driver began behind the wheel of an ambulance at the very beginning of the First World War.

In 1914, a 'thrilled', teenaged Dolly Wilde, dead set on adventure, stepped on to a boat-train going to Paris. She was probably not travelling alone, but her purpose was singular enough: she was running away from England to go to war in France.

Dolly left her Chelsea house in such a hurry that she barely had time to send her worried mother a brief, valedictory wire. 'SAILING!' Dolly telegraphed to Lily, adding the exclamation point as a marker of her mood.[3] This short missive launched Dolly on a lifelong career of authoring exciting telegrams — and it had one other distinction besides: it was probably the least expensive wire Dolly Wilde ever sent.[4]

Bed was where Dolly always felt safest — 'In bed I feel all right,'[5] she repeated with variations all her life – and the fact that she abandoned a bed in her mother's house to sail off to the uncertainties of war would ordinarily indicate some awful disturbance in her life at home. Lily's infatuated love for her second husband, Alexander Teixeira de Mattos,[6] could have been very painful for Dolly, who always required massive amounts of emotional concentration from all her intimates. But, apart from Dolly's suspicious refusal (or inability) to speak of her past – a survival tactic usually shared by *mythomanes*, molested children,[7] and near relatives of the notorious – there is no recorded or reported evidence, no biographical documentation of any kind, no instance of praise *or* blame, to attach to Dolly's relationship with Lily and Teixeira de Mattos.

There is only Dolly's eerie little anecdote about dipping cubes of sugar into Lily's perfume and eating them (a chilling, intoxicating attempt to incorporate her mother – and a fine measure of how Dolly's metaphorical mind worked) to represent her childhood for us and to provide a brief shudder of precognition.[8] After the baby photograph taken with Lily (Dolly at thirteen months, Lily at thirty-six years) described in Chapter 4, and the two or three vignettes in her mother's and stepfather's letters, there is simply a nothingness, a blank, an existential zero where accounts – however embroidered – about Dolly's growing up should be. No one – least of all Dolly – seemed to want to talk about it.

It is difficult to keep silent about one's childhood, especially difficult when that childhood is as punctuated with death and disorder and with as many emotional flights and financial drops as Dolly's was. Dolly must have worked very hard at her silence. Whatever her first, forming years meant to her, she preserved and maintained about them a vast, galactic hush. In the centre of that anguished stillness, unknown and beyond recovery, gape the black holes of her childhood. Dolly's first two decades, like her grandmother Jane Wilde's first twenty years, are confined to the curves of a question mark.[9] They can only be imagined from what they produced: a headlong, romantically impulsive plunge into the 'freedom' of dangerous and difficult conditions — a circumstance which Dolly was to repeat in a variety of forms throughout her life.

Still, Dolly's gestures spoke louder than her silence and she was to reprise her old childhood drama of emotional advance and retreat — of being sent out of the house and taken back into it — a thousand times in her most important love affair, the one with Natalie Clifford Barney. During this affair, Dolly began to speak extensively about her life in her letters, but always in the present tense, and always without reference to what Henry James called a 'visitable past'.

Dolly 'ran away', wrote Natalie Barney in 1951, from her mother's and step-father Alexander Teixeira de Mattos's London home at 9 Cheltenham Terrace to join a group of young women, Anglo-American ambulance drivers, on their way to the war front in France.[10] It was a brave and adventurous act for any British teenager to pull off in 1914; and, in an era when nursing was the conventional goal for women and young ladies were always seen home from parties by married women,[11] it was an especially brave and adventurous act for a girl. Dolly must have wanted to leave home very badly, and she seems to have left it in a very impulsive way. More importantly, she left it in and for the company of women — whole bands of women — who were assuming the risks and many of the responsibilities of regular soldiers.

Whatever situation Dolly was running away from in London could hardly have been more difficult than the one she found in France. Although she scarcely said a word about her war service and characteristically left no record of it, the testimony of a young woman from Boston attached to a British ambulance organisation in France leaves no doubt about the conditions under which young drivers like Dolly were trained for war:

The mud is ten inches deep here . . . and after four hours under my car making repairs, I am literally unrecognizeable . . . We live in a hut . . . We have a cot but no sheets, or chairs, fireless for days and no hot and often no cold water either for washing . . . I have been three weeks qualifying as a skilled mechanic and getting hardened before being entrusted to go into active service.[12]

Despite desperate preparations for war, Paris in 1914 was still the fascinating experiment in sexual, social and artistic possibilities that it had been when Dolly's uncle Oscar took up his own exile there in 1897. American and English writers had begun to settle into the narrow streets and cheap hotels of Montparnasse and French painters and poets were drinking and arguing in the cafés of Montmartre and the *rive gauche*. The many Modernisms (Dada was the first) which were to conquer Paris after it had conquered the Boche were on the boil when Dolly arrived in France; and they were, wrote Janet Flanner, what 'Paris always foments when the cerebral sap of the Gallic mind runs in two opposite directions at once, one aiming at the destruction of the city and the other at setting up a utopia on which nobody can agree'.[13]

Dolly's propensity for high risk and romantic attachment (not to mention a childhood she couldn't bear to talk about), would have made Paris – the Art and Sex capital of the world in the first third of the twentieth century – impossible to resist. Perhaps the city, with its fabled sexual freedoms and perverse poetic pleasures, exercised on Dolly the kind of attraction the Isle of Lesbos offered young Greek women 2,500 years before, when Sappho was still headmistress-in-residence in Mytilene. Pierre Louÿs, a friend of Dolly's uncle and a mentor of her future lover Natalie Clifford Barney, had already portrayed Lesbos in terms that were positively Parisian.

Lesbos was then the centre of the world [and] it had for its capital a city more elegant than Athens and more corrupt than Sardis: Mytilene, [on whose] narrow streets . . . there was no hour so late that one could not hear, through the open doors, the joyous sounds of instruments, the cries of women and the noise of dances.[14]

Natalie Barney, waiting in Dolly's Parisian future like an unexploded mine, had a more personal claim for her favourite city. 'Paris', Natalie said, 'has always seemed to me the only city where you can live and express yourself as you please.'[15]

Dolly was apparently already 'expressing herself as she pleased' when she arrived in France. Her first reported affair there was with a young woman, and she seems to have loved women by preference and made love to them by choice. Still, she was drawn in a sensual way to attractive members of both sexes and her later letters to her friend Honey Harris are full of admiration for the young men they knew together. The life available to Dolly in Paris during the First War gave social support to all her inclinations.

'Modern' experiments in sexual styles were the *specialité de la maison* of Paris, and nothing was more modern (or more ancient) than homosexuality. From the *belle époque* to the end of the 1920s, the social and legal constructions which now place 'homosexual' and 'heterosexual' in different categories (and on different planets) were still very recent inventions; it was possible for women as well as for men to carry on complicated emotional and sexual relationships with members of their same and opposite sexes without slipping into fixed, too-final self-definitions.[16] What became the Modernist *cri de coeur*, 'Make it new!', was finding application everywhere. Everywhere, that is, except in the lives of the major male Modernists who, perfectly reflecting the bourgeois world against which they railed, were themselves conventionally heterosexual and boringly misogynist.[17]

Although the Code Napoléon in France gave men full control over their wives' wages and choice of professions, the French official who drafted the Code was homosexual and so same-sex relations were left mostly unregulated in that country. Laws prohibiting such relations were confined to England and to English males alone, for Queen Victoria was famously unable to imagine women in bed together.

The three trials of Dolly's uncle had made the male homosexual act in England an unnameable one; and Oscar's imprisonment

rendered 'the love that dared not speak its name' – and the name associated with that love – truly 'unspeakable'. Ada Leverson's daughter
Violet said that if Oscar was referred to at all in London society it
was by his initials only. Lesbians and the female homosexual act – and
this was no compliment to women – were never mentioned in the
polite society of the British Isles. This left those women who preferred women the dubious, double advantage of freedom from both
identification and prosecution. Certainly, social stigma and persecu-
tion for lesbians were available for the asking everywhere in the
bourgeois world of London.

Unlike Queen Victoria, the French could all too easily imagine
women in bed together. Their response to this vision of felicity was
to legally prevent prostitutes – women who serviced men – from sharing the same bed.[18] With a clearer understanding of the relationship
between assumable power and women's fashions than the English, the
French – brought to the question 400 years earlier by that pesky,
cross-dressing teenager, Joan of Arc – also prevented women (by the
Proclamation of 7 November 1800) from donning the clothes of
men in public.

Whatever the laws or lack of them in France, homosexuality in
Paris in the first part of the twentieth century was still more or less
something one *did*, as the French-American writer Édouard Roditi
noted in a letter, and not yet something one *was*, and so homosexuals of both genders could and did contract 'heterosexual' marriages
with only a second thought for the consequences. Dolly, whose imagination, like Virginia Woolf's, was stirred mostly by women, was to
speak of marriage and of 'falling in love with my host' in quite a few
later letters. 'I really must marry my gentle, fox-hunting gentleman . . .'
she told her close correspondent 'Emily'.[19] And to Janet Flanner she
wrote, half-seriously, that either her friend Honey Harris's 'virginal
spinster look' or her own 'witty voluptuousness ought to win [the
richest man in America], in which case we will all live richly ever after,
you included.'[20]

Dolly was to receive – perhaps she encouraged – quite a few

proposals of marriage from men of all persuasions.[21] She usually spoke of these proposals practically and humorously with something like the narrative voice of a Jane Austen novel: 'He was infinitely relieved when I refused him . . .' Never shy of sexual matters, but by nature secretive, ambivalent, and uncommitted to a settled identity of any kind, Dolly preferred to keep her sexual secrets under the covers. In philosophy (too theoretical a name, really, for the spontaneous operating principles by which she lived), Dolly was an old-fashioned 'Aesthete' (as was her uncle Oscar before he made his too-rapid devolution to 'Decadent'): beauty, or rather, 'Beauty' ruled her attractions and she felt falsified by whatever social explanations she had to make about her sexual behaviour.

Though generally enthusiastic and open about all her tastes (flamboyant even), Dolly lived within – and, much of the time, *wanted* to live within – society, and high society at that; and so she saw the virtues of a certain kind of dissimulation. Dolly was always a déclassé woman in '*classé*' circumstances; she had a great deal to protect and when conditions warranted it and it suited her purpose, she lied her head off, insisting that: 'It's a pity that there should exist such walls of misunderstanding between Dorothy [a married woman friend] & me – I feel horribly sly at times & dislike the subterfuge. But her prejudice [against lesbianism] amounts to disgust – & why lose her friendship & pain Arthur.'[22]

As it turned out, prevarication was Dolly's only practicality.

Dolly was far more uncomfortable lying about her sexual activities – which were part of her aesthetic and of which she was inordinately proud – than she was lying about her later drug use – which was merely a shameful necessity and about which she felt guilty. The French way of dealing with lesbianism (and her uncle's way of dealing with his homosexuality before he got caught out) was to hide it in plain sight – and that method suited Dolly perfectly: 'Osbert Sitwell was at lunch & I brought you [Natalie Barney] into the conversation – at the risk of compromise – with devilish cunning.'[23]

Whatever the political climate for public or private sexual life, Dolly's impulsive voyage to Paris in 1914 would never have had to do with politics as we understand them – sexual or otherwise. The real summit of her world-view was the consciousness that one's friends should be looked after. And she expected, often infuriatingly, that her friends would look after her. She was much more likely to follow a friend or a lover to war than to follow a flag: her loyalties and her politics were always 'purely personal. Did you really think I'd work myself into a fever over England's downfall, distressing though it is to think that the balance of culture in the world is on the decline. National disaster spells *personal* ruin – that is all.'[24]

Personal, too, were her affinities for small, rebellious, hopeless causes. Her Irish blood was at all times high, and in this she was certainly Speranza's granddaughter and Oscar's niece. She had spiritual leanings towards metaphysical, self-improving practices, involving herself in Christian Science and in the various holistic healings of her time and recommending them strongly to friends. She had a clear, artistic sense of what it meant to be a lesbian in a world which did not condone such relations and she was, characteristically, far more irritated by works of art whose treatment of the lesbian subject was insufficient than she was by any societal, psychological or legal prejudices:

> Extraordinary Women [Compton MacKenzie's satire of lesbian life on Capri] – except for flashes of humour – *bores*
> me – & in a way that books of far less merit have never done.
> Literary photography is always meretricious. And how badly
> he envisages the whole question of Lesbianism – not the
> slightest insight. M. . . is sometimes well done as a character
> but never as a lover of women. I can't finish it even.[25]

Dolly kept her loyalties plain and her affinities quiet by keeping her sexual preference (she always spoke of it as a preference) and her social worlds determinedly separate.

Just before her death during the Second World War, when she was living in London, trying once again to dry out and taking maintenance doses of heroin, Dolly began to do volunteer work for an organisation that helped Polish refugees, the Polish Relief Fund. *That* was the kind of political work Dolly could lend her talents, her always-generous sympathies, and her understanding to. She had, after all, been a refugee all her life.

Once she arrived in Paris in 1914, Dolly, whose instinct for finding the bohemian centre of any city was irreproachable (and rather like her mother's), went straight to Montparnasse where she ended by sharing an apartment with four other female ambulance drivers. Bronia Clair, widow of the French film master René Clair, remembered Dolly in Montmartre after the war with people like Djuna Barnes and with her own sister Tylia Perlmutter.

'There were only five people there always together,' said Mme Clair, meaning women of course. Bronia Clair remembered briefly meeting Dolly Wilde in Paris ('she was tall,' thought the petite Mme Clair) and encountering a rather aggressive Natalie Barney at a lunch in Nice. Barney said to her: 'I heard you had beautiful eyes,' and pulled her over to the window to see them. 'I guess she was disappointed,' said Mme Clair drily.[26]

The apartment Dolly took with her sister ambulance drivers in Montparnasse was a cheap one because it had an unusual glass roof.[27] More than likely, it had been an artist's atelier. The five girls would have had some eerie evenings watching German bomber planes shelling the beleaguered city through the transparency of their own ceiling. One of Dolly's flatmates, Joe Carstairs, described in old age how the sides of entire houses fell down and people lay wounded in the streets, and how she saw an aircraft plummet in flames straight down on to the Place de la Concorde. Joe got out of her car and pulled the dead pilot out of the plane's wreckage.[28]

Like almost everyone close to Dolly, Joe Carstairs had a highly unusual character. Although she had trained behind the wheel of an ambulance, she always drove in her own direction. A determined cross-dresser from her earliest years, Joe was a stylish, commanding, Standard Oil heiress with cultivated muscles, a boy's haircut, and, later, startlingly tattooed arms. She grew up to become a notorious seducer of women (counting Marlene Dietrich — for whom she provisionally purchased an island — amongst her conquests), and a daredevil speedboat racer known as 'the fastest woman on water'. She adopted as her *alter ego* a preternaturally vital little boy doll named Lord Tod Wadley, whom she dressed beautifully, photographed carefully, and treated as though it were a sentient being. Joe Carstairs was seventeen at the time she met Dolly, just the right age for a massive crush, and she and Dolly went to bed together. Joe said they had an affair.

It must have been an exhilarating experience for the two adolescent girls — caught, as they were, between the horrors of war and the happiness of sexual experiment — to take charge of their lives in ways that women had not taken charge before: sitting in the driver's seat. In her later years Joe still referred to Dolly 'as one of the four women who changed her life'.[29] Since Joe Carstairs's field of past lovers numbered at least 120 interesting and beautiful women, this was not an inconsiderable distinction.

Joe said she found Dolly 'almost mystical'. Dolly *was* mystical and Joe was only seventeen, so the qualifier is understandable. 'I knew [her] excessively well,' Joe said. 'She taught me elasticity of thought. She taught me to think.'[30] That tutelary experience was only the first of the involved and infrequent connections Dolly and Joe Carstairs would continue until Dolly's death.[31]

A classic turn of phrase by Dolly almost a decade after the war ended indicates there may have been a faint reprise of Dolly's and Joe's teenage affair. Six months into her relationship with Natalie Barney, in December 1927, Dolly ran into Joe in London in an anemone-coloured Rolls Royce and wrote to Natalie — defensively, for Joe was notorious — that Joe '. . . is *quite* changed, charming, doesn't see any of that awful crowd she was with . . . is busy restoring her reputation. She comes to Paris in February, & you shall meet her — as she is stopping on purpose to see me on her way to Cannes to race her boat.'[32] That phrase 'on purpose' must have rankled Natalie considerably.

Although Dolly began the war by living in Montparnasse, she continued it by driving with an all-woman ambulance unit like the one assembled by her acquaintance, Barbara 'Toupie' Lowther.

Toupie Lowther was the eldest daughter of the sixth Earl of Lonsdale and she was a sometime-friend of that notorious writing couple, Radclyffe Hall and Una Troubridge. Toupie Lowther was also the sister of the actress Aimée Lowther – to whom Oscar Wilde made the famous remark which Ellen Terry famously did not understand: 'Aimée, if you were only a boy I could adore you.' A probably apocryphal story, too neat to be entirely credible, but wonderfully useful all the same, illustrates the confusing effect Toupie's appearance had on people who did not know her. It is said that Toupie Lowther, wearing pants, was arrested at the Franco-Italian border for masquerading as a man and, on her return journey – swathed in a conciliatory skirt – she was arrested once again, this time for masquerading as a woman.[33]

In 1917, Toupie Lowther and a Miss Desmond Hackett raised the money for an all-woman ambulance unit of twenty-five drivers and twenty ambulances. Despite the usual resistance to women wanting to do important things offered by men already doing them, Lowther's unit was finally allowed to accompany the French Army Ambulance Corps on the Compiègne battle front, where they motored thousands of casualties from the field back to the dressing stations, often incurring terrible dangers from shelling and bombed-out roads to do so.[34]

Radclyffe Hall used Toupie Lowther's ambulance unit as the basis for the 'Brakespeare Ambulance Unit' in the *The Well of Loneliness*, her highly melodramatic and self-punishing novel, published in 1928, on the subject of female 'inversion'.[35] Virginia Woolf found the book 'meritorious' and 'dull', though it is not exactly either. Colette loved the book's pastoral descriptions and deplored its tortured sexuality.[36] Dolly said that she was unable to finish it; reading it, she wrote, was 'like walking through a plowed field'. The *Well of Loneliness* is a *roman-à-clef.*

In the novel, Radclyffe Hall put her female hero Stephen Gordon into Lowther's ambulance unit, thinly disguised as the 'Brakespeare Ambulance Unit' – and *The Well of Loneliness* is full of other true-to-life details. Hall houses Stephen Gordon in Natalie Barney's *pavillon* on the rue Jacob and gives Stephen's young female lover who is, as Dolly was, a teenaged ambulance driver, the bedroom (blue and beautiful) that Barney gave to Dolly. Natalie Barney appears in the book, accurately described and ensconced (though in a flat on the quai Voltaire), as Valerie Seymour, as so do several other women in Natalie's circle.

As in Hall's novel, many of the British and American women involved in funding, sustaining or driving these First World War ambulances were women who preferred women. Among them was Dorothy Arzner, the only woman ever to achieve prominence as a film director in the golden age of Hollywood. Like Dolly, she was an ambulance driver in France and had an affair with the great stage and screen actress Alla Nazimova.[37] The war provided women who went to it with generous opportunites to enlarge their social roles, indulge their private tastes, and find a precarious but respected place for themselves in a world turned upside down. When the war ended, so did most of the women's opportunities – but their experiences of wartime driving altered them for ever.[38]

Twenty-four- and thirty-six-hour shifts were the norm for these young women drivers, who were regularly fired upon, accidentally blown up, and who suffered most of the pains of combat as well as the responsibilties of caring for its casualties.

Some ambulance drivers – one of them a man named Eddie Parker, married to that other interesting Dorothy, the American writer Dorothy Parker, whose swift ripostes and suicidal habits are so reminiscent of Dorothy Wilde's – turned to the ample supplies of morphine at the *postes de secours* to ease the horrors of war.[39] It is intriguing to think that Dolly might have had her first taste of what

Janet Flanner called the '*pays de Cocagne*' while driving an ambulance. Dolly, naturally, never said a word about it.

Natalie Barney wrote that Dolly emerged from battle with her 'first and only honours' – which, since Natalie uses the plural, were certainly Dolly's lieutenancy and perhaps a medal for wartime service – the Croix de Guerre or something like what Gertrude Stein and Alice Toklas received: the more routinely awarded Médaille de la Reconnaissance Française.

Bettina Bergery thought that Dolly might have wheeled into battle in Gertrude Stein's high-backed old Ford, 'Aunt Pauline'.[40] Although it is painful to imagine anyone motoring anywhere with the magisterial Gertrude, who regularly refused to drive in reverse and systematically disregarded all rules of the road, Gertrude, Alice Toklas and Dolly certainly made friends during the war years, and it is from that time that Alice remembered Dolly's 'almost mythical pristine freshness . . .' And Gertrude's pithy summary of Dolly's death captured both her life *and* her driving: 'Well she certainly hadn't a fair run for her money.'[41]

Natalie Barney called Dolly's ambulance unit 'that group of girls in uniform', slyly invoking Christa Winsloe's classic German film of same-sex desire in a girls' boarding-school, *Mädchen in Uniform*, and pointing to what was perhaps Dolly's most memorable wartime experience.

There is something poetic – something Byronic even – in Dolly's youthful flight to France and in her dashed-off telegram to Lily. Every adolescent's dream of romantic adventure billows out joyfully in that exclamatory wire: 'SAILING!' Bettina Bergery said that Dolly's 'real backbone was Byron', and that Dolly 'felt her parentage' with Byron,[42] whose extremes of rage and passion, dazzling poetic flights, and echoing reputation for uncontrollable indulgence had been a synonym for romanticism for almost a century, although his behaviour was often anything *but* romantic. Dolly must have felt many of Byron's chaotic promptings within herself: his plunge into the Greek wars for independence was the perfect paradigm of romantic behaviour – what is more exciting than a lost cause? — and Byron's poetry could easily have been one of her literary inspirations for that first trip across the Channel.

Both Dolly and Byron seemed to share elements of what we would now call, quite *un*romantically, a hereditary manic-depressive disorder: 'a singularly cyclic disease [whose episodes are] strikingly similar to [those in] the natural world . . .' and are characterised by chameleonic changes in mood, temperamament, and versions of self.[43] Dolly was, all her life, subject to large emotions that could turn on a sixpence (or, more accurately, change directions for want of a shilling); her impulsiveness in appearing (or not appearing) for appointments was the stuff of legend; and her physical and emotional flights, falls, and turns were more cyclic than the seasons — and often depended on them.

> You have no idea what a London winter is like with cold houses & damp grey days. My amusement in people gets less & less . . . worries of money seem trifling in comparison with this cloud of depression that settles on one — making suicide not dramatic but seductive which edges so much nearer danger point.[44]

In an acute piece of self-analysis written to Natalie Barney in 1927, Dolly said that the 'warm current of electric happiness is missing — & without the sun & the flowery summer life I feel devitalised & empty. Climatic depression?'[45]

The Wildean side of Dolly's family displayed — some would say theatricalised — many of these same characteristics. Both her father and her uncle shared Byron's (and Dolly's) mood swings, his excesses with alcohol, and his prodigality with money; and André Gide always insisted that Oscar was the most 'Byronic' of writers. Dolly's paternal grandfather was subject to these same burdens of character and Dolly told Bettina Bergery that Byron's mother and 'Oscar's mother' (she never said 'my father's mother') must have had 'the same kind of natures'.[46] While Byron found temporary respites from his malady in art, Dolly — too late in life — had to rely on the very inadequate understanding of doctors.

After the war in France, Dolly was still imaginatively preoccupied with Byron, even dispensing emotional advice in terms of his love life. Once, when Bettina Bergery was exceptionally 'love-lorn', Victor Cunard brought Dolly in as a sort of *ad hoc* amatory consultant. Dolly cautioned Bettina:

> The trouble is, darling, you've been behaving too much like Carolyn Lamb . . . Byron hated her because the scenes she made him were too picturesque. If you must show so much imagination — and masculine men don't really like women with imagination — you should try to be like a French actress who was called Sophie Arnaud. It's quite easy you know. You first read several books about her, and we've brought you one to begin with. Then whatever happens you just think what she would have done and do it. Do try, darling, it can't do any harm. Besides it will be so good for your French.[47]

And Dolly did not hesitate to telephone Bettina that evening to offer an even more literary suggestion:

> Darling, don't forget that Ninon de Lenclos said: 'Love never dies of starvation but often of indigestion.' That doesn't mean that you must stop eating, but you might go away for a while. Why don't you go see your family in New York? Darling, don't cry, tears are not becoming weapons for blondes.[48]

Applying the lineaments of literature to the lacerations of life was a characteristic act for Dolly. She was always a very smart and discerning reader — and a very avid one. '*Good* literature,' she said, is 'really my *favourite* drug of all' — and she never got beyond its intoxications.[49] Dolly might be the only woman on earth who ever really sacrificed her life to literature. She used books to think about herself, she used them as 'stimulants', (she loved the word 'stimulant') and she is surely the best example of her uncle's epigram about how all art is useless: it never helped *her* life for a moment.

One of Dolly's more creative acts was to turn the life around her into the literature she loved; and so she perpetually found resemblances between the people she knew and the literary characters who interested her. More deeply than Emma Bovary, but with some of Emma's same inclination to escape her circumstances, Dolly was 'corrupted' by her passionate love of good books. If she couldn't write a book, she seemed determined to live one and her advice to Bettina Bergery about imitating Sophie Arnaud through the absorbed reading of a biography sounds both professional – and practised.

By 1916, when Dolly was halfway through her war service, all conscriptable French males had been sent to the war front and Paris was virtually a city of women. This temporary feminisation of the population reflected one of the modes by which the city imagined itself: as a kind of 'society beauty' whose 'natural accoutrements' (the well-manicured parks, civilised woods, and fantastical gardens) had always been cosseted and kept up like living works of art – or like the kind of woman Dolly grew up to be attracted to. After the war, and with unmistakable intentions, Dolly regularly described variations on this kind of woman in her letters to Natalie Barney:

A very pretty girl is strumming 'Mozart' at the piano
(Reynaldo Hahn's piece) . . . She has fine baby hair – your
colour – brown eyes too gazelle-like – a nose that makes a
quick, unimportant little bridge . . . to her mouth which is
small & yet sculptured – so defined that one might almost
skate along the firm edge! – exquisite. She is small with an
absurdly fragile neck & shoulders like a doll's, funny little
round arms & hands that are pretty & incompetent . . . I
topple her over into unaccustomed channels of thought about
herself & so intrigue her that she leaves the young men & sits

bewildered on the arm of my chair, waiting like a little dog
for a bone! She should be saved — perhaps I will![50]

Now, in 1916, both the 'nature' in Paris and the women left to
populate it were enduring severe wartime privations. Such an obvious
set of paradoxes would have interested Dolly, whose later letters
often marked her natural surroundings in the same way that she
remarked on the allure of women.[51] Perhaps these paradoxes would
also have reminded her of her uncle Oscar, whose art had regularly
stressed the unnatural and who had never made an authentic comparison with nature until he went to prison.

It was in Paris, too, that Oscar had sought his own uneasy exile in
1898 and it was in Paris that Dolly's mother had visited Oscar at the
Hôtel d'Alsace about a month before he died in the autumn of 1900.
Lily certainly told the story of this visit to Dolly, probably repeating
Oscar's witticism about dying beyond his means. It would have taken
on the authority of all deathbed descriptions and Dolly would have
remembered it. Given the laxity of laws and customs in France, it is
easy (perhaps it is even correct) to presume that Dolly's early inclination for her own sex — whether or not it was as exclusive as it
clearly became — was one of her more interesting reasons for running
off to Paris.

Whatever its origins, this singular act, suffused with the high consciousness of Oscar's expatriation and ostracism, was the beginning of
her many self-enforced uprootings and her unceasing search for a
'home away from home' — the only kind of home she ever allowed
herself.

Dolly's crossing to wartime France also bears out Natalie Barney's
judgement that 'In spite of Dolly's inherent laziness, she could, on the
spur of the moment, prove more energetic and efficient than most of
us . . .'[52] and it prefigures Dolly's odd fearlessness in the next war.
When German planes were buzzing Paris skies during the late 1930s
and the formidable Natalie Barney hid herself in the little sixteenth-
century temple in her garden, Dolly unconcernedly remained in bed

upstairs in Barney's *pavillon* at the rue Jacob enjoying a good night's sleep.

Dolly emerged from the war in 1918 in an attractive, dark blue, lieutenant's uniform, fresh from her exhilarating tour of duty in the driver's seat. Until the end of her days, driving – driving too fast, that is – was an exquisite pleasure to her, but she seems never to have thought of buying her own vehicle. She made do instead with the borrowed cars of friends, a habit not always to her advantage. She and Natalie Barney were to have a series of less-than-pleasant exchanges about Dolly's persistent appropriation (and dangerous driving) of the stately pearl-grey Buick shared by Natalie and her far more conservative sister Laura. Janet Flanner thought there was something equine about this car, as though it had once been in some proximity to a horse.[53]

At the war's end, Dolly exchanged her blue uniform for some smart clothes provided by her mother's friends from Lady "Lucille" Duff-Gordon's shop in London, and 'spent her days posing in lamé scarfs and her evenings were spent refusing proposals of marriage or allowing her rejected suitors to escort her to parties where she scintillated with so many epigrams of her own, all delivered at once – that no one had time to remember any.'[54] And then, for the next nine years, chronicles of Dolly's wit and personality are obscured by the kinds of comings and goings – as frequent and as changeable as Dolly's feelings – that became her signature style of expression.

Like false fire on the lowlands, she flickers on and off amongst dimly lit and theatrically limned experiences, with only the occasional spotlight to mark her entrances and exits. Until she reappeared as the new star in Natalie Barney's firmament in the summer of 1927, Dolly surfaces in a traceable way with only an occasional flourish of the social oriflamme: a tea party in Neuilly in 1925, a country weekend at Wilsford in 1927, a chauffered motor trip to Algiers in 1924, and – still gossiped about in Hollywood in the 1970s – a brief affair with the exotic Russian-American film star, Alla Nazimova, in Paris sometime in 1925 or 1926.

It took a death in the family – the last death in her immediate family – to bring Dolly back to the social stage once again and to register the fluctuations of her presence in London, the city which had proved so unlucky for every single member of the Wilde family.

6

The Friends of Dorothy

*I feel too young to retire from life & yet I can't stay in bed
all the year round . . . How right you are never to go out,
people are simply dreadful – we must be solitary old
maids to the end of our lives. I wish we could marry each
other.*

Dolly Wilde to Pamela 'Honey' Harris

*I*n October 1922, Dolly's mother Lily, grieving terribly over
the demise of her second husband Teixeira de Mattos, died at
the age of sixty-two, leaving her 'beloved daughter Dorothy' a little
heap of pounds sterling, a socially adept executor to help manage
them, an apartment-full of furniture in trust, and a legacy of an
entirely different kind: an inherited experience of Oscar Wilde which
marked Dolly like a branding iron. Dolly mourned her mother: ten
years after Lily died, in a condolence note to Sacheverell Sitwell, she
wrote that she knew 'from my own experience the irrevocable sense of
sadness' that follows the death of an 'enchanting' mother.[1]

It is only after Lily's death that Dolly's movements begin to register, however faintly, on the minor historical barometers of the
moment: the street directories, the private journals, and the gossip.
And it is only after Lily's death that Dolly's movements – like the
aimless flight patterns or erratic railway journeys they so often

resembled – showed themselves for what they really were: the kind of persistent driftings that characterised so many of her post-war era's talented twenty-somethings.

In early October 1922, probably when she began to see the signs of some cash in her future, Dolly committed one of her few (and more unlikely) recorded acts. She took a service flat at 14 Queen Street, Mayfair, which she was to keep – occasionally occupied by herself, but mostly bothersomely let out or troublesomely empty – for the next twelve years.[2] Dolly gives every appearance of having taken it – now that Lily was dead and the Cheltenham Terrace flat dismantled – so that she would have a place to go away from.

It is characteristic of Dolly that the Queen Street flat's location would express all at once her social aspirations, her spiritual leanings, and her attraction to the louche things in life. The flat was: (1) in a very good street in Mayfair (like Oscar, Dolly was always attracted to good addresses); (2) around the corner from the Third Christian Science Church, constructed in 1910, twelve years before Dolly moved to the neighbourhood (Dolly was known to consult Christian Science Readers in times of trouble); and (3) near to Shepherd Market, which is just at the bottom of Queen Street (Shepherd Market is where all the better prostitutes once plied their trades).

Dolly, then, in late 1922 was a drifting twenty-seven-year-old with a flat to drift back to. She was parentless, though in actual fact she seems always to have given the impression that she was an orphan. She had a tiny income and she had her mother's executor, the art historian Tancred Borenius, to help her with it. And she was in the full flush of her roaring twenties in the very flush and roaring 1920s.

Moreover, Dolly was just far enough along in the chronological line – a full two decades after Oscar's death – to begin to reap some of the pride and not much of the prejudice of being both the niece of Oscar Wilde and his Chief Resembler. These rewards had eluded every other member of her family. She was now the last person in the world to bear the surname Wilde, and – coals to Newcastle – her name was *Dolly* Wilde, a name so perfectly insouciant that it would

have been difficult to invent a better one for her. It is a name that positively conjures up period giddiness, historical charm, and a shimmer
of inherited accomplishment. It was the perfect name for Dolly
Wilde, and it perfectly suited the era through which she carried it.

The 1920s, like their more colourful but less interesting epigone,
the 1960s, were, in London, Paris and New York, the first decade of
the twentieth century that consecrated itself to youth culture and
to the sort of self-indulgence which is usually explained away
by the term 'self-consciousness'. It was a self-regarding era: self-
mythologising, self-aggrandising and, at the same time, self-satirising;
dedicated to performances in living rooms, gender role exchanges
(mostly, but not always, limited to costumes), enormously silly social
games (treasure hunts and 'Truth' among them),[3] and the enhance-
ment of experience by chemical means (cocaine, heroin, and alcohol
being the front-running favourites).

If this summary of the 1920s sounds familiar, that is because it *is*
familiar, contemporary almost. The twenties was the period in which
everything we mean by 'modern', with the sole exceptions of the sil-
icon chip and the shopping trolley, was invented and/or popularised:
from buying on credit to high colonics to concrete to cult stars to
serious skyscrapers. And Dolly Wilde was just as modern as any
modern woman in her twenties (and in *the* twenties) could be. In fact,
Dolly, possibly taking the hint from her grandmother Wilde's and
uncle Oscar's fiddlings with chronology, seems to have remained in
her twenties several years longer than her birth certificate indicates
was possible.

During much of the 1920s, Dolly blew — a bright migratory bird
in what appears to be a heavy emotional headwind — from continent
to continent, from city to country, from Paris to London, perching
briefly in the borrowed residences, hotel bedrooms, villas, and the
guest apartments of her friends and lovers. She managed a nice mix
of social circles, from the high society of Sir Austin and Lady Cara
Harris and Lord and Lady Carnarvon, to the self-promoting qualities
of the literary Sitwells (Virginia Woolf was only 'fond . . . of parts of

them'; Alice Toklas judged Osbert Sitwell to be a 'lowbrow' writer), to the distinctly café society of her theatrical and/or homosexual friends. People marked Dolly's presence and remarked on its vividness: she is noted in a rather unprecedented way, as though her observers understood there was something original about her but did not quite know how to set it out in prose.[4]

Like any woman who has never stayed in one place, never owned property, never published a book, and never murdered anyone, Dolly Wilde was very difficult to locate.

'. . . I am living with Honey's Mama and Papa in a charming house in London – and once more find delight in 'family life' . . .

Dolly Wilde

Dolly's long-time friend, Pamela 'Honey' Harris, born five years after Dolly, in 1900, was a painter and sculptor who sacrificed (so her brother-in-law, the distinguished cartoonist, illustrator and theatrical set designer Osbert Lancaster, thought) what could have been a real career as an artist to the demands of her charming, erratic and imperious mother: Lady Cara Harris, the London painter, film maker and Surrealist prankster. Lady Cara Harris was the daughter of Mabel 'Ladye' Batten, the redoubtable society soprano who, as Lady Harris's granddaughter Cara Lancaster said, 'was surely the only woman to sleep with Edward VII, Radclyffe Hall, *and* Wilfred Blunt – though they all seem to have had Wilfred Blunt.'[5]

For Cara Lancaster (daughter of Osbert Lancaster and Honey's sister Karen), Honey Harris was a kind of fairytale aunt subject to the will of her fanciful mother, Lady Cara Harris, whose life revolved around home theatricals, expensive film-making, and registering, in the society columns of *The Times* and the *Tatler*, the births, deaths and marriages of the highly detailed dolls she sewed. Lady Harris made dolls of her friends Cecil Beaton and John Betjeman, and she created

Dolly Wilde and Lady Cara Harris.

Lady Cara Harris, painter, film maker, prankster, mother of Dolly's friend Pamela 'Honey' Harris.

Dolly at the wheel: Bembridge, the Harris's house on the IOW. Note the effaced man and woman seated beside Dolly.

Pamela 'Honey' Harris at Bembridge. Dolly called her 'pure Bronte.'

Lady Cara Harris crowning the artist Osbert Lancaster with laurels.

'Dolly Thame,' John Betjeman and Cecil Beaton: part of the doll family created by Lady Cara Harris.

Friday afternoon at 20 rue
Jacob: Berthe Cleyrergue
awaits the guests.

Romaine Brooks and Natalie
Barney: the Artist and the
Amazon.

Jeunesse Sauvage: Natalie in the wild woods.

A sitting room in the *temple*. Note the proscenium.

The *temple à l'amitié* in Natalie's garden of earthly delights.

The pavilion at 20 rue Jacob: 1909, the year Natalie Barney settled in.

Natalie Barney at 16: self-assurance to spare.

Natalie Barney in the costume she designed for
her first visit to Liane de Pougy.

Natalie as a *femme de lettres*: one of her many roles.

an exquisite doll in Dolly's likeness complete with fashionable clothes, a perky little hat, enormously soulful, dark-fringed blue eyes, a bright cupid's mouth, and a hennaed bob with a widow's peak. The doll's 'personality' is distinctly eerie; its eyes are fixed on a world other than the one in which it was made and it conveys a sense of almost unbearable melancholy. Lady Harris called the doll — perhaps hopefully, certainly ironically — Dolly Thame.[6]

Lady Harris and her husband, the banker Sir Austin Harris, had long ago determined that their lives would be far more enjoyable if they kept to adjoining residences. This they generally did, perhaps to prevent such picturesque incidents as the following one, which occurred when Sir Austin required Lady Harris's presence as hostess to the President of the Banque de France. In response to her husband's request, Cara Harris said, 'I'll come but you'll regret it,' and appeared at the banquet with a placard hung round her neck inscribed 'Deaf and Dumb'.[7]

With Honey's assistance, and with Dolly supplying the whimsical name and fictitious biography of the invented artist 'Rognon de la Flèche' (Sting in the Tail), Cara Harris painted the imaginary 'Monsieur de la Flèche's' works, giving them titles like: 'He was Mean with his Money' and 'She was Mean too!' — (Dolly could easily have been the title-supplier for these paintings) — and exhibiting them in Dorothy Warren's gallery in London in 1933.[8]

Dolly spent long, happy hours in the Harris family house at 10 Catherine Street, 'writing in Honey's romantic bedroom with lowered lights, a dreaming fire, and Honey tucked up like a Princess fast asleep!'[9] Dolly referred to Honey as 'the rich all understanding companion', described her as 'pure Brontë', and clearly adored her. Honey, said her niece Cara Lancaster, had a kind of perfected taste and everything about her was extremely refined and innovative; she began distempering the walls of her room with paints of her own devising decades before the technique became a staple of home decor. There is a William Nicholson portrait of Honey in half-profile, looking, characteristically, away from the painter.[10]

Everyone in the Harris family and their circle, particularly Honey Harris and Osbert Lancaster, loved Dolly and talked about her all the time. She was, they said, not at all an easy person, she never wore a watch and was never on time, but she was charming, captivating, enchanting – and they all made myths of her behaviour. Even Sir Austin Harris, Honey's father, a director of Lloyd's Bank and a stickler for punctuality, apparently countenanced Dolly's presence – though Dolly generally designed her sojourns at Catherine Street to coincide with his absence.[11]

Cara Lancaster remembers her father Osbert Lancaster and her aunt Honey telling wonderful anecdotes about Dolly that would always begin with: 'Do you remember the time Dolly said . . .?' but being very young at the time Cara Lancaster can't remember the gist of the stories themselves, only the sense of magic with which they were related. Dolly, she says, was always making you do things you didn't want to do, and you always ended up doing them anyway and *still* loving her.[12]

Victor Cunard, Dolly's close friend and a cousin of Nancy Cunard, whose Hours Press in Paris occasionally employed Dolly as a translator, was also a friend of the Harrises and an actor in Lady Harris's films. Victor went so far as to call Dolly's company 'addicting'. 'Once the habit had been formed,' he wrote, 'there was no disintoxication possible, and no price too high for the addict to pay. If only the drug in which she found her comfort had been as satisfying and as harmless as the one she dispensed to her friends!'[13]

One of the most interesting artefacts tucked away in the tin boxes that were part of Honey Harris's legacy to Cara Lancaster is Lady Cara Harris's notebook of personal evaluations. An obvious variant on the painful, popular parlour game of the 1920s called 'Truth' – a form of institutionalised cruelty in which game-players anonymously revealed their worst impressions of their best friends – Cara Harris's little book enjoins its signatories to give '*your* candid opinion of how the person strikes *you* . . . You are requested to fill in the numbers of marks you award without putting in your name. What you don't

know, or feel [a nice distinction], leave blank.' The qualities of each person are rated with marks ranging from 0 (the lowest) to 20 (the highest).

Cara Harris provided forty-three categories of qualities cross-referenced with the names of twenty-three friends, relatives and frequent house guests, of which 'Dorothy Wilde', an obvious late addition, is the last name listed. The book was created some time in the 1920s, for Karen Harris, the youngest Harris daughter, born in 1914, is judged too young to comment on by some of the people doing the marking, and Dolly's friend, the socialite Zita Jungman James, still appears under her maiden name. The book proffers a gruesomely candid report card (with a few terrified 'cheats' in favour of the imperious Lady Harris) marking personal reactions to such traits as 'Beauty of feature', 'Beauty of figure', 'Beauty of mind', 'grace & elegance', 'Brains', 'imagination', 'generosity', 'truthfulness', etc. An invitation to a beheading, in short.

Demonstrating the feckless lack of partiality with which the marks were generally given, the dignified head of the Harris family, Sir Austin Harris, received three 0s for 'moral courage', three 0s for 'truthfulness', two 0s and a 5 for 'charm', and a meagre 3 for 'joie de vivre'. Honey Harris did much better: she got six 20s for 'kindliness' and 'cleanliness of mind', and five 20s for 'brains'.

Dolly, who had a lot of blank categories under her name in the notebook (no one bothered to fill in the spaces for 'moral courage', 'obstinacy', 'spite', 'self-control', 'jealousy', 'sense of dignity' or 'love of gossip' – perhaps the ratings were too obvious to bother with), got a 19 and a 2 for 'moral sense' and four straight 20s each for 'good manners', 'sense of humour', 'intelligence', 'good temper', and 'kindliness'. She also ranked high on the scale for 'capability to do things well', 'joie de vivre', 'laziness' (two 20s, a 19, an 18 and a 17) and 'greediness' (three 20s and a 15). Explaining her tendency to regularly gain and lose weight, Dolly once said that greed and vanity waged a constant battle in her breast. For 'discretion', Dolly received two 0s and someone's very charitable 6.

Besides this uncomfortable game, the entire Harris family, sometimes accompanied by Dolly (who loved to stay at Catherine Street or at the Harris country seat, Smoglands, on the Isle of Wight, when Lady Harris was in a good mood), was always getting together for Cara Harris's theatricals. There are many photographs of Cara's daughter Karen playing the accordion accompanied by Honey Harris on the drums, and there are myriad stills from the elaborate home movies Cara Harris directed, with town houses and airplanes, and famous and titled players all very expensively costumed and disguised. It is a nice comment on the fluidity of upper-class English gender-role exchanges that it is impossible to decide if one masked figure in a movie still is Dolly Wilde *en déshabillé* or Cara Lancaster's own father, Osbert Lancaster, in drag.[14]

The pleasure Dolly took in all the Harris family doings and in simply being in repose in the Harris milieu is proved again and again in her lengthy correspondence with Natalie Barney, to whom, from 1927 onwards, she continued to write from the safe haven of Honey's family homes. The Harrises' homes embodied the beauty of taste that made life for Dolly a continuous thrill of exquisite sensations. In this letter to Natalie from 10 Catherine Street, she's in her element: 'To begin with, I am supremely happy in this house. Real taste possesses such enchantment that literally a glow of rich serenity seems to hang round every object in a diffused light.'

Dolly is surrounded by 'Such interesting people all the time. Imagine – Virginia Woolf was lunching but postponed at the last moment. I was so curious to see her, because of her books and Romaine's talk of her . . .'

Osbert Sitwell has just proposed to her 'with the sudden bravado of a suppressed nature. He was infinitely relieved when I refused him and we are happy together. Such fun at his first night. The 1st act pulled like a cracker.' And she has rented her ever-troublesome Queen Street flat 'to a charming American girl'.

Honey is perfection and all my pleasure is made manifest by

long hours with her alone – and always the getting back to her mellow elegance of thought. She is much less worldly than I am, and in answer to her somewhat questioning intolerance of people I told her we were more 'evolved'! She is delighted with the discovery and we carry that enviable epithet on our heads like crowns and fall asleep very proud of ourselves!

How flippant I am. And only love letters or business letters interest you.

You have set such a seal upon my lips that I still feel the line of suffering formed between them. I am bewitched by all around me but am willingly enslaved to you with deep and secret thoughtfulness.

So success comes easily to a preoccupied heart.

Dolly says in this letter that she's 'happy', even 'lucky', but her ironic eye (and tendency to underestimate herself) notes that 'the prize fortunately always goes to the unworthy!'[15] And she writes again to Natalie from the other Harris home, 'Smoglands', on the Isle of Wight:

Here I am embosomed in Beauty – wrapped in the scented sachet of summer. The garden rivals any Gardener's Catalogue; & we walk between its borders as [illegible] the Champs Elysées & superbly highly bloomed over green velvet into the sea. ('I have no love for the sea, but I respect it' I, or someone else once said.) We play tennis & disprove melancholy with rapid circulation of the blood. Its a lazy, exquisite life & we allow no one to intrude – hiding under the table at the first scrunch of a car in the drive with callers. I lie a great deal in the hammock which swings in the orchard by a bed of white stocks & roses, with a litter of books I never read. Today I lay

there and the bell of your name sounded in my ears all the time.[16]

Lady Cara Harris's best known film was *Treasons Bargain*, shot in 1937, more than twelve years after Dolly's frolicking twenties had come to a close – and ten years after the above letters were written to Natalie Barney. Cara Lancaster identified the extraordinary cast members in the film as well as she could for me, providing a nice no-nonsense run of commentary on the order of: 'The problem with all these people is that they just hadn't enough to *do*' – a fine counterpoise to any tendency to romanticise a film described as 'a dramatic and historical Comedy in 5 acts of 106 scenes'; featuring an indescribably villainous chase over several continents and an island; and starring an airplane, a suppositious elephant (a complicated gibe at Lady Sybil Colefax who is listed in the credits), Lady Cara herself, Osbert Lancaster, Victor Cunard, Lord Donegal, Tancred Borenius, David Herbert, Lord Berners, Willie King, Rosamond Harcourt-Smith, 'Fluff' Willes, John Betjeman, Adrian Daintrey, several males garbed as Girl Guides, and Cecil Beaton dressed up as a dowager.

It is a haunting experience to see all these people on film. Not only for their particular, individual notoriety and their fantastical sense of fun, but for their youth and their joy and the fact that they are almost all now dead. But none of them died as untimely or as unhappily as Dolly.

Dolly has three minor roles in *Treasons Bargain*. She plays a Kindly Lapp, a Venal Ballroom Agent, and an uncredited Spanish Lady (with her roles giving some idea of the geographic scope of Cara Harris's cinematic imagination), and in the few moments of screen time she gets, she is extremely self-assured, a very good silent actor, and forcefully beautiful. There is absolutely nothing languid about her and she seems to be piercingly alive. Her moving-picture appearance confirms a personal description provided by Charles Henri Ford, Pavel Tchelichiev's long-time lover, who remarked generally but emphatically on Dolly's 'intensity, her energy, her aura'. Ford added that

Dolly was 'swinging', giving that word the exact quotation marks it deserves – and she certainly 'swings' in this film.[17] Dolly, along with Honey Harris (who is wonderful in a series of false noses and moustaches), and Honey's father Austin are the only players in *Treasons Bargain* who don't overact woefully; and Dolly and Zita Jungman are the most striking women in the film – Dolly's dark hair and white skin make the kind of contrast that the camera loves.

Many of the people important to Dolly's life are players in *Treasons Bargain*: Tancred Borenius, who assumed the guardian-like role in Dolly's life after her mother died; Zita Jungman, whose 'golden beauty' and 'delicate loveliness' Dolly was always praising in her letters; 'Fluff' Willes, who soothed Dolly in her final days and identified and claimed Dolly's body after her death; Victor Cunard, whose presence, said Berthe Cleyrergue, always made Dolly's eyes 'sparkle like sapphires' and who probably proposed to Dolly; and Honey Harris and Rosamond Harcourt-Smith – all of whom went on to eulogise Dolly in the privately-published memorial volume edited by Natalie Barney.

Cara Lancaster told a discomfiting story recited to her by her father Osbert, the incident of which must have occurred in the mid-1930s, of how Dolly casually and openly injected herself with heroin or morphine at a dinner party and nobody at the dinner table thought twice about it.[18] The story supports what Dolly sometimes said, that she felt more comfortable in London than in Paris, where her 'dearest of all Professors', Natalie Barney, was always ready to teach her a lesson about sobriety. The story also testifies to Dolly's rather ominous social cool and to her ready kind of 'edginess': it takes a certain sort of wit, after all, to turn a serious addiction into an apparently casual dining room performance.

Berthe Cleyrergue told of the same thing happening at a dinner at the rue Jacob, only this time Dolly injected herself in the thigh, under the table, where she thought no one could see her, and slipped the syringe quickly back into her bag. But Berthe's sharp eyes caught exactly what Dolly was doing and Berthe never said a word about it

to anyone, not even to Dolly, until she told the story to me sixty years later, in 1996.

People had the same reaction to Dolly's flights of linguistic fancy as Cara Lancaster had to her family's stories about Dolly: they always remembered the aura and forgot the specifics. Honey Harris said that Dolly's 'wit was impossible to quote'. 'The quickest, lightest, most extravagant nonsense, with no bounds, no inhibitions, and often no sense of suitability. Dolly hardly ever talked about herself except to tell us how profoundly melancholy she was, and how much everyone was in love with her . . .'[19]

Honey was Dolly's very loyal and practical friend and there is no evidence – Honey Harris was discretion incarnate – that she might have been more than that. Berthe Cleyrergue said repeatedly that Honey was 'one hundred times better for Dolly than Miss Barney was'; but Berthe could not reconcile the many intrigues she had witnessed at 20 rue Jacob with what she observed of Honey Harris's sterling character, and so she never believed that Honey and Dolly had been lovers. Neither Honey's nor Dolly's behaviour indicates anything beyond the closest of friendships.

Cara Lancaster and her father Osbert used to speculate about Honey Harris's sexual proclivities but could never conclude what, if anything, they were. They always hoped that Honey Harris and Dolly *were* lovers and that Honey had had a satisfactory sexual life, but Cara Lancaster thinks Honey might have been too nervous and retiring for such a thing. 'My father always used to say that he hoped very much that she was,' said Cara, 'but he had a nasty feeling that she wasn't.'[20]

Dolly's and Honey Harris's letters to each other are giggly, witty, confessional, and, in the style of the times, openly loving and innocently flirtatious. They discuss catching rich husbands, Dolly's high-flying amorous hopes, and Honey's more tentative ones; Dolly is only half-joking when she finally writes to Honey in 1936: 'for the first time I don't wish for marriage having at last realized the unsuitability of the marital state for both of us . . .'[21] The letters refer to

their heartbreaks of the moment; Honey had a few and they all seemed to be about men. And the letters are full of Dolly's and Honey's friends and their mutual money problems, about which Dolly is alternately humorous and conniving:

> . . . these £3 ought to ginger you up on Christmas morning though I fear your heart may be strained [at the prospect of Dolly paying back a debt] . . . I won't apologize for keeping you waiting as I once waited ages for £15 from you! You can't appreciate the *agony* of it – pray God I do not weaken at the last moment. Well, here are my best wishes, darling, which thank heavens cost nothing.[22]

And Honey is both flippant and open about Dolly's lesbianism. Honey writes: 'We are longing to see you – please change your dinner jacket for a frilly blouse on the boat. I am very anti-lesbian having been slightly in love with a gentleman farmer lately . . .'[23]

Dolly and Honey knew many people in common – the Jungman sisters, Victor Cunard, Tancred Borenius, the Sitwells, two Peters – Coats and Green – and two Rogers – Senhouse and Hinks – as well as Allanah Harper, and a whole set of artistic and social people in London and in Paris. Dolly introduced Honey to Natalie Barney and perhaps to some of her fatal friends from Jean Cocteau's set: the writers Jacques Rigaut, René Crevel – of whose fantastic stories she was particularly fond – and the painter and designer Bébé Berard. She wrote about the talented and notoriously disorderly Berard to Honey: 'Bébé is in a hospital & won't leave even though he is cured, because he finds it's the only way he can keep clean without any trouble to himself.'[24]

Whether Dolly shared Jean and Jeanne Bourgoint – the doomed, drug-taking siblings whose lives Jean Cocteau used for his novel, *Les Enfants Terribles* – with Honey is not known. In a letter to Honey written from the Hôtel Montalembert in Paris in 1929, Dolly mentions that she and 'Jeanne' are using razors to scrape the paint from

some particularly beautiful perfume bottles which Dolly drew in the letter and immodestly compared to Cocteau's line drawings.[25] Since the letter refers to the suicide of 'Cocteau set' member Jacques Rigaut, the 'Jeanne' who is being so helpful with the razor blade might well be Rigaut's and Dolly's acquaintance Jeanne Bourgoint, who herself committed suicide with drugs in 1929. Still, Dolly was terribly anxious to hide her more serious drug use from Honey and its association with the Bourgoint siblings was so well known that Natalie Barney eventually banned the surviving Bourgoint from her household.

Dolly and Honey did many things together: they drew joint pictures, they travelled to Poland and to Paris, they issued joint invitations, and Dolly spent many months of her life recuperating from her various troubles in the Harris residences. She felt comfortable enough to angle shamefully for invitations – 'any chance of the yule log at Pittleworth?' – and she was, from time to time at Lady Harris's behest, a kind of paying guest at 10 Catherine Street at £4 a week – and was suitably ironic and characteristically resentful about that arrangement.

The forms of emotional expression available to women in the 1920s (before the cloven hoof of Freudian category stamped out anything but genital interpretations) were sufficiently elastic to make it likely that Honey's relationship with Dolly – whatever its seeming expressions and sexual reticences – was that rarest of things, a loving friendship. Honey said she 'felt safer' when Dolly was around and did her best to make Dolly feel safe as well. She once reproved Dolly's 'executor', the free-spending and apparently amorous Tancred Borenius, who was on the verge of making a kind of love-allowance to a mutual friend of theirs: 'I was very indignant & said that he had no right to do anything of the sort until he had paid your debts for you.'[26] Dolly, despite her well-documented seducing ways, needed a haven from the many turmoils of her life and she needed a friend to share it with – and Honey, to the end of Dolly's days, provided for her.

As it turns out, the paternal side of Honey Harris's family already

had a long history of friendship with the successful side of Dolly's family. In that odd referencing of Oscar's life that Dolly's life constantly displays, the previous generation of Harrises had supported and defended Oscar Wilde as vigorously as their children and grandchildren embraced and sustained Dolly. Honey Harris's paternal grandparents had a large house on the Chelsea Embankment near Tite Street and they saw the newly married Oscar and Constance Wilde – to whom they were devoted – almost daily.

Honey Harris's uncle, the well-known explorer and journalist Walter Harris, was godfather to Oscar and Constance Wilde's first son, Cecil. After Oscar's trial Walter Harris was forbidden to see Cecil, probably because Walter was homosexual. Fifty-two years after Oscar's death, Walter's sister, Honey's aunt Isabel Harris Graham, wrote a quietly furious letter to *The Times* defending Oscar from a book reviewer's gratuitous attacks.

Isabel Harris Graham's daughter, Honey's young cousin Barbara Graham, continued the tradition of cosseting the Wildes by attending to the last of them. She took over the handling of Dolly's finances during the summer of 1939 when Dolly was in one of her worst periods – drugged, drunk, and quarrelling with her lover, the actress Gwen Farrar – and while Honey was out of London for the summer. Barbara Graham, young enough to be dazzled by Dolly and wanting to help, volunteered to step in and manage things. But Dolly went on the warpath when Barbara tried to regulate her money, shutting herself up for weeks in a room she hadn't paid for in the Basil Street Hotel, weeping in terror and saying she had to have an operation.

Honey wrote exasperatedly about the whole business to Natalie Barney, saying that 'now . . . Dolly herself can look after her money affairs, as I will never do so'.

Being Honey, of course, she did not keep to her severely reasonable withdrawal from managing Dolly's affairs and on 24 October 1939 she wrote again to Barney:

. . . I had not meant to give quite such an impression of

relentlessness & never have any intention of dropping Dolly, but I do often feel maddened by her ways with money & am afraid I was rather cross with her when I wrote. . . . if you do really want to send such a huge & generous contribution to her welfare I will certainly look after it for her — let me say to her that you have said that you will try & help from time to time — so that I can eke it out gradually, without her knowing — otherwise she will try & get hold of it as quickly as she can. She has been most disagreeable with B.G. [Barbara Graham] when it has been withheld.[27]

Honey continued to do what any person attached to an addict does — and that is to try and manage her life for her. The attempt to apply convention to chaos and to control creative and/or destructive behaviour by the application of moderate principles (one drink and a few pounds at a time, in this case) is never a happy one. The bill-paying behaviour that would have satisfied the more conventional Honey was as foreign to Dolly's character — and as distasteful — as bad prose.

On 28 July 1927, at the beginning of her relationship with Natalie Barney, Dolly wrote to Natalie from the Harris house in London:

Honey *refuses* to let me leave earlier than the 4th — clings to me like a charming vine & I am weak. She . . . finds dispropor-tionate joy in breaking down reserve, shyness, aloofness, etc. with me. We are always together & I hear an agonized cry of 'Dorothy' 'Dorothy' if I leave for a moment! Tho' entirely dif-ferent in character she is my Romaine & not to be dealt roughly with . . .[28]

Dolly knew what she was doing when she equated her relationship with Honey Harris to Natalie Barney's relationship with Romaine Brooks, and it was not simply an attempt to remind Natalie Barney that she, too, had a friend as steadfast as Barney's long-time

The Romantic Teenager: Dolly, circa 1914. *Above*

The Virgin of Mayfair: Dolly posed by Cecil Beaton. *Above right*

The Full Flapper. 1920s' Piazza San Marco.

The Society Beauty: another — slightly altered — version of Dolly by Cecil Beaton. *Right*

Dolly at 13 months, Lily at 36 years.
Willie Wilde appears as a signature.

Lieutenant Dolly Wilde: post WWI,
possibly photographed by the Baron de
Meyer. *Above and right*

Heiress Eva Palmer, close friend of
Natalie, frequenter of the Barney salon.

Mina Loy and Djuna Barnes: Knights of Natalie's
Round Table. *Above*

Poet Renée Vivien, wearing
2 Siamese cats.

companion. All her life, Honey had habituated herself to 'partnering' difficult women: her mother Lady Cara Harris, Dolly herself, and the American expatriate Lady Barbara Moray, with whom she shared a house for many years after Dolly's death.[29] Honey's clear and classical sense of boundary (it was she who designed the 'kerbstone' enclosing Dolly's grave), was a match and a balance for Dolly's continual expressions of excess; and Dolly knew it and loved it. Honey never stopped helping and hoping for an end to Dolly's anguish, as this letter written to Natalie on 24 January 1940 shows:

> . . . I have told [Dolly] that I will pay for [the medical treatment], & indeed do so most gladly . . . because I think that the poor darling is now really frightened . . . She looks well & is amazingly brave & cheerful outwardly . . . in the meantime don't be too worried & unhappy because there is every reason to hope the treatment will succeed.[30]

In the only Will she was ever to write, the one that was walled up in Natalie Barney's safe deposit box for the duration of the war and caused such confusion between Barney and Vyvyan Holland's solicitors, Dolly made certain that Honey knew what her friendship meant to her. On her thirty-seventh birthday, Dolly wrote this sad little paragraph on Natalie's 20 rue Jacob stationery.

July 11, 1932

> I, Dorothy Wilde, in gratitude to my friend Natalie Clifford Barney of the above address bequeath everything belonging me to her as my sole heir, with the request that she helps my friend Miss Harris of 10 Catherine Street, London to the extent of £200 per year until such time as she should have inherited from her own relations.[31]

However they phrased their long friendship, it is certain that

Honey loved and cared for Dolly until her death and long beyond it, and that she was a moral imperative in Dolly's life. Dolly often tried to hide the things that shamed her from Honey — such as her suicide attempts, her drug overdoses, and the reasons for them — and she regularly vexed Honey terribly with her bad behaviour in town house boudoirs and hotel halls. In the end, of course, it didn't matter to Honey at all. In 1951, ten years after Dolly's death, Honey wrote of Dolly that 'I never think of her without blessing her beautiful, kind spirit and I think of her every day of my life.'[32]

It was Honey Harris, when the time finally came, who carefully laid out the plans for the marker that would designate the double grave in which Dolly was buried with her mother Lily. And it was Honey, with her exquisite sense of balance and proportion, who chose the stone, designed the marker, and selected the lettering, the language and the borders.[33] Because of Honey's unerring choices, the stone marking Dolly's and her mother's grave is one of the loveliest and most dignified ones left in what are now the ruins of Kensal Green Cemetery.[34]

7

Behaving in Public

Life goes on at break-neck speed here to the rhythm of dancing – dancing all the time. Youth is abroad with its inviolable beauty – its careless charming beauty – ensnaring me in its golden meshes . . .

Dolly Wilde

Pleasure is the only thing one should live for. Nothing ages like happiness.

Oscar Wilde

*A*way from the sheltering embrace of Honey Harris' friendship, Dolly displayed quite another version of herself. It was a version Bettina Bergery blamed on Dolly's resemblance to her uncle. Dolly, Bettina thought, simply could not bear to abandon her private audience – the 'effete young men boring themselves in Bricktops[sic] night-club, and the pale ladies caged in their daily worries and domestic irritations . . .'

So away with reform and pocket money, the frightening merchant would sell her something better than violets or a new dress or even an *appartement*, and that she could share . . . Dolly rushed about laughing again . . . Her words flew out like soap bubbles. She could still glitter for her public, but if one came upon her unexpectedly, sitting alone at a café table at Les Deux Magots, one was shocked by the apathetic look that so recalled the hopeless apathy of the broken poet Oscar, just before his end.[1]

Glimpses of the public life Dolly lived between the wars look like clips from a feature film whose plot line has been accidentally deleted. The logic of her 'narrative', the chronology of her 'story', is almost always missing, but there Dolly is, dancing till dawn at Lady Carnarvon's ball in London, or floating down the Seine in a luxurious houseboat, or driving in a diplomat's touring car to Tangier, or playing tennis at Count Wadcarzewnsky's country house in Poland: delightfully displaying a loose confederation of her several selves as though posing for a series of postcard vignettes, each one of which seems to lack a motive for her movement.

Still, Dolly's isolation in the midst of her vivid animation, her solitude in the excited circle that surrounds her, is often painfully apparent. Despite her legendary 'lassitude' (a disguise for the boredom that covered her depressions) and her seriously sculptural qualities (she looked like 'a statue made of fresh gardenia petals, with two huge violets for eyes'), Dolly's social manoeuvres spread out like talk at a marvellous party: they are everywhere at once – and nowhere for very long.

All of a sudden, Dolly is telling a story about a country dance in the South of France to which she has been taken by French friends who are the dance's patrons. Dolly's vivid account intensifies the atmosphere of the provincial *fête* the way an adverb mobilises an adjective, getting the details just right of the young girls in their pale blue dresses, and of the young men with their shirt collars riding outside their jackets. The tiny mayor of the town, whose head barely comes up to Dolly's shoulders, has asked her to waltz. The second time around the floor, breathing heavily, his head drooping sideways on to her breast in a trance of desire, the little fellow whispers hotly up at her: *'Mademoiselle, vous êtes la volupté même.'* ('Mlle, you are the essence of sensual pleasure.')

'I can see what the little man meant,' said Dolly's friend, the novelist Rosamond Harcourt-Smith:

> she was like a panther — softness, grace, purrs, and of course, claws. Her huge eyes were like grapes in a greenhouse before the blue bloom gets rubbed off. When she was pleased they had a velvety lustre, on the other hand, when angry her pupils retracted with the fascinating speed of a parrot's and the blue grapes became splintered glass.[2]

And here is Dolly again, back at the Hôtel Ritz bar in Paris, succinctly summing up a stuffed bird on Bettina Bergery's hat (it looks like a seagull with a parrot's behind) in a single, sufficient sobriquet: 'It must be a bird of paradox.'[3]

Or — a flashback to her Lieutenant Dolly days — she's in gold lamé scarves in London just after the First War, liberated from her ambulance driver's uniform, and posing languidly for a society photographer.[4]

Ten years later, she's taking tea in London, trading remarks with an improbable trio of literary figures: Ezra Pound, Una, Lady Troubridge, and Radclyffe Hall.[5]

Or she's back in Paris, where Victor Cunard has just seen her with her brand-new drug-supplier (naturally, he's a Surrealist writer) at a dinner party on the quai de Conti; she has never looked so 'radiant' and her eyes, enhanced by the drug, are 'of a dazzling blue'.[6]

And then a quick view of Dolly at the Surrealist nightclub, Le Boeuf Sur Le Toit, where 'the first, fine careless rapture' of the drug has come to 'a cruel end'.[7]

Still in Paris, Dolly is spending wild nights out on the town with Scott and Zelda Fitzgerald; her 'kohl-rimmed eyes' and 'total lack of discretion' impress Scott so much that he includes her in a 'canceled episode' of *Tender is the Night*, turning her into that 'hereditary achievement', a 'tall, rich American girl' named Vivian Taube.

> Nevertheless it was increasingly clear to him that Miss Taube had more immediate concerns – there was a flick of the lip somewhere, a bending of the smile toward some indirection, a momentary lifting and dropping of the curtain over a hidden passage. An hour later he came out of somewhere to a taxi whither they had preceded him and found Wanda limp and drunk in Miss Taube's arms.[8]

Then – another occasion, but still in Paris – Dolly is at a restaurant dinner party on the Quai Voltaire blooming with a bouquet of comparative adjectives so beautiful that she raises the table talk to the level of literature.

On this Quai Voltaire dinner party evening, Dolly is perhaps thirty-three years old, bored to death, and stripping the leaves from a sprig she has idly plucked from a vase of flowers on the table. All at once she lifts herself from inanition to redo Victor Cunard's dull introduction of a shy young man to Dolly's dinner partners, the Count and Countess Yorke.

> 'Darling you do introduce so badly, you don't know how to introduce at all: you just mention names he doesn't know, and that makes the conversation so general!' Now she addresses the boy directly: 'Victor, you don't need to be told, is the White Knight from Alice in Wonderland, and this,' pointing her twig at [Count] Yorke – a golden-headed German – 'is Siegfried. It's not red wine in his glass, he only drinks blood, dragon's blood, that's why he is smiling at the impertinent things the canaries in the cage over the *caissière's* desk have been saying about us. He understands them perfectly. She' – the twig now points at [Countess] Yorke – 'whose features are as taut as a red indian's, who knows what rites she performs

when the moon is full. As for me . . . you should have recognised me first and rushed to me — even without my turban, because I am Madame de Stael. If you've forgotten my face you should have remembered my branch' — here she waves her twig — 'and my beautiful hand and forearm.'[9]

The shy young man, utterly beguiled, forgets his social handicaps and seats himself at the table without being asked. 'Lost in Dolly's eyes which grow more and more laughing and luminous,'[10] and primed by the extravagant generosity of her language, he begins to talk as he's never talked before. Half in love with her before the evening is over, he turns up at the Ritz to meet her the next day for a luncheon engagement she casually makes — and just as casually forgets. And he goes on waiting at the Ritz every day, writing feverish letters to Dolly in between broken appointments, and becoming more intimate than he ever hoped to be with the circle of 'Dolly's young men', who, with more than a reminiscent nod towards her dead uncle Oscar's collection of stablehands, billiard markers, and rent boys, all wait together for her at the Hôtel Ritz. Each one of them is very busy 'inventing limericks and learning epigrams to please her until they all become "Dolly's old stand-bys:" sending postcards and new novels from London and Venice and appearing dutifully when telegraphed for.'[11]

Bettina Bergery, who told these stories of the Quai Voltaire dinner party and the boys in Dolly's band, met Dolly for the first time at one of Marie-Louise Bousquet's 'Thursdays'. Mme Bousquet was receiving in a suite of oblong rooms so heavily accented with red velvet that Dolly called them the 'chemin de fer'; she thought they resembled the first class carriages of ancient railways.

Bergery said that before Dolly went out to the dinner party on the Quai Voltaire in her 'shabby dark suit' Natalie Barney said to her, 'You must change, Dolly, you've got spots.' 'The leopard does not change his spots,' retorted Dolly, whose wit was sometimes smarter than her dress.[12] Dolly was so persistently in love with words that even the thick, white silk scarf she wore to dinner that night — the scarf that made her look portly and more like Oscar, the scarf she bought at Schiaparelli's in the hope that 'adding something new to the bill' would allow her to put off final payment a little longer – was printed all over with language, just like a newspaper.

At this time in her life, Dolly seems to occupy all parts of speech at once – with every part scored for performance. Her visible life – the traceable, presentational, public life – is very much like that of an opera libretto in action, with an opera's same elements of over-acting of emotion and under-representation of detail.

Dolly's linguistic extravaganzas are partly due to her persistent desire to force her life through the channels normally reserved for art. 'Reality' bores and frightens her; art is everything. In a letter to Natalie Barney, she makes a little Ruritanian operetta out of a trip she and Honey Harris made to Poland one month after she fell in love with Natalie.

<u>Black Thursday</u>!
Darling – darling

Here is my address. It's like an Alice-in-Wonderland affair & I feel very little confidence in it . . .
c/o Count WADCARZEWNSKY
ACUGOWO
VIA GNIEZNO
POLAND

O! Imagine leaving *Natalie* for Poland; Natalie & all the delights! . . .

. . . here we are in the Polish castle you see above – PURE Tchekov surroundings and we are enchanted. Such rooms darling – such portraits on the wall – such beds (with the sheets, blankets, and quilt all buttoned up together!) such mirrors on the wall – such bouquets of flowers in pale china vases — such sumptuous meals, etc., etc. . . . The servants are magnificent with lovely uniforms and serfs run out at every moment to wipe your shoes, take your coat, etc., murmuring words of homage! We drive in a carriage, gently rocked on luxurious springs — drawn by two smart bays with a coachman in white trousers and a coat with heavy gold braid, and a cockaded hat, through the fields of waving corn! . . . the Count . . . with lovely slender hips . . . pursues us with desperate but innocuous attentions. He *adores* us. Yesterday while I was leaning out of the window to listen to a peasant serenading us with sad Polish songs, he bit my calf! . . .

I have a thousand stories to tell you when I return to make you laugh . . .[13]

Honey Harris thought that this letter, which Dolly also sent in an almost identical copy to her friend 'Emily', was a rather unsuccessful attempt to turn their prosaic, Polish holiday into a parody of Russian literature. But the letter actually portrays Dolly 'truly'; that is, it shows her exactly as she wished to be seen on all her travels through life: in a luxurious *mise en scène*, having a wonderful time, the centre of some attractive person's sexual interest. In that sense — in the sense that Dolly wanted to be 'interpreted' — Janet Flanner was probably Dolly's 'ideal reader;' she saw Dolly retrospectively, as a work of fiction.

Flanner wrote that

Dolly Wilde, in life, was like a character out of a book, even if it never was written. On the street, walking, or at a Paris restaurant table, talking, or seen in the dim, sunset light of her Rue de Vaugirard flat, remote in its inner court, she seemed like someone one had become familiar with by reading, rather than by knowing.[14]

What Rémy de Gourmont told Natalie Barney to do – 'write with your life' – was something Dolly did literally and naturally; she was always turning her life into a work of fiction – without sacrificing the 'truth' of it or putting a word down on paper. Still, in her letter to Natalie, Dolly cannot forbear a reference to what she sees as her forlorn future 'in some strange house, far away [easing] my mid-Victorian heart with memories of the past.'[15]

Certainly Dolly passed some of her public time in places which slip more easily into the frames of fiction than into fact. She went from chauffeured trips to Fez and opulent balls in Paris and London where everyone dressed as sailors (an unfortunate tic of the twenties), to salons in Paris with Jean Bourgoint (the original of Paul in Cocteau's *Les Enfants Terribles*) where everyone smoked opium, and on to Venice and fevered visits in famous *palazzi*. In London, she would certainly have dined at everyone's favourite French restaurant, the Eiffel Tower, and frequented the fashionable new nightclub belonging to her friend Stephen Tennant's brother David, the Gargoyle Club. In the Gargoyle Club's mirrored and mosaicked halls (inspired by Manet) drugs and alcohol abounded, Mayfair French was heard everywhere, and the social embrace included foreign royalty, the Duke of Windsor, Tallulah Bankhead, Fred and Adele Astair, and Brenda Dean Paul, the infamous society drug addict.

In London also, Dolly was a friend of both Osbert and Sacheverell Sitwell and she loved to hear Edith Sitwell's later poem 'The Sleeping Beauty' repeated;[16] Dolly liked all things that had to do with sleep or beds. Since Osbert, Edith, and Sacheverell Sitwell were busy making themselves a part of the 'history of publicity' (though only Oswald kept his press clippings in a bowl on his table), Dolly would have attended all the premières of the Sitwell recitations, the Sitwell plays, and the Sitwell ballets when she was in town. Alice Toklas describes a Sitwell performance where 'Gertrude Stein had been asked by [the Sitwells] to sit on the platform. So that I was left alone for a moment when Dolly Wilde came up and said to me, Alice, where is darling Gertrude? I said, Darling Dolly, she is on the platform.'[17]

Dolly was all her life both a vividly social woman and a recluse in depressed or determined self-exile. She envied the reclusive Romaine Brooks's 'flight from life & think she has the better exchange'[18] and continued to alternate her post-First War existence between the high visibility of society appearances and the low profile of engineered absences. Her twinned and mutually exclusive desires for (1) ballrooms bursting with beaded beauties and (2) a bookish life in a country bed, pursued her like yoked Furies. These desires were most soulfully expressed in her rather jokey (but Dolly was always most serious when she was only *half*-serious) charge to Natalie Barney that 'When you come to write "The Life & Letters" (if I should acheive [sic] fame) two salient qualities I hope you'll stress – that I'm une grande amoureuse & a lover of Nature!!'[19]

Grandes amoureuses do their best lovemaking in cities, where the population guarantees a plethora of attractive choices; their environment is exactly the opposite of what a lover of Nature requires. In the country, Dolly was often happy to be alone with a bed and a book. But with the continental divides that were always present in her own personality, Dolly usually vacillated (the right verb) between country and city, London and Paris, with a set of friends, a set of habits, even a way of thinking that suited the occasion and the environment in which she found herself.

What is most interesting about Dolly in this specimen post-war period cannot be reproduced by photograph, linguistic image, or by any sifting of what William James called the 'calculable universe'. Dolly's fascination lies in the questions provoked by some of her public behaviour, a very extreme behaviour for a woman with no social standing who wishes to circulate in society.

Why did Dolly raise herself from quelled boredom to the Life of the Party so often, and what happened when she subsided? What *were* those strange trances – she called them 'daydreaming in public' — that she fell into at odd moments in front of everyone?

What did she really *feel* about being compared so often to Oscar? And what happened to her sense of self when she heard herself sounding like him? Cecil Beaton thought that Dolly seemed to be *astonished* at what she said.

What signals did Dolly send out to attract all the men who flocked around her, the men with whom she presumably did not sleep? And what about the passing and past affairs with women she alludes to in her letters: did those women go completely out of her life? After her death, Nancy Mitford said, emphatically, that Paris 'still harbours many an old mistress of Miss Wilde . . .'[20] Apparently, Dolly attracted many people of both sexes and seems to have revelled in social seduction.

In a journal entry written two days after Dolly died, Vyvyan Holland called her behaviour with men 'half-hearted cock-teasing' — though cocks were usually not Dolly's target. Dolly occasionally hints at a little experience in that area, as in her 'disappointed' perambulation around Brussels that led her to the famously vulgar fountain of the spouting boy which 'appealed to my newly acquired sense of virile indecency!' But such hints are usually followed up with a direct reference to women. 'And it was nice walking amongst those endless, pearly, naked women [in the picture gallery at Brussels]. I feel a little like an aesthetic young bachelor doing the Grand Tour! . . .'[21]

Vyvyan Holland wrote that as far as men were concerned, 'one of [Dolly's] great faults was that she was always taking her horse to the water and then refusing to let him drink' and that he had told her so.[22] He also remarked, with a kind of cousinly irritation, that Dolly later stole this remark from him.

In the event, it was exactly Dolly's seductive style, great natural charm, and boundless need for love that allowed her to arouse desires and raise expectations which she had little or no intention of satisfying. Dolly adored the feeling of living with her senses saturated and half-drowned in desire. Tranced and spellbound, she found most intense sensations intoxicating and her fabled ability to listen so well to other people seems to have come from this compulsion to lose herself, to dissolve herself in the fascination of a compelling presence or a riveting narrative. Here she describes a meeting – probably with the notoriously grotesque Princesse Violet Murat[23] – in which opium has conspired with her senses so successfully that she can ignore what she sees, but still draws back.

> . . . 'Madame la princesse' – legend, tradition, the great name . . .
> The next meeting in her hotel, in the anonymous sitting-
> room, people, opium, drinks, the stimulant of artificiality
> leading to flirtations, exaggerations, the target of our wit, of
> our inner eye being the monstrous creature on the sofa who,
> through the haze of her smoke and drink, still retained a
> startling lucidity: the befuddled oracle, the unfallible débauchée
> with blind eyes and shapeless mouth – a presence rather than
> a human being. Her magnetism, defending the insolent ravages
> of time, consoled her vanity . . . Initiated into opium
> smoking . . . I found myself alone for the first time with this
> telepathic presence. Bemused with illusory happiness, affec-
> tion became electrical between us. But her élans towards
> me . . . met with an unconscious drawing back, and her flat-
> tery met only the impertinence of surprise. Night succeeded
> night, her magnetism crystallizing slowly – I was confused, my
> mind enthralled, my senses subordinated to my vision.[24]

It was probably during this post-World War I season of high sexual spirits and open prospects that Dolly began to fall into the dangerous attitude of a dazzling (and bedazzled) creature very probably meant for one form – good writing – and fatally settling for another one – high living.

In London, the disturbing rasp of Dolly's 'real' sexual proclivities against the smooth social silk in which she tried to clothe herself must have chafed her constantly, like a too-tight chemise. As late as

1918, a London production of Oscar's *Salome* sparked a five-day trial in which Maud Allan, the lead actress, and her producer were both branded as homosexuals because of their association with such a 'tainted' work. In Paris, however, a woman could have opinions and run a brilliant salon; a woman could 'experiment sexually' – even fashionably – with women; a woman could flout convention by breaking *all* the conventions; but no woman could take her provocations as seriously (and own them as lightly) as Dolly went on to do.

Dolly was far too passionate, much too obstinate, and a good deal too impetuous to practise for very long any of the deceptive *modes de vie* which would have given her a fixed position in the luxurious social swirl to which she felt herself suited. She was always breaking appointments with important people to go off and 'take a ride in the country', or doing drugs semi-publicly (she had plenty of company in this),[25] or making rapid conquests and hurried exits, or insulting the rich simply because she felt like it. One of Dolly's most creative insults was directed towards Elmer Harden, an American expatriate who courted Dolly socially, and perhaps otherwise.

Elmer Harden was an aesthete from Medford, Massachusetts who went from the First War to studying music to a close friendship with a Frenchman, and thence into easy familiarities with Gertrude Stein, Alice B. Toklas and Edith Sitwell. He was a great reader, said Alice Toklas, and he knew all of *Paradise Lost* by heart. It was Elmer Harden who first brought Edith Sitwell to Gertrude Stein and Alice Toklas on the rue de Fleurus in 1924[26]; so among his other qualities can be counted a certain social courage.

Dolly, who cared enough for Elmer to occasionally joke in letters about marrying him, concentrated all the complexities of her relations with her male admirers in a social jape aimed at Harden the way a nocked arrow is aimed at a target. Lorna Lindsley, a friend of Dolly whom Janet Flanner referred to as the 'constant nymphomaniac', relates the story in a verdant little memoir set in a fashionable restaurant in the Bois de Boulogne. Lindsley begins by insisting that Harden loved Dolly 'very much':

When I got off my horse they were sitting in the light and shade of the horsechestnut trees. Dolly in a bright spring muslin, Elmer very elegant and polished, with a gold-headed cane. The green light from the trees flickered on them, they looked like beautiful static fish in a bowl.

Tea was ordered and brioches, a whole silver salver full which Dolly asked to have left on the table. She sipped her tea and leaned forward and removed the little round top-knot of a brioche and ate it; she leaned forward again and decapitated another . . . When the tea was finished two dozen headless brioches lay on the silver platter. Elmer was raging. 'Why did you do that? Only you would do a silly wasteful thing like that!' And Dolly replied open-eyed – 'But they are the best part of the brioches, I didn't want the rest.' . . .

We let him get well away and then Dolly and I left, I sensed a quarrel deeper than the brioches but I said: 'After all, Dolly, it was a silly thing to do, it was like a naughty child, why did you do it?' Dolly was evasive, 'I don't really know,' she said, 'but I think it was to reproach him for his riches.'[27]

Dolly, who usually affected airy unconsciousness of her misbehaviour, and half-heartedly begins to do so here, ends by reading this gesture for exactly what it was: an extremely artistic version of the *bras d'honneur* (that universal proclamation of anger and contempt usually expressed by a raised middle finger in America and an erect forearm on the Continent), presented to a milieu without which she felt she could not live, but whose apparent and essential frivolities often disgusted her deeply.

There is a poignant postscript to this vignette of Dolly's rebellion against the monied classes: when Natalie Barney briefly eloped with an actress in 1931, leaving Dolly to slash a vein in anguish at the Hôtel Astoria, Dolly threw a great quantity of pounds sterling out of the window of her hotel room before she put the razor to her wrist.[28]

In her wilfulness, and in the capriciousness of her advances and retreats — what Natalie Barney called Dolly's 'resort to rudeness' — Dolly resembles Lily Bart, the American heroine of Edith Wharton's tragedy of manners, the haunting 1905 novel, *The House of Mirth*. Wharton's description of Lily Bart, who, like Dolly, was a lovely woman of limited funds in love with *luxe*, reads like a premonitory sketch of Dolly's predicament:

> She had learned by experience that she had neither the aptitude nor the moral constancy to remake her life on new lines; to become a worker among workers, and let the world of luxury and pleasure sweep by her unregarded. She could not hold herself much to blame for this ineffectiveness, and she was perhaps less to blame than she believed.
>
> Inherited tendencies had combined with early training to make her the highly specialized product she was . . . She had been fashioned to adorn and delight; to what other end does nature round the rose-leaf and paint the hummingbird's breast? And was it her fault that the purely decorative mission is less easily and harmoniously fulfilled among social beings than in the world of nature? That it is apt to be hampered by material necessities or complicated by moral scruple?[29]

When Dolly was in Paris and London and visible (which wasn't so often), she gravitated, like her uncle Oscar thirty years before, towards the prominent, obvious, artistic and social circles, and to the *haute bourgeoisie* haunts where the money, the hospitality, and the good company could be found. In London, she saw people like Allanah Harper, the wealthy young English editor of *Échanges*, the Franco-American literary journal; her 'guardian' Tancred Borenius, editor of the *Burlington Magazine*; the Sitwells (she was close to Osbert); Una Troubridge and Radclyffe Hall; Lord and Lady Carnarvon and the Harris family; and many of the *jeunesse dorée* later gathered under the journalists' favourite, invented rubric: 'Bright Young Things'.

There is one sighting of Dolly's 'invisible' social life in London, the life involved with drugs and drink and the kind of associations that are kept secret. Dolly is reported to have been present at a party (probably at the Variety actress Gwen Farrar's house) during which Joe Carstairs's partner, Ruth Baldwin, began to die of a drug overdose while her friends were listening to a boxing match on the radio.[30] There is something awful in the picture of Dolly absorbed by the sound of blows (shades of Queensberry) as Ruth Baldwin convulses to death; a kind of flashforward to Dolly's own slam-down death in a service flat four years later. Still, Dolly must have seen other overdoses in her time — and, like all addicts, she must have ignored them.

Aside from her obvious social circles, Dolly was developing at least two other identities (and two other corresponding forms of behaviour): one as a lesbian and one — in the lovely, lurid French word — as a *morphinomane*, and she was generally careful to keep these hidden identities from casting shadows on the more visible sides of her social life. Zita Jungman James, for instance, when queried about Gwen Farrar, said *very* definitely: 'Gwen Farrar was someone one saw on the stage . . . One didn't see her socially.'[31] But Dolly did.

And Joe Carstairs, Dolly's outré, adolescent, wartime romance, was so much an exile from regular society that she retired to an island in the Caribbean, visibly shunned by many of the people to whom her wealth or her tastes should have united her. Dolly, however, renewed her acquaintance with Joe and even tried to recommend her to Natalie Barney. Dolly loved to walk on the wild side — and she certainly took far wilder walks than can be documented at this remove. But her yearnings were always romantic and just slightly to the left of *bourgeoise*. What she really thought she wanted was an orderly home life, a regulated social set, and drawing rooms full of lovely gentlemen and learned ladies with whom she could flirt and jest and talk about literature.

And somewhere in this dream of ordered miracles and domestic bliss would be a handful of Sloane Street physicians who would steadily dispense heroin and morphine to her by prescription and without question.

Unfortunately for Dolly, when the shadows from one side of her life began to lengthen on to the sunny sidewalks of the other side, it was not in the careless 1920s but in the somewhat more publicly constrained 1930s (W. H. Auden called it that 'low, dishonest decade'), and then much of her social life was overcast by the disapproval of people she wanted most to impress. It was the drug and alcohol use that did it, of course; and who knows what final performances of outrageous behaviour snapped the threads to her social connections.

Eventually, Lady Carnarvon, for whom she had sometimes acted as a kind of social secretary, refused to have anything further to do with her or to help her financially, despite, or perhaps because of, drafted pleas from Natalie Barney. Tancred Borenius said that if Cara Harris had known of Dolly's drug use, she would have cut their connections.[32] In the 1920s, unless Dolly was with people who understood her various lives or who lived in a similar way themselves, she managed to keep her existences partitioned by special vocabularies, separate companions, and actions specific to each *mode de vie*.

Only when Dolly was very comfortable or, like her uncle, very deliberately careless, did she allow one of her existences to leak into another one – as in the London dinner party during which she casually injected herself with heroin in full view of her perfectly accepting fellow diners. Or when she lingered too long in *salles de bains* in Paris or exited from them 'ostentatiously blowing white powder out of her nose', as Aileen Hennessy disapprovingly described. On this occasion, Hennessy's sister said: 'What a waste.'[33] Lily de Gramont – but this again was in the more political 1930s – concurred with the Hennessys and told Natalie Barney's sister Laura that Dolly Wilde was wasting her life.

Although she later complained in letters about the social dodges she felt obliged to employ to separate her 'lesbian' life from her conventionally 'social' one, and how 'the faint plucking of the Sapphic harp might be a little upsetting'[34] to her friend 'Emily', after the First War Dolly began to drive — metaphorically now — down three separate roads: the socially acceptable, the sexually suspect, and the chemically addictive; and her great traffic-management problem was to prevent an inconvenient intersection of the three. Her intermittent success in partitioning her *modes de vie* — she was particularly anxious to keep certain dark acts from Honey Harris and certain other ones from Natalie Barney — is one reason why so much of Dolly's life has disappeared into anecdote or oblivion.

Still, while Dolly was enjoying them, it would be hard to say which of her social connections provided her with more pleasure. As long as there was beauty or excitement to be found in the milieu, and as long as that milieu was supported by the 'expensive' classes or the most enchanting people, Dolly could be divinely indifferent to the ethical considerations which might have given other people pause, particularly when they involved sex or money or politics. Dolly often operated on a kind of 'contingent' morality (another of her very contemporary qualities); but her aesthetic standard — her only categorical imperative — was always inviolably high.

Gertrude Stein's old maid Hélène once admirably phrased the attitude that Dolly struggled with in France when she was ducking below (or rising above) the current social radar to indulge in what appears to be perfectly contemporary behaviour. It is a peculiarly French attitude and it explains why — even though Paris was more apparently liberal than London in these matters — Dolly seemed to be more censored by her friends in France than by her friends in England when one part of her life leaked into another. When Gertrude Stein asked her maid Hélène if the subject she did not wish to speak about were a secret, Hélène replied: 'Oh no, madame, it is not a secret, but all the same you do not tell it.'

8

Smart Society

. . . I have been socially distracted, keeping the coloured top of conversation madly spinning, whipping it accidentally when it slowed down & showed signs of over-balancing ungracefully! Yet . . . I have felt so depressed that it seemed as if no blood ran in my mental veins & that I must die of spiritual anaemia!

Dolly Wilde

When critics of Oscar Wilde tired of complaining that he was a poseur, or a contaminator of youth, or not an English gentleman, they usually brought out the accusation — it was one of George Bernard Shaw's chief complaints — that he was a terrible snob. Dolly, who spent a good amount of her visible time performing in high society, seems to have inherited Oscar's inclination for social tone.

Whether she came into society by the back door, because of her utility as a quondam aide-de-camp to people like Lady Carnarvon;[1] or by the side door, because of her mother's executor Tancred Borenius took her under his wing; or whether she entered by the front door, because of her name, her wit, her translations for titled ladies or attractions for wealthy socialites, Dolly did seem to gain entrée (and, more importantly, *wanted* to do so) into places where the titled and rich made themselves at home.

Who might have recorded Dolly's presence in this moneyed milieu? The answer, by degrees, became obvious: someone like that accomplished social alpinist Cecil Beaton, who was already friends with Dolly's friends, the Jungman sisters and Allanah Harper. And, indeed, there were four photographic portraits of Dolly hidden away in the Beaton Archives at Sotheby's in London.

Sometime in the late 1920s, Cecil Beaton dressed Dolly up as a beaded Virgin (or as Lady Diana Cooper *playing* a beaded Virgin) for two photographs. On the negatives of two other photographs — this time Dolly is garbed as a suave, society beauty — Beaton carefully air-brushed out the baby fat on her face, his way, always, of improving on the reality. And Cecil Beaton was probably responsible for a series of composed snapshots in which Dolly appears with friends at Sir Austin and Lady Cara Harris's homes (there were two of them) on the Isle of Wight. In 1934 Beaton also painted a pensive watercolour of her for *Vogue* magazine in London.[2]

Dolly appeared, young, attractive, and amusing, at a time the painter Adrian Daintrey said was exactly the right moment to be young, attractive, and amusing in smart society. After the First War, artistically inclined Londoners were beginning to look beyond their starched, Edwardian upbringings, seeking 'experiences such as art and music provide, and a wider range of personal relationships than was to be had in more conventional circles . . . The really poor, the young and the unattached were entertained without any return at all.'[3]

One of Dolly's guides into this world was Professor Tancred Borenius, executor of her mother's will, Regius Professor at the Slade, and a well-known art historian. Borenius was the editor of a respected art journal which still flourishes today, the *Burlington Magazine*; he was a dealer in old masters and served as art authority to people like Lord Harewood; and he was one of the founders of Sotheby's of London.

Lauretta Hugo, widow of Victor Hugo's grandson, the painter Jean Hugo, used to assist Borenius at the *Burlington* and remembers him as a fabulous figure, a witty polymath who spoke every language in the world (Romany included) except Russian, which he refused to learn because he was a Finn. Borenius was received everywhere; even Queen Mary and the Princess Royal enjoyed his company and saw him socially. For Dolly, having this deeply literate, highly cultured male as her escort must have been a bit like having a posthumous sampling of her uncle Oscar; and Borenius certainly brought her to places where Oscar had been made welcome and where he could exercise his own colourful talents.

Once, Tancred Borenius had to go up to Oxford to lecture on Italian art. The thought of it bored him so much that he asked Lauretta Hugo to give him a list of improbable words to slip into his lecture. She provided words like 'cold cream' and he amused himself by working them seamlessly into his talk on Italian painters. During the Second World War, Borenius ran the Finnish Boadcasting Service and was most likely involved in secret war work.[4]

Because of his social and artistic expertise, Tancred Borenius moved freely among the kinds of people who could afford to buy the kinds of paintings he sold. He acquired paintings for Osbert Sitwell and was probably responsible for Dolly meeting the Sitwells as well as the Jungman sisters. And it was either Tancred Borenius or Zita Jungman who was Dolly's entrée into Wilsford, the phantasmagoric country seat of Stephen Tennant's family near Amesbury.

On the weekend of 15 January 1927, Dolly was on her way to a sojourn at Wilsford to join her London friends, the beautiful Jungman sisters, Zita and Teresa (known as 'Baby'), society beauties whose stepfather was Richard Guinness. Dolly was particularly fond of Zita Jungman and loved to rhapsodise later on in letters to Natalie Barney over her somewhat unearthly beauty. 'Golden Zita', Dolly called her, and that beauty is preserved in the many photographs of her by Cecil Beaton, who was given his first camera by Lady Eleanor Smith, the Jungman sisters' and Allanah Harper's great friend. Beaton actually began his photographic career, as Zita Jungman James said, by 'starting on us'.[5]

Mrs James, now in her nineties and living in retirement in Ireland with her sister Teresa (Baby) Jungman Cuthbertson, insists that she knew nothing of Dolly's addictions; proof, perhaps, of how well Dolly was able to separate her various lives from her various friends. But Mrs James was not shocked to hear of them. 'Well she was so animated I'm not surprised to hear she was a heroin addict,' said Mrs James, 'though I knew nothing of it at the time. I mean these animated people have to keep it up.'[6] In fact, Dolly took drugs to *cut* her consciousness, not to sharpen it: Dolly had, she told Natalie Barney, 'an understanding of things that is almost too knife-like in its inevitable suffering.'[7] Mrs James thought she and her sister might have met Dolly through Honey Harris or Tancred Borenius, widely accepted as Dolly's 'guardian' (though he was not), and always around the Guinness household. In any case, the Jungman sisters and Dolly all had the same friends, they all read the same books, and they were all always meeting each other in different places or going to Paris together.[8]

On her way to Stephen Tennant's country house this particular January weekend in 1927, Dolly took the train with Cecil Beaton, Eleanor 'Baba' Brougham, and Stephen Runciman, an old classmate of Beaton.[9] Cecil Beaton's journal entries attest to his discomfiting suspicions of Dolly, whom he must have regarded as being as much of an outsider as he was. Beaton, who could shape a phrase very well when he had to, was not a reader; his natural style in describing women was waspish and rancorous and Dolly's particularly Wildean vividness may have been too extravagant, too self-consciously 'literary' for him. Dolly may also have been too sexual: his later photographs and a watercolour of her tend to suppress her natural voluptuousness.

To the twenty-two-year-old Cecil Beaton, Dolly seemed exactly as her uncle Oscar had seemed to the aesthetician Walter Pater: 'rather vulgar' with 'bad-style smartness'. Beaton described Dolly the way Oscar's observers sometimes described him: he thought Dolly wore 'vitriolic purple', that she 'reclined like a decadent Roman empress', and that her 'oyster face' was 'plastered with powder'.[10] This last is a surprising judgement to find in the circle of Stephen Tennant's friends, where too much make-up would barely have been considered enough. All the young men around Stephen painted and powdered and creamed their faces at night, then seriously discussed their complexions in the morning.

Beaton, himself no stranger to the powder puff and a man who made free with both eyeliner *and* make-up at evening get-togethers with Raymond Mortimer and Nancy Cunard, delivers his opinions of Dolly's *maquillage* in contrast to his later photographic portraits of her which are rather sympathetic and sweetly theatrical. The watercolour he painted of Dolly for the 21 February 1934 edition of English *Vogue* is a wistful, womanly quotation from Oscar's best, melancholic looks; and her resemblance to her famous uncle is clearly the point of the picture as Beaton's caption (which was not printed) indicates: 'Dolly Wilde who has her uncle's wit . . .'

Dolly did personify – sometimes unfortunately – the Bright Young Noel Cowardish style of the twenties, which Beaton, who was jealous of Coward, volubly disparaged. And she was, like Cecil Beaton, a foreigner to the circles she frequented, both socially and financially. In his journal, Beaton seems to be descriptively critical of someone whose behaviour is threatening to him: he characterises Dolly's screams of joy as 'vulgar', for instance, as opposed to the 'girlish screams' of Zita and Baby Jungman, who were probably just as noisy as Dolly was but somewhat more socially secure.

This was not the last time Dolly was to be criticised for fashion vulgarity, however. Bettina Bergery, who worked for Schiaparelli, thought Dolly got herself up badly, or at least messily. The majestic Romaine Brooks, a woman who dressed, painted and decorated in black, white, and grey, firmly discouraged Dolly's very British wearing of the colour pink. And in *Oscaria*, the book of memoirs she edited about Dolly in 1951, Natalie Barney dropped the following footnote to Dolly's boast: 'I seem to be the best dressed woman in Vittel'.

'Although Dolly considered it a "civic duty" to be "well-dressed" and "look one's best" — she rarely lived up to this — or any other duty perhaps also because it may be a superior form of vanity to please not because but in spite of one's clothes.'[11]

In fact, Cecil Beaton's remarks on Dolly's habits of dress evoke an immediate image of Dolly's grandmother, Lady Jane Wilde, who also loved mauve, and whose overstated *maquillage*, outrageous costumes, and overly theatrical postures as a *femme de lettres* in her dimly lit salons in Dublin and London caused fairly constant comment. Even Marie Corelli(!) thought Jane Wilde's habits of dress were 'eccentric'.

Once Dolly began to speak, however, Beaton's impression of her enlarged. 'Dolly, never expecting that she might have inherited her uncle's wit, continually managed to say clever, funny things as if by a fluke. Her eyes widened with astonishment at each *bon mot*, and she exploded as heartily as anyone in the ensuing laughter.'[12]

Dolly's and Cecil's weekend host, Stephen Tennant, was very rich, perpetually delicate, wonderfully artificial, and raised to be a genius — with the usual dreadful consequences: Osbert Sitwell called him 'the last professional beauty'. His family's famously lovely Elizabethan-style manor house, Wilsford, was so originally decorated by young Tennant — fishnets, shells, mirrors and startling collages were everywhere — that Tancred Borenius thought its doors should be sealed and the whole place preserved as a kind of museum for future generations.[13]

Beaton thought the entire weekend was 'like being at the most perfect play' and he modelled his leopard-print dressing gown for Stephen Tennant and then 'managed to let Dorothy Wilde see me in it too and she too was amazed and enraptured'. Beaton was still young enough to consider this weekend 'the beginning of a new life'. He wrote: 'I was at last among really lovely people, the sort of people I want to be among — not middle-class brainless idiots. These delightful people were perfection to me. I was gloriously happy and thankful.'[14]

The month after this hibernal house party, Stephen and his

mother Pamela rented the Villa La Primavera on the Riviera in Cap Ferrat. Cecil Beaton came and photographed everyone upside down; Edith Olivier, Mrs Belloc Lowndes and her daughter were there; the painter Rex Whistler came, and so did the future Duchess of Westminster, Loelia Ponsonby, who also photographed the guests, remarking: 'The young men certainly look smarter than the girls!'[15]

Dolly was also staying at the Villa La Primavera and seems to have been a fairly regular Tennant guest, one of 'Stephen's crowd' according to his biographer. She had probably come to Cap Ferrat with Zita Jungman. This winter sojourn is simply another example of Dolly amusing herself in a circle which her uncle Oscar had obviously influenced, a circle which he might almost have authored.[16]

Most likely, it was Tancred Borenius who introduced Dolly to the adorably unconventional Viva King, one of the first women in café society to have an open affair with a black man. Viva, who wrote about Dolly with affection in late life, was one of those women who seems to have been everywhere. She went to Brian Howard's famous Greek party dressed as Sappho, and she was dubbed by Osbert Sitwell, who seemed to like distributing rubrics, 'The Scarlet Woman', presumably for her many affairs. According to Viva's friend, the transgendered performer April Ashley, Viva's initiation into the more rarefied practices of 'upper Bohemia' began in the 1920s when she was secretary to the artist Augustus John and found Mr John 'in the study one day beating the desk with an erection and shouting "no no no no no."'[17]

Viva King loved Dolly's 'gratifying quality of appreciating and laughing at your most humble bon mot, so that you really did feel witty . . .'[18] and Viva and Dolly met many times at the Harris homes and at smart dinner parties, like the ones Leigh Ashton gave, in the various subsets of literary and artistic London. Viva provides a useful description of 'the gossip and wit of Tancred Borenius', Dolly's 'guardian', in her autobiography, *The Weeping and the Laughter*:

[Borenius was] a tall fat Finn who had brought his family to live in England. His face was brown and his eyes round and black, which gave him a seal-like appearance. As adroit as a seal, he had to juggle with the precarious business of picture dealing and needed all his wits and charm to counterbalance a reputation for sharp practice — something which many successful dealers have to contend with. He was criticized for the collection of pictures he bought for Lord Harewood. 'So that is the man who robbed my cousin Harry!' exclaimed Helen Maclaglan (née Lascelles) when I mentioned him.[19]

Borenius, 'the man who robbed my cousin Harry', continued in his role of agent-without-portfolio to the art-buying rich of London. He also continued as a chronically recurring figure in Dolly's life — sometimes indispensably so. Rather like a character in a Borges story, Tancred Borenius's life history has been recorded in a biography, but that biography is in the Finnish language and entirely untranslated.

When Lily Wilde died in 1922, Tancred Borenius, who said to Viva King, 'I'd eat dirt if it would turn to gold in my mouth,' took over in an advisory capacity the management of the £2000 or so that she had left to Dolly. Although Borenius was no more than ten years Dolly's senior, he became a kind of elder confidant and adviser for her. They sometimes travelled together, they gossiped with each other about each other's love affairs, and later on, in the 1930s, when the bad days were coming down on Dolly like acid rain, Borenius did his painful best to offer comfort to Dolly and to warn Natalie Barney (who by this time needed no warning) of the unlimited disaster Dolly's life was becoming.

Adrian Daintrey, who had been Borenius's student at the Slade, provides a glimpse of Tancred Borenius and Dolly together out on the town:

I was surprised and delighted when Dr. Tancred Borenius, whose inaudible lectures in his own brand of foreigner's English and whose solemn appearance I remembered from

Slade days, swam into my ken again in this circle. Now he was, it appeared, the most gallant social butterfly possible: rotund, a little stertorous, and infinitely good-natured, he was usually escorting the delightfully funny, and charming Dolly Wilde – niece of Oscar Wilde. Tancred not only adored pretty ladies but company generally: for the purpose of enjoying as much as possible of it, at one period, one day a week at lunch-time he held open house at a table in Prince's restaurant in Piccadilly. Any of his friends who were passing were welcome.[20]

Borenius's daughter, Clarissa Borenius Lada-Grozicka, was certain that Tancred Borenius had slipped Dolly quite a bit of money over the years and thought that her mother disliked and was jealous of Dolly because of this.[21] Dolly's cousin, Vyvyan Holland, indicated in his diary that he suspected Borenius of slipping money *out* of Dolly's trust. Although there is no evidence of defalcation on Borenius's part – Natalie Barney, who would have noticed, said that Dolly died with five hundred 'disregarded pounds' to her credit and Dolly herself wrote of several instances in which Borenius helped her with pressing bills – Tancred Borenius was regarded as a sharp dealer who always got his commissions and then some. Honey Harris referred to him in a letter as Dolly's 'foxy old guardian' and noted that in a transaction over a Joshua Reynolds painting with her banker father, Borenius prevailed completely and got 'his 15 quid'.

Cecil Beaton had a more aesthetic (and classically vitriolic) objection to Tancred Borenius, formed when they were both staying at Sacheverell Sitwell's during the war and quoted by Hugo Vickers in his biography of Beaton: 'Oh! that halitosis. It's so thick – a greyhound couldn't jump it. It would kill a mosquito at a yard.'[22]

Clarissa Borenius Lada-Grozicka had memories of Dolly from early youth, when, after Dolly's mother's death in 1922, Tancred Borenius assumed a more central position in Dolly's life and Dolly came often to the Borenius house:

I was dazzled by Dolly when I was a girl – she was so much
more glamorous than my mother's friends & wore beautiful
big hats & wonderful clothes. As a child I used to follow
Dolly around and call her 'the pretty lady . . .' Dolly listened
to me very sympathetically because I was always falling in love
with boys who were not in love with me & she gave me very
good advice I must say. I adored her & of course she liked me
for that . . . I used to visit her at the Hôtel Montalembert in
Paris – no one knew what she lived on or how she afforded
it.[23]

And Mrs Lada-Grozicka's uninhibited memory of a visit to the
Barney salon in the last, difficult years of Dolly's connection to it,
shows how separate and secret Dolly could keep her social connections – and the kind of social comedy this separation could produce:

Though I visited the Barney salon in 1937, I can assure you I
was not molested in any way . . .

But when I saw Natalie Barney [sixty-one years old at this
time] . . . passionately kissing a beautiful, blonde, young
American college girl whom she called 'Venus', I telephoned
to my mother & asked her to make some excuse & get me out
of there. I had no idea, you see, what they were up to. Really
no idea.[24]

Back in Paris, Dolly is harder to trace since she often stayed in
hotels or with unrecorded friends or lovers. But in the mid-1920s,
like invisible writing blooming under the heat of inspection, Dolly's
name starts to appear in society guest books, those magnificently self-
referential volumes by which the entertaining classes congratulate
themselves. One of the guest books in Paris with Dolly's name in it
belonged to Mme Valentine Fauchier Magnan.

Valentine Fauchier Magnan was the elder sister of Marcelle

Fauchier Delavigne, the biographer, dramatist, and socialite, and they both descended from the brother of Casimir Delavigne, the eighteenth century French playwright whose name adorns one of the small streets spoking out from the hub of the Place de l'Odéon. Dolly was to have a huge effect on Marcelle Fauchier Delavigne's emotions in the 1920s and 1930s and Marcelle remained deeply attached to Dolly long after her death. Berthe Cleyrergue, who liked Marcelle Fauchier Delavigne very much, said that the attachment was a profound one.

Marcelle told her grandson Hervé of the time she found a book of André Gide's writing on a train, read it, and, finding the writing wonderful but too 'dangerous', tossed the book out the window. The thought of a book sailing out of a train window would have driven Dolly to kicks and screams and might account for Dolly's occasional avoidance of Marcelle; but Marcelle continued to find Dolly enchanting and continued to seek her out. As late as 1951 she was still writing to Natalie Barney about Dolly, whose image continued to haunt her.

> It's already 10 years ago [since Dolly died] but I see [her] everywhere here as if she had just left rue Las Cases a few days ago. I discovered in a film a woman who reminded me of her . . . she had her hair set in the same way on her large beautiful forehead and at times [she had Dolly's] gesture in lighting her cigarette. I went back to see this film every day for a week![25]

Marcelle Fauchier Delavigne took Dolly on trips to Rome and to the French countryside and she may have been the 'married woman', the one Dolly referred to as 'the pocket Napoleon', who put Dolly up at the Ritz in Paris. She made Dolly welcome in the *hôtel particulier* she occupied with her husband in Paris's fashionable 7th *arrondissement* and at her country estate in Normandy where Dolly, characteristically, complained of bad food and lack of distraction. Marcelle supplied Dolly with money and comfort in times of trouble, sending presents to her, when war was declared, in a diplomatic pouch. She put up with Dolly's rudenesses, her ambivalences, her spotty correspondence, and her little rebellions, and, like all Dolly's friends, she felt amply rewarded for her loyalty. Marcelle mourned Dolly profoundly when Dolly died, making a 'veritable pilgrimage' with Honey Harris 'to all the places Dolly occupied', and writing about it to Natalie in April of 1951: 'Thank you for thoughts about she [Dolly] who has left us taking with her the harmonious clarity she gave to life.'[26] And before Dolly's death, Marcelle suffered deeply from her compassion for Dolly's illness; a generous suffering inspired by love.

> . . . Dolly *is and will always be* my sole thought (*mon unique pensée*): the idea that she suffers, & that one day perhaps this atrocious pain can make her suffer even more makes me insane . . . I would like to draw the blood out of my veins to give to her. (*Je voudrais me tirer le sang des veines pour le lui donner.*)[27]

Dolly's name first cropped up in Marcelle's sister's (Valentine's) guest books in February 1925, when she was invited for lunch with Tancred Borenius. Since Mme Fauchier Magnan's lists included only the socially respectable (Natalie Barney is notable by her absence in the early years and in later years was only invited to the more public gatherings), Dolly must have been busy making herself respectably social and, in fact, she continues to appear rather infrequently (perhaps she was not that respectable – or not that inclined to go to Neuilly-sur-Seine) on the Fauchier Magnan guest lists until 1936.[28]

At large gatherings and at small lunches in Valentine's elegant Palladian villa in Neuilly, Dolly was invited with people she knew or would come to know: Marcelle Fauchier Delavigne, the photographer Baron de Meyer, the American party-giver Elsa Maxwell, the American decorator Elsie de Wolfe, the duchesse de Clermont-Tonnerre, the actress Marguerite Moreno, and Katy Fenwick, the socialite. Mme Fenwick's sister, Antoinette Gentien, the glamorous resident of Avenue Kléber with whom Dolly reportedly had an affair, was sometimes invited when Dolly was there. Antoinette was the mother of the French tennis star, '*le tennisman*' Coco Gentien, and it was into Antoinette Gentien's husband's trousers (a pleasure, clearly, of quite another kind) that Dolly told Janet Flanner she had slipped in order to appear as her uncle Oscar at the duchesse de Clermont-Tonnerre's costume ball in June of 1930.

In the first part of the 1900s, Neuilly was a far cry from the overdeveloped, elegantly commercial, upper-middle-class suburb it has now become. Then, it was a leafy bower, a pastoral paradise for the rich, whose great houses and lovely greenery ran right down to the River Seine. In the first decade of the century, Natalie Barney, Dolly's future lover, was just beginning to invent her fabled salon in a house in Neuilly-sur-Seine, on the right bank of the river near the Bois de Boulogne. She rented it until 1909 when she moved to her *pavillon* on the rue Jacob. Barney's artistic, social, and overtly sexual intentions were of a much different order from the entertainments chez Fauchier Magnan.

At one of Barney's garden parties in Neuilly, long before Dolly arrived in France, the one at which Mata Hari appeared naked on a white horse hung with a turquoise, cloisonné harness, the writer Colette (a future lover of Barney) and the beautiful American hotel heiress Eva Palmer (a former lover of Barney) performed a kind of Greek dialogue written by the French *décadent* Pierre Louÿs, who had been a friend of Oscar Wilde. Colette said that she and Eva Palmer were both so nervous that they each reverted to their native accents in French: Eva Palmer's speech turning pure American and Colette's rolling Burgundian 'r's' becoming 'positively Russian'.

> Pierre Louÿs, author and guest, listened. Or perhaps he did not listen, for we were undoubtedly pleasanter to look at than to hear. But we believed that the whole of Paris under its sun-shades and its hats, which were immense that year, had its eyes upon us. After the performance I plucked up the courage to ask Louÿs if 'it hadn't gone too badly'.

He answered gravely: 'I have experienced one of the greatest emotions of my life.'

'Oh! dear Louÿs!'

'I assure you! The unforgettable hallucination of hearing my work spoken by Mark Twain and Tolstoy.'[29]

It was around 1925, the year she began to sign into the Fauchier Magnan milieu in Neuilly, that Dolly started and ended a brief affair with the great Russian-American theatre and film star, Alla Nazimova. Nazimova was the actress who had brought the plays of Ibsen and Chekhov to America and then settled in New York and Los Angeles. At the age of forty, she became a major American film star and the highest paid actress in Hollywood. By the early twenties, Nazimova had already beggared herself producing and starring in a film of Oscar Wilde's ever-controversial *Salome*. Her version of *Salome* was filmed during the winter of 1922 with hallucinatory, Aubrey Beardsley-inspired sets and costumes by Natacha Rambova, Mme Nazimova's companion (later the wife of Rudolph Valentino); it was cast with three of the court ladies played by men in drag.[30]

Mme Nazimova was a small, slight, luminously pale Russian Jew, who had a highly charismatic and sexual aura, wonderfully blue, 'tragic' eyes, a soulful and authoritative presence, and a reputation as a brilliant actress who disappeared into each role she interpreted. She was also the godmother of Nancy Davis, whose second marriage to sportscaster-turned-movie actor Ronald Reagan would make her Nancy Reagan, First Lady of the United States. In a feature article in the December 1972 issue of *Films in Review*, theatre scholar DeWitt Bodeen wrote of Alla Nazimova: 'There has never been any doubt about the greatness of Alla Nazimova as an actress. I would not hesitate to name her the foremost actress of the 20th Century American theatre . . . She reformed and revitalized acting in America just as Eleanora Duse did throughout Europe.'[31]

It was Nazimova's estate in Hollywood, the Garden of Alla (with an added 'h'), which became the Jazz Age hotel that eventually housed such notables as Dorothy Parker, Scott Fitzgerald, Frank Sinatra, and Orson Welles. The Garden of Allah was also home to Nazimova herself at the end of her life: broke, out of work, a paying guest in a town that had no position for a great international star who was getting old.

According to Nazimova's biographer Gavin Lambert, a likely time for Dolly and Nazimova to have begun their affair was during the summer of 1925, when Mme Nazimova was in Paris, staying at the newly built Hôtel Montalembert, Dolly's favourite hotel. But the Montalembert did not open its doors until 1926, so perhaps Dolly and Nazimova met in another hotel or in another year.[32] If Dolly had any money at all (and even if she didn't), she would have been at the Montalembert in its opening season.

However they found each other, Nazimova would have been delighted to meet the niece of the man whose play she had sacrificed so much to put on film and Dolly would have been fascinated by this great actress, whose stage work later inspired Tennessee Williams to become a playwright and who gave to Eugene O'Neill 'my first conception of modern theatre'.

The story of the affair between Dolly Wilde and Nancy Reagan's godmother was told by Nazimova herself to the American film director George Cukor, 'that great connoisseur of the secret life of Hollywood'.[33] Cukor preserved the story in his 'formidable memory' for fifty years.

Djuna Barnes was in New York City in the spring of 1930 working as a journalist, and she interviewed Alla Nazimova for the April 1930 issue of *Theater Guild* magazine during one of those precipitous dips for which Nazimova's career was famous. Djuna noted perceptively: 'There has never been any reasonableness in her "fate", a glance backward shows a meteoric condition that almost no one could cope with.' And when Nazimova, shying away from personal revelations in the interview, said that she had 'never known what it is to be in love'

Djuna, who quite likely had heard all about Nazimova's affair with Dolly in Paris – perhaps from Dolly herself – wrote slyly: 'What a gorgeous lie that was, a brazen effort to say, you do not see this face as you look at it.'[34]

Dolly's next recorded affair began in June 1927 with another extraordinary woman, the American expatriate *femme de lettres* and *salonnière* Natalie Clifford Barney. It was to last, in one form or another, for the rest of Dolly's life.

Like Alla Nazimova, who was deeply involved with Oscar's art before meeting Dolly, Natalie Barney had been eerily caught up in Oscar Wilde's life and work long before she met Dolly. During her relationship with Natalie, Dolly seemed to grow increasingly like her uncle Oscar – and in all the wrong ways.

4

The
Knights
Of
Natalie's
Round Table

9

Natalie Clifford Barney

What have you loved the most?
– Love.
And if you had to choose several things?
– I should choose love several times.

Natalie Clifford Barney

I miss nothing and nobody.

Natalie Clifford Barney

Natalie Clifford Barney, who was exactly the sort of wilful American heiress Henry James wrote about in his international novels, grew up to become one of Paris's more interesting literary figures, and one of her most seductive *salonnières*. She begins *Aventures de l'esprit*, the book recounting her intellectual education, with this story.[1]

In 1882, when Natalie Barney was five years years old and vacationing on Long Island with her artist mother, she was pursued down a long hotel hall by a group of taunting boys throwing preserved cherries at her small, blonde head. The cherries were a marvellous touch on the boys' part – or on Natalie's. Henry James, whose definition of evil includes the sudden sighting of 'a bad-faced stranger' in a quiet country house corridor, would have richly appreciated the little girl's predicament. Suddenly, a very kind, very tall gentleman 'dressed in the most extraordinary way' with hair almost as long as hers, scooped Natalie up in his arms, routed the urchins with his cane, and forbade her to cry because he was going to tell her a story. He sat down on a bench, arranged the child on his lap, and began to invent what Natalie said was 'a wonderful tale.'[2]

The fairytale figure who rescued young Natalie Barney from ignominy at an American seaside resort in the summer of 1882 was none other than the twenty-seven-year-old Oscar Wilde, on his first, triumphant lecture tour of the United States. Natalie grew up to remember his charitable act to a child all her life. She insisted on being painted by Carolus-Duran as Wilde's Happy Prince when she was eleven; she wrote to Oscar sympathetically when he was in Reading Gaol and she was a teenager; and she briefly and improbably engaged herself in her early twenties to his fiendish little lover, Lord Alfred Douglas, when Douglas was fortune-hunting in America. To round the matter off — for Natalie was as thorough as she was practical — she had a love affair with the English poet Olive Custance, Alfred Douglas's fiancée and then his unhappy wife, an affair which Natalie in later life would include among her major *liaisons* on a list written in her own hand.

Natalie Barney went on to memorialise Oscar Wilde in other ways in her famous Parisian salon. She served up his emblematic cucumber sandwiches, and, later on, she served on committees in Paris that commemorated both his birth and his death. And in June of 1927, in a turn of events Henry James would never have published, Natalie Clifford Barney fell madly in love with Oscar's only niece, Dorothy Ierne Wilde.

Natalie Barney's life, and the writers', artists', and scholars' salon she created and maintained in Paris for more than sixty years, were so extraordinary, and have made such bewilderingly little impact on the written history of literature, that the story of who Barney was and how she stayed that way for most of a century deserves to be told over and over again – until every person still interested in twentieth-century Modernism understands how important this wayward American from Ohio was to the flourishing of the Modernist movement and to that movement's radical, humorous subversion by the brilliant women for whom the Barney salon provided a local habitation and a name.

Natalie Barney was born in Dayton, Ohio in 1876, on 31 October, an appropriate birthdate for a woman whose lifelong love of costumes and masquerades influenced her social life, her writings, and her love affairs.[3] Natalie and her younger sister Laura were the daughters of a handsome, conventionally minded, Midwestern railroad heir, Alfred Clifford Barney, and his flamboyant and unnhibited wife, Alice Pike Barney. ('I wish I were more like my happy confident enterprizing enjoyable mother,' Natalie wrote to Dolly after Alice's death.)[4] Alice Pike Barney, in turn, was the art-making daughter of a German-Dutch-Jewish entrepreneur, Samuel Nathan Pike. Samuel Pike married into the genteel (and gentile) Miller family of Cincinnati and became both a distinguished American business man and an intensely philanthropic supporter of the arts. He built opera houses in Cincinnati and New York City and his charitable and artistic propensities were inherited by both Alice Pike Barney – who founded theatre companies, painted seriously, and wrote fifty plays (she won the Drama League of America Award for 1927) – and by Natalie herself, who experimented with everything.

Natalie and her sister Laura grew up first in Cincinnati and then in Washington DC with all the advantages their father's money and their mother's artistic and theatrical inclinations could provide. Alice Barney's unusual medley of artistic interests are still evident in Washington DC where she was known as a portrait painter, a stager of *tableaux vivants* (Natalie was rumoured to be nearly nude in one of them), founder of a theatre company and designer of her wonderfully built Arts and Crafts-style atelier, Barney Studio House – whose façade bore a close resemblance to the painting studio of Alice's friend in London, James MacNeill Whistler. Studio House still stands in Washington DC, stripped of its highly theatrical and idiosyncratic furnishings and appointments, and put up for sale by the Smithsonian Institution to which Alice had willed it.

Natalie's upbringing and education were those of a ruling-class James heroine, an 'heiress of all the ages', and her manners – but not necessarily her sexual etiquette – always reflected a gracious sensitivity to life's civilised pleasures, a sensitivity encouraged by her beautifully extended childhood. The Barney houses in Ohio, Washington DC and Bar Harbour, Maine were maintained as mansions and Natalie had cosseting governesses, lessons in the arts, more social life than she desired, and a stint at a Swiss boarding school, Les Ruches, under its extraordinary headmistress Marie Souvestre. Marie Souvestre was the teacher so loved by Eleanor Roosevelt when she was her pupil in England that ER detoured her honeymoon with Franklin Delano Roosevelt especially to call on Mlle Souvestre. Natalie also had a great deal of luxurious, supervised European travel with her exigent, alcoholic father and, sometimes separately, with her restless, flirtatious, painting mother.

What was less (and more) than Jamesian about Natalie Barney is what caused her incensed father to slap her when he found some telltale letters: her enthusiastic and relentlessly sexual pursuit of the women she found attractive. Natalie had always displayed a heightened, if selective, awareness of women. She said that her feminism was fixed at the age of eight when she saw a man sauntering along smoking a pipe and his wife limping behind him hauling all their goods on a milk cart like a beast of burden. It is quite likely that the nature of her sexuality was apparent to her at an even earlier age than her feminism. From the beginning, Natalie Barney was remarkable for the clarity of her desires and for the uninterrupted way in which she named and pursued them.

Accustomed to a life of privilege, a sense of her own intellectual superiority, and the feelings of entitlement with which her magnetic, blonde looks and privileged background endowed her, Barney combined a publicly correct social life with a not-so-private and sometimes chilling libertinism in sexual matters, in ways which exemplified a new *façon de vivre* for women in love as well as in art.

Like Dolly, who defeated time again and again by always being late for appointments, Natalie ignored the conventional clock and dated her life only in terms of the eras of her lovers. Her clothes — costumes, really, many of them — made for her by designers such as Paul Poiret and Mme Vionnet, also seemed to be fashioned outside time and she presented herself as a kind of 'period piece', never quite belonging to the present, always invoking an indefinable, literary past.

On the other hand, Natalie could appear in photographs as though she represented every whim and phase of fashion: from the correct young Amazon with a crop and a bowler who rode side-saddle in the Bois de Boulogne in the 1890s, to the sorceress with flowing robes (designer robes, with all the constellations on them) and unruly, shoulder-length hair in the late 1940s in a Florentine villa. And, always in these photographs, Natalie Barney, like Dolly, faces directly into the camera — but Natalie faces it with an audacious expression and with one hand defiantly on her hip.

Natalie, perhaps rephrasing the title of her lover the duchesse de Clermont-Tonnerre's intelligent memoir, *Aux temps des équipages*, always said that Dolly was of the era of motor cars and that she, Natalie, was of the era of carriages. Still, Natalie's astonishing experiments in love and in her own kind of 'work' can make her seem, like Dolly, to be absolutely contemporary — but with this interesting prolepsis: Natalie's conscious devotion to lesbian love and to its expression in a variety of literary forms — *minus* the support of a politic — puts her very much in *front* of what is now contemporary.

Natalie's unusual interest in maintaining a social and artistic community made her a wonderful friend, and friendship gave the fluctuations of her amatory life its enviable stability. She said she was so lazy that once she made a friendship, she never revoked it, and she often preferred to give back as a friend what she had taken away as a lover. But her pursuit of women also made her a dangerously overextended paramour; her high feelings of amity and control never allowed her to relinquish a relationship once the sexual connection had subsided. Her current lovers always had to put up with all her former lovers and Natalie's focus on sex never retreated. She once told Dolly – for whom literary discussion was a sustaining pleasure – that she 'preferred her body to her thoughts'. And she complained to the man who became her French biographer that some of her lovers were more interested in the *mot à mot* than in the *corps à corps*.

Someone once said that three was Natalie's favourite number, and to her relationship with Dolly she brought her long-established and deeply felt love-relations with the very intelligent duchesse de Clermont-Tonnerre, Lily de Gramont – known as the 'red duchess' in her communist phase and spoken of (mercifully) without rubric during her Mussolini period – and with Romaine Brooks, the wealthy and richly gifted painter who was Natalie's companion for life. And then there were the numerous women with whom Natalie simply had affairs.

A list in Natalie's own hand, made in old age, divides her longest relations into three categories ranked by importance: '*liaison*', '*demi-liaison*', and '*aventures*'.[5] There are twenty-seven names under the three headings and Dolly's name is in the major *liaison* category along with Romaine Brooks, Lily de Gramont, Renée Vivien, and Olive Custance. Colette was included as a *demi-liaison* and Eyre de Lanux, who had something like a seven-year relationship with Natalie, only made it into the *aventures* class. Berthe Cleyrergue, who had a cataloguing mind, calculated that Natalie had had forty major affairs and hundreds of minor ones. To Dolly, Natalie was both an excellent friend *and* a dangerous lover; on the one hand offering the 'home life' Dolly craved, and on the other hand regularly crushing that possibility beneath the heap of multiple affairs into which she regularly plunged.

Dolly's own emotional pattern of advance and retreat was as native to her as her restlessness, and her long relationship with Natalie Barney produced some extreme and highly contradictory feelings. One moment, she is addressing Natalie as the queen of hearts, the next, characterising her – always delicately – as the knave.

It was more than kind of you to leave me so many things —
just what I needed — though the pretty little watch was extravagant of you. I could have wished your kindness to have gone
even further & not left evidences of your [other] love in the
book by my bed — amongst the writing paper etc. Horrid
stabs — unnecessary hurt. Tout Paris pours endless stories into
my ears — but acceptance of the rhythm of destiny becomes
easier & easier — & like a ghost I feel I have no hands to struggle, no voice to lift up, no heart to break.[6]

Of course, Dolly was capable of giving as good as she got. She
provocatively dangled her other attractions before Natalie in letters;
and she caused Natalie deep and intermittent distress by going word-
lessly away or walling herself up and refusing to continue their
communication, particularly when she was drugging or drinking.
When Natalie travelled hurriedly and worriedly to London after
another of Dolly's suicide attempts, this note from Dolly was delivered to her hotel:

It sounds ungrateful not to see you but really I only want to
get well . . . Please don't stay over here with indefinite
expense . . . I feel *quite* alright when I am alone & surely the
fact that I leave a message every day shows I am alright . . .
Only I *can't* see people.[7]

But Dolly was too enamoured to regularly sustain these defensive
poses — they were contrary to her heart and mind and feelings — and
she often collapsed under the weight of what she felt were Natalie's
abandonments. While Dolly was still sexually attracted by Natalie —
and there is some evidence that Dolly's sexual interest lapsed before
Natalie's did — her romantic nature was always subject to injury by the
coolly classical way, the way of a confirmed, controlling sensualist, in
which Natalie Barney conducted her life.

There is a story that, when Natalie was fifteen, she seduced her governess, her father came to know of it, and he sent Natalie *and* the governess to Paris with enough money to keep them both until the affair (or the possibility of scandal) blew over. Esther Murphy, Gerald Murphy's sister and another brilliant talker in love with Natalie, regaled the writer Sybille Bedford with this anecdote.[8] Although it is quite likely an embellished tale (given Barney *père*'s frantic and multiple attempts to derail his daughter's lesbian ways, including trying to buy up every copy of a book of lesbian poetry she had privately printed), it is just the sort of narrative Natalie *would* have entered into if she had thought of it – and just the sort of story Natalie's life always provoked.

The famous Barney libido could be kindled in Barney's early sixties by a blonde American college girl whom Tancred Borenius's daughter observed her to be passionately kissing during one of her Friday receptions; and it could be aroused in her late seventies by an eleven-year-old telegraph girl whose delivery interrupted Natalie's bored slumber during a tea party. At the little girl's entrance, Natalie snapped awake, her eyes sparkled, and she began to praise the child – '*Quelle jolie fille*' – breathing over her and stroking her arm the way an old man might croon over a chorus girl.

'It was really extraordinary,' said Sybille Bedford, at whose tea party at the Hôtel des Sts-Pères the telegraph girl appeared, 'the way Natalie would suddenly come alive in the presence of sexual possibility. And she did this all her life in the centre of a great group of people who regarded her as a legend and worshipped her.'[9] Bettina Bergery, who had ample opportunity to observe Natalie's doings over the years, thought that sex for Natalie was always connected with power. 'The iron fist in the velvet glove.'

In the 1960s, when she was in her late eighties, Natalie rejected a serious proposal from the seventy-three-year-old painter, writer, and furniture designer, Elizabeth Eyre de Lanux, with whom she had conducted an affair forty-five years before. Eyre de Lanux had been an intermittent rival of Dolly in the old days, although not a rival Dolly took very seriously, and Natalie rejected Lanux's request to see her (a breathless letter with a delicate drawing of a breast on it) with the kind of practised diplomacy which allowed Lanux to retire from the field with dignity:

> My dear and still beautiful Past, whatever may have occasioned your 'flare-up' I feel that your memory of my being is better than any new encounter. You are too strangely emotional to realize that in about eleven years — if I go on living — I shall be a hundred! So stay with the 'source' and may it bring you the happiness of existing, through looking backwards — where I await you.[10]

Natalie wrote this letter when she was eighty-nine years old and concentrating on her latest flame, the sixtyish wife of a Romanian diplomat.

Interviewed in 1996 at her 102nd birthday party, and for some months afterwards, Eyre de Lanux, who was Natalie Barney's last surviving intimate, still showed every evidence of the personal charm, artistic talent and linguistic preoccupations which distinguished all the Barney circle, and which kept the heart of the Barney salon beating and bleeding every Friday afternoon for sixty years. (See Appendix 2: I Don't Remember Dolly Wilde.)

In general, the things Natalie Barney actually did were more daringly inventive, and sometimes sillier, than the stories people were inspired to tell about her. As in, for instance, the early years of the century, when Natalie kept two coaches (one made of glass), two coachmen, and two sets of horses, to accommodate, at all hours, the volume of her sexual pursuits. Then there was the afternoon she had herself delivered to the poet Renée Vivien in a large box of white lilies, dressed for the boudoir. Or the evening she and the great mezzo-soprano Emma Calvé (another of Natalie's serious lovers) stood outside Vivien's house in Paris while Calvé sang the 'J'ai perdu mon Eurydice' aria from Gluck's *Orphée et Eurydice* and Natalie pelted Vivien's balcony with flowers.

And, *pour couronner le tout*, there was Natalie's carefully planned and smoothly accomplished seduction, at the age of twenty-two and in the green velvet costume of a medieval page, of the most famous member of Paris's *demi-monde*, the lovely, literate courtesan, Liane de Pougy. So successful was the youthful Natalie in winning the affections of this notorious *belle horizontale*, that Liane wrote a novel about Natalie — *Idylle sapphique* — and continued to correspond with her intimately for the rest of her life.

The affair between Natalie and Liane de Pougy was quite a coup for the twenty-two-year-old debutante to pull off since her rivals at the time were male millionaires and princes of the blood; and it perfectly illustrates Natalie's tastes, talents, and total powers of concentration.

Both Natalie Barney's American and French biographers thought Liane de Pougy was the first, the death-obsessed poet Renée Vivien (née Pauline Mary Tarn) was the second, and Dolly Wilde was the third of the much-loved ladies whom Natalie Barney wanted to 'save' from themselves. Although Natalie's habits in loving usually exposed her lovers to at least as much danger as they were in *before* she began her attempts at salvation, Natalie did go regularly, though *never* selflessly, to the rescue, and her history and character conformed to these missions: she had her father's alcoholism before her as the type of all bad examples; she was a born 'instructor'; she was an ardent feminist by nature and an active one where it suited her purposes; and her habits in everything but love were abstemious and temperate. In a larger way, however, Dolly, Renée, and Liane represented something very like failures for Natalie. They all loved her, they all listened to her, and they all continued to do exactly as they pleased — perhaps in reaction to the multiplicity of Natalie's attachments, perhaps for the pure pleasure of thwarting Natalie.

In the cases of both Dolly and Renée Vivien (who died anorexic and alcoholic at thirty, drinking perfume in an odd quotation from Dolly's childhood habit) Natalie took on two women who were preternaturally drawn to death, and there were many people who said that Natalie had hastened Dolly's and Renée's untimely ends. Renée Lang, the scholar who abandoned a prospective biography of Natalie in the 1950s, thought Renée Vivien, Romaine Brooks, the duchesse de Clermont-Tonnerre and Dolly Wilde were the four great loves of Natalie's life; Lang was one of the people ready to blame Natalie for Renée's and Dolly's deaths.

Liane de Pougy, who had none of Dolly's and Renée's desire to dissolve themselves, continued to find pleasure in both sexes, married one of the princes Ghika, and, at the end of her life, adopted a style of living calculated to annoy Natalie (who thought of Liane as 'my most voluptuous memory') far more than her prostitution ever did: Liane joined a nunnery.[11]

It was not just women with whom Natalie was successful, although it was women in whom she was sexually interested. The greatest humanistic intelligence of pre-war Europe, Rémy de Gourmont, fell completely and utterly in love with Barney's mind and character and body, and made her a famous *femme de lettres* by addressing a series of profoundly reflective and adoring letters to her — *Lettres à l'amazone* — and publishing them in the leading literary journal of the day, the *Mercure de France*. According to Jean Chalon, Natalie's French biographer, Natalie used to allow Gourmont a single intimacy: he could stroke her hands.

The art historian Bernard Berenson wrote to Natalie intensely, lengthily, and very flirtatiously for years; Pierre Louÿs, Anatole France, Sir Harold Acton, Paul Valéry, André Germain, Paul Eluard, Ezra Pound, Philippe Berthelot, Max Jacob and many more notable literary males were all happy to name her as friend, quote her epigrams, and turn to her for help. It is said that without the support of Barney's salon, Paul Valéry's career would never have launched itself into the Académie Française; and Natalie had plans for literary journals with such diverse writers as Sinclair Lewis and Ford Madox Ford. The suggested title for one of those journals is still provocative today: *How to Live by Those Who Have*.

Natalie Barney's writings — more interesting and more anarchistic than they have been understood to be by many of the writers and film makers who have engaged with her life – run through a myriad of forms and a plethora of styles. There are dialogues, an 'interior' novel, memoirs with structures so loose as to include drawings and criticisms (she has a chapter called 'What Men Think' in one of her memoirs), plays, and poetry. And there is a kind of unpublished novel in aphorisms, *Les Amants feminins*, as revealing as a Proustian analysis and as coldly sensual as *Les Liaisons dangereuses*, which details with chilling precision the innumurable sexual and emotional combinations of three women – M., L. and N.[12] This work, like most of Natalie's writing, appears to be autobiographical and has not, like most of Natalie's writing, been translated from the French in which she wrote it. (One work has been badly translated.) And so her quite unusual *aperçus* about women, pacifism, sex, and love are unknown in the English and American languages.

Natalie, who always maintained the pose of writing carelessly, in fact wrote as carefully as she could. Her archives reveal many scratch copies of letters and prose pieces and voluminous diaries and drafts for creative work. She wrote and rewrote and rewrote, tweaking her 'pensées', her prose, and her little paradoxical stories, until she was satisfied with their implicative superficiality or with their shape. Her handwriting, on the other hand – cramped, tiny, conscious of every time-saving gesture – is that of a woman in a terrific hurry, belying her self-promoted image of 'lâche-ness' and laxity. Her 'carelessness' was simply a pose, like any other. Her ability to concentrate herself and her thought on paper, and her distaste for long, literary forms resulted in several books of *pensées*, written in wonderfully precise French and marked by subtlety and ingenuity. Like much of her work, they, too, have resisted translation.

Although her American prose is sometimes awkward (she had a rather leaden nineteenth-century style in her native language and – far more successful – an ornate and highly polished eighteenth-century style in French) and her poetry school-roomish, the *pensées* are chiselled and wittily exact in a Wildean way. But they lack the encompassingly

Parnassian quality of Oscar's epigrams — often to their advantage. They are far less like proclamations from Oscar's Imaginary Academy of Fine Ideas and far more like crystalline splinters from Natalie's Golden Bowl of Life: the biography in them is always obvious. Natalie called her first book of *pensées*, the book that attracted the attention of Rémy de Gourmont, '*Eparpillements*' — 'Scatterings'; Harold Acton described it as 'scintillating'. Here is a sample:

La gloire: être connu de ceux qu'on ne voudrait pas connaître.
Fame: to be known by those whom one does not wish to
  know.

Toujours: trop longtemps.
Always: too long.

Jésus Christ a séduit beaucoup plus de femmes que Don Juan.
Jesus Christ has seduced many more women than Don Juan.

Marié: n'être ni seul ni ensemble.
Married: to be neither alone nor together.

Si j'hésite, c'est qu'il ne faut pas.
If I hesitate, it is because I shouldn't do it.

Ce parasite: le passé.
This parasite: the past.

*Vous avez peut-être raison, mais avoir raison n'est peut-être pas avoir
  grand-chose.*
You are perhaps right, but to be right is perhaps not so
  important.

Il vaut mieux être un amant qu'aimer un amant.
It is better to be a lover than to love a lover.

*Le duo d'amour est une invention d'opéra; en amour on ne chante que seul
ou l'un après l'autre.*

The duet of love is an invention of opera; in love one sings
only alone or one after the other.[13]

These are the *aperçus* of a literary and civilised *femme de lettres* who
has thought clearly — although perhaps not very deeply — about what
it means to lead a voluptuous life. Like all well-wrought *pensées*, their
charm is in the concentrated availability of their surface and in the
vague promise that something more lies beneath it.

Natalie's classical temperament, best suited to the protected life
that all eighteenth-century *hommes de lettres* lived (Natalie recreated
that style in the female mode well into the twentieth century), finds
its fullest expression in these aimed little arrows of wit. Natalie's reap-
propriation of male forms — the *homme de lettres* pose, the epigram, and
the erotic narrative — not to mention the many photographs of masquerades and temporary gender transformations attending lesbian
love that she staged, directed and starred in with her lovers, deserve a
far wider audience than they have had. And her advanced sexual
ideas — classically Greek in their provenance, occasionally Roman in
their practice — could support an entire volume of their own, as
could the chronicle of her mostly successful attempt to reconstruct a
City of Women in the very heart of literary Paris.

Feminist historians have always tried to represent Natalie Barney as
the unique, pioneering re-creator of Sapphic society that she certainly
was, while Barney's other interpreters have concentrated on her sexual
tastes and flamboyant liaisons. In fact, the Barney salon, the longest
running and most unusual salon in all of Europe, was a place where
lesbian assignations *and* appointments with academicians could co-
exist in a kind of cheerful, cross-pollinating, cognitive dissonance, due
as much to Natalie's brilliant social sense, developed intellectual interests, and lion-hunting tendencies (and to the ameliorative presence
and famed cuisine of Berthe Cleyrergue), as to the times, customs,
and communities which made such exchanges possible.

Natalie Barney was a genius at having it all ways. Her life represented a genuine revolt against what Gertrude Stein called 'patriarchal poetry', yet she consulted and managed to befriend many famous and highly accomplished male writers, all of whom admired her mind, attended her salon, and supported her various causes. She carried on multiple affairs to the despair of her women lovers, yet finagled to keep them all as friends *and* lovers. Her openly lesbian sexual tastes put her outside the pale of society, yet she established a distinct community of her own, into which the very people who initially excluded her wanted, in the end, to be invited. 'I left society before it left me,' she wrote. Natalie Barney was a formidable woman.

Natalie turned the old criticism of women — that they can't get their minds out of the salon or their bodies out of the bedroom — on its head. She made a virtue of that criticism. Her salon, during its heyday, was so famous that nobody wanted to get out of it; her bedroom was so notorious that everyone wanted to get into it. Natalie actively pursued the accomplishments of *both* the salon and the bedroom: she pursued them fully and completely and she made certain that she had an unusually good time doing so.

The accomplishments of her salon — one of which is surely its longevity — can be seen in the revolutionary way that it welcomed male Modernists and Academicians, while supporting the female subverters of both those styles. Like its *salonnière*, the Barney salon could hold two contradictory ideas in its head at the same time. And this doubling of intention and multiplying of purpose really all emanated directly from Natalie's remarkable character, which was rather like the that of Elizabeth Tudor in its self-assertions, its manipulations, its emphasis on a constant rotation of compliments, its political dispersal of favours, and its insistence on having things all ways.

Unlike Elizabeth Tudor, however, Natalie's pursuits were direct and unambiguous; she was able to sustain the contradictions in her life — supporting male artists and sustaining the work of the women who subverted them — without recourse to a contradicting conscience. And she always attracted homage. Even Dolly, unless she was playing the impertinent, frolicking role of 'Puppy Wilde', first applied the sobriquet 'The Knights of Natalie's Round Table' to Barney's inner circle and always treated Natalie like a queen regnant, plying her with high-flown and fulsome compliments, assuring her that she had every right to exercise her *droit de seigneur*.

Behind Natalie's back, however, Dolly was sometimes apt to refer to Natalie as a '*vieille toupie*', or a '*vieille folle*' and complain that the only place at 20 rue Jacob she could get good champagne was in Berthe Cleyrergue's tiny apartment. (Natalie tended towards *vin mousseux* and could be very mean with the servants.) In everything but love, and then frequently even in love itself, Natalie's character was cool, temperate, and classical, and she took a certain geometric pleasure in the complications that a human triangle — her favourite figure in love relations — could engender.

Dolly, who was always a shrewd evaluator of her own and everyone else's love affairs and whose metaphors are vulnerable and revealing, thought that Natalie was something of an accountant in love: always figuring just how much emotion she had to dispense to get the desired amount back. Dolly refers persistently to Natalie's 'American business-man's telegrams' and letters, and alludes to her as regularly calculating a spreadsheet of *amours*. 'Toughness disguised as great femininity,' said Sybille Bedford, who thought that Natalie was 'heartless and artificial' like 'all the French'.[14] At the end of her life, when some fissures in her sixty-year loyalty to Barney were finally beginning to appear, Berthe Cleyrergue said that Natalie Barney enjoyed watching her lovers suffer.

But Natalie could be touchingly vulnerable where Dolly was concerned and wild with worry when she did not hear from her, as she often did not. In a 21 August, 1937 letter to Honey Harris, sent from her villa in Beauvallon, Natalie is trying to track Dolly down:

> How are you and how is our Dolly? I know how happy she
> has been with you from a long letter she wrote Romaine, but I

would like to hear more directly through you. Has she left Bembridge — is she *apparently* all right? — the most we can hope for? and how is she filling up the gap between August 15th and her stay at La Brière with Madame Fabre-Luce, and her trip to Austria with T. B. [Tancred Borenius]? I'm always a little anxious at this time of the year when I loose [sic] sight of her — and she is always so all present or all absent isn't she? . . .[15]

Since Natalie had no 'politics' in the sense that we understand the term today (a fact regularly misunderstood by her contemporary interpreters), questions have arisen about just how actually 'fascinating' she found fascism. Natalie was an outspoken pacifist during the First War, when she held anti-war meetings in her garden at the rue Jacob, boasting that she and Romaine Brooks were the only two American women in Paris *not* driving ambulances. In her personal life, she seemed to loathe discord and was always clever about defusing disagreement in both her salon and in her bedroom. She feared the communists far more than the fascists (whom she praised because they would uphold 'traditional' values) and she entertained the usual upper-class American's horror of a communist-controlled Europe. In this, Natalie was like every wealthy expatriate whose worst nightmare was the socialisation of her or his financial capital and the destruction of the ordered and orderly world of Western Europe.

With the exceptions of Mina Loy, Lily de Gramont, and Janet Flanner (who reported politics far better than she understood them), most of the women who surrounded Natalie did not make political analysis a subject of thought or interest or serious conversation. Elisabeth Hardwick's opinion that 'art was the religion of the 1920s', along with Scott Fitzgerald's judgement that the 1920s were 'not interested in politics', certainly remained true long after the twenties were over for many of Natalie's cohorts. Most of them, anyway, were old (or new) style Aesthetes or sensualists: from Gertrude Stein — who could excitedly describe a secret *Croix de Feu* meeting near her

country home in Belley without remarking on its reactionary implications and who was as conservative as a monarch in money matters;
to Colette – whose interest in current events was confined to 'crimes
of passion', who published work in occupation journals during the
Second World War, and who neglected to cover any political crisis of
the 1930s in her journalism; to Eyre de Lanux – who had affairs with
both the communist Louis Aragon and the neo-fascist Drieu La
Rochelle without concerning herself with the views of either man; to
Djuna Barnes – who protested because all her fellow writers at the
WPA in New York were communists trying to convert her to a
theory of 'the masses', when she was simply 'an Elizabethan' who
cared only about 'beauty'; to Dolly Wilde – who could take an artist's
pleasure in precisely describing the conformation of Mussolini's head
without worrying about what was inside it.

Natalie had a conflicted and predictably torturous relationship to
her Jewish ancestry, although she often boasted about it. Dolly once
addressed her with clearly affectionate and sexual intent as 'my little
Jew boy' and Natalie counted women of Jewish extraction among her
lovers (possibly the artists Sonia Delaunay and Chana Orloff) and
men of Jewish heritage among her closest friends (Saloman Reinach
and Bernard Berenson). Her ambivalent, unpublished essay, 'Jews',[16]
which manipulates every stereotype of anti-Semitism in trying to
figure out what manner of people Jews are, seems, actually, to be
Natalie's attempt to figure out exactly what kind of Jew *she* is. She
really thought about the subject and, like so many of her generation
who were part-Jewish, subscribed to nineteenth-century ideas of
fixed, racial identities. She was Jewish enough for Hitler, but not
Jewish enough to identify or to particularly sympathise with her partial birthright. But her Jewish ancestry was surely one of the reasons
she had to withdraw from Paris (where she was notorious) to 'winter'
the Second World War quietly in a Florentine suburb (where she was
unknown and where there was a community of like-minded
women) – instead of refugeeing, blamelessly, to the swimming pools
of Hollywood as Christopher Isherwood and W. H. Auden did.

A nice recycling of contemporary anti-Semitic gossip had it that Natalie was paying for rhinoplasty to alter her presumptively 'Jewish' nose, which looked, said Berthe Cleyrergue, 'like the neck of a goose'. The appropriate and unconscious bit of *Yiddishkeit* that accompanied this false piece of information was that what the plastic surgeon had put into Natalie Barney's nose to straighten it out was . . . the bone of a chicken.[17]

Natalie's failure to acknowledge the carnage fascist policies created on all sides is perfectly consistent with the way she lived the rest of her life: in a world of her own creation, shored up by her money, exercising her iron will to keep things just as she wanted them. Closer to home and twenty years later, she showed the same, regal unconcern for the activities of the *soixante-huitards* just outside her salon door, where, said her French biographer Jean Chalon, the popping of champagne corks in the salon coordinated nicely with the sounds of the paving stones thrown by the students.

Berthe Cleyrergue summarised the situation precisely when she said of a carping letter Natalie wrote to her from Italy about the garden at the rue Jacob during the worst of the Second World War: 'Voilà bien Mademoiselle. Ici, on croule sur les bombes, et elle, là-bas, ne pense qu'a sa pelouse de lierre.' ('That's Mademoiselle to a "T". Here, we collapse under the bombs and down there, she thinks of nothing but her ivy ground-cover.')[18]

The fact that Natalie Barney was both the major seducer that her male biographers claimed her to be, and as 'politically' unresponsive as some of her female critics have suggested, must not obscure the much farther-reaching fact of her life: Natalie Barney was the radical sustainer of an unprecedented community of art-making women in Paris who formed by their work and their relations with each other the only serious critique of Modernism as it was practised by male artists in the twentieth century.

In this Natalie was absolutely unique. She was a pioneering supporter of women artists and writers, a shrewd cultivator of the male artists, politicians, and academicians who interested her, and an alert and sexually adept seducer. What, in gentler days, used to be called the 'libido', played as large a role in Barney's salon as did what, in quieter days, used to be called the 'intellect'. Barney's own unquenchable sexuality guided her into her ninety-sixth year – nor did her intelligence desert her.

Although Natalie's friendships and affairs were innumerable, although her longest and dearest partnership was with the painter Romaine Brooks, although she and Dolly had a turbulent and frequently mutually painful relationship, Natalie's best feelings for Dolly never abated. She was haunted, she said, by the twitch in Dolly's smile at their final parting and she spoke of her always as a charmed and charming being – although perhaps a little easier for Natalie to deal with in memoriam.

On the third anniversary of Dolly's death, in April 1944, Natalie wrote to Honey Harris from her refuge in Florence: 'My thoughts have gone out in search of your thoughts all these months, and especially during Aprils – "April is the cruellest month" – as since April 1941 – when we left off living for the doubtful pleasure of surviving.'[19]

1 0

The Knights of
Natalie's Round Table

*Ma liaison avec le 20, rue Jacob s'est transformée en un
durable mariage.*

Natalie Clifford Barney

*I*n 1948, seven years after Dolly's death, the twenty-three-year-old
prose writer Truman Capote was brought to Paris by his
French agent, Mme Jenny Bradley, to be the 'American literary lion' of
the winter season.[1] Jenny Bradley had been a good friend of Natalie
Barney since 1913, and Sybille Bedford remembers Capote at one of
Natalie's Fridays sitting on a sofa 'like a little Pekinese between two
Duchesses, who were feeding him cream cakes on either side.'[2]

Almost thirty years later, Truman Capote was interviewed in the
Paris Review about an evocative afternoon he spent alone with Natalie
Barney, an afternoon that sums up all that was left of the seductive
circle of wit, beauty, and intrigue that enveloped Dolly when she first
crossed the cobbled courtyard of 20 rue Jacob and walked into
Natalie's life.

On the day Capote remembered, Natalie Barney stopped by his
hotel to take him to luncheon, saying that 'she wanted to show me
something very unusual and extraordinary which very few people

had ever seen . . .'³ Natalie conveyed him to an unknown neighbourhood near the Eiffel Tower, gave him a meal in a curious little
restaurant, then led him on a long walk to a nondescript building
whose creaky elevator hoisted them both to an upper floor. Capote
had the impression that they 'were going into Ali Baba's cave'.

They walked into an enormous room, 'really enormous, like a sort
of "super-loft"'. It was about four o'clock in the afternoon and the
huge space was suffused with 'that strange, gray pearly light' that
overcasts Paris in winter.

> The whole room was well kept but it had the quality of total
> desertion – as if no one had been there for years. In the
> middle of the room was an easel with a half-finished painting
> on it, and beside it a table covered with tubes of paint, but all
> of them rather dry and desiccated-looking. Around the room
> the walls were covered with paintings shrouded with cloth,
> each of them with a little pull-cord next to the frame so you
> could pull it and the cloth would fold back and you could see
> the picture.
>
> And Miss Barney said, 'This is the studio of my beloved
> friend, Romaine Brooks . . .'⁴

Natalie led Capote around the vast studio, pulling the cords next
to the picture frames to reveal what Romaine Brooks had left there
for all those years: portraits of some of the most extraordinary
women in Europe, women who had frequented Natalie Barney's salon
between the wars. It was, said Capote, 'the all-time ultimate gallery of
all the famous dykes from 1880 to 1935 or thereabouts'.

> . . . Lady Una Troubridge with a monocle in her eye;
> Radclyffe Hall in a marvellous hunting outfit with a terrific
> hat . . . The paintings were wonderful . . . with terrific quality
> and style, and we looked at them, one after the other . . .
> Renée Vivien, Violet Trefusis . . . and of course Miss Barney

herself in a wonderful outfit with a pair of gloves here and a whip in the foreground . . . on the canvas she was this wild thing wearing a cravat, with her hand on her hip like *this*, and a *whip* over there . . . and I said, 'Miss Barney, my goodness, really, is that really *you?*'[5]

Natalie said later that she feared Capote was turning into 'a one-book boy.' And Truman Capote said he thought the milieu he had discovered with Natalie Barney on that grey Paris afternoon was just like an 'international daisy chain'.

Back in the United States, people were playing a chic little parlour game of the same name, the International Daisy Chain. The goal of the game was to link one famous person to another through the shortest possible chain of lovers. One of the most valuable links in the Daisy Chain Game was the playwright and screenwriter Mercedes de Acosta. It was usually possible to get from Mercedes de Acosta to almost any one else in under five sexual acts.

As a screenwriter in Hollywood in the 1920s, Mercedes de Acosta insisted on wearing a tricorn hat, a black cape, and long trousers, long before trousers were remotely associated with women in the American imagination. She knew everyone in the American and European artistic worlds of the 1920s and 1930s – and she knew Dolly well enough to mention her in her memoirs and to keep a photograph of her.[6] Acosta began to make very occasional appearances at the Barney salon in the 1920s, perhaps through her acquaintance with Una Lady Troubridge and Radclyffe Hall.

But it was Acosta's advent into the Barney salon with her current lover Greta Garbo that guaranteed her a place in the salon's oral history. Alice B. Toklas, who took an accountant's pleasure in such tallyings, is reported to have said: 'Say what you will about Mercedes, she has had the three most important women of the 20th Century.'[7] Which three women Toklas was referring to is a matter of conjecture, but Mercedes de Acosta was surely the only married woman – no, the only *person* – to have partnered Marlene Dietrich, Greta Garbo, Eva

Le Gallienne, Alla Nazimova, and Isadora Duncan in one short writer's lifetime.[8]

Although Acosta was an infrequent visitor to the Barney salon, the variety, interest, quality and complications of her love affairs (they *were* complicated — at one point she was seeing Marlene Dietrich and Greta Garbo simultaneously), were perfectly representative of the lives of the more regular female visitors to 20 rue Jacob. And they point up the *real* phenomenon of the Barney salon: it was a loosely structured social organisation, a sodality of women joined by intricate ties of art, love, sex, friendship, and money, who kept up with each other's activities, supported each other's work, and encroached on each other's emotional territories. Dolly often referred to this sodality in her letters: 'My love to Romaine. Is she fading under prosperity? And to Mina & Djuna & darling Lily.'[9] The word 'sodality', with all its Catholic implications, is properly applied: Claude Mauriac once referred to Natalie Barney as 'the Pope of Lesbos'.

The private heart of the Barney salon was composed of this association of mostly lesbian writers and artists whom Dolly dubbed 'The Knights of Natalie's Round Table'. Just as unusual as her creation of this women-only enclave, was the fact that Natalie welcomed both women and men at her public Fridays and encouraged as 'international' an atmosphere as she could manage. These private and public faces of the Barney salon probably had their provenance in Natalie's romantic idea of the 'school' of Sappho and in her classical interpretation of the 'tradition' of Oscar Wilde.

In 1903, the young, wealthy, in-love Natalie Barney travelled by boat with the equally well-fixed and enamoured poet Renée Vivien (née Pauline Mary Tarn)[10] to the isle of Lesbos (Mytilene) in Greece. Inspired by the fragments of Sappho's poetry discovered in 1895, and excited by Pierre Louÿs's imitations of Sapphic style in *The Songs of Bilitis*, these two rather self-important young women were making a private Odyssey to the Capital of their Imagination. It seemed perfectly natural to them to try to establish a lesbian colony — they would be its First Citizens — in the very place where 'burning Sappho' had sung and played.

That colony was never established. Natalie was perhaps deterred by the bad gramophone music, the unattractive women, and the cohorts of short, hirsute, male shepherds she said she found there. But the spirit of her youthful journey to Lesbos and her idea of founding a society of like-minded women in the manner of Sappho slowly made its way into the afternoons she began to hold in her house in Neuilly-sur-Seine and, later on, into the association of attractive, brilliant women who met in the salon and garden of her *pavillon* at 20 rue Jacob.

Vaunted with as much enthusiasm as her neo-Sapphic ideals were Natalie's profound feelings for Oscar Wilde, who had rescued her as a child just as Natalie would repeatedly rescue Oscar's niece. Natalie's sense of the injustice of Oscar's fate, and the identity she felt with Oscar's overt homosexuality (though not with his manner of express-ing it) were added to by her attachments to at least three characters in the Wilde Family Drama: Alfred Douglas, Olive Custance, and, of course, Dolly Wilde herself.

Natalie's motives for creating her salon uncoiled somewhat lazily over the years and were not nearly as defined as my explanation of their origins makes them seem. Nonetheless, Natalie Barney estab-lished a literary salon that would invoke and invite a male world like the one in which Oscar had shone so brightly. And then she carefully preserved the centre of that salon as a secret garden where Oscar's niece and the interesting women writers of the day could make liter-ary, social, and sexual connections.

For a salon to succeed, as Jane Wilde (one of Natalie Barney's unofficial grandmothers-in-law) noted in an essay on the subject, it requires a *salonnière* of extraordinarily supple character, a 'queen reg-nant' who is also an 'actress' and 'a slave to . . . literati, artists, and all the notabilities of fashionable circles'. Natalie Barney, who privately had a will of iron, was capable of summing anyone up in an epigram, wielded power like a head of state, and never in her life was anyone's slave, was publicly the most flexible of hostesses.

But a successful salon – particularly one as visibly and ambitiously successful as Natalie Barney's was to become – needs more than just a brilliant hostess. It needs an identifiable location (a house with literary associations will do), a memorable cuisine (the French, as Virgil Thomson noted, are 'terribly greedy' at the end of the day), and a large and rotating assortment of wits, political luminaries, and socially-and-career-minded artists, each one of them willing to be audience and/or performer, and each one available for verbal seduction on a weekly basis. It also needs the coincidence of an era and an ethos able to support the extravagant expenditures of time, mind and resources that enhance the life of a salon. The Barney salon at 20 rue Jacob had all of these things – and it had the added advantage of being in a *quartier* of Paris located, physically and intellectually, halfway between the formal pleasures of the Faubourg and the looser ones of Bohemia.

The rue Jacob, on the left bank of the romantic River Seine where Dolly Wilde was to spend so much of her life and so many of her emotions, had a history of residences by distinguished European writers. Lawrence Sterne and Prosper Merimée both sojourned on the rue Jacob and most of the American writers living in Paris between the wars began their expatriate careers at the rue Jacob's Hôtel d'Angleterre. Hemingway, Djuna Barnes, and Robert MacAlmon all stopped there, and Janet Flanner lunched constantly in the hotel's dining room in the company of minor Surrealists who regularly and for the fun of it insulted priests and spat upon sidewalk nuns.[11]

The rue Jacob, in short, was the perfect location for Natalie Barney's famous Friday salon and for *le tout Paris* – or almost all Paris, for Natalie, as Janet Flanner said, still 'lived as an oddity because of her tastes'[12] – to come and hear Mina Loy introduce Gertrude Stein, to see Natalie herself launch Paul Valéry towards the Académie Française and Djuna Barnes into literary Paris, and to watch Colette and Paul Poiret act scenes from *La Vagabonde* and Dolly Wilde represent – that's how the guests thought of it – her uncle Oscar's style and spirit.

The now-legendary house where Barney lived and entertained for more than sixty years is at the end of a cobbled courtyard, hidden from street view by the great, deep-green carriage doors at the courtyard's entrance. The house is a relatively small, two-storey *pavillon* in the classical style, free-standing on three sides, with the ceiling of every room inscribed with a circle within a square. The salon room was one of two downstairs drawing rooms with an alcove at one end where, on special Fridays or during meetings of the *Académie des Femmes*, the reading writers stood and declaimed from their works. The salon room gave on to an unusually large, unusually neglected garden, where Racine was supposed to have strolled with his mistress *La Champsmesle*.

The light in Natalie's *pavillon* is always characterised as aquarium light: aquatic, shadowed and mysterious; produced, perhaps, by the refractions of sunlight through the greenwood just beyond the windows. When Natalie was in residence, the rooms were always dusty and rather carelessly arrayed: books by all the authors Natalie knew were piled about; lumbering, inherited Arts and Crafts furniture, all wood and leather and large brass nails was backed against the salon walls downstairs (Natalie's mother gave her all the furniture that was 'not good enough' to be shipped to America). Bric-à-brac was everywhere, a Carolas-Duran portrait of Natalie in a cloud of blonde hair was on a wall, a famous lute (or was it a mandolin?) with a famous rift was perpetually on display, and, usually, an open box of chocolates was within reach. Dolly, with her customarily wicked accuracy, called the house a '*musée de province*' and a provincial museum is no doubt what it resembled.

Upstairs, Natalie's bedroom and the blue guest room she gave over to Dolly were separated by a small dressing room with eighteenth-century cane furniture, and a wicker dressing table laden with every conceivable item for a lady's toilette.[13] Dolly, who was both highly sexed and profoundly gendered, probably loved it. The items on the vanity were all from Guerlain. Natalie, true to her *arrière* style, favoured Jicky, a scent created by Guerlain in 1889. Dolly, who also

powdered, puffed, and scented with Guerlain, went for more contemporary products: possibly Shalimar, launched in her thirtieth year,
was one of them. A blue counterpane picked out with white stars covered Natalie's bed, a piano was in the chamber, and beside the bed lay
an old, white rug made from an old, white polar bear which figured
prominently in many of the photographs Natalie had taken of herself and her lovers in period costumes and flamboyant poses.

Even in the 1920s, the furniture in Natalie's *pavillon* looked
démodé, as though it had come from another, not-quite-ascertaina-
ble era; like her house, Natalie Barney retained an outside-of-time
quality. And like a fairy queen or like the heroine of a fairy tale
which she certainly resembled, she continued — unconcerned by wars
(she was a lifelong pacifist), untroubled by political sympathies
(except the stiffly conservative ones of the monied classes) — to use
her will, her absolute concentration on her own pleasure, and her considerable financial resources to keep herself alive, and well, and doing
exactly as she pleased to the end of her long life.

When Natalie first rented the *pavillon* at the rue Jacob in October
1909, the façade of the house was traced by ivy, and the floors were too
weak for dancing, so, as she remarked rather flippantly in old age, she
began to make her gatherings more literary and less performative. Backed
by its wild garden — in the English Romantic style rather than in the
French — with a tangle of weedy trees and a tiny conservatory (long since
disappeared) to admire them from, Natalie's *sous bois* was also famous
for the lovely little stone Doric *temple à l'amitié* built, it was said, for the
eighteenth-century French actress-courtesan Adrienne LeCouvreur.

The garden at the rue Jacob quickly became the imaginative centre
of everything Natalie Barney stood for: a kind of New Eden whose
gates were opened wide to those who consented to bite into the
Lady-Apple of Knowledge. Or perhaps Natalie's garden was more
like a Greenwood where Dolly's well-named 'Knights of Natalie's
Round Table' met for the delights of art, and the pleasures of social
performance and sexual connection.

Unlike Dolly, Natalie really didn't care for the outdoors and she

didn't like to dine in her garden. She much preferred nature in a subdued state (represented by the Bois de Boulogne or seen through the
walls of the glass coach she used to keep), and she couldn't be bothered with paying a staff to tame the garden. She used to stage *tableaux
vivants* in front of the *temple à l'amitié* and there are wonderful photographs of daisy chains of dancing women in Greek costumes looking
risibly Classical and striking affected poses amongst the trees. During
the First War, Natalie, opposed to all conflicts for any reason and
none too fond of patriotism of any kind, held pacifist meetings on
the temple steps, filling the garden with women journalists. Everyone
who saw the garden at the rue Jacob remarked on it; it was an unusual
place — a kind of physical illustration of the French idea of a *jardin
secret* — and unusual things happened in it.

In her salon, Natalie offered a forum for male writers such as T. S.
Eliot, Ford Madox Ford, André Rouveyre, Valéry Larbaud, Bernard
Berenson, Max Jacob, Ezra Pound, Thornton Wilder, Anatole France,
Paul Valéry, Paul Eluard, Marcel Schwob, Phillippe Berthelot, René
Crevel, Scott Fitzgerald, Pierre Louÿs, Somerset Maugham, Edmond
Jaloux, Phillipe Soupault, André Germain, Paul Géraldy, Carl Van
Vechten, Sinclair Lewis, Harold Acton, etc., etc.[14] In her *Académie des
Femmes*, she hosted unprecedented honourings of women writers such
as Gertrude Stein, Lucie Delarue-Mardrus, Rachilde, Mina Loy,
Anna Wickham, and Djuna Barnes. But in her garden she conducted
for her own amusement some far more private (and certainly more
erotic) revels both in the outdoors and in the little *temple à l'amitié.*

The names of the female *fidèles* of the Barney salon read like an
inventory of the women who were making art and interesting trouble
in Paris and London in the first third of the twentieth century. From
the beginning of the *belle époque* to the end of the 1930s, Rachilde,
Marie Laurencin, Liane de Pougy, Colette, Wanda Landowska,
Radclyffe Hall, Una Troubridge, Eva Palmer, Emma Calvé, Ida
Rubenstein, Dorothy Ireland, Isadora Duncan, Mina Loy, Gertrude
Stein, Alice Toklas, Jeanne Galzy, Florence Gould, Miriam Harry,
Dolly Wilde, Germaine Beaumont, Lily de Gramont (duchesse of

Clermont-Tonnerre), Janet Scudder, Georgette LeBlanc, Romaine Brooks, Nancy Cunard, Eileen Grey, Anna Wickham, Eyre de Lanux, Gwen Le Gallienne, Marguerite Moreno, Nancy Cunard, Djuna Barnes, Janet Flanner, Cécile Sartoris, Solita Solano, and many more women of talent and ability came to Barney's Fridays or to the more intimate lunches and receptions she reserved for women only.[15]

The Barney salon was far from the only one (and far from the first one) to welcome women. Salons were traditionally initiated by literary women and many salons were flourishing in Paris at the same time as Natalie's; each *salonnière* having her own special focus such as music, politics, the *beau monde* or literature. The comtesse de Fitz-James, Marie-Louise Bousquet (Dolly's second favourite *salonnière*), Mme Strauss, Gertrude Stein, the duchesse de la Rochefoucauld, the comtesse Marthe de Fels, the comtesse Greffulhe, the Princesse de Polignac (née Winaretta Singer, the American sewing machine heiress), Mme Arman de Caillevet, and Rachilde are among the women who opened their homes to friends and rivals alike during the period from the *belle époque* to the Second World War.[16] But none of these women created a salon with the 'international' flavour of Natalie Barney's and none of them made Natalie's deliberate attempt to *feature* the work of women.

And so the Barney salon became the only salon in Paris (and the only serious salon in Europe) to acknowledge the possibility of a community of art-making women, and to bring them together for regular discussions and expositions of their work. Natalie crowned a select few of these women with a rubric which would have been revolutionary in its time and which sounds subversive even now: the *Académie des Femmes*. She printed the rubric in her book *Aventures de l'esprit* as *académie de femmes*.

This '*Académie*' was both a flippant response and a living reproach to the collection of *immortels* in the Académie Française, whose gendered name in French is practically the only female thing about it. (The Académie Française admitted its first woman member in 1974; sometime later, it admitted a second one.) Natalie, who said she preferred to be the friend of men and the lover of women, nonetheless made patient and comprehensive efforts on behalf of the art of her women friends, whether or not she had other interests in them as well.

Although Natalie mixed the Faubourg with the *quartier latin*, and entertained people of all nationalities, persuasions, sexualities and economies, her salon rested on the oddly stable society of women composed of 'The Knights of Natalie's Round Table' and the *Académie des Femmes*. Some of the female 'Knights' had been Barney's lovers (and/or each other's lovers); all of them read and admired each other's works, knew each other's intimates, gossiped, sometimes bitterly, about each other, and forgave each other each other's indiscretions. And two of the most prominent – Romaine Brooks and Lily de Gramont – continued as Natalie's intimates throughout her relationship with Dolly.

The painter Romaine Brooks was the most important person in Natalie Barney's life – and a sometimes difficult figure in her salon.[17] Romaine hated crowds and she hated small talk. Natalie, on the other hand, hated the smell of paint – which is the reason, said Berthe Cleyrergue, why the walls of 20 rue Jacob were rarely repainted. Romaine was Natalie's lover, friend and acknowledged life-partner from about 1915 onwards.

Romaine Brooks came from a background similar to Natalie's – American-born, monied, Europeanised, and rootless – but she had been emotionally marked by a madly aversive mother and a pathologically diseased brother. She was withdrawn, she could be paranoiacally suspicious, and she lacked Natalie's social pliancy and sense of humour. But Romaine had qualities of concentration and dedication to art which Natalie never could develop, probably because Natalie lacked Romaine's great gifts as a creator. Romaine continued to paint her beautifully acute and psychologically remote portraits well into her nineties, when she broke off her sixty-year relationship with Natalie over Natalie's final, intolerable infidelity with the Swiss wife of a Romanian diplomat.

Romaine was Dolly's utter despair at the beginning of her affair with Natalie, but Dolly quickly recognised and appreciated Romaine's artistic gifts, her unusual physical beauty and her strength of character — all of which commanded from Dolly, as superior qualities always did, the most profound respect. Romaine also inspired something like a schoolgirl crush as well. Dolly regularly sent Romaine little messages like these in her letters to Natalie:

> Remember me to Romaine & tell her I often envy her her flight from life & think she has the better exchange.[18]

> How is Romaine? Please remember me to her — she is always an exciting thought in one's head![19]

> This is to convey my love to Romaine — dear Romaine! What a lovely name. I should use it all the time if I was in love with her, thus: Romaine, do you love me Romaine? & so on![20]

And Romaine, between jealous bouts of having Dolly banished from the rue Jacob and insisting that Natalie 'shake this rat from out of your skirts',[21] used to lunch lingeringly with Dolly, and send her money, warm clothes, and sound, conventional advice.

The other great figure in Natalie's life and salon — and a woman who figured in Dolly's life as well — was Lily, the duchesse de Clermont-Tonnerre, who wrote under her family name of Gramont. By late middle age when Romaine Brooks painted her portrait, Lily de Gramont was maintaining a statesmanlike demeanour while bearing a certain resemblance, as Virgil Thomson remarked, to 'a washerwoman'. But in her youth she had a Gainsborough-like beauty and her character was always fearless, independent and intellectually original. Her four volumes of memoirs give an active participant's look at the social intricacies that Proust chronicled, the intricacies of the Faubourg St Germain.

Lily de Gramont was descended from Henry IV and raised in the time when all the young males in her family were dukes.[22] Her parents had entertained some 90,000 people in their lavish household in the Faubourg and the family maintained an unimpeachable social standing. But none of this kept Lily from separating from her husband (who spanked her when she took their automobile out without his permission), or from earning her living with her pen when the Great War reduced her finances. And she radically shifted her political views, first to communism, then to a support of the far right, with a fine disregard for public opinion.

Lily and Natalie were lovers for some years before the First War and continued their intimate friendship until the duchess's death in 1954. Dolly seems to have known Lily almost before she knew Natalie. There was a kind of intimacy between them; Dolly did some translating for her, and provided an excellent description of one of the qualities for which Lily was beloved.

> Dear Madame de C.T. was with us, exquisite, wonderful and so sensitive to someone she likes, that after an outwardly amusing evening she got up in the middle of the night and came to my room because she felt I was feeling sad — and indeed I was in tears! Such sweet rough comforting![23]

Lily, however, was also one of the people Dolly irritated by the intermittent breeziness and occasional rudeness of her social manners; whatever philosophies Lily embraced, she remained, in outlook, a duchess to the end.

After Romaine, the next American member of Natalie's inner circle was Djuna Barnes, the 'red-haired Bohemian' from Greenwich Village.[24] Barnes was a pioneering American journalist, a brilliant writer of prose fiction and poetry, and a painter and illustrator. She had early on been recognised by the entire expatriate community in Paris as a woman of exceptional talent — genius even. She was virtually the only woman writer who had the support and respect of men like James Joyce and T. S. Eliot, as well as the admiration of all of Natalie's 'Knights'. Natalie gave her money, featured her in the

Académie des Femmes, and counted her among her intimates. Djuna Barnes said she was bisexual, although her longest, most painful, and most creative relationship was with the sculptor and silverpoint artist, Thelma Wood, who had also been the lover of Berenice Abbott. Thelma Wood inspired Djuna's masterpiece, *Nightwood*.

Djuna and Dolly had a difficult relationship, perhaps because of a certain rivalry for Natalie's attentions, perhaps because Djuna had fulfilled her literary promise and Dolly had not.[25] Although they were closely associated through Natalie's salon and the inner circle of Natalie's 'Knights', as well as through their family histories, Dolly seems always to have felt that Djuna was working against her. In fact, the bluntness of Djuna's speech sometimes caused troubles between Natalie and Dolly.

In middle age, Djuna wrote that she found Dolly Wilde hard to take – 'so damned conceited'. And in her embittered old age, during which she became intensely critical of women and much less accurate about her relations with them, she apparently told an assistant two unflattering and perhaps inaccurate stories about Dolly: (I) that Dolly said that if anyone should be a genius, it should be 'me' – and that Natalie had replied 'But it's Djuna'; and (2) that Dolly had persuaded Natalie not to let Djuna dedicate *Ladies Almanack* to her because it would ruin Natalie's reputation.[26]

Both Dolly – because of her delightful presence and eternal potential, and Djuna – because she had already realised many of her possibilities – were the recipients of more gifts of money and attention than most of the other women in the Barney circle. Their odd, underground rivalry (which their economic dependence must have exacerbated) and their suspicious preoccupation with each other continued during Dolly's lifetime and long after Dolly's death. On her seventy-ninth birthday, when Djuna ate her birthday dinner with Vivian Eliot, T. S. Eliot's widow, she spent the entire time talking 'inordinately' to Mrs Eliot about Dolly Wilde.[27]

Mina Loy, the famously beautiful Anglo-Jewish poet and artist, was the only exclusively heterosexual woman in Natalie's *Académie des*

Femmes. Along with Djuna Barnes and Gertrude Stein, she was the other 'genius'. The uncompromising experimentalism of her formal poetry, her independent and intellectually feminist spirit, her subversion of both Futurism and Modernism, and the socially conscious preoccupation of her subject matter brought her the usual rewards: her work in both literature and the visual arts was forgotten for half a century, much of it lost or buried in private collections, and she suffered the deprivations of poverty and the humiliations of patriarchal responses all her life. Mina thought: 'Our social institutions of today will cause future generations to roar with laughter.'

Mina was much admired by the Barney circle and Natalie asked her to introduce Gertrude Stein at one of the very first convenings of the *Académie des Femmes.* At another meeting, the works of Lily de Gramont and Mina were featured together. Everything Mina Loy turned her hand to was unusual and somehow unlucky; Peggy Guggenheim set her up in a shop to sell lampshades – no one had ever seen such beautiful shades, but she couldn't make a profit. She invented things – and then the patents were stolen. After the Second World War, when she was living in poverty on the Lower East Side of New York City, she continued to make wonderful constructions, designed to be hung on walls. The poet Kenneth Rexroth thought Mina's poems were forgotten because they 'defied category'. Mina, like so many of Natalie's inner circle, was an original.

Mina Loy had an unusual relationship with Dolly. Not only were they friends, but Mina's second marriage had been to Dolly's cousin-by-marriage, the quondam boxer, braggart, and all around Dada hero, Arthur Cravan, né Fabian Lloyd, son of Constance Wilde's brother Otho and his first wife. Fabian, like Dolly, had been touched by the myth of Oscar; he was presumed drowned when fleeing conscription from the same war in which Dolly drove an ambulance and Oscar's oldest son Cyril Holland lost his life. Mina mourned Fabian Lloyd until she died; it is very likely that she and Dolly talked together about the strange fates of all Oscar's relations. Dolly, as she did with

Djuna, admitted to being envious of Mina. Even Dolly's taste in envy was excellent.

Lucie Delarue-Mardrus, the least recognised member of Natalie's salon, was one of its better writers, and a very acute observer of Natalie. Renée Vivien thought Delarue-Mardrus was 'the greatest poetess of our time'. As with too many other members of the Barney salon, Lucie's letters and life-circumstances have been suppressed or denied publication by her heirs. Natalie had initiated Lucie into sexual love with women in 1902 when she was still married to the orientalist, Dr Joseph-Charles Mardrus (it was a *mariage blanc*) and Lucie knew Natalie for a very long time. She called her

> *My joy and my pain, my death and my life,*
> *My blond bitch!*

Lucie wrote plays, poems, novels and memoirs and in 1930 published a *roman-à-clef*, *L'Ange et les Pervers*, which contains a particularly subtle, complicated, and piercing portrait of Natalie Barney in the person of the character Laurette Wells. The portrait limns Laurette's (and Natalie's) most inescapable identity.

> For you are terribly American, for all your cosmopolitan airs. You make twenty-five rendezvous all over Paris for the same hour, not counting five minutes for the theater and a quarter of an hour for a concert. You have the restless disease which comes from being dragged around ocean liners, trains and hotels while too young, like all little Yankees who are too rich.[28]

And in her memoirs, Lucie concluded:

> . . . after a little while Natalie became simply the bosom friend, the sister, the pure and faithful companion, whose

pride, loyalty and nobility I have esteemed so highly for more
than thirty years, despite her intolerable faults and vices,
which would probably not exist but for the literary pose she
adopts.[29]

The two other Americans who frequented Natalie's inner circle
were novelists and journalists as well as lovers, Janet Flanner and
Solita Solano. Janet Flanner, who had some of Natalie's habits in
love — she seems never to have had less than two or three intimate
friends at once — was the upholder of the best of the old *New Yorker*
magazine style: witty, allusive, *mondaine* and uncommitted. Natalie
liked Janet, but did not value her work particularly; nor did the
other women of Natalie's circle. Janet was the author and originator
of the *New Yorker*'s 'Letter From Paris' column, which ran for fifty
years, and she was a shrewd and subtle observer of the social scene.
In her many letters from Paris, Janet always managed to tuck in
little items of gossip from the Barney salon and news about its
habitués. In July 1930, Janet mentioned the duchesse de Clermont-
Tonnerre's costume ball at which Dolly appeared in the 'habiliments
of her uncle looking both important and earnest'. Dolly was flattered and wrote to

Darling Janet
    How earnest & important I felt as I read your article in the
New Yorker . . . 'Dolly Wilde' took on unexpected reality in
that implacable print. (Most of the time one lives in a grey,
nebulous photographic world of unreality) . . . Dear Janet, the
housemaid has left & I have a new one to look after me called
Molly who has become, of course, Moll Flanders to me. But I
haven't forgotten you, even without this spur of memory: in
fact I think it would be *difficult* for us to forget each other now,
wouldn't it? . . .

And among the Flanner/Solano papers in the Library of Congress, there is this scribbled, somewhat intoxicated note from Dolly to Janet:

> <u>Midnight</u>
>
> Dear grey & white Janet
>
> Your hair is your fortune & there is a nuance about you that makes you rare & exceptional. I want to thank you for the bouquet, the pleasure is indescribable – like all enchantment & there is something sad about being unable to tell the secret of pleasure. Be clever enough to enter the core of secret magic & leave me the tedium of explanation.
>
> I seem to know everything – even things dark & gloomy & fresh young green things the colour of lily of the valley leaves that spell youth & luminous light. Do you understand? If this letter is incoherent – it is nervousness & hopeless clarity.

Judging from the oblique references in these letters (but Dolly could never really be oblique about sexual matters) Janet and Dolly went to bed together. In two separate essays about Dolly – one a slight revision of the other – Janet wrote about Dolly with the authority of a thinker and the physical precisions of a lover. Janet's interpretations of Dolly are as subtle and allusive as Dolly herself and Janet obviously found Dolly fascinating.

Solita Solano, a lovely woman with a smooth bob and large, expressive eyes, lived with Janet Flanner for years, published three novels, was a theatre critic, a journalist, and a woman very much aligned with the community of women in Paris, and later on with the Gurdjieff community. Her response to Dolly's memorial volume shows the instinctive sympathies for which she was noted: '. . . I must tell you at once how deeply touched, benefitted, wounded, inspired and grateful I am – I feel – for the book. It has enlightened for me many mysteries in Dolly's nature, character and conduct . . .'[30]

Natalie's *Académie des Femmes* was already ten years old when Dolly began seeing Natalie and was distinguished from the inner circle of 'Knights' by being more artistically promoting and public than socially convivial and private. It initially included journalists like Rachilde and Aurel, the writers Colette, Lucie Delarue-Mardrus, Lily de Gramont, Djuna Barnes, Mina Loy, Gertrude Stein, Anna Wickham (whom Lucie Delarue-Mardrus called the 'English Verlaine'), the painter Romaine Brooks and, posthumously, the poet Renée Vivien. Natalie had devoted afternoons to the works of these writers and Colette's play *La Vagabonde* premièred in Natalie's salon in 1927, with Colette and Paul Poiret, the great couturier, acting scenes from it. Later on, Germaine Beaumont, Marie Laurencin and several other women of distinction came into Natalie's intimate circle. Dolly, of course, was a charter member of 'The Knights of Natalie's Round Table'.

Over time, the smaller circle of Knights and the wider circle of women artists who came to the Barney salon developed, under Natalie's direction, their own variations on established socio-political forms. The fact of their association created a kind of body politic based on an aristocracy of talent, wit and attractiveness. Intelligence, imagination, and good looks were the tickets of admittance, while friendship and romantic love were part of its social adhesiveness.

Most of the Barney 'insiders' were unusually handsome, gifted women with beautiful speaking voices. Lily de Gramont had a laugh which the French describe as 'a string of pearls', and Janet Flanner, Eyre de Lanux, Romaine Brooks and Dolly Wilde all had sensual, clear, low theatrical voices which people remarked on as 'beautiful' and which remained in memory. In short, Natalie presided over a tea-table full of accomplished, attractive intimates who convened in regular meetings outside the Friday salon for art, love, gossip and for Berthe's wonderful food, which played, as food always does in France, a very large role in everyone's memory of the Barney circle. One of Berthe's recipes is printed in *The Alice B. Toklas Cookbook* and Natalie's favourite food, a classic chicken and rice dish from the American South, was interpreted by Berthe as '*Poulet Maryland*' and served regularly to Natalie's close friends at private dinners. (See Appendix I: 'Poulet Maryland')

These intimate women friends also had an informal economic system, a kind of 'taxing of the advantaged', which worked out to the voluntary support of the poorer women of the circle by the richer women — usually when the poorer women were in circumstances of extremity. Eyre de Lanux, for instance, received without explanation a cheque from Romaine Brooks when she'd been in a car accident and was without funds. This form of donation alleviated temporary distress, but did nothing to redress the inequalities of wealth and power around which Natalie's circle turned. And the giving was sometimes based on the incredibly intricate connections — sexual, affectional, sororital, rivalrous — among the women, connections which would take a separate book, almost, to divulge.

In Dolly's case alone, while her affair with Natalie continued, she had possible sexual affairs and/or intricate emotional connections with Janet Flanner, Lily de Gramont, Marcelle Fauchier Delavigne, Mimi Franchetti, Mme Fabre-Luce, and Antoinette Gentien, as well as uncounted others outside the Barney circle. She had a complicated relationship with Romaine Brooks; and she continued to receive employment as a translator as well as outright gifts of clothes and money from Romaine, Lily, and Marcelle. Even Berthe Cleyrergue regularly loaned Dolly money. And Natalie herself, a woman not noted for her loose ways with finance, went on responding to Dolly's financial exigencies to the end of Dolly's life.

The supportive 'economics' of the Barney salon circle extended beyond its centre; many of the wealthy women who came to the salon and many of the women who were not wealthy and only rarely went to the salon practised a like-minded generosity. Shipping heiress Bryher, the writer born Winifred Ellerman, the only woman in the general milieu of European lesbians richer than Natalie Barney, gave money to Djuna Barnes, Sylvia Beach, Edith Sitwell and Dorothy Richardson, among others. Janet Flanner made certain that a near-destitute Alice Toklas did not want for necessities after Gertrude

Stein's death; and she assisted Djuna Barnes as well. Solita Solano supported her lover Margaret Anderson, founder of the *Little Review*, and Margaret's other lover, the soprano Georgette LeBlanc, out of her own meagre funds. Alice DeLamar, the retiring American heiress who came to Paris as an ambulance driver during the First War, bequeathed Eyre de Lanux and Eva Le Gallienne enough money to keep them through extreme old age. Even Peggy Guggenheim, a woman well out of the Barney circle although acquainted with it, managed to support at least one of its members: she provided Djuna Barnes with a grudging monthly allowance (ungratefully received) that helped sustain her for the rest of her life.

Perhaps taking their cue from Natalie, who never gave *anyone* up if she could help it, all the women in the Barney circle continued to take an interest in each other long after they were scattered by war or personal misfortune. Before the war, they went out together in small groups in the evenings to enjoy themselves at concerts, plays, film premières, restaurant dinners and, as Dolly indicated in a note to Natalie, somewhat more private pleasures: '*la voiture va me conduire à l'hôtel ayant laissé "la bande" au restaurant Lesbien!*' ('the car is going to take me to the hotel, having left "the band" at the lesbian restaurant.')

In the Court of Natalie's Round Table, Dolly often had the responsibility of Master of the Revels and she could remark with irony on her position as not only the Resident Performance Artist but as the Dignified Sufferer of Sexual Jealousy in the face of Natalie's maddeningly multiple tastes.

> . . . with all of you I am the performing animal – eternally criticized, alternatively approved & disapproved according to the temper of the audience . . .[31]

> I at least feel guilty of indulging grief, & will use subterfuge if necessary rather than spoil your happiness at the moment with your oldest friend, your newest mistress, and a newly-found companion of wit and humour![32]

Nowhere is the existence of these 'Knights of Natalie's Round Table' made more apparent than in the 'slight satiric wigging' given them by Djuna Barnes's *Ladies Almanack*, privately printed in 1928, hand-coloured by Djuna herself and by Mina Loy and her two daughters (one of whom was Oscar Wilde's grand-niece), and hawked about the streets of Paris by eager young women. Djuna's stylish and sometimes belligerent self-presentation, and her obviously rich gifts had already persuaded Natalie to dedicate an afternoon to her work in the salon's *Académie des Femmes* long before *Nightwood* was in flower.

Ladies Almanack provides an arch, anonymous, insider's view (Djuna signed it 'A Lady of Fashion') of the intense emotional and sexual entanglements of Barney's circle. It decks Natalie out in the tropes of redemption and the talismans of heroic fashion. The form – that of a medieval calendar – combines with a style that seems to invoke the various vernaculars of the Duchess of Malfi, the Wife of Bath, and a monologue by Molly Bloom – if Molly Bloom were a seductive, *soignée*, international lesbian. The effect of *Ladies Almanack* is intensely female and very deliberately antique, both of which qualities – as well as the 'satiric wigging' – are obvious in this description of lesbian love.

> Nay – I cannot write it! It is worse than this! More dripping, more lush, more lavender, more mid-mauve, more honeyed, more Flower-casting, more Cherub-bound, more downpouring, more saccharine, more lamentable, more gruesomely unmindful of Reason or Sense, to say nothing of Humor.[33]

George Wickes thought the book was a countering of Proust's glum vision of Gomorrah; and Djuna Barnes herself wrote that her intention was to provide a 'neap-tide to the Proustian Chronicle'. Both Djuna and Natalie criticised the way Proust depicted lesbians in his work and Barnes was just the writer to throw cold water (the 'neap tide') on Marcel Proust.

Ladies Almanack certainly provides an opposite view to Proust. It is a jolly, lusty tale of sexual adventure and female complications in love, satirically presented, with so many links to the inner secrets of the Barney circle that parsing its particulars is like trying to decode an encryption. Still, its larger meaning is always clear: a jocose reminder of 'the Consolation every Woman has at her Finger Tips, or at the very Hang of her Tongue', as it celebrates the sexual and social possibilities of the like-minded and very exclusive community of women who met regularly at 20 rue Jacob.

Natalie's close friends are all given aliases in this chronicle. Natalie herself is Dame Evangeline Musset, a sort of proseletising lesbian Pope whose desires are without end, whose bed is never empty, and whose death at ninety-nine results in her tongue being preserved in an urn on the altar of the Temple of Love. Janet Flanner and Solita Solana are Nip and Tuck, a breezy couple of journalists, exactly what they were in life; Lily de Gramont is the duchesse Clitoressa, Romaine Brooks is Cynic Sal, Esther Murphy is Bounding Bess, Mina Loy is Patience Scalpel (the only heterosexual figure in the book), Dolly Wilde is Doll Furious; Mimi Franchetti, a former lover of Natalie, is Senorita Fly-About. Dolly is first depicted pursuing Mimi: 'Merry Laughter rose about her, as Doll Furious was seen in ample dimity, sprigged with Apple Blossom, footing it fleetly after the proportionless Persuasions of Senorita Fly-About, one of Buzzing Much to Rome!'[34]

Dolly is next shown – displayed, really – in bed, wanting more of something than she has apparently just enjoyed.

'And,' said Dame Musset, rising in Bed, 'that's all there is, and there is no more!'

'But oh!' cried Doll.

'Down Woman,' said Dame Musset in her friendliest, 'there may be a mustard seed!'

'A grain, a grain!' lamented Doll.[35]

Barnes produces a sharp-eyed parody of Dolly's habits of keeping to her bed — 'my great big beautiful bedridden Doll' — and of her delight in telling stories. Doll Furious repeats a tale of sexual recognition and fidelity while walking through the Luxembourg Garden on Dame Musset's (Natalie's) arm. The fidelity part of the story seems to make Dame Musset quite nervous. 'There is a parody of these above preoccupations and of such sentiments . . . in the almanach's [sic] "July" which brings you evasively into focus,' Natalie wrote to Dolly about the *Ladies Almanack*, after telling Dolly that she had 'laughed myself sick' over the book.[36] The 'preoccupations' Natalie is talking about were the anxious coordinations of their respective menstrual cycles that Natalie and Dolly engineered every month in order to meet and make love when they were 'well'. Djuna, anyway, was in on all the jokes of Natalie's 'Knights', and she was also privy to their sexual excitements, Natalie's in particular. Dame Musset, who is thinking of putting together the Ideal Woman, says that she would like it to have 'the Hips of Doll'.

A visual record of the outer life of the Barney salon — the life that met regularly on those Fridays when both women *and* men were present — exists in a diagram drawn by Natalie Barney herself to illustrate her book, *Aventures de l'esprit*. The name of every important guest the salon received — there are hundreds of them — is carefully printed inside an outline of the salon and the garden of 20 rue Jacob along with several '*belles du jour*' and '*un group de mondaines*'. So crowded is the diagram, that the names of deceased guests — Isadora Duncan, Alan Seegar, Proust, Renée Vivien, Rachilde, Rilke, Miss Pankhurst, Eyre de Lanux, Pierre Louÿs, Rodin, and Robert de Montesquieu — spill out of the salon into the woods around the *temple à l'amitié* and into the garden.

Natalie represented herself in the diagram by a sinuous line which winds in and out of the thick forest of nomination she has printed. The line curves very close to the name 'Dorothy Wilde' which is written in right next to the name 'Jaloux' (Edmond Jaloux, French Academician, critic and novelist of distinction, and Dolly's admiring friend) at the left end of the drinks table. Rather hopefully, Natalie has angled Dolly's name so that it is turned away from the sketched-in glasses of port and whisky and directly faces the tumblers of water and the orangeade.

Never again, since those Fridays at 20 rue Jacob, has there been such a time for literary ladies. Never again has there been such an arena for their social presentation. Without the *mise en scène* of the Barney salon, without the reciprocity of possibility by which the conversational 'star' made the reputation of the salon and the salon provided a kind of oral history of the 'star's' verbal achievements, the eccentric gifts and killing wit of someone like Dolly Wilde would have vanished into anecdote, or into footnote, or into the unmarked, crossroads grave Virginia Woolf reserved for Shakespeare's brilliant, imaginary, suicide sister in *A Room of One's Own*, a work whose subject uncannily suggests some of the trials of Dolly's own life.[37]

Whatever the emotional currents it sustained, Natalie Barney's salon always maintained an outwardly impeccable and determinedly international decorum. 'International', said Berthe Cleyrergue, was one of Barney's favourite words. William Carlos Williams had bitter memories (he felt excluded) of women with foreign accents dancing together in Barney's garden in the moonlight, and everyone else speaks of Berthe's wonderful cuisine, of the hundreds of exquisite tea sandwiches ('folded up', said Bettina Bergery, 'like damp handkerchiefs'), the rich cakes, the fruit cup, and the exquisite company.

Throughout the hiatuses of war and illness, and along with the death of many of its principals, the salon at 20 rue Jacob continued to retain the rather démodé character of its *salonnière*. In its later life people not privy to the salon's complicated ties of literary and sexual kinship could find it rather museum-like. 'A lot of old moles looking for crumbs' is how one visiting American described the salon's senescence in the 1960s; and some of the invited gentlemen were wont to wax sarcastic on the artistic elevation of some of the invited ladies.

Sir Harold Acton, an admirer of Natalie who thought her 'dry

French wit belonged more to the eighteenth than the twentieth century' and who described her Friday receptions as 'literary agapes', brought the American writer Sherwood Anderson to one of Natalie's Fridays in the rue Jacob. Anderson was under the impression that Natalie was giving the tea for him that afternoon, but, no, said Acton, it was to honour the work of the 'burly Anna Wickham, who had evidently fortified herself with garlic and wine in advance'. Miss Wickham, the English poet, had obviously enjoyed what all the guests at the salon had also enjoyed that day: a good French lunch. Acton's remark is characteristic of the way some of the men at the salon spoke about some of the women.[38]

But in its heyday, which coincided with Dolly's own years of shine and sparkle, and in its stated purpose of bringing together writers of distinction and partners (sexual and otherwise) of promise from several cultures, the Barney salon was the longest and most successful enterprise of its kind in Paris, and it mingled genders, tastes, talents, ages, sexualities, and cultures for sixty years and more; always on Fridays, always in the same place.

The full history of the Modernist women writers and artists whom Natalie entertained and sponsored in her salon challenges the dominance of the work of the far more celebrated Modernist male writers and artists who also came to the salon — and that challenge is so serious that it has only begun to be explored in the last decade and a half. For the most part, the emotional and artistic history of those women — and of the unique salon that sponsored them — still continues to be the *real* 'love that dare not speak its name'.

The simplest proof of this assertion is perfectly visible in Paris — or rather it is *invisible* in Paris: marked by an absence rather than a presence.

Paris is a city which worships the past. It is a city where people actively go to seek out the past, and Parisians are inclined to put the name of every petty under-controller of finances on the building where he lived and died so that his little significant moment in the city's history will not be forgotten. Even the histories of buildings are marked with their own paddle-shaped signposts, in the event that someone might want to know exactly what happened at, say, the Hôtel de Varennes in 1643.

But there is not a paragraph posted anywhere in the city of Paris to mark the sixty-year-long existence of Natalie Barney's 'Fridays' and the gatherings of 'The Knights of Natalie's Round Table'. Nor is there a plaque at the courtyard entrance of 20 rue Jacob to memorialise the life of Natalie Clifford Barney: the remarkable, 'essentially American' woman who created the most important Parisian literary salon of the twentieth century.

I I

Oscaria

I know you think that your past letters will one day be agreeable reading – but they won't, darling, they won't. Forgotten sentiment goes rotten – & love letters rarely contain the interest of incident & the pleasure of wit.

Dolly Wilde, letter to Natalie Barney

What Natalie Barney did not accomplish in Dolly's lifetime – saving Dolly from herself – she managed to accomplish after Dolly's death. She rescued Dolly for posterity. Dolly's natural tendency to erase her history gave Natalie a lot of extra work to do: 'I am already tearing up letters, telegrams, and notes – that sad history of past months always collected wherever one is,' wrote Dolly to her friend 'Emily'.[1] But in the end, Natalie made certain that Dolly *did* leave a book behind her. It was the book that Dolly had written with her life and in the autumn of 1951 Natalie privately published *In Memory of Dorothy Ierne Wilde: Oscaria* with Darantière in Dijon, the printer who had set the type for both James Joyce's *Ulysses* and Djuna Barnes's *Ladies Almanack*.

Oscaria, faithful to its subject, is a rare, oddly attractive, ambivalent little volume full of colloquial charm, edited and sometimes altered sources, brilliant anecdotes, glittering vignettes, ill-concealed irritations, and some of Natalie's best editorial behaviour and slipperiest self-justifications. Natalie paid for the publication of *Oscaria* using, apparently, some of the money from Dolly's 'estate', and, as its editor and the writer who provided its prefaces, its introductions, its end notes, and all of its poetry, she never lost sight of the practicality of putting her purposes on every page.

Natalie's purposes were what they always were in such instances: to memorialise her brilliant and much-loved dead friend and to make certain that Dolly had her due *in this world*, the only world Natalie considered important. (Dolly once called Natalie a 'fourth dimensional materialist'.) Natalie also wanted to remind everyone that she, Natalie, had been the object of the lovely departed's deepest affections, and that she was entirely blameless in the tragic, early death of Dolly Wilde, who was, by the way, suffering from a 'relentless disease' and had a few other serious problems besides. In *Oscaria*, Natalie managed to hit all her marks. It was no mean feat.

'Oscaria' was an inevitable nickname for Dolly and it was certainly the name Natalie would have invented for this book if it had not already been available. Natalie, who loved both nicknames and Oscar, may even have given it to Dolly – or perhaps it was one of Dolly's *jeux d'esprit*, rather like Oscar's familial fantasy of himself as his great-uncle's protagonist, Melmoth the Wanderer. Dolly, anyway, never shrank from being identified as a Wilde. The look of the book *Oscaria* is as unusual as its title: a smallish paperback with softly pebbled, ivory boards, rich as *crème anglaise* and restrained as good linen; the hue probably recalling to Natalie the much-vaunted opalescence of Dolly's skin. The coverleaf printing is just as Natalie ordered: the 'exact colour of the green of Ireland' banded by two 'Irish green' stripes.

Twenty copies of *Oscaria* were inscribed with the names of Dolly's closest friends and were struck off on '*velin de rives*' and Berthe Cleyrergue got one of those. The ordinary copies, printed in a first edition of perhaps two or three hundred *exemplaires* on regular paper, are deceptively heavy; they seem to be weighted according to their contents rather than according to their size. On the book's frontispiece is a blurred photograph of Dolly dressed up as Oscar with her hair slicked back and a large 'aesthete's' cravat, bow-tied, at her throat. She looks fragile and sealed up in her impersonation and Natalie must have deliberately included the image to underline the significance of *Oscaria*'s title. Even in death, and especially in the publicity necessary to 'push' a book, Natalie did not hesitate to identify Dolly with her uncle.

Like Dolly's life, *Oscaria* is divided into two parts, one in English, one in French, and Dolly is presented through the remembrances of twelve of her 'fervent friends' and 'casual acquaintances' in many versions, mostly double ones. She is at once an English Rose and the incarnation of French *volupté*; she is Dolly to the core and a living reminder of Oscar; she is a woman with many male suitors and an ardent wooer of women; she is a brilliant comedic performer and she is trapped in a tragic role; she is a weary sophisticate and she yearns for spiritual purity; she has all of Oscar's 'feminine' qualities but she has come too late to make use of them, etc., etc., etc. Hardly an antinomy is missed, but because Dolly's friends are so smart themselves — and so charming on paper — their readings of her are terrific and convincing. From the archaeology of *Oscaria*'s rich mixture of gossip, regrets, vivid vignettes, and Natalie Barney's (barely) passable poetry, Dolly arises alive, exasperating, and very lovable.

Oscaria also includes a generous selection from Dolly's correspondences with Edmond Jaloux, Antoinette Gentien, 'Emily', and Natalie Barney, and the letters, Natalie noted, are 'much more charming and characteristic of her than our contributions'. Dolly was 'involved' in various ways with the three female letter writers represented; the male correspondent, Edmond Jaloux, was a famous critic and a highly respected member of the Académie Française who knew very well how to appreciate Dolly: his letters to her are charming, worldly, and literarily flirtatious.

The remembrances — six in French, six in English and American, with an 'Interlude' from Bettina Bergery — were, most of them, terribly late for the publication deadline, or written at the last moment, or were prised out of their contributors in circuitous ways. Many people Natalie had counted on for contributions did not make them and she could scarcely conceal her displeasure at their failure. 'The following contributions somewhat console us for the lack of those who failed to seek and find, and so deprive us, and perhaps themselves, of so enriching a fidelity.'[2]

Many of Dolly's friends, having spent a lifetime criticising her for not doing what they felt she was born to do, which was write, found that putting words on paper, especially words about Dolly, was more difficult than not. Could it have been all those appointments that Dolly failed to keep, or postponed, or cancelled, or was late to, coming back to retard this sole record of Dolly's life? Or was it the thought of Dolly dead that was so impossible to understand? All the charm of Dolly's youth and vitality — and the writers' youth and vitality as well — seems bound up in the memoirs. But there is surely some irritation in the tardiness of some of the contributions — and there must have been quite a bit of time spent on what *not* to say about Dolly. *Oscaria* is as much marked by what was left out of it as by what was put in.

Alice Toklas got off with a few lines, albeit a few good ones.

Gertrude and I did want to do a few words in appreciation of
Dolly's youth and her so lovable qualities. But how to give
them her joyous spontaneity? For in spite of the war she had
an almost mythical pristine freshness in 1916 — that, alas,
later became a bit tarnished, though she never really completely lost it.[3]

Gertrude Stein's recorded summation was pithier: 'Well, she certainly hadn't a fair run for money.'[4]

Rosamond Harcourt-Smith said that all Dolly's 'fictional instincts' turned every conversation towards a higher truth and gave a sharper point to life.

I miss Dolly always . . . I should like to see her sitting with her elegant legs crossed at the ankle, her long hands quiet in her lap (she never gesticulated), and her nostrils indrawn with mock severity as she pried open the oyster of my heart. I should like to hear her dismissing my enemies with one apt word, revealing my friends to me, picking up my life and massaging it with the oil of her approbation, giving it a few well-aimed slaps to bring up the circulation, then handing it back to me with all the falseness and lies sweated out, rejuvenated and firm.[5]

Honey Harris wrote that what Dolly cast over her friends

. . . almost amounted to a spell. She would fly down in our midst like a beautiful exuberant cuckoo, and in one moment I would find myself transformed from the rather shy and reserved person I was at the time . . . into a jocular garrulous chatterer – a very intoxicating change . . . a great many people reacted [to her] in just the same way. It was due to . . . all the nice things in her nature which rushed with delighted response to meet anything the other might manage to bring, even if it were only a turned up nose, provided it wasn't a dull one.

. . . although she was completely self-confident and made a great show of sophistication, she never lost a naive simplicity of heart which was very endearing and which turned the world into a place unfailingly full of surprises.[6]

Honey used to draw Dolly a lot and her 'pencil learned to do an almost automatic switchback run round the curves and points of her charming forehead, down her delicate teapot spout nose, and end up with the swoop of her rather heavy mouth and chin'. But it was the 'oddly touching quality' in Dolly's rather 'awkward' walk that was most vivid to Honey. 'I used to watch her from the window when she left the house, and even in her gayest days it seemed as if she was starting off alone into unknown sorrows – as indeed she was.'[7]

Janet Flanner's portrait of Dolly is extremely subtle; she and Lily de Gramont were alone in thinking that Dolly shouldn't have been a writer. Janet's idea was that Dolly was rather more like 'a character out of a book', still seeking the uwritten novel that might have provided her with 'resolute action'. She saw her as having the 'very delicate, civilized, uncertain psychological frontiers of an infinitely expanding and retracting person . . .' And as someone who 'had as many versions of herself, all as slightly different, as could have been seen in views of her supplied by a room lined with mirrors'. Dolly was 'utterly singular' and 'unique, in the way that only one, no two other youngish, foreign women were in that particular circle and her Paris decade'. One of the other two 'singular' women meant by Janet Flanner must surely have been Djuna Barnes; the other one could have been almost anyone in Natalie's circle.[8] (But it was probably Nancy Cunard or Mina Loy.)

The novelist and journalist Germaine Beaumont met Dolly for the first time at the opening of a *grand magasin*, one of those huge Paris department stores, where Dolly appeared in the centre of a group of social and literary personalities. Dolly was 'at the zenith of her brief destiny', in a 'shining, intelligent, modern milieu', and possessed of the slow majesty of 'those who are either indifferent or goddesses'. Beaumont thought even then that of Dolly's 'celebrated spirit' only 'brilliant powder in a broken crystal vase' remained.

Germaine Beaumont, observing Dolly from the outside, agreed with Janet Flanner that Dolly seemed to be 'a fictional being'. Dolly dramatised nothing, said Beaumont, but drama turned around her 'like crows around a belltower.' Dolly was like someone who had arrived a little too late 'on a beach when the tide has gone out'. The only thing left for her was to 'gather shells, plait seaweed for her hair, and watch the veils of the horizon diminish'. Dolly, thought Beaumont, always looked like an exile and 'carried this fate of exile' with her.[9]

Lily de Gramont's memoir invokes Dolly's ability to fascinate, her Irish beauty, her talent for warming a room, and the 'extraordinary verbal gift' which 'she had inherited from her famous uncle' and which she 'nourished with everything she heard and saw'. Lily also dwells on Dolly's 'grand impertinence', the effects of which had obviously stung her over the years, but, like Allanah Harper, Lily said you couldn't stay angry with Dolly because her criticisms simply showed her deep interest in you. Lily apparently did stay angry, however, since she describes a lunch at Natalie's when she and Dolly were '*en froid*' following an 'excess of impertinence', and Dolly kissed everyone there, even the people she did not know, to point up Lily's chilly reception – which, after such an extravagant response, certainly could not survive the occasion.

Lily compared Dolly to the runner who can never run fast enough, the gambler who can never put down enough money on the green baize: like them, she had to augment her verbal gifts with artificial means and she died '*encore jeune, encore belle, encore avide*.'[10]

Marcelle Fauchier Delavigne remembered Dolly as a kind of fairy-tale figure who brought magic into her life – and so she describes an afternoon she spent with Dolly in the terms of an enchanted fairy tale. Like Lily de Gramont's contribution, Marcelle's remembrance of Dolly leaves much unsaid; it goes further than Lily's, however, in providing an allegory of Dolly's profound effect on Marcelle's life.

Marcelle recalled one of those lowering, grey Sunday afternoons in Paris when, oppressed by the weather, irritated by the sound of buses, and bored with her empty house, she was just about to get the tea things herself when Dolly appeared. Like a full-colour figure on a black and white ground, Dolly transformed the surroundings. Suddenly the sky turned blue, the air was clear, the buses were silent, everything had changed its 'color, its form and its aspect'. Dolly, incidentally, is regularly described as making entrances like this one, entrances that change someone's day, or someone's mind, or even someone's life. On this afternoon, Dolly appeared, wrote Marcelle extravagantly, 'like a star, like a flame'. Tea was a wonderful experience.

After tea, Dolly lit her inevitable cigarette and went over to the cage where Marcelle kept two doves. She reproved Marcelle for never speaking to the doves, saying they must be boring themselves, and she opened the door to their cage. The doves flew around the room, came to rest on Dolly's shoulder and spoke, wrote Marcelle, in Dolly's ear. And Dolly

> understood very well the doves' language because she lived also in the domaine of spirits . . . and just as she opened the door of the cage, she opened as well many other doors, and behind the doors the horizon was vast and full of clarity, and she led you by mysterious and flowery roads towards these radiant clarities across so many unknown regions . . .[11]

Edmond Jaloux, whom Natalie had counted on for the introduction to *Oscaria*, died before he could write it, thus offering the only acceptable excuse for failing to contribute. But Natalie managed to represent him in the epistolary section and wrote that 'Mr Jealous', as Dolly used to call him, 'was enchanted by her as by no other siren'. In his letters, he always addressed her as 'darling'. Victor Cunard, the man who was to lunch with Dolly on the day she died, turned in an entry so late that it was couched in the form of a letter of apology. Lorna Lindsley recounted the story of Dolly and the Headless Brioches, Antoine Gentien gave the poignant history of Dolly dressing up as Oscar, and Katy Fenwick and Allanah Harper provided intimate details of Dolly's interior life that only old friends could have observed and absorbed.

Each contributor represents an interesting and intimate rotation of Dolly's social and emotional life. Only Guillot de Saix, the Wilde scholar, didn't know Dolly at all and had scarcely met her. Saix, who had served with Natalie on a French committee to commemorate the fiftieth anniversary of Oscar's death, was Natalie's 'Oscar' note in *Oscaria* and was probably a replacement for some far more *au courant* but more recalcitrant contributor.

Saix provides two small anecdotes of Dolly which are valuable for their consistency, showing that Dolly behaved with strangers exactly as she behaved with friends. Guillot de Saix met Dolly at one of Natalie's Fridays in October 1936 where a woman was speaking in support of the Oxford Movement. A just-published spiritual biography was discussed and Dolly thought that reading such a book was unnecessary and that those who did so were interested in exhibitionism. 'They want one to perform a striptease of the soul,' she said. Then someone began talking about the candour of undressing the soul, how it was like the Swedes on their beaches: completely nude and without shame.

'Ah,' breathed Dolly, 'how melancholy the Swedes must be! They have not even the taste for sin.'

Dolly promised to meet Guillot de Saix at the Hôtel Montalembert where she was staying. She was late, of course, and somewhat 'absent inside', but full of 'static dignity'. She asked him if he knew about Oscar's letters to Sarah Bernhardt, said that one of her friends owned a thin edition of them edited in America, and that she would ask this friend to lend it to M de Saix. He never got the book.[12]

The list of *Oscaria's* putative contributors was varied – and often Natalie did not get who or what she originally wanted. Harold Acton and Osbert Sitwell as well as Jean Bourgoint were thought of, but whether they were actually invited to contribute is unknown. Nancy Cunard and Tudor Wilkinson were on the list of possible contributors, as was Jocelyn Bodley, probably a relative of Dolly's old friend Ava Bodley.[13] Vyvyan Holland responded to Natalie's careful, flattering request for a remembrance with a negative so distressing to Natalie that she did something uncharacteristic: she did not keep his letter. And when Natalie was discussing the possibility of Secker & Warburg putting the book out under its imprimatur, she said that she could get a page out of Colette about Dolly.[14] Colette had liked Dolly and no doubt Natalie *could* have got something from her for *Oscaria*, but she did not manage to do so.

Editing *Oscaria* was a difficult undertaking for Natalie. She had to make substitutions because of death or dilatoriness and the remnants of her struggle to smooth over omissions or late contributions have left deposits all over the book — like calcium spurs irritating its softer parts — so that the elastic of her connecting comments sometimes creaks where it should be most supple. She had uncredited editorial help from Germaine Beaumont, the novelist and journalist who had been Colette's protegée, and credited help from Honey Harris, whom Natalie referred to in letters as a kind of co-editor. 'Our book', she called *Oscaria* when she wrote to Honey about it.

The memoirs are arranged on either side of Bettina Bergery's very entertaining 'Interlude'. This lengthy submission came to Natalie so late that it had to be given a special place in the manuscript. Bergery's remembrance is couched as a personal remembrance-cum-summary of other, absent friends' impressions of Dolly. Perhaps this example of Dolly advising the lovelorn with citations from literature and the 'Psychopathia Sexualis' was the reason for Bettina asking Natalie to introduce her 'Interlude' in a lighter vein than it merits.

It's not hopeless, [Dolly] says, nothing is hopeless, darling. Have you tried Lysistrata's system? Oh, he's trying it! Really! Then what about Krafft-Ebing? Have you tried feather boas and perfumed them? and lace petticoats and wigs and whips and masks? (Do you suppose Allanah Harper got the idea of her white rabbit suit from his 'case' book? Its effect on several people at the reincarnation ball was remarkable.) Have you tried spells. Remember how Dickey succeeded with her Duke, you should try that. It's better than Isolde's magic philtre, and you don't die of the after-effects, but I've found a receipt in a book of magic I bought on the quais and can loan you, but don't try it on Italians, they can't digest it. Lucretia Borgia used it and you know what happened at her parties . . . [15]

Prompted by Bettina, Natalie wrote that Bettina 'liked Dolly and was acquainted with her for a long time [but] she never knew her very well really'; and that her memoir was 'just a resumé of what other people imagined they remembered'. But imagination and memory were exactly the right qualities to apply to Dolly, and Bettina applied them liberally, wonderfully recreating two of Dolly's monologues and giving new descriptions and vignettes of Dolly from some of her unknown friends.[16]

Every part of *Oscaria* is presided over by Natalie's active literary presence. She is the author of both the Epilogue and the Introduction, and she positions herself solidly as Dolly's chief mourner with poems (uncharacteristically sentimental poems), evocations, prefaces, and little vignettes. The editorial 'Natalie' moves through the book in the same manner that she must have presided over the 'Knights of Natalie's Round Table': with a little linguistic intervention *here* to make things go more smoothly, a heavier editorial presence *there* to keep things in line, etc., etc. All done in the low tones and modulated gestures of a well-bred *femme de lettres* making this one, final point about the life of Dolly Wilde — who, after all, was not just any woman but was Oscar Wilde's Exceptionally Talented Niece, His Rightful Heir, and the Very Last of the Wilde Line. And look here, Gentle Reader, Natalie seems to be saying, I place before you Dolly's beautifully written letters to prove both her linguistic talents *and* her undying love for me.

Natalie's intervening hand is especially evident in the unedited version of Bettina Bergery's reminiscence of Dolly. For publication, Natalie cut out Bergery's direct references to Dolly's erotic life as well as some sharp little vignettes of her more unconventional behaviour — such as the time Dolly settled the matter of a persistent flasher by flashing the fellow herself one night with a branched candlestick concealed under her cloak.

Natalie also removed some of Bettina's most revealing anecdotes about Dolly's relations to Oscar. One of them concerned the famous photograph of Dolly got up as her uncle. Dolly, wrote Bettina, used to wash copies of this image in tea to give them a "worn, ancient look," then, adding dedications and Oscar's signature (which Dolly could imitate to perfection), she presented them to Oscar's more celebrated admirers. Bettina insisted that several of the photographs "have since appeared as authentic in books written about him."

Dolly's letters were included in *Oscaria* over Honey Harris's strong objections and Natalie removed the headings which would have indicated that certain letters were coming from the Harris family homes in London and the Isle of Wight, 'as I don't want to not only shock you by Dolly's letters but not in any way give you trouble with your family'.[17] *Oscaria* sometimes gives the rather decorous and false impression that Dolly was actively bisexual – though, given Dolly's freewheeling flirtatiousness, her social viability, and her sensual apprehensions of the world, bisexual attractions were certainly available to her. Honey Harris, always anxious to keep private things private, notes that Dolly 'hardly ever talked about herself except to say how profoundly melancholy she was and how much everyone was in love with her (usually her companion of the moment's own young man would be specially mentioned – "But darling it isn't you he's in love with, it's ME – He ADORES ME!" was a phrase we all had to get used to) . . .[18] And Bettina Bergery describes Dolly's ease in charming young men and getting them to fall in love with her – but Bergery slyly hints that the core crowd of Dolly's 'regulars' were 'effete young men' who had much the same sexual tastes as Oscar's blackmailing boys.

Natalie had made memorials like *Oscaria* – though not exactly like *Oscaria* – before. At one time or another, she assembled volumes of the verses of Renée Vivien, Lucie Delarue-Mardrus and Milosz; established the Renée Vivien prize for poetry; formed a plan to extricate T. S. Eliot from his bank job; dedicated salon afternoons to writer friends like Gertrude Stein, Djuna Barnes, Mina Loy and Anna Wickham; and served on committees in Paris to honour Oscar Wilde. But commemorating a woman like Dolly, who didn't have a public profile or a published oeuvre, was a different matter altogether and it was clever of Natalie to turn Dolly's friends into her biographers. How else, after all, to map out Dolly's killing wit, her sexual allure, the charm that kept a party going and friends feeling brilliant, the letters that seemed to look into your face while so cleverly hiding her own? And what to do with the apparent tragedies of Dolly's wont and use, her high-flying heritage gone to hell in a fashionable handbag?

While Oscar's very cadences were transcribed as carefully as music[19] — so that we know even the pitches, stresses, and junctures of his speech — what remains of Dolly's brilliant arias is snippets of half-rendered wit, two handfuls of recounted 'incidents' by her friends, and Bettina Bergery's contribution of one fully recreated monologue. Most of Dolly's gifts were written out on the air, where spoken language always resides. And while no one who met Dolly Wilde would ever forget that encounter, Dolly's life, although *noticed*, was not surrounded by the self-importance that other 'performers' have used to make the world pay attention.

The things that Dolly did best — brilliant repartee, sympathetic understanding, lovely language, and a magnetic physical presence — were as unsustainable in temporal terms as a cooling soufflé and very difficult to render in prose. With the exception of Guillot de Saix, who didn't know Dolly at all, the memoirs in *Oscaria* insist on *interpreting Dolly personally*, as though, fifty years before the personal memoir became a dominant literary form, the Friends of Dorothy understood that there was really no other way to discuss her.

Natalie began imagining ways to remember Dolly during the first few years after Dolly's death. In April, 1945, after a very long gap in their communication, she sent an exploratory letter to Honey Harris in London which contained the beginnings of her interest in a book to honour Dolly. Natalie wrote the letter from the Villa Saint Agnese in Florence where she had wintered the war with Romaine Brooks. Many of her friends had scattered or died or found themselves on opposite sides of indelicate political questions and Natalie sounded as lost as any refugee:

I know hardly anything about you, nor my friends in France

etc. Nor indeed whether or where I shall move after all these arrested years . . . So many who are at home like my sister [Laura Dreyfus-Barney] and Lady T [Una Troubridge] – minus Johnnie [Radclyffe Hall] – wish to return here, while those who are here are booking very doubtful passages back home.[20]

Much of this letter is about Dolly – it was provoked by the month of April, Dolly's death month – and it is into this letter that Natalie drops the line about leaving off living 'for the doubtful privilege of surviving' since Dolly died. And she recalls how Marie Laurencin visited the rue Jacob just before 'everything broke off', how she had met Dolly in 'our Parisian garden' and how she had liked her.[21] Natalie wanted to go back to the rue Jacob 'to at least secure all the (to me) precious memories it contains – along with Dolly's many letters and some photographs' and to 'forward her "will" to you . . . to assure our interests.' Natalie meant the interests that she and Honey had in Dolly's estate, for she had recently been plagued by letters from the law firm of Holmes, Son, & Pott insisting on her presence in London or on the presence of Dolly's actual Will. Natalie also sent deliberate greetings to 'Victor, Nancy, and whoever else may somewhat share our love for Dolly Wilde . . .' Natalie was on a fishing expedition.

In more or less conscious preparation for *Oscaria*, Natalie was 'looking backward'; thinking about Dolly and about some way to secure her memory. Writing to Honey Harris was a prelude to the work she had in mind. Honey balked at prospective disclosures from the beginning; the portcullis of her privacy quickly closed off further confidences.[22] Dolly, she believed, wouldn't have liked to have her letters exposed like this. And were all those letters really well enough written to be published?[23] And, by the way, would Natalie take the trouble to remove that little passage from Dolly's letters to her about Honey waiting up for Dolly like an anxious bridegroom – she wouldn't want people to get the wrong idea.

Natalie assuaged and consulted Honey in her responses and then did as she always did — which was just as she pleased, including publishing that delicate little passage about Honey waiting up for Dolly that Honey had asked her to delete. Honey's reserve about revelation had always been marked — her own life was kept strictly private — and Dolly herself had written: 'old love letters don't make for good reading'. Still, Honey's delicacies and artistic tastes were responsible for many of the arrangements that had to be made about Dolly's memorial book and for the stone that marked the double grave that Dolly shared with her mother Lily.[24] Honey's design for Dolly's grave pleased Natalie very much and the stone in the Cimetière Passy which Natalie shares with her sister Laura rather resembles Dolly's stone, perhaps in imitation.

Memories of Dolly didn't stop giving pleasure and pain to her friends after her death — people might die, but their patterns are immortal — and her friends seemed very glad to have *Oscaria*. And Natalie did not omit to ask Honey to help her with another kind of remembering: Natalie wondered if Honey could possibly send half a dozen hard-boiled plovers' eggs from London to the duchesse de Clermont-Tonnerre in Paris — 'an old custom on my part & excuse my asking this of you'.[25] So Natalie's patterns did not change either. Natalie had once asked the same favour of Sybille Bedford. Mrs Bedford said that she and Esther Murphy had practically killed themselves making sure that the plovers' eggs were properly wrapped, cooked for just so many seconds, and transported on a train, all in the service of Natalie Barney's custom of memorialising her old lovers.[26]

Characteristically, Natalie made sure that *Oscaria* appeared in the tenth anniversary year and in the season of Dolly's death: spring 1951; and that it was sold in bookshops such as Heywood Hill's in Curzon Street, Mayfair, London, the social bookshop where Dolly's friend Nancy Mitford had once worked. Natalie paid attention to the book's distribution — she had originally hoped that Roger Senhouse, an old friend of Dolly at Secker & Warburg, would give it his firm's imprimatur — and she noted with pleasure that Nancy Mitford's slight mention of the book in the London *Times* Supplement had produced an order for six more copies. She took Dorothy Strachey Bussy's (author of *Olivia* and sister of Lytton) suggestion that she bring out a second edition of the book — two or three hundred copies — if the strength of the original sales warranted it and she charged Honey Harris with speaking to Heywood Hill about this. The sales of the original edition apparently did warrant further effort, for in 1952 Natalie brought out another edition of *Oscaria*. Dolly once remarked that even in love Natalie displayed a certain talent for accountancy.

In a serious way, Dolly had always been sitting on a mountain of magnificent accomplishments, a mountain which no one quite knew how to map. It was intelligent of Natalie to take the trouble and to find a way — when no one else would or could — to record what was left of Dolly's life and what her life left behind. The best way to read *Oscaria* is to read between the lines for what is hidden there; but many of the lines themselves are terrific ones. Dolly's friends were very smart and mostly observant and they wrote about her with vivid feeling and terrible regret.

Small comfort to Dolly, who always preferred to cover her tracks and who was, anyway, ten years dead when the volume was published. But without *Oscaria*, every personal idea of Dolly would have died with her death. And all the love and exasperation and enchantment that Dolly elicited from her delighted friends — to whom she had perhaps listened even more carefully than they had ever listened to her — would have gone entirely unrecorded.

5

Living
Up To
Oscar

12

Living Up To Oscar

I am more Oscar-like than he was like himself.

Dolly Wilde

*I*magine Dolly Wilde in London and Paris in the early 1920s: sheathed in mauve, swathed in gold lamé, and trailing several definitions of decadence. She would have appeared to many people — she *did* appear to many people — as an uncanny revision of her outlaw uncle, living his life all over again as a woman. She must have given quite a start to her friends' parents, many of whom had shuddered through 'the love that dare not speak its name' in the year of Dolly's birth, and most of whom could recognise trouble when they saw it. Especially when they saw it in a form that superficially, at least, resembled Oscar Wilde's.

To those who had experienced Oscar, watching Dolly — as she plumped her body with gorgeous foods, enhanced her sparkle with contemporary chemicals, and descanted her wit for a circle of screaming society bohemians (the twenties were filled with the shrill sounds of Bright Young Things tarnishing quickly) — would have been like looking forwards and backwards at the same time. That must have been what Janet Flanner meant when she said that Dolly had a 'pivotal quality'. Of course, Dolly also had Oscar's sexual proclivities, kitted out for a woman.

Dolly, however, was at once more imaginative and more conventional than her uncle in choosing her lovers and her suitors. She could count among the former women of brilliant talent, and among the latter men of serious accomplishment.

Starting in the early 1920s (and in her *late* twenties), what was to become Dolly's 'tragedy' began to be apparent. Dolly was charming to a fault, evidently brilliant, and extraordinarily witty.[1] She possessed the extensive, eclectic literary tastes of both her grandmother Jane and her uncle Oscar. She had the *Oxford Book of English Verse* by heart and most of Shakespeare's sonnets. She loved the Brontës and Tolstoy, Madame de Staël and Ronald Firbank, and she revelled in Krafft-Ebing and Charles Dodgson and Barrie's *Peter Pan*. She felt her mythological 'parentage' with Byron, though less so than with Oscar, and thought that if 'Allegra [Claire Clairemont's daughter by Byron] had grown up, she might have been very like me'.[1]

Perhaps Dolly felt that Byron's daughter was 'like her' because she imagined herself more as Oscar's artistic daughter, bred through the brain because of Lily's admiration of Oscar, than as Willie's biological child. Dolly resembled, in charm and intelligence, the Wilde brothers' brilliant little sister, Isola, whose death at the age of ten Oscar had so sincerely mourned. And Dolly's self-comparison to Byron's daughter is apt. Little Allegra was callously dumped by Byron in a Catholic convent at about the same age that Dolly suffered a similar fate — but Allegra died there. Dolly did not die in the 'country convent' to which she had been consigned before the age of four — but many of her family feelings apparently did.

Dolly's bookish links with Oscar were undeniable and she possessed what he called the artist's 'instruments of an art': 'thought and language'. Just as Oscar had done, Dolly read and met most of the authors of her time and made astute comments on their work. What she hadn't read, she could improvise upon and most of her references were literary ones. Dolly saw things in phrases rather than in pictures, and life for her was, as Bettina Bergery wrote, like a 'new novel'.

Just now I'm in love with Mlle de Maupin which I've just read in an excellent translation. *Do* read it — the beauty of it sets one's head buzzing with heavy honeybees.[2]

In De Quincey's Studies of the Poets he says 'Miss Wordsworth stooped in her walk in a most *unusual* manner' — Now, what can that mean — could any adjective be more surprising? '*Mrs* Wordsworth was sexually dignified' thank God *we* are sexually dignified.[3]

Her initial instinct, however — the one she could never quite abandon — was to live life rather than to write it. As time passed, she would be unable to reverse her priorities.

The novelist Rosamond Harcourt-Smith wrote that Dolly's lightning-quick comprehensions and passionate curiosity gave people the impression that she was an intellectual but

. . . actually her knowledge, her understanding, was of life itself, of human motives, but her passion for truth, her perfect taste and quick perceptions carried her triumphantly through a thousand subjects of which she possessed little or no real knowledge . . . 'Don't worry, darling, I shall catch up in a moment,' [she would say], and 'catch up' she inevitably did, arranging, docketing and storing the knowledge gained in the vast index-card of her formidable memory.[4]

Unfortunately for her, Dolly resembled Oscar enough to be constantly compared to him by almost everyone who met her. These comparisons were especially evident in the mid-1920s and 1930s when, through her association with Tancred Borenius in London and through the Barney salon in Paris, Dolly made friendships with people for whom Oscar's life and work were a touchstone. The exceptions to this chorus of favourable Oscar-comparers were her cousin Vyvyan Holland (who liked her earlier, didn't like her later, and had his own, obvious reasons for refusing to consider her Oscar's spiritual heir) and Oscar's old 'Sphinx', Ada Leverson. Leverson, responding 'loyally' to someone's praise of Dolly, replied that Dolly had perhaps inherited Oscar's mantle 'but none of her own'.[5]

Everyone else — how could they help it? — made automatic, favourable connections between the niece and the uncle. 'How nice to meet a feminine Wilde,' said H. G. Wells on encountering the niece at a PEN meeting, though Wells could just as well have been paying a back-handed compliment to the uncle. Lady Una Troubridge remarked in comparing the two that Dolly was 'much the better man'. Mercedes de Acosta wrote that in her wit and her alertness, Dolly was 'mentally very like [Oscar]'. Philip La Selle often imagined that Dolly was the ghost of Oscar. Germaine Beaumont thought that all the things in Oscar Wilde that could not be expressed through him were diverted on to Dolly, all the unclaimed feminine traits of the uncle found themselves in this niece without the proper frame but as his 'perfect expression and as his justification'. Bettina Bergery wrote that it had been within Dolly's possibilities to be a 'famous conversationalist' like her uncle but that Dolly's preparation was lacking and she knew it. Rosamond Harcourt-Smith said that Dolly had Oscar's same oval face, 'without the lines of self-indulgence and dissipation', his same dark hair and widow's peak, and his same long hands. Sylvia Beach thought that Dolly much resembled her uncle Oscar, but was 'better looking'. Janet Flanner said that Dolly looked just like Oscar 'except that she was handsome'.

The comparisons go on and on, adding no final lustre to the reputation of either Wilde. Between Dolly's installation in 1927 in Natalie Barney's significant salon — which staked its stick on Oscarian aesthetics and dandled Dolly as their avatar — and the long shadow that the Wilde family's always-arresting mythologies cast over her life, lies a biographical trap which Dolly would have been too modest to appreciate. It is the trap of summoning up a version of Dolly Wilde whose originality is contaminated by comparisons to her famous relative.

Certainly, resemblances to Oscar are what made (and make) Dolly so initially attractive: they present the painful pleasures of a myth continued and a genius diluted. But Dolly herself would have protested against the more extravagant of these comparisons with her uncle; perhaps — *because* she was Dolly — she would have protested too much. To understand Dolly only by familial comparison is to miss the point and pathos of her life, which had much more to do with the way she evaded her heritage than with the way she exploited it. Brian Howard, another brilliant Londoner who laid waste to his talents, said that what the English meant by 'character' was 'the power to refrain' — and that he lacked it. So did Dolly, in that definition. Like Oscar, Dolly is better imagined than she is defined, and she is *best* imagined as a complicated series of 'characters', which were only partially created in response to the Wilde Family Romance.

Although Dolly was noted for the ways in which she resembled Oscar, the ways in which she differed from him were at least as interesting. In her letters and in her life she displayed a serious gift for describing nature (something Oscar could not do well); a lack of authorial pomposity (Oscar's admonition to Walter Berry: 'in so slight a matter . . . feelings need not borrow stilts' is a perfect description of much of his own prose); an early and excellent grasp of the psychology of human relations (Oscar's work was never driven by character analysis); and a fluidity of metaphorical line that seems to justify Janet Flanner's decription that 'Dolly was not like anybody else . . . she was utterly singular'.

Moreover, Dolly was content to confine herself to the kinds of audiences her uncle never would have accepted. Oscar's ambitions and talents were historic and global. He went for the wider world and for a reputation that would last — and he got them both. But the circle Dolly wanted to inscribe, the circle her very personal talents fitted her for, was a much smaller one, and Dolly was perfectly happy to entertain a handful of friends at dinner, a set of admiring artists in the salons, some avid aquaintances at the Ritz bar, or a clutch of duchesses at a tea party. (Dolly did love duchesses, although she reserved her deeper sympathies for their maids.) Like her grandmother Jane and her uncle Oscar, Dolly was dazzled by royalty or by the appearance of it. In 1937, when many of the writers she knew were decrying fascism, Mussolini in full parade dress provoked a rather admiring miniature from her:

> . . . The entire square was filled with his militia & it was an amazing sight to see, suddenly, ten thousand daggers flash in the sunlight as they were raised in salute. Mussolini gave the curious impression of being very human in his short corpulent figure, but the head compressed into the rigidity of a statue, the expression never changing; the maximum of will power & force stamped as on an effigy once & for all.[6]

Dolly even reproved Janet Flanner for her staid New Yorker portrait of Queen Mary; Dolly thought it was too 'pert.'

So personal was Dolly, so interested in private expression, that she was guided almost entirely by her amorous feelings and wayward affinities, never by overt ambitions for a larger life. Certainly, this ability to focus intently on a small audience must have accounted for a great deal of her charm, both sexual and otherwise. Any other ambitions she might have had were firmly kept down by her indulgence in alcohol and chemicals; and her letters were always meant for an Audience of One.

> And now darling I am having eggs and bacon and hot rolls on a tray (Do you know that neatly curled fern-like bacon that grows like a spring bulb in a glass bottle?). It is *so* good, all of it and I am experiencing that warm glow and dreamy indifference that I imagine De Quincey felt after a long inhalation of opium.[7]

Since Dolly's writing was not available for public consumption, the source of her 'celebrity' came to rest partially upon resemblance and analogy, on the 'reflected glory' that her friend Lorna Lindsley talked about. Dolly was Oscar's niece, she knew her family history, and she kept it in mind. And almost everyone who had ever stretched out a hand to her — either in friendship or in desire — knew her family history as well and also kept it in mind. Dolly's relationship to Oscar launched her from the beginning into a kind of 'satellite life': 'I used to revolve — satellite — round people . . .' she confessed to Natalie Barney.[8] She was accustomed to reflecting the light of larger stars.

In putting Oscar first, Dolly and her admiring friends managed to turn the tables on Santayana's much-quoted formulation about the value of history: those who don't know history are condemned to repeat it. Dolly repeated Oscar's history (and some of her father's) partially *because* she knew it so well, enacting that collapse to the inevitable, the 'paralysis' that regularly gripped her, that all the Wildes exhibited under life's reversals. Still, Dolly continued the tradition of putting Oscar forward, but in her own, peculiarly 'retrospective' way: simply by *being* there in her public character — a walking quotation from the Wilde canon: body, soul, and wicked wit — two decades after the fact.

One of Oscar Wilde's best traits as a writer has always been his ability to 'corrupt' (in the strict, lexical sense of 'breaking in pieces') the imaginations of flexible youth. He has as many literary identities as adolescents have personalities and his talent for producing the superficies of contradicting forms and philosophies is perfectly adapted to the shifting attentions of the young, whom Oscar always said he loved and admired and whose natural extremities rise delightedly to meet his outrageous paradoxes. An excellent and entirely undemeaning case could be made for Oscar Wilde as a brilliant writer of adolescent literature.

There must be hundreds of thousands of literarily inclined young people in the twentieth century (and quite a few in the last decade of the nineteenth) who plunged themselves into Oscar Wilde's exaggerated work as into an exotically tiled Turkish bath. Its perfumed waters, its hanging velvet swags and trailing *peaux de soie*, its plumes of opium smoke and proscribed oppositions of sense and sentiment, have seduced many a would-be young writer to the cult of beauty (or to the Cult of Beauty) and the Superiority of Self-Regard.

It is that much sadder, then, that in the most obvious case of Oscar's influence – his niece Dorothy – the results seem to have been so disastrous. Certainly, the full extent of Oscar's influence on her is impossible to calculate. Although Dolly's life sometimes seems to be a gloss on her uncle's most cynical epigrams, Dolly, said everyone who had tried to do so, was impossible to influence; she followed her own wilful ways always. Within her 'inability to refrain', there lurked an unusually strong will. Moreover, she had never met her uncle and she had her father's hideous example before her. And there was the larger, looser question of her genetic inheritance.

But the superficial outcome of Dolly's relation to Oscar was fatal enough. Wherever Dolly went, whatever social performance she was giving, someone in the charmed circle of her listeners was certain to be watching for traces of Oscar Wilde; trying to see the uncle *through* the niece, trying to see the uncle *in* the niece, trying to see the uncle somewhere *near* the niece.

Dolly bore a burden much heavier than any burden Oscar carried before his imprisonment. For Oscar, at his apogee, had only to invent or reinvent himself to suit his circumstances. Dolly, throughout her life, had to serve as a constant literary allusion to a notorious dead male writer, a dead writer whom she resembled in every way but the way that would have been important to her. She did not, she could not write for publication. Dolly was a strictly private writer.

Germaine Beaumont imagined that the tide of Oscar's legend engulfed Dolly's own 'story' long before she wrote it, leaving her alone on the empty beach of her ambitions. Bettina Bergery suggested that Oscar had usurped Dolly's narrative, rendering her mute and paralysed in the face of a wish to work. Dolly could not have avoided feeling – particularly after she began her descent into destructive habits – that Oscar had already written with *his* life *her own* biography – and before she'd had the chance to fully live it. He certainly provided her with endless opportunities to ruminate, pen in hand, on the difficulty of living up to the perfection of the dead – and on the ease with which one could 'live down' to them.

Dolly once confided to her friend Allanah Harper, the editor and intellectual spark of a clutch of Bright Young Things, that 'she longed to write' but could never put down on paper anything that remotely conveyed what she meant.[9] Natalie Barney, with Dolly's talents in mind, repeatedly told Berthe Cleyrergue: 'Dolly *must* write.' But Dolly didn't write. Or rather, Dolly didn't write what everyone *thought* she should be writing. Bettina Bergery put it another way. She said that Oscar must have 'seized Dolly's pen to prevent his works from being rivalled after his death.'[10]

Actually, Dolly's 'natural' intellectual resemblance to Oscar was as radical in its style as Natalie Barney's earlier appropriation of male literary forms. The paradox, for instance, came easily and organically to Dolly's lips; and her wit was as swift as a swallow's swoop. But Dolly never for a moment gave the appearance of annexing a 'male' style (Oscar's style is 'male' in the sense of its concentrated assault on worldly success and its unwavering focus on the importance of being Oscar). Dolly used her wit the way a naturally talented cook with a fine set of Sabatiers would use her knives: as a matter of course, on the material at hand, and with some of the cruelty and *brio* for which cooks are known.

Allanah Harper, who felt that Dolly was 'irreplaceable', nonetheless wrote that 'to the vulnerable, the teasable – like myself – Dolly was merciless; she took great delight in making me appear ridiculous in public'. There was a terrible evening when Dolly inveigled Allanah into slipping into a too-tight rabbit costume – a silky white plush affair lined with pink crêpe de Chine and accompanied by long pink plush ears – given her by the Aga Khan, and doing a less-than-graceful Rabbit dance in front of assembled guests. Dolly provided some sharp running commentary on the order of: 'Only Allanah would get nothing but a Rabbit's dress out of the richest man in the world.' Harper was crushed by Dolly's satire — and, even worse, couldn't think of a timely retort.[11]

But Dolly's pleasure in watching her victims squirm was such an integral part of her 'great charm' that no one really seemed to want her to change. 'The startling originality, the pertinence of her ridicule was so illuminating.'[12] Harper thought that Dolly lashed out with her swift wit because she could not bear vulgarity or cliché and that her horror at either condition was so great that she could not let them pass unmarked. The novelist Rosamond Harcourt-Smith agreed and repeated a favourite sentence of Dolly: 'Now don't exaggerate, it's only interesting if it's true.' Harcourt-Smith said that the razor edge of Dolly's wit was rarely turned towards 'the individual but at the flatulent opinion, the easy cliché, the fashionable, false ecstasy'.[13] Dolly's gift for satire was natural and it was irrepressible; but there had to have been quite a tangle of interrupted desires and invidious impulses to make her alternate — sometimes painfully — between a cutting edge and a profound compassion with so many of her dearest friends.

Dolly's real friends never seemed to take offence when her sharper side was turned towards them — at least not for long. Harcourt-Smith noted that

> I never minded her criticisms of my behaviour or character. They came, I knew, from a passionate interest inspired by affection, and what more can one ask of a friend? She once said to me, 'I must tell you something very extraordinary! So-and-so thinks you are very intelligent! I said to him that of course we both loved you, but *intelligent*? Really, darling. I find I shall have to reconsider my opinion of you!' Who but a ninny could have taken umbrage at that?[14]

Vyvyan Holland was the exception: he took umbrage and saw

Dolly without sympathy or empathy. He wrote in his journal on the day of Dolly's death that 'mischief-making was one of the joys of her life' and that she had permanently enlarged the breach between himself and the Sitwells 'though . . . this did not break my heart to any considerable extent'.[15] Holland didn't like Dolly, mostly because he thought she talked behind his back (a good bet, since she talked behind everyone's back – and to their faces too). It could not have been easy for Holland, 'being', as Natalie Barney wrote, 'neither like Oscar nor bearing his name', to see this cousin's startling resemblance to his father and to see her hailed as the only remaining successor of the 'Wilde *répartie*'. Dolly herself left no written record of any critical feelings for Holland – she praised his book-sense, in fact, to Natalie Barney – and there are faint intimations of a submerged and rather cousinly attraction between the two of them: the kind of attraction that sometimes produces sharp comments on both sides.

Dolly was certainly capable of using her wit amelioratively, sometimes in league with her real tenderness of heart, sometimes as part of her irrepressible 'hostess spirit'. Viva King, who spent the evening of Dolly's funeral with Vyvyan Holland, told of a house party at which Dolly was present along with the two Rogers – Senhouse (Lytton Strachey's lover) and Hinks (of the British Museum) – who were known to the party's hosts as pretty Roger and ugly Roger. 'Roger Hinks heard of his namesake's flattering nickname and enquired what he himself was called. Quickly Dolly replied "Clever Roger."'[16]

Allanah Harper had a very clear memory of one of the first times she met Dolly, in a setting where Dolly's wit electrified the room. It was in the 1920s in an apartment on the rue du Bac in Paris. Harper said she 'was shocked and delighted by [Dolly's] *phrase d'entrée*'.

Dolly entered, her face radiant, her eyes sparkling with malicious disdain. Like the wind she came, blowing away the banalities of the talk. Boredom that a moment before had hung like a thickness over the room, was chased away, she said, 'You all look as if you were waiting for the Coffin to be brought in.' A famous review actress was there – severely dressed in a tailored suit, pretending to read a book of poems by one of the ladies present. Dolly who had not met her before, on being introduced, raised her beautiful voice and said, 'It can't be you, I've always imagined you in tights and ostrich feathers.' And to our hostess, very slightly aside, 'What is she here for? Darling, it can't be for her mind.'[17]

This is Dolly in a sarcastic, theatrical mode, but it is not the teasing, theatrical mode of her uncle. And Dolly only dressed publicly as her uncle when the occasion warranted it. Though there were other dressings up as Oscar (notably for a singular photograph in a faux frame), her one publicly recorded impersonation of Oscar was a spur-of-the moment affair. The occasion was the duchesse de Clermont-Tonnerre's costume ball in 1931. 'Coco' Gentien, the tennis star son of Dolly's 'ravishing and unreal' society lover Antoinette Gentien (who, like Natalie Barney, used to play tennis with Suzanne Lenglen) said that 'despite [Dolly's] marvellous sense of humour, despite her glittering language and childlike laugh, I have never known a being who emitted such anguish'. Gentien left a painful picture of Dolly's transformation for the duchess's ball:

My mother was wearing a sailor's costume that the House of Lanvin had created for Yvonne Printemps . . . and I put on the kilt of a Scottish friend. Dolly hesitated to accompany us. Suddenly, she had an idea: 'I am going to get myself up as Oscar Wilde, lend me an outfit, darling.' It was very amusing to dress her. 'I am much fatter than you, but it doesn't matter, my uncle loved straight trousers!' [Janet Flanner's version of this story, more piquant and presumably conveyed to Flanner by Dolly herself, has Dolly getting into Antoinette's *husband's* trousers.]

My mother said to her: 'You're ready, let's go along.' But Dolly could not leave the mirror. She had lost her gaiety. With an anxious eye she contemplated herself disguised and unmasked (*travestie et démasquée*).[18]

The only photograph of Dolly dressed up as Oscar is the image Natalie Barney chose for the frontispiece of *Oscaria*. In its sole extant version, the photograph presents itself wittily as being at two removes from Oscar (as Dolly was) by being the photograph of a photograph of a niece got up as her uncle, deliberately positioned to show that the first photograph is in a frame. The photograph was printed in *Oscaria* without the frame, as though to establish a more direct connection between the niece and the uncle. Whether the frame was present in an original photograph – or whether the photograph was staged as a commentary – is open to question.

If Dolly ever dressed up as Oscar in private – and beyond the probability of a request from Natalie Barney (who loved both Oscar *and* costumes) there are nothing but rumours to suggest that she might have done so – the occasion could have been recorded in one of the many photographs that were burned as 'pornographic' (they were merely erotic) after Natalie Barney's death. All Dolly's friends stressed the fact that Dolly remained extremely 'feminine' in her self-presentation while managing to evoke the dead male who was her uncle. But Dolly did it with enough of his *esprit* to make some people feel they were seeing double. Her cross-dressing was a question of personal psychology, natural talent, and a direction dictated by her genes; it was never a matter of common cloth or mere material. Her mental resemblance to Oscar, never simply a question of an 'adopted' style, came from the inside and then it worked its way out.

In public Dolly must have experienced the frequent feeling that she was emotionally garbed as Oscar. Not because of her own self-consciousness (she was famously spontaneous) but because of the responses of the people who surrounded her. They all reacted to her as a participant in an act of spiritual transvestism, an act to which she was both the legitimate heir and in which she performed as a kind of counterfeiter. There could have been no rest in either of these positions, and only when alone in a room did Dolly produce the quiet character which she felt was her 'true self'. 'The house is quiet, – books lie all around me and I am once more that *very* serious, puzzled, earnest Miss Wilde that is my true self . . .'[19]

Dolly confided to Allanah Harper that she had become tired of herself. And she came to feel that 'Parties bore me, dinners and lunches too . . .' and her 'inability to play the part of a boisterous, gossiping Dolly' took a toll on some old friendships which she sometimes felt she'd 'out-grown'.[20] 'Don't please mention any of my feelings to Victor or Antoinette,' she told Natalie, 'I more & more dislike their participation in anything but the superficial in me.'[21] Only Allanah seemed to realise what a burden of family history Dolly packed on her back; how much 'she felt that she was expected to amuse, to play her part, to carry on the tradition of her famous uncle – to be a brilliant conversationalist'.[22]

Oscar once said, self-dramatisingly and with some accuracy, that he had 'died in prison'. After his release he sought out a palmist in Paris who told him that his life line ended physically on his palm at a place that exactly corresponded to the time when he'd been sent to prison. Amongst those people who also believed Oscar 'died' as an artist in prison (he was imprisoned in 1895, the year Dolly was born), Dolly was a convenient hinge upon which to swing some interesting speculations. Philip La Selle, a friend of Dolly in Paris, was so taken with her resemblance to her uncle, that

he wanted to know the hour of Oscar's death and at what exact time Dolly had been born. He also wanted to know when she first found out she looked like Oscar. He always wondered what alchemy could have transformed the lovely girl . . . could there have been a spell which enabled his [Oscar's] spirit to enter her body?[23]

There was a year and a half between the death of Willie Wilde in March of 1899 and Oscar's own death in November 1900, when Oscar and Dolly were the only blood relations still alive who carried the Wilde name. All her life, Dolly was shyly interested in stories about her uncle and in meeting people her uncle had known. Her delight in Carlos Blacker, who had been a good friend to Oscar until Oscar carelessly made light of the Dreyfus scandal, was unfeigned: she clearly felt Blacker as a link to her 'family romance'. And Blacker's extravagant insistence on Oscar's being the illegitimate son of the King of Sweden was one of the 'family stories' that intrigued and pleased Dolly mightily.[24]

It is impossible not to speculate how much different Dolly's life would have been — perhaps how much better — if Oscar and the *myth* of Oscar had not played before her continually like a beautiful, poisoned fountain.

Dolly's few references to her own immediate family were usually couched in terms of Oscar. Lady Wilde was rarely 'my grandmother', and never 'my father's mother', but almost always 'Oscar's mother'; Vyvyan Holland was not 'my cousin', but 'Oscar's son'. When Dolly referred to her father, she did so in terms of her uncle, saying 'in a nostalgic way' to Janet Flanner that Anglo-Irish people had always told her that Willie was even wittier than Oscar 'but the drink had taken him early before anybody had time to set it all down on paper'.[25] Natalie Barney and Bettina Bergery both repeated the opinion, which they could only have had from Dolly, that Willie Wilde was as gifted a talker as Oscar. And Ethel Smyth said the same thing. Oscar, however, still remained the standard to which her father was compared, and what Dolly said about Willie Wilde reveals that Lily Wilde had been generous in speaking about Willie to Dolly, and that Dolly wanted a father she could be proud of.

After the First War, when Dolly began assembling the witty

character – the Bright Young Social Butterfly in Baudelaire's 'artificial paradise', one wing dipped in love's languorous potions, the other wing dusted with cocaine – with which she flew in and out of drawing rooms, dining rooms, and private parties, her distinction from all the other Bright Young Characters became obvious. Dolly's self-presentation never made reference to any childhood history; and yet she seemed to be enjoying a perpetual adolescence. Her life continued to be phrased in a kind of permanent present tense impossible to conjugate into old age.

Dolly's deletion and/or repression of the 'real' details of her past – her father, her mother, the ways in which she had been abandoned by both of them – had a specific effect on her present. It made her connection to her uncle more conspicuous, more direct, more unavoidably *paternal*. Oscar began to appear, at least in people's imaginations, as the paterfamilias in Dolly's Family Portrait. (What a pity *that* picture was never painted!) Since the world knew everything the tabloids could print about Oscar – and very little about Willie and Lily Wilde – Dolly's abridgement of her Delicate Family Subject could only have enhanced the view that she was Oscar's real, reincarnated heir, replete with physical resemblance, literary references, same-sex affinities, and killing wit. All that was missing was the writing, but in the 1920s Dolly was still young, the writing could still come.

Of course, there were those two Wilde cousins to counteract Dolly's primary position as Oscar's imaginative heir: Oscar's own sons, Cyril and Vyvyan. But their surnames had been changed to Holland after Oscar's imprisonment and with that change much of the Wilde glamour seemed to evaporate. Their mother's family rigorously suppressed any information of their father's life and works; they had been separated and sent to different schools so that they couldn't discuss Oscar, and Vyvyan Holland, the surviving brother, was left with a distinct aversion to the notoriety attached to being a Wilde.

Jean Cocteau remembered meeting Vyvyan Holland in Venice in September of 1908 when Vyvyan was making a two-week attempt, 'as an experiment', to resume his father's name. So many Italian journalists wanted interviews with him when they heard the name 'Wilde' that he gave up the painful trial.[26] Cyril Holland, the favoured elder brother, was to die in the First War, the same war that Dolly ran off to. Some people conjecture that Cyril's way of dealing with his share of the Wilde heritage was to step in front of a sniper's bullet.

There was one more cousin faintly in the family picture, a son of Constance Wilde's brother Otho, who called himself Arthur Cravan and whose real name was Fabian Lloyd. Cravan was a self-described 'hotel thief, muleteer, snake-charmer, chauffeur, ailurophile, nephew of Oscar Wilde, poet with the shortest hair in the world', as well as being a boxer of dubious reputation. Cravan edited and entirely wrote a literary journal, *Maintenant*, while living on the rue St Jacques in Paris in 1912. He showed enough originality and bad behaviour to be of some interest along Wildean lines.

At his 1917 lecture on art at the Grand Central Gallery in New York City, Arthur Cravan cursed the audience, disrobed on the podium, and was carried from the stage dead drunk and in handcuffs. Marcel Duchamp, who was in the audience egging him on, remarked: 'What an excellent lecture.' Cravan married Mina Loy, Natalie's and Dolly's friend, and had a daughter, Fabienne, with her. Cravan was presumed drowned in 1918 off the coast of Mexico. Unlike Dolly, Arthur Cravan was not a blood relative of Oscar and he lived his later life far from the salons in which Wildean reputations are made.[27]

So, really, the position of Oscar's social and literary heir was an open one, the other familial successors being unavailable, or uninterested, or not necessarily Oscarian. Dolly had the supposititious talent, the looks, the flamboyant wit, the name, and she had — and this must have pushed her further towards identification than almost anything else — the outlawed sexuality. Why not accept the role for which the world (and very likely her own chromosomes) was casting her?

Although Dolly, when she was in the mood, could connive like a courtesan and manipulate like a marquise, she was not at all a conventionally calculating person. So it is interesting to think about whether this alignment with her uncle might be accidental — simply the by-product of a need to suffer her immediate family story in silence combined with the easy opportunities with which her looks and her wit presented her. Or whether the identification with Oscar was the result of a more calculated campaign to present herself as 'Oscaria' — heir to all the Wilde legend.

In the details of her life, Dolly was the world's least organised woman. She could be — and was — wilful, heedless, impulsive, episodic, and intermittent. Her personal finances were regularly in ruins and her attempts to calculate them mar the margins of even her tenderest love letters. Her laboured plans to make elaborate ren-dezvous with lovers often went awry because her inability to hold to an appointment — with the great world rushing by her and proffering so many unplanned, natural pleasures — was the only thing you could count on. Friends and lovers alike accused Dolly of a want of method, complaining that their letters to her went unanswered, that her visits to them were irregular, and that she failed to appear when promised.

In an uncharacteristically bitter moment (Dolly must have done something dreadful), Natalie Barney once remarked, 'Dolly will always have friends, but they won't always be the same friends.' Dolly's beautiful lover Antoinette Gentien repeated this remark with fervour to her son after she had waited out a long afternoon in her avenue Kléber apartment for Dolly, who did not appear — once again — for their usual tea.[28]

And Dolly regularly enraged Natalie Barney's long-time friend, the writer Lily de Gramont, duchesse de Clermont-Tonnerre, whose employment of Dolly as a translator was important to Dolly's flag-ging finances. Dolly cancelled appointments with Lily at the last moment and, worse, used the intimate form of French address with her, the *tu*, in public. Lily feared that Dolly's *tutoy*-ing would cause gossip and repeatedly asked Dolly not to do it. Dolly went right ahead with the provocative intimacy and continued to stand Lily up. With a history of broken appointments and rebuffed socialites behind her, a Grand Plan to present herself as Oscar's social and literary heir – and the constant effort and attention to ambition such a campaign would have required (the kind of effort that had carried her uncle into every salon and newspaper column in London and Paris) – is just exactly *not* the kind of programme that Dolly would have sustained or wanted to continue.

Moreover, considering her endowments, Dolly was actually a very modest woman. She suffered bouts of verbal conceit, but they never lasted for more than half a page and had more to do with assertions of need in love – 'I can accept superiors as rivals but never inferiors' – than with establishments of Self in literature. She knew perfectly well what would allow her to assume the Oscarian mantle: it was writing, writing, writing. And in the face of that act, Dolly was extraordinarily humble. 'Oh! For a little talent & to be – like you – dispassionate amongst the things one loves!' she wrote to Natalie Barney.[29]

Natalie noted how ready Dolly was to erase her writing self.

> . . . while staying with me in Paris, and in spite of a cold in her head, seized with a sense of responsibility towards a new-born review, [Dolly] sat up through the night translating a promised essay by Paul Valéry on Stendhal – occasionnally [sic] using me as a sleepy partner or human dictionary in pursuit of just the right word; for this translation had not only to be 'perfect' but handed in the following morning. So, without relaxing, she went with it to the publishers, but fearing to put her name to anything destined to print, she left it unsigned, and the editor was only too glad to reap the entire benefit of it.[30]

And then there were the two 'wealthy and titled *femmes de lettres*' who took advantage of Dolly's translations – and of 'her generous nature' – without ever paying her. Even when writing in someone else's voice (which, in a way, is what translating is), Dolly could not bear to raise it.

Aside from her letters, Dolly made other, intermittent attempts throughout her life at putting words on paper: a brief and conscientious twenty-seven-page journal[31] undertaken for a 1924 trip to Morocco, a few translations, and some various prose fictions she said she was working on, now lost. In at least two notes to Natalie, she indicates the rare pleasure she was able to associate only with creation – and the immediate feelings of insufficiency which followed it:

> If I knew what time it was I should be less pleased with what
> I have written I suppose! Anyway the amusement of writing –
> even if tomorrow brings calm criticism – has been fun. And if
> it all seems bad in the morning, I at least have enjoyed several
> hours happiness![32]

Certainly her Moroccan travel journal lacks every bit of the charm and felicity of phrasing that make her letters such discoverable delights to read. Dolly, whose voice in verbal entertainment and letters was so unusual, uses none of her range of expression for this journal. But the journal provides a few clues as to why she seemed able to put language everywhere but on paper.

Dolly bought the notebook she used for her travel journal on a trip to Morocco in the first or second week of December 1924; its yellow-ochre cover is almost the colour of the buildings she saw from the long touring car in which she travelled from Algiers to Fez with her friend Ava Bodley, obliquely referred to in Nancy Mitford's comedy of bad manners, *Love in a Cold Climate*.

This Moroccan journal is the only private record Dolly left of the countless pleasure-trips she took. Her entries are obvious exercises in recording impressions and setting out descriptions. There is one vivid picture of her upper-class companions descending their touring car and allowing the British newspapers wrapping their lunch to fly free in the desert 'to spread a bit of Hampstead around', but, in general, her expression in this journal suffers mightily from a lack of direct address to an imagined audience. It also suffers from the absence of the enlivened 'I' which so enriches her letters. Dolly herself was so bored with her attempt at impersonal, linear prose – an imitation of 'male' reportage – that she couldn't bear to sustain it for more than five days.

What is missing from this truncated chronicle of a de luxe journey on the dark continent are Dolly's feelings about where she is and what she is doing. Dolly's own personal style was spontaneous and original, and she is both uninteresting and uninventive when she imprisons herself in reporter's prose. Rather like Oscar in his early attempts at poetry, Dolly is exhausted and imitative in this form, her inventiveness disappearing into laborious attempts at describing desert sands. Sand was not a subject for Dolly Wilde and when she couldn't be 'herself' (or one of her 'selves'), Dolly wasn't anything at all. After the full feast of her letters, the dull fare of this early journal is disappointing.

The form she might have been happier working in was the one her uncle controlled by 1895, the year of her birth. Dolly's ability to enliven a conversation, her electrically quick repartee, the voiced, almost *vocalised* imagination so generously displayed in her letters, the ability to launch herself into the emotional centre of her friends' lives and speak from it, all point to Dolly being a natural (perhaps a naturally *born*) writer of theatrical dialogue; a playwright manqué.

Like her uncle, Dolly not only loved going to plays (and later to films); she dearly loved being with actresses and sometimes identified with them. She thought, for instance, that the flamboyant, dramatic Constance Collier was delightful and looked 'just like me'. And unlike Oscar, who only courted them, Dolly also slept with actresses: Alla Nazimova, with whom she had a brief affair, was perhaps the greatest stage actress of the last century; Gwen Farrar, though from a County background, was a Variety actress; several of Dolly's other lovers, notably Natalie Barney with her love of costumes and Joe Carstairs with her love of disguises, had a distinctly theatrical bent; and Dolly's own self-presentation was dramatic enough so that people remembered and commented on it as something belonging more to art than to life.

When Dolly said that the second act of Osbert Sitwell's play 'pulled like a cracker' or when she wrote that she and her friend the playwright Édouard Bourdet (author of the famous play about lesbianism called *The Captive*) went 'groaning' to half a dozen plays in London because they were so bad, or when she claimed that she and Honey Harris were more disgusted with the *audience's* good reaction to a bad play than with the play itself, she uses the vocabulary of one who is not only used to making a spectacle herself — and to making a spectacle *of* herself — but of one who is accustomed to the form of theatrical spectacle and is quite comfortable with it.

Dolly made a few other attempts at writing original prose besides the Moroccan journal — she told Natalie Barney of having tried some short stories — before giving up, defeated and unexpressed. Since playwriting and literary criticism, the two forms which might have allowed her an expression closest to her natural talents, were arts very fully occupied by Oscar's reputation, she may have felt prohibited from practising them.

Having balked at the first great hurdle all writers must take — the establishment of her own voice on paper — Dolly gradually seems to have taken herself out of the writing race. She totally lacked the aggressive quality which would have made it possible for her to bring concentration, discipline, and a belief in the flare of her talents to the work of writing. Janet Flanner described this quality very well when eulogising the death of the much-admired Parisian chanteuse Yvonne George, a cult favourite whom Dolly probably heard performing in the *boîtes* of Paris just after the First War. 'She lacked', wrote Janet of Mlle George, 'the lion-tamer's quality which marks big artists'.[33]

Although there are almost no references to her direct connection with her uncle in her letters (Janet Flanner said Oscar was too 'obvious' a topic for Dolly to refer to) Dolly retained a familial, historical sense of what it meant to be the niece of Oscar Wilde. Of a dinner party, she said, 'I blame myself for not being more disciplined tonight — but I *couldn't* resist the "bon-mot" which sprang to my lips — (Oscar's lips after all!) . . .'[34] And from the actress Gwen Farrar's topsy-turvy, alcoholic ménage on the King's Road in London where she was living in 1939, she writes of how the '. . . slovenly, impossible atmosphere, with the *constant* worry of someone incapacitated through drink driving the car, arriving home hours late etc undermined what little discipline a "Wilde" possesses!!'[35]

Dolly's tacit recognition of her 'Wilde' qualities did not stop with these references. Like her uncle, she carried with her a vivid sense of destiny, so related to Oscar's own fate that the poem she chose to represent her future was written by Lionel Johnson, the unhappy man responsible for first introducing Alfred Douglas to Oscar Wilde.[36] The poem's first stanza begins: 'Go from me, I am one of those who fall.'

Compared to Oscar's extraordinary self-aggrandisements in *De Profundis* — surely the longest *tua culpa* in the language — Dolly's extravagant statement, 'I am more Oscar-like than he was like himself,'[37] seems like a self-mocking little simile referring to her own depradations. One of the ways Dolly was more 'Oscar-like' was that she simply skipped the social shaping of her talents that confinement to an art form brings, and turned her gifts to a long and publicly performed self-destruction.

Dolly adopted her famous uncle's mantle, just as Oscar had adopted *his* famous uncle's mantle — and in the same spirit of irony. After his release from prison, Oscar took as his *nom de plume* the name of his great-uncle Charles Maturin's most famous fictional character, Melmoth the Wanderer, the despised outsider, adding with a flourish the pronomial Sebastian for his favourite, pierced saint. Adopting the guise of Melmoth was Oscar's rather witty strategy for having it both ways: he could express his outcast state and at the same time place himself securely within his family's distinguished literary history. Dolly, however, had no acclaimed career or present publications to recur to. Even if her self-comparison with Oscar were not entirely ironic, she still had to put Oscar first.

A crucial indication of what Dolly's 'Wildeness' meant to her may be seen in the only objects she inherited from the Wilde family, the two portraits of her paternal grandparents Jane and William, passed down to her from Willie on Lily's death in 1922. For the whole of her adult life, Dolly held on to these portraits of her grandparents through periods of money difficulties so severe that she seemed to go out of her mind with worry.

On Dolly's death, the portraits were passed – perhaps not quite legally, since Dolly's will specified that her entire estate go to Natalie Barney – to her cousin Vyvyan Holland. Holland, who wrote in his journal that he hated 'the whole idea of family', sold them as soon as he could.

To Janet Flanner, Dolly seemed interested in Oscar only in a 'receptive Proustian fashion'; she would receive new, legendary stories about him as if 'he had been an uncompleted Guermantes'. Flanner once told Dolly about a trip she made in Louisville, Kentucky to view the façade of a rather ugly new house designed to fulfil aesthetic suggestions Oscar had made to its future owner during one of his lecture tours to the States in the 1880s. Dolly was interested 'beyond reason' in this story because she had never heard of an Oscarian-inspired house before – Janet Flanner thought privately that Dolly had never heard of Kentucky before either – and to hear of it from someone who had actually seen it in years gone by, 'furnished a tripod of presentation' that suited her to a T . . . It satisfied Dolly's 'real preference for old stories' – her retrospective quality again – 'like rediscovered blurred first editions'.[38]

Flanner told Dolly another story about her pilgrimage to Père Lachaise Cemetery in the early 1920s to lay a single black iris on Oscar's grave. She arrived to find the grave closed off even to literati because the local *lycée* students had been hopping the fence at night to hack the genitalia off the famous androgynous Sphinx, sculpted by Jacob Epstein, which topped the tomb. (The Sphinx bears Oscar's face and looks startlingly like Dolly.)

After Flanner's initial telling was over, Dolly insisted that the story be broken down into sections to be retold, reconsidered, probed, wondered about, and partially explained — deconstructed, in short. Janet Flanner said that a full explanation of the story would have been an absolute disappointment to Dolly 'because the inexplicable attracted her, like something to fiddle with, to finger with her lovely, idle, opulent hands'.[39]

In a letter to her friend 'Emily', Dolly once expressed what happened to her sense of her self in the exercise of her 'Wildean' traits, by using a kind of circus-performer's comparison, a busker's analogy, really, which is all the more painful for its accuracy and stark suggestions of homelessness:

> I feel sometimes like a clever man balancing a billiard cue on his nose — one false slip and the cue will topple — fall. I mean my whole *life* seem[s] just that — no reality and yet this lack of reality passing unnoticed because the trick is so amusing and clever. It's terrifying at times — Emily — and I think absurdity can only stand *one* more day — that one day the cue will fall and I shall fall to pieces on the pavement! Write to me PLEASE.[40]

This self-portrait appears to be the result of a wave of painful revelations — when did the revelations start and how many times did she reject their evidence? — by which Dolly saw, in incomplete flashes, what it *really* meant to don the Magic Dancing Slippers of the Wilde family. Her feeling is the one that awaits any enchanted performer on the other, more precarious side of her self-created fairy tale; when, after countless bewitching balls and private manifestations, the magic slippers she has donned so carelessly begin to cut horribly into her feet, become impossible to take off, and force her to dance so fast that she starts, literally, to die of exhaustion. How wonderful those dancing shoes must have seemed to Dolly when she first tried them on!

In his biography of Oscar Wilde, Richard Ellman wrote that Oscar had to live his life through twice: first at great speed, then very slowly. Like her uncle, Dolly began fast, but there must have come a time for her when every day that she was a living (but not a working) reference to Oscar was an awful one. From London, in one of the great depressions that always succeeded her attempts to shake off 'the ill effects of drugs', Dolly wrote to her friend 'Emily': 'Like Cezanne I *long* to seize "la petite sensation" and write it down as he painted it. The vicious circle – I see something, I can't express it, the double vision of pain and sterility. What do you think of suicide?'[41]

6

Body
Of
Evidence

I 3

La Main Heureuse

Wisteria waves from walls,
– Faint-handed a farewell –
Its gestures' droop recalls
The hands we loved so well.

Natalie Clifford Barney, poem about Dolly Wilde

There is a very small black and white photograph of Dolly Wilde taken *en plein air* somewhere in France. The image is suffused with the high contrasts of light in late autumn. Perhaps the photograph was taken in Beauvallon, where Natalie Barney's country residence was. Or perhaps it was made in the garden of Barney's *pavillon* in the rue Jacob. It is the closest thing there is to an unposed 'snapshot' of Dolly.

The photograph is quite powerful for its size — barely two inches square — and it pictures a radiantly sensual Dolly, caught off guard by the camera, in the act of shielding her eyes from the light. On first viewing, there seemed to me to be something besides Dolly's eyes that was concealed in the image, but it took many months before I found — in plain sight — exactly what was hidden there.

In this particular photograph, Dolly is sitting back on what appears to be a deckchair draped with an overcoat. The crook of one long, lovely arm — the right one — hides her eyes from the penetrating light. Her mouth is rouged, sun-swollen, ripe, and she seems, in her languorous way, ready for any season. Even with shaded eyes, she is perfectly beautiful. There is a *pli amer* under her bottom lip, accentuated by the sun's bright rays. It looks like a punctuation mark.

The overcoat covering the chair is thick and expensive-looking, made of merino wool or camel's hair, but a little moth-bitten and cigarette-burned like so many of Dolly's clothes. It suggests the extra protection an invalid might need from the deceptive winds of a warm November. Her blouse is a light-coloured, linen, short-sleeved affair. She has folded the sleeves back to make them almost disappear, and opened the neck two buttons too low for modesty. The arm not covering her face – the left arm – is bent at the waist and her left hand rests unselfconsciously on her right breast, making it a *point d'appui* and drawing attention to it. Her arms, crooked and bent, create two open isosceles triangles that frame her upper body. Their Classical geometry accentuates the Romantic carelessness of her pose.

Someone – the photographer most likely – has just called out, 'Look up, Dolly, look at the camera,' and Dolly just naturally fell into this completely graceful attitude of concealment and revelation.

So strongly did this photograph engage my imagination that I began to rehearse a variety of narratives to explain it. It was that double quality of revelation and concealment, the unbuttoned blouse and the hidden eyes – Dolly's signature style after all – that kept drawing me back to the little paper square of reflected light. If only I could understand it, could 'read' what was written there, I might make some sense of the perplexing paradoxes that surrounded Dolly Wilde's life and death.

Perhaps Dolly was recuperating when the picture was snapped – she did have a kind of invalid air – from one of her terrible *grippes*, and a solicitous friend or lover (probably Natalie Barney) was offering her sun and solace. On the other hand, Dolly might be in the midst of a painful disintoxication, watched over by one of the various *démorphiné* specialists whose names Natalie had so carefully copied into her *carnet d'adresse*: Docteur Borel, Docteur Simon, Docteur Moreau.[1]

Or perhaps Dolly wasn't recuperating at all, perhaps she just looked that way. Perhaps she was failing, worsening, recidivating — whatever the opposite curve to recuperation might be — and she was in that chair nursing a ferocious drug or alcohol hangover, the kind that contracts the pupils to mean little dots and turns the mouth into a wayside comfort station. That might account for the hidden eyes and the punctuating pleat beneath her bottom lip.

And what about the two other extant photographs of Dolly which were also taken in the open air and in which she was also wearing that same linen blouse? One is of a dryad-like Dolly in profile against a tree, looking barely twenty-five; the other is of a tragically ruined Dolly, her full face towards the camera, looking older than she was even when she died.

If all three photographs, each depicting a wildly different Dolly Wilde, had been taken on the same day (a reproduction of the Dolly-in-profile photograph is marked, inconclusively, 1935, but the same blouse and the same *mise en scène* are compelling evidence of them being taken all at once), then Janet Flanner's perceptive memorial essay on Dolly must be read much more closely, especially the marvellous passage in which Flanner tries to fix in prose Dolly's constantly *chatoyant* 'selves':

> While still alive she had a gift — probably it was that — of seeming to exist in retrospective as well as in perspective. It was a kind of pivotal quality. Even then one could look back on Dolly if one had seen her only a half hour before, because she was interesting to cull over and think about and also because often one wanted to locate in immediate recollection the particular version or vision of her which had been visible on that special day, and she had as many versions of herself, all as slightly different as could have been seen in views of her supplied by a room lined with mirrors . . .

She was not like anybody else or at any rate not like anybody else I ever met and so there was no point in comparing her, if only to stabilize one's self. Within her boundaries — those very delicate, civilized, uncertain psychological frontiers of a constantly expanding and retracting person which was what she seemed to me to be — she was utterly singular. In that way she was unique, in the way that only one, no two other youngish, foreign women were, in that particular circle and her Paris decade. Even in being unique Dolly was very pervasive.[2]

I put the photograph away for some months and when I took it out again it looked like a completely new composition. The picture — I could see it clearly now — was all about Dolly's arms and her beautiful hands. It was a kind of architectural display of their properties, arranged as if by accident. Suddenly all the explanatory narratives I'd been entertaining contracted into a single knot of terror and pity. Something awful had appeared on Dolly's right wrist, something I had missed before when I was looking too hard.

Starting just above the right hand and trailing up the underside of her forearm, were a series of ugly, defiling scars. A bit like the cross-hatched tracks skis make on virgin snow, the scars were not at all regular the way ski tracks are supposed to be. They looked jagged and raised, like the marks a knife or a razor might leave: messy, keloidal marks, the hieroglyphs of lost hopes, the kind of marks that are left when you hack away at your writing wrist with something sharp in the hand you *don't* write with. Dolly's left wrist, pressed to her breast and vein side down, was hidden from sight.

Like everything else to do with Dolly Wilde, these 'scars' presented large questions and little mysteries. Certainly it was possible for someone not conversant with Dolly's history to decide that the 'scars' were the product of an uneven application of photographic developing solution, or of smears on the negative, or even of a print removed too soon from its acid bath. And could it also be possible — in my altered 'biographer's state' I thought it might be — that, like other miraculous relics of the Catholic faith Dolly had re-embraced before her death, the little photograph was developing 'sympathetic' wounds reflecting Dolly's own suicide attempts? If that were the case, then what a pity that the image, unlike the portrait of Dorian Gray, had not suffered all of Dolly's sorrows for her as well.

There is no serious way to determine if this photograph was taken before Dolly's first recorded suicide attempt at the Hôtel Astoria in Paris in 1931 (the one precipitated by Natalie Barney's elopement with an actress), or if it was taken *after* that sad act but *before* her almost-successful second try at her service flat in London in September 1934, when she was saved only by the quick-wittedness of her Irish housekeeper, Nora O'Shaughnessy.[3] The little picture is not dated and the underside of Dolly's left wrist (which presumably would be similarly marked if the markings are 'authentic' traces of her 'suicides') is hidden from view. Though it is remarkable that the scars on the photograph appear where Dolly would have cut herself, the question of whether the marks themselves are 'real', or mistaken, or merely miraculous is unanswerable, and the picture remains a paradigm of concealment, revelation and mystery – a paradigm, in short, of Dorothy Wilde herself.

In any case, the image itself, even if only half-understood, helps to explain something about Dolly's ambiguous and solitary death, a death which some people certainly considered a suicide. For it was a recurring pattern with Dolly that, when she was at her most desperate, she would regularly 'cut herself off' from whatever she loved. She did it actually by barricading herself in her various rooms for days and weeks, and she did it symbolically by attacking her hands. More than anything else about her physical self, Dolly adored her hands and arms; they were her 'only vanity'. And when she was most serious about killing herself – and she was *very* serious about it on at least two of her four separate attempts – she would begin by hurting what she loved the most: she always took a razor to her wrists.

The hands are the most significant part of the body that the Self can see without a mirror. Dolly Wilde, who disliked what she saw in mirrors — 'Never believe in mirrors,' she told Philip La Selle, 'mirrors are more lying than photographs . . .'[4] — was fascinated by her own hands. She was not alone. In the world in which she lived, everyone seemed to notice and to have something to say about Dolly's beautiful hands.

When Dolly wrote, she wrote with her right hand, and when she opened things it was with that right hand as well. She was careful not to move her hands too much in conversation, preferring the statements they made when she displayed them, simply and regally, in her lap. She found her unadorned hands to be decoration enough and she never wore rings or bracelets or coloured nail polish. She kept her nails manicured, lacquered, and buffed to a high shine; they looked like expensive, unshelled, Spanish almonds. Her 'ten moons' always glimmered pristinely in the cradle of their cuticles.

Once, when she coquettishly rested one 'precious' hand on his shoulder, Vyvyan Holland exclaimed with obviously mixed emotions: 'Dolly, your fingers look like beautiful white slugs!'[5] Dolly would have recognised this allusion as the contrapuntal echo of Lady Campbell's disgusted remark about Oscar — that he looked like a 'great, white slug' — and she repeated the reference as though flattered by the comparison. Tancred Borenius said Dolly's hands were 'Bronzino hands'; Rosamond Harcourt-Smith wrote of Dolly's 'just pride' in her hands and described 'the narrow palms . . . as soft as a kitten's paw, the fingers exceptionally long and slender'.[6] And Janet Flanner, whose interest in Dolly was not strictly artistic, called her hands 'lovely, idle, opulent'.[7]

Natalie Barney wrote that Dolly's 'wrists and hands were so perfect that they seemed less expressive than the rest of her unique person'; that she 'prided herself on nothing but these hands', and that she displayed them 'with guilty vanity' on social occasions.[8] Natalie meant that Dolly's hands were her only *visible* vanity, for Dolly had little physical self-consciousness and so her tendency to a less-than-discreet 'show of hands' was remarked on with affection and amusement by her friends.

One of Dolly's other vanities – she seems, for such a fascinator, to have been touchingly without the usual conceits of appearance – was her success in sexual adventure. She wrote in an early letter to Barney that if she ever 'achieved fame' (the subject was rarely on her conscious mind, but when it was it must have gnawed like a rat), 'two salient qualities I hope you'll stress – that I'm "*une grande amoureuse*" and a lover of Nature . . .'[9] With regard to her first 'salient' quality, there may well have been a double reason for pride: women who make love with women often use the hands as one of their principle instruments of sexual expression. In the memoir of her sensual life, *My Blue Notebooks*, Liane de Pougy, Paris's most celebrated courtesan, refers with nostalgic pleasure to the 'agile little fingers' of Natalie Barney.

Dolly's letters contain a myriad of poignant references to hands. She uses hands in her writing as a kind of synecdoche for human connection and for her own intensely developed emotional vocabulary. Here are a few examples (a handful, in fact) from thirteen years of correspondence with Natalie Barney.

Parties every night but I am refreshed in the mornings with your letters on my tray. I decide to open them *after* I have drunk my coffee, adding anticipation to delight: but hardly have I scrunched the first mouthful of toast then resolve goes to the wind & I have the envelope open with absurdly feverish hands![10]

I love you & am sad, & feel full of presentiment & foreboding: & angry, too, at your intolerant acceptance of anything but classified emotions. Where is Romaine's small hand to comfort me with moody sympathy?[11]

I am still faithful to you – a week yesterday! *et dans tous les sens.* Like Saint Sebastien I am pierced with a hundred arrows – hands bound, limbs twisted – anguish on my brow![12]

But you give me glib assurances in your letter & I am comforted, altho' I sense a certain tired aptitude of phrase . . . You have held so many hands . . . so many waists . . . written so many love letters . . .[13]

Tout Paris pours endless stories into my ears – but acceptance of the rhythm of destiny becomes easier & easier – & like a ghost I feel I have no hands to struggle, no voice to lift up, no heart to break.[14]

Yes, darling, I close my eyes & immediately my spirit hands push open your door & I am by you on the bed with impatient arms around you . . .[15]

I seem to gather together all my love & appreciation for you the moment your back is turned, & am seized with a longing for you that leaves me empty-handed with despair.[16]

Darling – darling – I can't let the night close up without stretching out a hand towards you.[17]

And this final one, too obvious, almost, in its reference: 'From which romantic sighing you must gather that I am in love – tortured of course, vanitous & repressed! Already I am struggling to get my hand out of the trap – squeaking in my usual cowardly way at the first twinges of pain!'[18]

Dolly is always wanting to 'stretch out a hand', and always hoping to join her hands to 'sister hands'. She refers to hands variously as 'grateful', 'feverish', 'listless', 'sympathetic' – in short, they are everything that Dolly feels or that Dolly feels other people feel for her. Her hands, she thought, were 'Valentine hands', heart-shaped: Dolly didn't wear her heart on her sleeve, she displayed it directly in her hands, and when she is broken-hearted she often describes herself as 'empty-handed'. Her interest in hands elicits from her an exquisite scrutiny, with consequences that are almost taxonomic. At the end of an undated letter to her friend 'Emily', a letter containing what must be one of the most richly accurate and densely pictorial descriptions of Virginia Woolf ever written,[19] Dolly adds this casual post-script:

> Darling,
>   Of course I meant to tell you about Virginia's hands — things I always notice and am affected by. At first they looked like delicate but capable hands with all their beauty frost-bitten by the cold outside so that they had a certain touching awkwardness and redness. Then as the evening wore on they paled to natural softness and one remarked the *young* wrist amongst other things. They aren't Valentine hands like mine or petals like yours — but they have a beauty of sensitiveness and delicacy . . .

Like many obsessive themes in her life, Dolly Wilde's intense feeling for hands — 'the first thing', she said often, 'I notice about people' — can be matched in certain family facts; patrilinear facts, because those are the available ones. There was a history of 'handedness' in the Wilde family: Oscar and Willie both painted landscapes at Moytura, the family's country home in Ireland, and Willie delighted in playing the piano. ('Speranza', Lady Wilde, on the other hand, was described by Bernard Shaw as being splay-handed, fumble-fingered and obscurely groping in the use of her hands. He also thought she suffered from 'gigantism'.) Both Willie's obituary in the *New York Times* on 15 March 1899, and the memoirs of a childhood friend from the Portora Royal School attest to his facility at the keyboard; and the composer Ethel Smyth, one of Willie's many short-lived 'fiancées', described his evident pleasure in his odd hobby of making up new endings for Chopin études.

Like Willie and Oscar, Dolly also painted and drew and had once allowed herself a rarely combined creative and financial pleasure by selling some paintings she made in London for a much-needed £15. There are only a few desultory sketches amongst her letters to Natalie Barney and to Pamela Harris, and most of them are of objects: a series of elegant and outlandish perfume bottles she bought for Honey Harris and a clutch of annotated drawings of high-fashion dresses she designed and had copied by this seamstress or that maid. She did do one rather outré drawing of herself and Natalie Barney, separately ensconced in Natalie's bed, each of them wearing fantastic masks of a sexual, surrealistic felinity.

The most touching 'hand-made' sketch Dolly did in her letters to Barney, is the one she completed for her forty-second birthday.[20] The drawing, done in pencil on creamy folded paper, shows a romantically frayed page from a personal calendar.

This is a surprising and profoundly childish image to come from a forty-two-year-old woman. It almost deliberately reprises the drawings children make in primary school to please their mothers and delivers yet another aspect of what were Dolly's clearly complicated feelings for Barney. The hands of the clock are 'hands' of another order and the phrase, 'And time the enemy!', had a particular significance: Dolly was always late for everything.

Wherever Dolly's feeling for hands came from, there is no doubt from whom Dolly inherited the *look* of her hands. They are very much Wildean hands – Oscar's and no doubt Willie's hands – considerably 'feminised' and refined. Comparison of a plaster cast of Oscar's hands and an ink-print of Dolly's right hand made in 1936 displays a striking similarity: their hands both have the same lengthy fingers, the same narrowed palms, the same languid, liquid display of possible poses. In his rare photographs, Willie's hands are often half-obscured or folded, but from the length of his body and from what is visible in the pictures – long palms and artistically turned wrists – it is probable that Dolly's hands were also very like her father's. And, although people often reacted with repugnance to Oscar's hands – indeed every part of both Oscar's and Willie's anatomies elicited, at one time or another, shudders of repulsed description – that was

The date

Sunday
11
JULY 1937

9.A.M. Dolly's Birthday!
1.30. Luncheon Romaine
5.p.m. Lady Westmacott.
6.30. Laure
8.p.m. Dinner Rue Jacob.

SUNDAY JULY 11 1937

and time the enemy!

never the case with Dolly, whose hands and every other feature were praised almost beyond reason. She was discussed, as Janet Flanner wrote, as though she were 'someone one had become familiar with by reading, rather than by knowing . . .': regarded as a work of art, rather than as a fact of life.

The first, now famous, public focus on Wildean hands occurred two years before Dolly's birth, the night Oscar's play *A Woman of No Importance* opened in London, on 19 April, 1893. At the gala dinner party honouring the author at Blanche Roosevelt's town house after the opening, the guests were beguiled by the palm-reading abilities of Cheiro, *soi-disant* Count Louis Hamon, a society palmist in considerable vogue at the end of the 1890s. Cheiro would figure later on in the life of Natalie Barney's long-time lover, the painter Romaine Brooks, but on this evening he was reading palms thrust through a curtain so that his predictions would be 'blind' ones. In his book of reminiscences, *Cheiro's Memoirs*, Cheiro describes what he saw in the hands of the guest of honour, Oscar Wilde:

> I pointed this case out as an example where the left hand had promised the most unusual destiny of brilliance and uninterrupted success, which was completely broken and ruined at a certain date on the right hand . . . Almost forgetting myself for a moment, I summed up all by saying, 'the left hand is the hand of a king, but the right hand that of a king who will send himself into exile.'

> The owner of the hands did not laugh. 'At what date?' he asked rather quietly.

> 'A few years from now,' I answered, 'between your forty-first and forty-second year.'[21]

Oscar repeated the prediction gravely and left the dinner party without a further word, to the consternation of his hostess. Cheiro, or so Cheiro said, was one of the mourners who followed Oscar's coffin to its grave in Bagneux in 1900.

Given Dolly's inordinate interest in hands, it is not surprising that she, too, might have found someone to read her character through her hands, someone whose scientific accomplishments were as attuned to the *Zeitgeist* of her era as Cheiro's 'spiritualism' was attuned to the *esprit* of Oscar's. When Dolly went to consult a psychiatrist, she found the only one in the world whose original theories of human psychology and sexuality began with the human hand.

Dr Charlotte Wolff was a brilliant psychiatrist with revolutionary ideas and an intuitive, highly individualistic approach to science.[22] In her lengthy career she wrote five pioneering books on the human hand, all of them intensely and originally researched and focused on interpreting hand shapes and palm lines as well as specific gestures. She did serious, scholarly investigations of bisexuality and wrote the classic psychological treatise, the only one of its kind, *Love Between Women*. Her papers now lie uncatalogued in the British Psychological Society's archives at the University of Liverpool in England. No one, said the Society's honorary curator when I telephoned, had inquired for them since her death in 1986. Aldous Huxley wrote about her in 1936, the year Dr Wolff treated Dolly:

> Nobody who has had a sitting with Dr. Wolff . . . can doubt her ability to make a diagnosis of physical conditions and tendencies that is often astonishingly detailed and accurate; can doubt her power to specify past events and date them correctly to within a few months; can doubt her knack of describing character, and the secret springs of action with a penetrating and often disturbing insight.[23]

Charlotte Wolff was a German Jew, born near the rapidly shifting territorial borders of Danzig in 1897. Small, intense, and electrically charged with originality and self-assurance, she went to Berlin to study for her medical degree during the heady days of the Weimar

Republic and began her investigations into the human hand there. She left Berlin in 1933, when it began to be apparent that the *Lebensraum* in Germany would leave no room for Jews, and paused for almost three years in Paris where she attracted the full attention of the Surrealists. Among the hands (and psychologies) she 'read' in Paris were those of: Romola Nijinsky, Paul Eluard, René Crevel, Max Ernst, Julien Green, Ravel, Princesse Edmond de Polignac, Prince Armande de Polignac, Antonin Artaud, and Man Ray.

In 1936 Charlotte Wolff emigrated to London with the help of her friends and strong supporters, Aldous and Maria Huxley. She worked with Julian Huxley for a while in London (on the palms of the apes in the London Zoo, among other things), and continued her 'reading' of human hands. Sybille Bedford said that Charlotte Wolff 'deliberately lost the gift of prescience' because she couldn't bear the consequences of what she could see: when Dr Wolff examined Virginia Woolf's palm and saw her suicide there, she fled the room.[24] It was in London, during the first year of her residence there, that Charlotte Wolff probably encountered Dolly Wilde.

1936 was a difficult year for Dolly, as were all the years of her later life. Judging by her letters to Natalie Barney – mailed from her usual unsettled locations in Fontainebleau and in Cannes (where she was staying with the professional 'hostess' Elsa Maxwell and her companion Dickie Fellowes-Gordon), in London and in Paris, where she was riding a dreadful rollercoaster of emotional distress and physical debilitation – she could feel both her luck and her power to attract love running out. Dolly wrote to Barney:

Neither you nor Providence (the only people I believe in & the only important factors in my destiny) can stretch the elastic of tolerance & forbearance any further. It's come by infinite stretching to the last tenuous thread that is almost transparent with strain, like the thread in an old torn suspender.[25]

The father of Dolly's Parisian doctor died on the very day that she was to begin a 'cure' in Paris and she had to postpone it. She compared herself on the eve of her next 'disintoxication', unpromisingly, with Mary Queen of Scots on 'the night before her execution'. Dolly, to whom narrative was the supremest fiction and the world's great delight, wrote sadly that now 'Fiction is out of place, somehow, in this stark period, a luxury for leisured days that has no place now.'[26] She was distracted enough to commit the stylistic *gaucherie* of repeating the noun 'place' in one sentence – a solecism she would have noted with self-critical disgust in the old, exigent days of her letter-writing career.

Dolly spent the summer of 1936 in the English countryside. In October she was living in an attic at the Berkeley Hotel, and her furniture had been repossessed for the usual, debt-ridden reasons. She wrote to Natalie in Paris saying that she had 'had a very happy summer staying in the country – but London is lonely & depressing . . .'[27] It was quite likely in late 1936 (after she had returned from an October visit to Paris where the Wilde scholar Guillot de Saix remarked on her 'static dignity' and 'interior absence') that someone she knew or knew of – it could have been Aldous Huxley who had just written the introduction for the 1936 edition of Wolff's *Studies in Human Hand-Reading* – directed Dolly to consult with the newly arrived Dr Charlotte Wolff.

In an interview conducted by Romaine Brooks's biographer, Dr Charlotte Wolff is reported to have said that Dolly Wilde came to see her as a patient in 1936 suffering from overwhelming depressions. 'She was very sick at the time,' said Dr Wolff, 'but she was so beautiful; she was radiant. I shall never forget how she stood in front of the fireplace. I've met hundreds of women in my life, but this woman I never forgot.'[28]

There is no record in Dolly Wilde's very sparsely preserved correspondence for the year 1936 of her treatment by Dr Wolff, but there is an unusual piece of evidence that, along with Dr Wolff's reported assessment, suggests that this treatment could certainly have occurred.

Among the souvenirs of Dolly Wilde that Berthe Cleyrergue kept for sixty years (or retrieved on Barney's death from Barney's papers), is an ink-print of Dolly's right hand, taken exactly the way Dr Wolff took all the handprints that she used for her chirological researches. The print is signed, in unmistakable handwriting, 'Dorothy Wilde' and quite likely it was Dolly who added, in fat green capital letters down the upper left-hand corner of the paper, the two mysterious words: 'ADDA NARY.'

Could the words ADDA NARY be a kind of name? Dolly loved making up names and witty sobriquets. Were they a bit of baby talk? A love-designation of some kind? Dolly had provided plenty of those *dans ses jours*. Perhaps ADDA NARY was an anagram. I tried out a few bad combinations in English: DADA YARN, ARYAN DAD, NARY A DAD. Too many missing fathers came up, as they did in Dolly's life, and Gertrude Stein's epitaph for patriarchal poetry – 'fathers are depressing' – seemed the right epitaph for my investigation.

Still, this handprint, a touchingly personal relic of Dolly in itself, displays the same qualities of concealment and revelation and mystery I found in the little photograph of her. There is the almost shockingly intimate revelation of every line and whorl of her palm, the mystery of the circumstances of the 'reading' as well as the apparent loss of its result, and the odd arrangement of words on paper and their reminiscent green colour – green being her uncle Oscar's favourite colour for mischief.

And of course, it was Dolly herself who must have traced the distinct and careful black pencil line around her handprint so that – and there is no other reason she would have done this – its lovely shape could be more fully appreciated.

as dangerously as her emotions, and she fainted, occasionally and gracefully, in public and private places — often regaining consciousness with a diverting quip. She had *la grippe*, a particularly virulent form of European influenza, recurrently in and out of season. Her throat produced abscesses and had to be cauterised and cut. Her ears ached with the cold and the heat, and her nacreous, opalescent, lustrous skin, the skin that an unknown admirer likened to the petals of an extravagant gardenia flower, developed allergic rashes, produced frightening boils, and scorched in the sun. She almost died of diphtheria in hotels, *palazzi* and private hospitals in Venice; she was frequently indisposed with a bad head or a minor nervous breakdown in Paris and London. She came close to expiring in flocks of inexpensive flats in far less desirable locations (and for far less desirable reasons) and always — in the last years of her life — she was torturously insomniac, seeking sleep like a lover.

Dolly was so frequently ill that she could write about her maladies with the minute and hyper-real attention of a witty hypochondriac: 'I am feeling better & better for my medicine & far less depressed. Alas! that all tragedy is glands.'[2] But Dolly was not a hypochondriac, she was merely a woman extraordinarily interested in her own body.

> I've had cold after cold or rather grippe after grippe leaving
> me exhausted & without will power to do *anything*. *I can't* get fit
> & have lost so many pounds. How I admire the Rubenesque
> figures now — how lacking in all quality are these skinny
> modern figures. I like a plump dove's breast & the milky skin
> to be swollen like a bird — or rounded & crisp like popcorn! I
> am no longer your 'puppy' but a gaunt Dolly who could tick
> off the days of her discontent on her ribs![3]

Along with her creative involvement in the pains of love (she once suggested that a jilted friend try both Lysistrata's cure *and* something from Krafft-Ebing),[4] Dolly continued to pursue solutions to the problems and pleasures of inhabiting her body. Her fascination with the body caught Dolly up in a paradox of which she was only half-conscious: the conundrum of keeping her spirit (she called it 'vitality' and valued it more than her body) alive in a physical form that seemed more subject than most to the depredations of gravity, early menopause, and infection.

Did this embroilment in somatics begin for Dolly with a vision of the anaesthetised Mary Travers sexually spread out on Dr William Wilde's examining table? Mary Travers was the obsessive young patient who accused Dolly's paternal grandfather, Dr Wilde, of chloroforming and then raping her. A Dublin jury believed her.

Or was it the looming image of Dr Wilde himself, that curiously gifted physician for whom her father had been named, which was so fatally inscribed on Dolly's imagination? Until she died, doctors continued to play an enormous part in Dolly's life – and in the complicated series of permissions she needed to go on living it.

The first portrait that exists of Dolly is of Dolly as a sick infant. In a letter to Oscar Wilde's friend More Adey, a letter dated by Adey 14 March 1896, Dolly's mother Lily Wilde writes from her Oakley Street residence: 'Of course I would have come to see you, but I am leaving town tomorrow as my Baby is *very* ill & the House must be left quiet for her.'[5] Given that Dolly's father had by this time no other career than that of drunkard, and that each of his wives had accused him of behaviour that was both violent and abusive, Lily was perhaps taking Willie Wilde to North Malvern to spare the terribly ill, eight-month-old baby her father's drunken outbursts.

From this fragmentary, dimly lit look at the infant Dolly, a vignette of physical and emotional abandonment assembles itself. It was to be repeated (some would say invited) and keenly felt by Dolly in one form or another for the rest of her life.

As an adult, Dolly once told Janet Flanner 'in a nostalgic way' that her father died [of hepatic liver failure in 1899] when she was so young, that she could not remember 'even having been dandled by him'.[6] In fact, Dolly was old enough – almost four – to remember her father perfectly well had there been something about him that she wanted to remember. Many of her later medical problems would now be considered the products of an immune system invaded too early on by the mad excesses — and even more maddening lacks — of Willie Wilde's household at Oakley Street. Just as Dolly's central emotional drama kept repeating its particular agonies and ecstasies all her life, so, too, did her diseases.

Before Dolly developed cancer, before her wilfulness and her will had been eroded by her habitual addictions to pills, powders, and potions, she was beset by many small illnesses and 'nervous collapses' and she began tentative little withdrawals to bed. Many of her letters are written from the bedroom and she affirmed, again and again in various ways, that 'in bed I feel alright'. The frantic activities in pursuit of 'health' that filled up her later life after the cancer began to grow, the activities that *became* her life in the way that searches always become their own subject, began with these small retreats to bed with a fever, a cold, the doldrums, or a depression. Confinement to bed for Dolly was the beginning of an attempt to bolster a body compromised by late nights, bad drugs, and a justified fear of the future. When anything threatened — and everything eventually *did* threaten — Dolly was always capable of contracting her operating territory to the conformation of a counterpane.

Dolly seems to have passed almost as much time conversing with her doctors as she did sparring with her lovers or fascinating her literary friends. Some of this time was spent in charming prescription drugs out of them, and she bragged about these successes proudly. It was unfortunate that the physicians and matrons of the various sanatoriums and *maisons de santé* where she spent so much time in the 1930s enjoyed her company so thoroughly. Some of their medical statements about her conditions read like favourable reports from a finishing school, praising her wit, her humour, and her excellent comportment, and glossing over the frequent little 'relapses' she suffered.

In September 1939, from Chiswick House, Dolly's nursing home in Middlesex, the directing physician Dr Douglas Macauley wrote an assessment of Dolly's progress for Natalie Barney, who was, as usual, paying Dolly's doctor's bills.

> She has been wonderfully better since she has been here although on one or two occasions she has not been so well. This has usually been after coming back from a trip to London . . . as she is a voluntary patient, we cannot prevent her from doing so . . .

> She is looking a good deal better and is very cheerful.

> She is now only taking ¼ grain of heroin and I am very anxious to try to get her off it altogether, but she feels that she is not really strong enough at present to do that . . .

> As you know, some time ago I got her to see . . . the chief expert in London on cancer of the breast. Unfortunately, she will not take his advice to have an operation with radium as well . . . . She has been most co-operative, except for this one or two occasions when she has become emotionally out of control . . .

> I knew Miss Wilde personally 20 years ago.[7]

This letter shows who was *really* in charge of Dolly's treatment at Chiswick House – and it was definitely not the dependable Dr Macauley. With her usual *brio*, Dolly has raked the thin soil of her nursing home for advantages and wrested control of her disintoxication and her cancer therapy from Dr Macauley. She is dipping into London from time to time for something that leaves her returning to Chiswick House 'not . . . so well', she has refused breast surgery, and she has declined to have her daily heroin supply reduced. Dr Macaulay's wistful last line about knowing Dolly 'personally 20 years ago' makes it clear why and how she ran up the enormous consultation bill at Chiswick House that Honey Harris complained about. Dolly was plying her charms and her talents on an old friend, possibly an old admirer. It was the last strategy of control left to a woman taken into 'care' – and it seems to have got Dolly what she wanted.

Dolly had two other notable exchanges with doctors in 1936, a bad year for both her physical and psychological health. It was in 1936 that she apparently consulted with the psychoanalyst Dr Charlotte Wolff, who found her disturbingly memorable. The infections which characteristically flickered throughout Dolly's always-too-receptive immune system, were running rampant again in 1936. She had an inflamed eye at the end of the year and an 'anthrax' caused by infected glands in the middle of it.[8] In the summer, the prescription drug on which she had come to depend so desperately (it must have been heroin or morphine) ran out in Cannes, and this prescription was so 'dangerous' that it could not be legally renewed in that city. Dolly found herself at the end of a short rope.

Characteristically, she managed to charm the necessary drug authorisations out of a young provincial doctor, who, she wrote (continuing her long habit of turning life into literature), looked like 'Trilby's brother'. 'I called Trilby's brother & argued, coaxed, threatened, frightened, hypnotised, touched, reassured, & finally suceeded [sic] in making him "risk his career . . ."' – all the while providing the beguiled young physician, through her 'distraction of pain', with a brilliant legal defence in case he was arrested for obtaining the drug for her. Dolly's final authority was always literature and she cited in her persuasive arguments, 'J.-Jacques Rousseau, Voltaire, St. Theresa & the weeping Niobe herself!'[9]

So great was her need for the drug in question that she literally couldn't function without it. She sent this rare description to Natalie Barney about what happened to her after she had filled the prescription.

In an hour I could walk, dress, *pack*, talk lucidly to the Wagon

Lits on the telephone, drive 20 kilometres to the station, & journey for 12 rattling, swaying, rocking & bumping hours to Paris in comparative comfort. Darling if I burlesque the whole incident to you it is because the real horror of it is insupportable to me as much as to you . . .[10]

By calling the doctor 'Trilby's brother', Dolly revealed who the real Svengali (or the real Svengali's sister) of their exchange was. In *Trilby*, Gerald du Maurier's eponymous novel of art and control, the music master Svengali has the beautiful young Trilby performing completely under his direction. A Trilby-like doctor was Dolly's dream: a physician of her very own to fill out any prescription Dolly/Svengali wanted. Turning her doctors into 'Trilbys' – and ignoring their advice – was Dolly's last line to liberty, her only defence against a sanatorium life and the 'real horror' of her condition. The 'weakness' her friends were always accusing her of was one of Dolly's versions of strength: she knew what she needed, she got it, and she damned (and was damned by) the consequences. Dolly didn't want to be cured, exactly, but she *certainly* didn't want to be controlled.

The 'Trilby' episode occurred while Dolly was visiting the compulsively social, internationally connected party-giver Elsa Maxwell and her companion Dickie Gordon-Fellowes in Cannes at the end of July 1936. One of Elsa Maxwell's autobiographies was entitled *I Married the World*, and the kinds of nuptials she liked to invite the world to are made plain by photographs of Maxwell dressed up as Benjamin Franklin, J. Edgar Hoover, and a jolly Austrian burgher in lederhosen and a Tyrolean hat. It was obvious, even from Dolly's airy references, that Dolly's inability to function without the drug she required (as well as her anxieties about not getting her hands on it) frightened the vulgar, hearty Maxwell to death: although Maxwell 'was *very* sweet and understanding . . . she decided on *instant* departure'.[11]

Like most heroin addicts, Dolly knew a great deal about medicine. She understood more – much more – than most of us about the dosages and dangers of any drug, but seemed to want the imprimatur

of a 'doctor' to prescribe them. Her attempts to find medical diagnoses she could live with after the lumps in her left breast became
obvious, led her to both the highways and the byways of medical
practice. She consulted everyone from Christian Science practitioners
to 'sorcière-healers' and a host of respectable ordinary doctors.
Eventually, a pantechnicon of cancer specialists, X-ray specialists,
serum specialists, distinguished surgeons, and general practitioners
were added to the list, all of whom provided her with contradictory,
compelling, and totally confusing diagnoses. In February of 1939
Dolly wrote to Natalie:

> I am bewildered by the extraordinary disagreement of doctors.
> A says an incision for the microscope is easy & feasible & con-
> clusive: B says any incision is dangerous as the result might
> mean poison percolating into the blood stream with conse-
> quent damage: C says any incision is inconclusive . . .[12]

Displaying another one of her oddly contemporary qualities,
Dolly feared the 'Harley Street doctors with their expensive society
fleecing – counselling operations when they are not necessary, charg-
ing enormous fees etc. (a book called 'The Citadel' written by an
ex-doctor exposes the whole camp ruthlessly & is terrifying to me).'[13]
And this fear became her bulwark against submitting to any diagnostic incisions or larger 'surgical' cures. Up to the beginning of 1940,
the year in which she immersed herself in the waters of Lourdes for
four days, Dolly, with all her doctoring, managed not to know if the
lumps in her breast were actually cancer. She rejected many inter-
mediary diagnoses of malignancy, including one by a special research
physician Natalie hired in Paris, Dr Marbais. Dolly saw him in April
1939, he told her she had cancer, and '. . . luckily, [he] didn't convince
me. If he had made any sort of injection – taken any blood test etc
etc – I should have been in the depths of despair. As it was – accompanied by Honey – I shed two tears & then dismissed the whole
thing.'[14]

Dolly didn't care for Dr Marbais's diagnostic procedures *or* for his diagnosis and, by now, she was a discerning medical client. But her rejection of Dr Marbais's judgement had more to do with what she was ready to accept as a diagnosis than with what she was competent to judge as a patient. Perhaps it was this statement by her old friend Dr Macauley in a letter to Natalie Barney on 19 April 1940 that finally persuaded Dolly to go to Lourdes in early May: 'The X-ray treatment can only be ameliorative. The condition itself should have been operated upon long ago. It is now quite inoperable.'[15]

Miracles, anyway, were Dolly's preferred form of revelation and at Lourdes she found the two smaller lumps in her breast disappearing and the larger one 'much diminished'. Although the waters at Lourdes were icy, Dolly said she did not feel the cold at all. On 7 May 1940 she sent a telegram to Natalie signed with her pet name: PROGRESS EVERY DAY DEEPLY IMPRESSED ALL LOVE CARD POSTED PUPPY WILDE[16]

Presumably Dolly did not know what her autopsy – her very last appointment with a doctor – finally revealed: although the lumps in her breast had apparently shrunk, there were 'small deposits of cancer dotted throughout the lungs'. Had Dolly lived longer, she would have faced an intolerably medicalised future.

The year Dolly went to Lourdes, 1940, began with a flurry of contradictions, retractions, and indecisions, all related to Dolly's medical conditions. Dolly was back in Chiswick House, and she was collecting herself for a trip to Paris to seek out yet another doctor to treat her breast tumours.[17] Natalie and Marcelle Fauchier Delavigne were expecting her.[18] Then 'specialists' told Dolly she couldn't travel for at least six weeks. On 4 January she sent a telegram to Natalie saying she was trying to get to France, vowing 'endless love', a belief in 'miracles', and begging Natalie not to 'leave me'.[19]

Then came more contradictory diagnoses from more doctors, including the judgement that Dolly's 'regular doctor' was 'unreliable' and that her 'symptoms' were increasing.[20] Ever more specialists were consulted, and finally the decision was taken that there would be no breast operation. On 17 January Honey Harris wired to Natalie Barney that 'immediate radiotherapy' was required for Dolly and that Dolly would not be travelling to Paris after all.[21]

These contretemps of the first two weeks of January 1940 are just a small sampling of the confusion of diagnosis and expectation that followed Dolly's cancer like a pair of evil eyes. The emotional effect this whipsawing had on Dolly couldn't have been more destructive. It drove her deeper into drink – which she could get without her doctors – and more regularly to drugs – which she preferred to get *from* her doctors (though she seems to have got them anywhere she could). Perhaps this 'medicalisation' of her drug habit had something to do with Dolly's intermittent desire for repectability, a desire which led her into some astounding acts of personal corruption: she turned most of her lovers into loan sharks and all of her doctors into drug dealers.

On 24 January 1940 Honey Harris sent a letter to Natalie Barney asking Marcelle Fauchier Delavigne and Natalie to continue to contribute to Dolly's support: 'It hasn't been her fault at all – she has been so frightened & wretched, & Fate & the doctors were entirely responsible for her not arriving in Paris as she intended . . . I think that the poor darling is now really frightened . . .'[22]

For Dolly's friends, her breast cancer was almost a moral relief, something to focus on besides her 'hopeless habits' and her increasingly 'weak will'. Here, finally, was a disease they couldn't blame her for; there, at last, was a condition which had nothing to do with Dolly's 'inability to refrain'.

Dolly, of course, managed to destroy even this option for innocence by continually refusing to have the kind of treatment her friends all thought she should have. True to form, and in the midst of terrible confusions and terrors herself, she regularly turned down the operations recommended by the expensive surgeons her friends hired or suggested, and looked to alternative therapies when and where she could.

As in the case of Dolly's 'suicides', which often involved her 'unconscious' self committing actions that her 'conscious' self rejected, Dolly must have known, profoundly, that she had cancer. But she made sure that the hard diagnostic facts wouldn't reach her until very late in the day, at a time when conventional medicine couldn't cure her (if, indeed, it ever could have). The cancer, her friends thought, was becoming almost another Dolly-con, another condition she couldn't (or wouldn't) be cured of, just like her alcoholism and her drug addiction. It was one more justification for Dolly to annul her consciousness with drugs, to forget herself in a bed. How like Dolly to contract a disease for which there was no cure but a course in miracles!

For all her interest in somatics, Dolly had even greater spiritual yearnings and sensitivities. She was always recommending Christian Science 'treatments' to people and sending them 'cards' for practitioners. Acts of sorcery appealed to her as much as the Catholic rituals of her own intermittent faith. Dolly thought the music of Bach was 'like God, so perfect that I can't believe it's true'.[23] Had she even been baptised? She was housed in a convent as a child and her metaphors are shot through with Roman Catholic references – mostly, and appropriately, to mortal sins. At the end of her life, she took to wearing a gold cross around her neck and appearing at odd moments in churches; a priest presided at her funeral. Her uncle Oscar had received the Catholic sacraments on his death bed while semi-conscious.

Dolly believed in and consulted 'healers'. Her overwhelming interest in, and penetrating analyses of, other people's love lives could itself be ascribed to the possession of a sense beyond her ordinary senses. She could reach out of herself uncannily and inhabit another person's life; perhaps it was more comfortable for her to occupy lives other than her own. Even the translations she did for Nancy Cunard, Natalie Barney, Lily de Clermont-Tonnerre, and other writers were a kind of adoption of another person's territory; a way of speaking in a voice not her own.

Vyvyan Holland wrote in his journal that one time Dolly

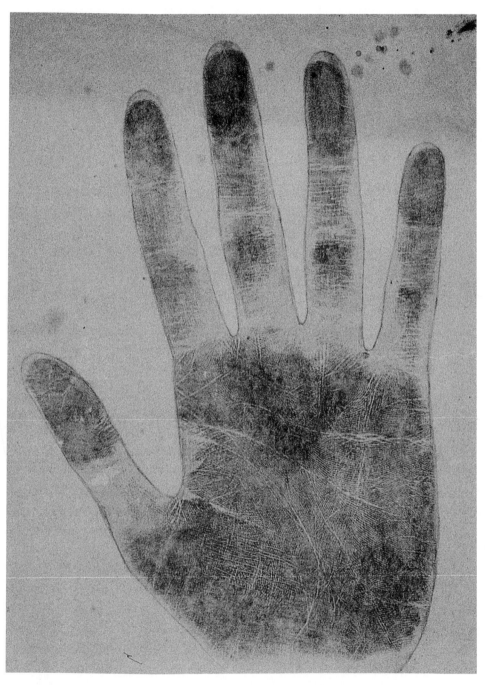

(See Appendix 3, 'Dolly's Right Hand' for Dr Josephine Day's reading of this print.)

I 4

Dolly and the Doctors

The last two days I have had a bad cold & a tempera-
ture – but I am paying for not allowing my pleasures to be
interrupted & to-day am in bed – my death bed I feel.
Mourn for me, dear, tender, heartless paradoxical ama-
zone & mingle your love & regret!

Dolly Wilde to Natalie Barney

Your fever is my temperature . . .

Natalie Barney to Dolly Wilde

ll her life Dolly Wilde was interested in doctors and
illness – and with good reason: she was so often ill herself.
After the drugs had compromised her immune system, there was the
alcohol to add assault to injury. And before the alcohol and the
drugs, there was Dolly's constant, restless travelling that seemed to lay
her open to every microbe and bacterial infection anxious to hitch a
ride on the *Flèche d'Or*, the Golden Arrow, the luxury boat-train Dolly
used to ride from Paris to London, always taking with her a fresh
brioche wrapped in a napkin to eat on the way.[1]

Dolly's lovely blue eyes developed infections, styes, and chalazions.
Her lungs filled up with water. Her physical temperatures fluctuated

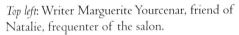

Top left: Writer Marguerite Yourcenar, friend of Natalie, frequenter of the salon.

Top right: Writer Marcelle Fauchier Delavigne, one of Dolly's '*deux amies incomparables*,' painted by Ochsé.

Centre right: Journalist Janet Flanner: more than an artistic interest in Dolly.

Bottom left: Raconteuse Bettina Bergery contemplating her opposite. 1948.

Bottom right: Painter Marie Laurencin, who met and appreciated Dolly at rue Jacob.

Amateur theatricals, malicious intentions: lawyer Nadine Hwang and friends.

Valéry Larbaud, Nadine Hwang, and Natalie Barney in middle-age, looking, said Bettina Bergery, 'like Benjamin Franklin.'

Dolly, Baba Beaton (Cecil's sister), Karen Lancaster, and friends at Bembridge.

Natalie Barney in her garden in old age, still swinging.

Antoinette Gentien. 'Yes Paris still harbours many an old mistress of Miss Wilde . . .' wrote Nancy Mitford.

Katy Fenwick and Dolly Wilde travelling: on a postcard.

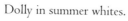

Dolly in summer whites.

Nature morte:
Dolly and tree.
1935?

Dolly as her uncle Oscar: posed as the
photograph of a photograph.

Oscar as Oscar. Dolly 'looked
most like Oscar when she was
dressed up as herself.'

The lion in winter: Natalie in late life, still accompanied by a photograph of Romaine Brooks.

Dolly in distress: perhaps one of the last photographs.

Natalie on her 95th birthday: dedicated to Berthe Cleyrergue. 31 October, 1971.

The mysterious snapshot of Dolly: *'encore belle, encore jeune, encore avide.'*

Berthe Cleyrergue speaking about Dolly Wilde to the author. 25 November, 1995.

suspected (rightly) that he had 'a sleeping appointment' with a woman she knew and that she tried her best to get the information out of him. Holland, stating the case largely, said he believed Dolly would as soon have slept with him herself as let him get away to that appointment.[24] Dolly's anxiety to have her intuitions confirmed is a measure of how much they meant to her — and of how much of her emotional attention she put into other people's lives.

'Love's Intelligence Service' was definitely Dolly's major contribution to military matters. It was part of the imaginative work she did in changing the life around her into a semblance of art. Some of this instinct to transform she practised on herself: she had a performer's unconscious ability to change her face or her apparent age at a moment's notice. '. . . With my usual facility for looking ill or well, pretty or ugly, at short notice, I feel much better & *very* happy,' she wrote to Natalie.[25] Her slippery, mutable spirit liked to move around and multiply itself into various characters and attitudes. People were always noticing how 'different' or how 'changed' she looked. Dolly's resemblance to Oscar was only one of her many ways of presenting herself.

Dolly's nearly alchemical capacity for conversion showed up most creatively in the relations she invented between her friends and the literary characters she admired; making the friends feel witty and wonderful by turning their lives into literature, and exercising some of her gifts by turning *her* life into a work of art. Bettina Bergery wrote that life for Dolly was

a *roman à clés*. The people she knew were really people from books: George Beckwith, for example, was Peter Whiffle by Carl van Vechten, Daisy Fellowes . . . was the Empress Elizabeth of Austria. [Princess] Violet Murat came out of Grimm's Fairy Tales: 'The Princess who was changed into a Frog' . . . Natalie was Balzac's Serepheta, Lucien Vogel was Mr. Pickwick . . . 'Darling,' Dolly would telephone, 'Eleanor Wylie's Venetian Glass nephew wants to meet you.'[26]

And Dolly thought Anne Green, the novelist Julien Greene's sister, was really Louisa May Alcott.

Dolly's metaphors always display an Ovidian sense of instability and of the easy way matter can be transformed into something less weighty, something lighter and lovelier to bear. And so her 'addiction to drugs' could be converted into a kind of respectable insomnia through the magic medium of a doctor's prescription. And her 'cancerous tumours' could be changed by the waters of Lourdes into nothing more than troublesome cysts.

There was something in Dolly's make-up – something to do with her restless spirit and its tentative attachment to her body – that evaded all attempts by doctors to 'treat' her. Whether it was drug cures or cancer protocols, conventional medicine entirely failed her, as Natalie Barney thought she herself had done, 'first and last'.

Those constant fevers Dolly had that expressed themselves through so many different little illnesses; the heightened emotional temperature which added such vividness to her performance when she was 'up', and then crashed it like a light plane when she was 'down'; all the precipitous peaks and dangerous drops were so much a part of Dolly's *chatoyant* character that 'treating' her medically was like trying to coax the mercury back into a broken thermometer: when the doctors got too close Dolly just divided into bright little bits of glittering material and rolled away. The subtlety of her biological systems, her success in evading anything she didn't want to do, her distracting charm, were altogether too much for the simple crudities of 'modern' medicine. Dolly's doctors were placed in the impossible position of crane operators trying to pick up a quark with a bucket loader.

'I am a darting trout,' Dolly wrote, 'shifting, glancing & flashing iridescent tail in a hundred pleasant pools!'[27]

Many times in her life Dolly tried to leave her body, presumably for a better world. Drugs and day-dreams and sex and suicide were only four of her more expedient ways of extracting her soul from her flesh. If she'd had the discipline for a spiritual practice – she wished she had (and once spent an extra hour in a car just to hear Allanah

Harper discourse on a System of Metaphysics), but knew she hadn't.
Or if she could have settled for her friend Jean Bourgoint's ascetic
solution, life in an African monastery looking after lepers . . . but, of
course, that wasn't Dolly. Dolly was a voluptuary. She lived in the day,
in the moment; and the moment, like Dolly herself, has no conception of time or of what she called 'reality'. 'The dead level of reality',
Dolly said repeatedly, is 'flat & terrifying'; it always stole 'in on imagination and disturbed my heart'.[28] Truth, for Dolly, 'was like Loie
Fuller: a rather ugly lady always on the stage, who twirled continually
in draperies and whose appearance and shape depended on the colour
of the light reflected on her . . .'[29]

One 'grey day' in February 1939 when Dolly was visiting the
unhappy disorder in Gwen Farrar's house on the King's Road and
hearing 'the monstrous rhythm of worries ringing in one's ears', a
package of seductively 'feminine' presents — silk pyjamas and a beautiful handbag — arrived from Natalie Barney.

> Like the endless reflections of mirrors in your bedroom, these
> delicate presents refracted thoughts — as mirrors refract
> light — making me aware of an order of life where all is
> disciplined routine, & fastidiousness & the niceties of life the
> greatest common denominator! As if during a period of mun-
> dane worries over servants, bills & ugly details of life one
> suddenly plunged one's face into a bunch of lilies-of-the-
> valley . . .[30]

Dolly's desire for a life 'out of time' and 'out of this world' was
both the stance of an accomplished escape artist and the position of
a woman with strong spiritual yearnings. It was also a dangerously
impractical way to live. Dolly knew this and wondered seriously if she
would 'ever get through life'.[31]

Getting through life means applying discipline to time. Without a
sense of time passed in disciplined occupation, Dolly could get nothing measurable done — least of all joining the split between her

attachment to her body (the most 'real' of all her worldly baggage) and her interest in leaving it. She could 'prove Pascal wrong' by staying unhappily alone in a room, but she could never disprove Descartes. Dolly 'loved life and didn't like it'[32] and she brought the doubleness of this attitude to all her many meetings with the medical profession.

Dolly's persistent illnesses had a distinctive way of placing her in custodial relationships to both friends and strangers, on whose kindnesses she then depended. Every public breakdown of health or nerves (there were awful ones in private as well) allowed her to be cosseted and cared for, gave her a temporary 'home life' and the kind of 'family' which only Natalie Barney's personality and establishment provided with any regularity. 'Darling Natalie, Am I in disgrace? I should be! I have had a very happy summer staying in the country — but London is lonely & depressing & I am longing to get back to family life with you!'[33]

Of course the sole home Dolly could allow herself was an impermanent one like Natalie Barney's *pavillon* — and the only way she could sustain her feelings for it (the most recurrent one being regret for its loss) was to run away from Natalie repeatedly, or to suffer Natalie's running away from her. 'Am I to prove myself stronger in resistance than you?' Dolly wrote. 'You usurp my territory & would take possession of the whole map!'[34] Within the caretaking arrangements Dolly made for herself by being ill (rather than the ones she made for herself by being in love) she managed to find another interesting way of exerting control: she used her doctor's diagnoses and prescriptions to suit herself.

Dolly's very serious illness in Venice in 1928 — it was diphtheria and it almost killed her — began when she went to bed with a 'stupid temperature & sore throat and woke up almost in delirium' with a raging fever and an abscessed throat. The abscess was cut out by a doctor, but the infection spread. One side of her face and throat swelled up alarmingly and she had to be transported to the British American hospital in a closed launch, accompanied by a nurse and a specialist. She was so rheumatic that her whole body had to be wrapped in bandages; she looked, she said, like 'a white China doll'. It was feared she would suffocate or die of septicaemia.

The 'darling Cunards' – Victor, Edward and Nancy – who were renting Lady Juliet Duff's famously beautiful Palazzo Vendramin at the time, and whom Dolly had principally gone to visit, danced attendance on her during this crisis. They even slept in the hospital one night. 'I was too ill to do anything so they did it all,' wrote Dolly, who loved having 'all' done for her. She was thrilled with the 'deep kindness' of the Cunards and delighted to have found a 'clever doctor' – 'I couldn't have done better even at home.' She had to have expensive serums sent from Bologna and a special nurse brought in from Rome. Of course Natalie Barney paid and paid.

Natalie wrote to Dolly too – persistent, worried, and very loving letters offering to rush to Venice and to rescue or give aid to 'my darling, my Dolly Wilde'. 'What a separator illness is – that I should have to be considered a 'visitor' and perhaps not even admitted to you is hard to get into my head and heart . . .'[35] Natalie wanted to secure a room at the American Hospital at Neuilly for Dolly when she was well enough to travel, reassuring her that the American Hospital was so comfortable that patients stayed in it long after they were cured just to enjoy the care. But Dolly, who loved Venice because 'it satisfies almost everything in me', continued to put Natalie off.

Natalie suspected that she was being deterred because of the presence in Venice of a 'very occupying damzel', a Miss Pater, and continued to inquire about her in her letters. Dolly avoided the subject of Miss Pater – although she must have been pleased to entertain someone with the same name as Walter Pater, the man who had so affected her uncle Oscar – and pleaded the dangers of infection, her inability to write lovingly because of her worry over a motor trip that Natalie was taking, her illness, her weakness, etc., etc.

Dolly sometimes liked to use medical opinion to turn her convalescences into avoidances (another kind of transformation), while she toyed with other, more interesting possibilities – although it was often Natalie who did the actual postponing. But Dolly had also written that 'distance creates enchantment' so perhaps she was merely allowing herself the full-blown feelings of love that were available to her only in separation and solitude.

Solitude was a state Dolly often craved after one of her crises, and carefully measured doses of solitude usually restored her soul. But Natalie suspected and said that Dolly was using her convalescence to remain in Venice's 'strange fancy dress society' (Byron had called the Piazza San Marco 'the drawing room of Europe') for far less innocent purposes. Naturally, Dolly was to remember this Venice episode as an occasion when Natalie had 'abandoned' her. 'Perhaps I expect too much from you & should have realized that Lily & Romaine are the only people you give spiritually to, to the others material gifts, & I should have learnt this as long ago as Venice, when you didn't come.'[36]

Dolly's 'suicides' – both the conscious and the unconscious ones – usually brought out the very best in the people who 'saved' her. Her character and her plight, like her uncle Oscar's, continued to elicit sympathy and acts of kindness from even the most casual of contacts. In her 1934 suicide attempt in London, a Dr Duseau looked after Dolly 'with great sympathy and infinite sacrifice'. In Dolly's suicide attempt in Paris in 1931, Berthe Cleyrergue stayed with Dolly night and day for an entire week, then cosseted her for a month. Nora O'Shaughnesey, the Irish housekeeper of her service flat in London, saved Dolly's life on two occasions and was perhaps 'the Irish nurse' who accompanied her on her last trip to Paris. And Natalie Barney, sometimes complaining, sometimes silent, always requiring receipts, continued to handle many of Dolly's medical bills, sharing the burden a little with Marcelle Fauchier Delavigne and Honey Harris. It is a measure of Natalie's solicitude that in her address book there is a list of doctors who dealt only with Dolly's various 'conditions'.

Although Dolly was generally efficient about distributing her debts amongst her friends for these expensive 'suicides', when she couldn't do so it was disastrous for her and added to the weight of worries – 'the dull reality' which she knew she had no business dealing with. Still, Dolly usually managed to wake up from her 'suicides' to the very best medical care and continued to have it even after she died. Her last doctor — from Dolly's point of view an unsympathetic one in that he refused to increase her heroin dosage — was an expensive Sloane Street physician and the two physicians and the coroner who took the evidence for her autopsy were all celebrated specialists.

Each of Dolly's four documented attempts on her own life occurred during her relationship with Natalie Barney. The timing of these attempts supports the widely whispered opinion that Natalie, with her multiple-choice relationships and powerful will, was hell on wheels to love. But Dolly's own deep need for separation — a true character trait that sometimes masqueraded as a response to Natalie's infidelities — did not exactly allow for close and comfortable pairing. For the most part, responsibility for the turbulence of their relations can be shared with something like relative equality. Still, there is little doubt that Dolly became increasingly addicted as Natalie continued her *laissez-faire* behaviour — and Dolly continued hers. And there is no doubt at all that it was Natalie's grip that was on the purse strings. The money was always Natalie's, the overt power was hers as well, and so was the control.

Still, it was not just that Dolly's recorded 'suicides' happened during her lengthy love affair with Barney; it was also that Dolly's attraction to death and/or unconsciousness seemed to be *sparked* by troubles in love. Love and death were Dolly's magnetic North and South — and if she couldn't go in one direction, she usually went in the other.

Dolly never tried to kill herself in a nursing home, a sanatorium, or a hospital. She got enough 'home care', enough of a simulacrum of 'family life', in those various establishments to keep her away from suicide while she was still a patient; and she never tried to kill herself in Natalie Barney's house either. It was only when she was alone too long in her service flat or shut up in a public hotel after some kind of emotional crisis that she went for the most extreme solution. Splitting her attempts on her life as she split her life, Dolly tried twice to kill herself at the Hôtel Astoria in Paris and twice at her flat in London.

But it was a nursing home — or more precisely, it was the prescription of a *doctor* in a nursing home — which provided Dolly with the drug that probably helped her to her death.

On Dolly's October 1939 requisition lists and receipts from the Wilbraham Nursing Home are many items that should never have been placed anywhere near a potential suicide.[37] Among the products she was given are quantities of unspecified drugs, razor blades, hypodermic needles and aspirin. Wine — a standard item on the nursing home receipt — is always cancelled out on Dolly's bills. By 1939 alcoholism had become a threat and Dolly was not allowed to order wine or spirits.[38]

On her receipt from the Wilbraham for the week of 25 October 1939 the name of the drug paraldehyde is written in over the crossed-out category of 'Wine'. Paraldehyde is the over-the-counter sleeping draught that figured in Dolly's death. In a 1941 letter dated three months after Dolly's demise, the British novelist Nancy Mitford wrote, inimitably, to her sister, Jessica Mitford Romilly, the story of Dolly's death she heard from Victor Cunard:

> Oh dear I minded very much about Miss Wilde. So many of my best friends are now dead — still it will make heaven more matey in a way. Miss Wilde did not exactly commit it — she was terribly ill & the [doctor] said if she went on taking some drug it would kill her in the end so she did & it did. But that's not *quite* the same as holding one's head under the tap is it? Victor Cunard says she was quite jolly & herself to the end.[39]

Only Dolly, with her instinctive attraction to paradox, could have checked into a nursing home to get rid of one drug — and come out saddled and bridled with another one. In the process, she created a whole new category of medical irony: the heroin whose daily dosage she had presumably reduced at the Wilbraham Nursing Home was illegal and dangerous to procure, while the paraldehyde she came back addicted to could be bought without prescription at any chemist's in Chelsea. The drug that turned out to be the most dangerous drug for Dolly was the one a doctor had introduced her to.

The very last story told about Dolly, other than the Chesham Place waiter's careful report of her solitary final meal, is a medical one. At least it involves a quasi-medical diagnosis. The story comes from a man whose name was in Natalie Barney's *carnet d'adresse*, Dr Robert LeMasle. Dr LeMasle was a friend of Proust's doctor-brother, a frequenter of the Barney salon, a friend of Marie Laurencin and of Berthe Cleyrergue and her husband Henri, but beyond that, what? His connections with the Barney circle were aesthetic, but what did LeMasle mean to Dolly – with her too-convenient, ever-expanding collection of narcotic-prescribing physicians? Was he another one of the many doctors who supplied her with morphine and heroin?

A fortnight before Dolly's death in 1941, Dr Robert LeMasle knocked on the door of Berthe and Henri Cleyrergue's small apartment at 20 rue Jacob while they were still having breakfast. Knowing Berthe's special relationship with Dolly – and perhaps reluctant to relay such a story to Natalie herself who had, anyway, refugeed to Florence – LeMasle arrived to tell the Cleyrergues that he had just returned from London where entirely by chance he came upon Dolly Wilde passed out on a bench in a square in Westminister. She was dead drunk, he said. *Ivre-morte.*[40]

As a doctor, LeMasle would certainly have tried to minister to Dolly's condition. Perhaps he took her back in a taxi to the Normandy Hotel, her last residence before her move to Chesham Place the following week. If Dolly came to any kind of consciousness, she would have been astonished and embarrassed to be seen intoxicated by someone she knew from Paris, someone who also knew Natalie Barney. There may have been some conversation between Dolly and Dr LeMasle: perhaps some final words of admonition and medical advice from him, perhaps an attempt at witty diversion from her. But the story ends – as did Dolly's life – without the crucial details that would allow a resolving finish to this strange

I5

Dolly's Addictions

I feel a drug-fiend dipping secretly into a packet of cocaine – ever-exhilarated, ever tremulous, ever comforted at the thought of you.

Dolly Wilde, letter to Natalie Barney

. . . I can scarcely keep count of the various doctors I have got hold of from time to time to disintoxicate her.

Tancred Borenius, letter to Natalie Barney

No one knows into how many icy baths Dolly – in her pretty party dresses – was dumped to counteract an overdose. Or how many times she was slapped awake so that a fatal doze could be walked off. Who pounded her chest to start the heart stopped by a drug rush? Who helped her tie off the punctured veins that would not stop spurting?

Dolly died violently – a pop-star end we would call it today – face-down and cyanosed on a rented floor. Before her death, she had experienced many of the ugly 'realities' that injecting heroin entails. But Dolly, who was also addicted to beauty, never wrote about them.

The surprising thing was how many people made efforts to help her when her worst days came on. So many doctors, lovers, maids, and companions were willing to see beyond their anger at her 'paralysis of the mind' and 'hopeless habits' of self-destruction, and to go beyond their exasperation at her 'satellite' life and profligate 'waste' of talent. Friends and strangers alike continued to spell each other in the work of watchful attention that keeping Dolly alive turned into — until, at the very last, their numbers dwindled down to a handful of loyalists.

Perhaps Dolly's susceptibility to drugs began with her delight in day-dreaming, in the kind of self-hypnosis that produces a pleasurable trance.

> Strange this last week how dazed I've felt — charmingly
> drugged — in a dream . . . I feel asleep — with all sleep's soft
> indifference. How dangerous to tell you all this — . . . when
> tonight or tomorrow that strange drug will wear off & every
> vibrant feeling will sweep over me — drowning me deliciously
> in its flood — if you are there.[1]

'Day-dreaming' presents different conditions from the crude realities of finding a viable vein in your arm or sticking a needle into your thigh. But the ends of day-dreaming are exactly the same as those of injecting heroin or morphine: an exit — with anger suppressed — from the 'sense of reality'. Dolly wrote often and eloquently about how much she hated 'flat reality'.

The closest Dolly ever came to describing an 'altered' state was in a letter to Natalie Barney written sometime in 1928. Natalie was in Algeria, Dolly was feeling neglected, and she dropped a hint about 'day-dreaming' in public. The condition she described to Natalie could have been a self-induced trance or it could have been a veiled allusion to a blissed-out, opiated high. Whatever it was, the pleasure Dolly took in it was almost criminal: 'That illicit dreaming done under the very nose of everybody — that apparent attention that sublime inattention — has a certain strange excitement that the unchartered dreaming of solitude lacks. All is perverse.'[2]

The Cures

There is a fatality about all good resolutions. They are invariably made too soon.

Oscar Wilde

On 21 July 1939, ten days after Dolly's forty-fourth birthday, Natalie Barney received this letter from a Monsieur Toulouse, the manager of Dolly's favourite hotel in Paris, the Hôtel Montalembert, where Dolly had been an intermittent guest since its opening in 1926.

HÔTEL MONTALEMBERT, 3 RUE MONTALEMBERT, PARIS 7e

Madame,

You have been suggested to me by various friends of Miss D. Wilde as being the person who has the greatest influence upon her . . . At this very moment she is drinking so much alcohol that a crisis of fever and delirium tremens cannot help but follow, as well as further consequences up to and undeniably including the possibility of suicide.

In addition to which, Miss Wilde emits piercing cries all night long alternating from time to time with groans which disturb her neighbours.

I would be infinitely grateful to you if you could use your

influence over her to make her listen to reason and if you could remove her to a sanatorium.[3]

Drinking was almost the least of Dolly's addictions, but it was the noisiest. Dolly raged and wept when she was intoxicated. She shut herself up and howled out the terrors that her daily dose of self-mockery usually deterred. Dolly's drunken misery at the Hôtel Montalembert — grotesquely preserved in M Toulouse's sober formalities — moved Natalie quickly to action. Natalie and probably Marcelle Fauchier Delavigne and Honey Harris persuaded Dolly to go to Chiswick House, a suburban nursing home in Pinner near London, from which Dolly sent this reassuring telegram: ARRIVED PINNER ALL LOVE ALL WELL[4]

Dolly and her friends were embarking on yet another attempt to separate Dolly from what Gertrude Stein would have called her 'bottom nature'. The hell of rage and despair into which Dolly had just tumbled was an habitual one: it always opened up just before or just after Dolly began one of her 'cures'. Her quick wit and transformative talents usually prevented these appalling falls into the pit, but not when she was drugging or drinking. At those times, after the first 'careless rapture' disappeared, she dropped into a misery as palpable as fact.

On 4 August 1939, Dolly telegraphed Natalie that she had come up to London from her nursing home, Chiswick House, 'for treatment' (X-ray treatments for the cysts in her breast). The telegram reassured Natalie that Dolly was 'returning tonight' to Chiswick House, that she was 'unrecognisably well', and that she would be 'writing'.[5]

On 15 August 1939 Jessie Wadsworth, the Matron of Chiswick House, sent Natalie this cheerful, bluff, optimistic report on Dolly's progress.

Dear Miss Barney,

I cannot tell you how delighted we are with Miss Wilde, there is really a marvellous improvement.

Her average injection [of heroin] for the past eight days has
been cut down to ¼ grain a day, in comparison to I grain a
day which she was taking before this. The whisky has been cut
right out of the menu & two ½ pint bottles of lager, seem to
be quite sufficient.

It is such a pleasure to have her with us as she is such good
company, & we are all so delighted at the very determined
effort she is making.[6]

Dolly, like the darling daughter she yearned to be, reverted to her
best behaviour for the staff of Chiswick House and the kindly
Matron fell before her social charms. But Dolly's repeated disintoxications were *always* punctuated by hopeful letters like Miss
Wadsworth's, *always* provoked by alarmed warnings like M Toulouse's,
and *always* underlined by Dolly's own sincere, telegrammed assurances
of recovery and reform. And the pattern of despair, false hope, and
eventual disgust and/or anger (in both Dolly and her friends) created
by Dolly's regular relapses continued also to repeat itself in each new
situation — altered only by the circumstances and intensity of Dolly's
very real distress.

Since the early 1930s, Natalie Barney, Tancred Borenius, Honey
Harris, Marchelle Fauchier Delavigne, Lady Carnarvon, Victor
Cunard and many other friends of Dolly had been witnessing her
'breakdowns' and stage-managing her 'cures'. What, exactly, she was
being cured *of* was never a simple matter — nor was it often properly
diagnosed — and this will be taken up later in the chapter. The by-now
familiar report from the manager of the Hôtel Montalembert to
Natalie had a prototype in a letter sent from London in the fall of
1934 by Tancred Borenius to Natalie at her country villa in
Beauvallon. The picture it draws of Dolly — a hopelessly abandoned
child, drowning not waving — seems so horrifyingly beyond repair
that Natalie's and Borenius's obvious reluctance to once again hoist up
the wreck of Dolly's life is understandable.

<u>Private & Confidential</u>

Dear Miss Barney

. . . Last night in a moment of great depression [Dolly] took an over-dose of sleeping draught, *and* cut an artery in her wrist: the excellent maid of 14 Queen St. found her collapsed and with blood streaming. The Dr . . . writes me that the important thing . . . is that she should be with a *friend all the time.* That is why he asked me to communicate with you, asking you to come & take her away, giving her *companionship & home life*, which, however much I try to see her, I cannot give her . . .

If therefore you can come, do come; that *will* save her — I see no other possibility, or I would not have wired . . .[7]

Natalie's response, pieced together with interpolations and deletions from a scratch copy in her files, sounds petulant and ungenerous, but by now Natalie had come to Dolly's rescue many times, offering love (but not exclusive love) and money (but Dolly was made to keep a strict account of her debts to Natalie) to the recidivist Dolly, who was sometimes ungrateful and always relcacitrant.

Dear Doctor Borenius,

. . . Will you kindly give me news of D's state, explain minutely the situation to me . . . — has she no friends in London nearer than I am who could come to her aid — is Lady C. [Carnarvon] in spite of her . . . great resources not to be counted on? Have you tried?

Aided by my sister I helped D. out of her crisis at Hôtel Astoria last fall . . .

In late summer 1933 Dolly swallowed a whole bottle of sleeping pills in the Hôtel Astoria, writing afterwards: '. . . I had *no* memory of it – & certainly didn't intend to do it . . .' She told Honey Harris that she'd been in a taxi-accident. In 1931, after Natalie ran off with an actress, Dolly cut her wrists in the same hotel and was saved by Berthe Cleyrergue.

> I also paid bills for her this spring & am now stranded & obliged to live on my capital or borrow money.

Natalie's fortune at this time was about four million dollars; like all wealthy expatriates, she had a horror of invading her capital.

> So as I have for years releaved [sic] the strain & rescued D & paid her debts with rent etc time after time I think it unfair that more of her other friends should not do their parts – and you as Dolly's legal guardian can surely manage to move to the best of her advantage.

> . . . because of the suspicious friends D. brought to my house during my absence some time ago [Natalie here means the 'Cocteau set'.] . . . Paris is therefore fatal to her . . .

> I do not wish to default or fail D. in my untiring friendship for her but simply ask to be aided & not always called upon at the last moment to see her through.[8]

Both Tancred Borenius and Natalie knew that Dolly had made another suicide attempt in March 1934. Lacking the funds for a nursing home and back on drugs again, Dolly tried to disintoxicate herself. She began by taking a normal dose of sleeping draught and then '*unconsciously*, in my sleep, I took the whole bottle. I couldn't *imagine* I should do this, especially as they are tablets rather difficult to swallow without water, & the thought never even crossed my mind.'[9]

The quick-witted housekeeper of 14 Queen Street, Nora O'Shaughnessy, once again saved Dolly, who lay unconscious for two and a half days. Lady Carnarvon assumed financial responsibility for Dolly's expensive nursing, but Dolly was left with the 'ruinous' doctor's bills.[10] She woke up to the same reality that had driven her back to drugs: 'endless worries that never seem to be right however much I economise in food, clothes, taxis, etc.'[11]

Dolly wrote pathetically to Natalie at the end of March 1934 that she was eating enough 'but in *very* cheap places where the food is very good but the surroundings awful – no clothes & buses everywhere & I look back even on last year with expensive fancy dresses as madness!' And she wondered what '. . . strange impulse makes me head for destruction, so that even my subconscious dictates death to me? And, stranger still, what guardian rescues me from ultimate disaster over and over again – to what end?'[12] And Dolly once more sincerely promised Natalie that

> this is the end of all that sort of thing . . . and in a week or two this paralysis of the mind will pass: and then I'll come to you (if you will have me darling) and we'll spend a happy spring together and forget all this sort of horror . . .
>
> I should think you'd be finished with me: but *please* don't forsake me, ever . . .
>
> I really mean to take a new lease of life and I feel, somehow, that things are going to be different in every way as if a new star had risen in my firmament which would alter the course of my wavering fate![13]

The 'happy spring' Dolly hoped for, cradled in the 'home life' of Natalie's *pavillon*, was apparently interrupted by the introduction to 20 rue Jacob of Nadine Hwang, Natalie Barney's newest lover. Dolly's September breakdown in the Hôtel Montalembert probably had a lot to do with Nadine.

Tancred Borenius answered Natalie's reluctant letter immediately, writing — as everyone always wrote — to Natalie:

> . . . you are the one person remaining who can do something for her . . . From [Lady Carnarvon] no help can now be got, nor from Honey's mother, who is the only other wealthy friend D. has got; in fact, if Lady H. [Harris] ever knew the truth about D., she would instantly break off all relations with her.
>
> As I explained in my last letter, the only thing that can save Dolly is if she, for some time to come, shares a home & family life with someone . . .[14]

Doctors and friends, as well as Dolly herself, clearly understood that Dolly's aimless wanderings from hotel rooms to bed-sits to borrowed apartments — a pattern begun in the poverty of her childhood when she was moved in and out of her mother's rooms and continued in adulthood with her twinned search for equilibrium and oblivion — was both a source and an expression of her chaotic emotional life. The ambivalence of her suicide attempt in early spring of 1934, when her 'subconscious' prompted her to swallow a bottle of pills 'in her sleep', was entirely absent here: as in her 'suicide' attempt in the Hôtel Astoria in 1931, Dolly hacked away at her wrist and was 'found with blood streaming'.

What is new in the prescription for Dolly's recovery is the acknowledgement that 'family life' — as well as 'home life' — was crucial for her. But despite receiving the regular assistance of friends for the next seven years, Dolly's most consistent 'home life' would be the protocols of sanatoriums; her most frequent experience of 'family life' would come in the care she received from doctors and matrons.

Natalie refused to see Dolly until Dolly had been disintoxicated in a nursing home, sending instead a cheque and a letter to Lady Carnarvon on Dolly's behalf, hoping, obviously, to provoke Lady Carnarvon into sharing the responsibility. And she repeated her opinion to Borenius that Dolly was more likely to have a relapse in Paris than in London and that she, Natalie, was 'not in a position to again resume the whole responsibility of Dolly . . . which has so often fallen on me alone'.[15]

It is possible that this September crisis was the one that finally did provoke Natalie to come over to London to 'rescue' Dolly. In the event, Natalie came – whenever she came – in vain, for Dolly, covered in shame, stung by embarrassment, and craving oblivion, absolutely refused to see her.[16] Whatever else Natalie did at this time, she made certain special ampoules of medication were sent to Dolly by Dr Simon, her own doctor in Paris. Typically, the arrangements for the mailing were made by Natalie's new lover Nadine Hwang – whose presence in Natalie's house had perhaps caused Dolly's collapse in the first place.

The physical and emotional life afforded Dolly by her constant 'cures' affected her like a succession of whiplash injuries. She was violently and repeatedly jerked from the pole of 'health' to the pole of 'addiction' – and back again; with the added burden, in the late 1930s when lumps in her left breast appeared, of contradictory cancer diagnoses coming at her from all quarters. Only someone with Dolly's proven ability to re-enact the drama of the death-rebirth cycle could have born it; on the eve of one disintoxication in July 1936 Dolly compared herself to Mary Queen of Scots 'on the night before her execution'.[17]

Jean Cocteau, whom Gertrude Stein described as priding himself on being 'eternally thirty', had almost certainly supplied opium to Dolly and certainly did supply it to their mutual friends Jean Bourgoint and Jacques Rigaut. He makes a good case for its use in his book *Opium* – in the introduction to which he quotes Dolly's uncle. 'Opium', he wrote, 'becomes tragic in proportion to how it affects the central nerve centres which control the soul. Otherwise, it's an antidote, a pleasure, an extreme siesta.'[18]

Cocteau's experiences with the many 'cures' he underwent struck him as more dangerous than the drug. 'After the cure comes the worst moment, the greatest danger. Health, but with a great hole in it, and immense depression. The doctors loyally hand you over to suicide.'[19]

Almost as bad for Dolly as the failure of her 'cures', was the toll her friends' moral judgements took on her diminishing self-esteem. The judgements are understandable: too many 'cures' had ended in too many relapses, and the people paying for these treatments felt, naturally, that they had an absolute right to issue ultimata about Dolly's 'bad habits'. Meaning to treat her medically, her friends always ended by faulting her morally. Although Dolly's intimates came to her aid in ways that seem almost incomprehensibly generous, the effect on Dolly was awful: these reiterated interventions in Dolly's drug use and self-injury — and Dolly's reactions to them — began to assume the shape of addictions themselves.

All Dolly's letters of apology to Natalie Barney — there are quite a few of them — are pocked and pitted with the complicated explanations that guilt, anger and a disintegrating sense of self produce. She felt horrified by her cancer (a word she never used), afflicted with the alcohol, and damned by her inabilty to keep off heroin. And there was that apparently 'inherited' Wilde passivity — she was always aware of it and called it a 'paralysis of the mind'- which encouraged her to fall apart in circumstances requiring abstinence or decision.[20] In the summer of 1939 (after her 'crisis' at the Montalembert and 'cure' at Chiswick House), her next breakdown was just weeks away.

By the middle of October 1939 a terrified Dolly had shut herself up in the Basil Street Hotel in London — apparently drinking and drugging — weeping that she had to have an operation on her breast tumours and that she wanted Natalie to come over from Paris. Things got so bad that Honey Harris advanced Dolly money to pay her hotel bill and Dolly moved herself 'into a nursing home which I know nothing about — not even where it is'.[21] This relapse, provoked by abscesses under Dolly's arm, which she mistook for a metastasising cancer (the abscesses were brought on by Dolly's dainty use of Odorono, a deodorant powder),[22] provided the occasion for Dolly's first stay at the Wilbraham Nursing Home. On 17 October

Dolly telegrammed to Natalie that she was safely ensconced there.

One of the things Dolly was supplied with at the Wilbraham was Kotex pads.[23] Dolly was still getting her periods, or thought she was. She had, in fact, already entered into an early menopause and could have confused the bleeding from her fibroid tumour (identified in the autopsy report) with her menses. During the week of 25 October 1939 Dolly was introduced to paraldehyde, a drug in liquid form prescribed by a doctor at the Wilbraham.[24] Paraldehyde had another use – it calmed the withdrawal pains of heroin addiction – but it was mostly applied to insomnia and Dolly, as usual, was having a terrible time sleeping.

Dolly, who never used the word 'addict' (just as she never used the word 'cancer') got many of her drugs from prescriptions written by doctors; but she also got them in other places. Berthe Cleyrergue said that when Dolly returned to Paris from Lourdes in 1940, she went out at night continually to buy drugs on the street and no one – not even Berthe – could stop her.[25]

In April 1940, Dolly was again back in Chiswick House, and was once again planning to come to Natalie in the rue Jacob to be looked after by both Natalie and Marcelle Fauchier Delavigne.[26] On the Friday of her proposed departure to Paris Dolly suddenly began to balk at going and by Saturday she had flatly refused to travel, giving 'the International Situation' as her flimsy excuse. This from a woman who had run off to wartime France as a teenager.

Honey Harris thought it was such a shame 'that there were you [Natalie] & Marcelle, so kind & loving & eager to welcome & help her – & there she is with nothing to prevent her coming to you but her own weakness & hopeless habits'.[27] Dolly was four months further along on her dissolving curve of contradictory cancer diagnoses, disintegrating sense of self, moves in and out of nursing homes, regulated amounts of hard drugs, and free access to paraldehyde, and she clearly did not want to conduct a complete disintoxication under the clear, judgemental gaze of her 'dear professor', Natalie Barney.

Honey wrote sadly to Natalie about Dolly:

Since Saturday I hear that she has simply lain in bed in a sort
of stupor . . . drinking Paraldahide (this is phonetic spelling, I
don't know how it should be written) . . . She started to do
this some time ago & then when taxed with it promised to
pull herself together & give it up . . . I must tell you that all
this time she has *seemed perfectly normal to talk to & be with* . . . but
now I find that Dr. Macauley & the Matron both consider her
in such a bad mental state & so difficult to control as she can
buy this stuff anywhere & anytime! that they think she ought
to be temporarily under much stricter supervision which I
suppose means a hospital under certified registration. This
seems dreadful to me . . .[28]

Dolly hadn't paid either her board or her bills for Dr Macauley at
Chiswick House, although she was regularly sent monies by Marcelle
and Natalie for that purpose.[29] Honey's observation about Dolly's
ability to conceal her new addiction from both doctors and old
friends explains why Dolly did so well in nursing homes: she simply
took what she wanted from them, turning them into a kind of
grotesque parody of 'home life'. No one knew where Dolly's money
was going — it could just as easily have been to street drugs or needy
friends — but the Matron at Chiswick House had an interesting
theory: she thought there was a possibility that Dolly was being
blackmailed and said as much to Honey Harris.[30]

Five months before her breakdown in the summer of 1939 —
when her present multiplication of horrors began — Dolly had been
living in London with her lover of more than a year, the Variety
actress Gwen Farrar. Gwen's house was on the King's Road, literally
around the corner from Jane Wilde's house in Oakley Street where
Dolly was born — and a few short blocks from Cheltenham Terrace
where Willy and Lily Wilde lived after Jane Wilde's death. As Dolly's
difficulties increased, she began to circle painfully back around the

landmarks of her Chelsea childhood, lodging herself, emotionally and physically, in the neighbourhood of her earliest memories, perhaps in an attempt to connect the problems of her life with their unspoken, familial causes. Dolly seemed magnetised by her old environs, unable to leave the familiar streets even in reponse to invitations from her worried friends in France.

She haunted hotels in Chelsea, Knightsbridge and Belgravia – the Royal Court and the Basil Street among them – and one of her favourite nursing homes, the Wilbraham, was in Sloane Square, Chelsea's centre. And now this house of Gwen Farrar's on the King's Road was a two-minute walk from the house where Dolly had been born. The apartment she moved to briefly when she separated from Gwen – a flat in Joe Carstairs's Mulberry Walk house – was also in Chelsea; and her final lodging at Twenty Chesham Place was within view of a Chelsea landmark that had a terrible significance for the Wilde family: the Cadogan Hotel on Sloane Street, where Oscar was first taken into custody and where his creative life effectively ended.

Gwen Farrar, the woman with whom Dolly was living at this time, was a tallish woman with a black bob, a deep singing voice, and a comedic flair. She was the daughter of a baronet and had been left a comfortable fortune and a trustee to manage it. (Trustees are usually allocated when an heir is considered untrustworthy: Gwen probably had a *mis*-trust fund.) She fell in love with Dolly sometime in 1937 or 1938. Gwen was a talented and, for a time, highly paid musician and comedian; she had acted, sung and played the cello with her partner Norah Blaney in a series of well-known Variety acts in London and New York, and in provincial Variety theatres in England. She also produced plays, wrote revues, and appeared in operas. She was a prize-winning horsewoman, had been a lover of Dolly's old wartime lover, Joe Carstairs, and was a friend – and had been a lover – of Tallulah Bankhead.[31]

Gwen was also an intermittent alcoholic and she, too, was to die at forty-five, three and a half years after Dolly. Although Gwen was deeply concerned with Dolly's various 'conditions' and spent time, trouble, and money on them, she was unable to provide the orderly home life that Dolly craved. In a letter to Natalie Barney in February 1938, apologising for some rude incident sparked, probably, by a custody battle for Dolly's emotional welfare, Gwen wrote: 'Please try to forgive me & realize my only aim & ambition in life is for her to be cured really cured because I really love her as much as you & shall worry always until she is well.'[32] Dolly thought Gwen was 'intellectually starved' and couldn't help making comparisons between the demi-literacies of Gwen's theatre crowd and the elevated exchanges of the 'Knights of Natalie's Round Table'.

Gwen earned the contempt of Natalie and the unspoken dislike of Honey, both of whom thought that her alcoholism and constant partying added a new terror to Dolly's cancer worries and drug use. Dolly had written to Natalie that Gwen's house often resembled a 'bar' and that when she was with Gwen, she began to drink defensively and 'too much'.[33] Lauretta Hugo, the widow of Victor Hugo's grandson Jean Hugo, who described Gwen as 'very lesbian', went to a party at Gwen's and had the same experience that Tancred Borenius's daughter had at Natalie Barney's: she was frightened by what she saw the women doing.[34] During her relationship with Gwen, Dolly added alcoholism to her list of addictions.

In November 1938 Dolly was feeling somewhat hopeful about her relationship with Gwen Farrar. Gwen was a disciplined worker when it came to her *métier* – and it was too bad for Dolly that she couldn't diagnose her own distress with the same cold eye she cast on Gwen's drinking: 'I know it sounds great weakness on her part – but only companionship or work keep her straight . . . While working she is always as good as gold & it is unfortunate that the last two years she has not worked . . .'[35]

But Dolly's need for solitude in the relationship was immense and unsatisfied – and her craving for literate companionship was unfulfilled. Even Gwen was bemoaning the fact that there wasn't a 'London Natalie' for Dolly to talk to. Dolly's 'addiction' to good conversation was as unbreakable as any of her other habits. Dolly felt obligated to Gwen, who was probably helping to support her financially and certainly emotionally, and she made an effort to bolster Gwen up for a return to the stage. But Dolly's lack of spontaneous enthusiasm for the project of bolstering Gwen is expressed in this unironic sentence she wrote to Natalie from Gwen's house: 'How lucky we have all been to have been in love with you – where no duty prevailed, no obligations – only those of love & enjoyment!'

In February 1939, Dolly 'parted for good' from Gwen and was once more without a 'home life' – even such a one as Gwen had provided.

> With all Gwen's sweetness & devotion our whole relationship has been in the nature of a bargain it seems to me. 'Give me stimulation, enchant me, make up for all my years of mental starvation & I'll be your slave' has been her motif. But 'be depressed, lose your vitality, cease feeding my desire to be amused, enchanted & you no longer interest me'. . . A slovenly, impossible atmosphere . . . undermined what little discipline a 'Wilde' possesses!!

> . . . I rescued her from miserable boredom & unhappiness among a crowd of spongers whom she hated, & for the most part gave her a year of devotion & stimulation, ending in a nervous breakdown on my part from which I recovered in the sanctuary of a small hotel bedroom.[36]

Although Dolly described herself as a 'stimulant', she was not interested in being used as one – and there is distinct irritation in her remark that the hotel bedroom she 'recovered in' was a 'small' one. Gwen and Dolly were still going back and forth about their relationship many months after it had supposedly 'ended', and Dolly wrote to Natalie that Gwen was:

> . . . what I used to call Marcelle [Fauchier Delavigne] – 'le cheval pie' – every virtue with a paradoxical contradiction . . .

I am *really* fond of her, nearly always worried over her, &
always touched by her. We have made it up as I told you, but
her reliance on me for stimulation apart from her suffering by
my not being in love with her makes companionship very difficult . . .[37]

Dolly did love Gwen's 'pretty house' but the pallor of her 'fond'
feelings for Gwen and 'the burden' of Gwen's love are apparent in
Dolly's letters — and must have been especially apparent to Gwen. An
'excess of love' on Gwen's part, unmatched on Dolly's, was making
Dolly ill-tempered. '. . . To "love" someone is, it seems to me, as
painful as to be "in love" — & to witness pain in that person is to have
a perpetual ache in one's heart.'[38]

The turmoil caused by the drunken parties and disorderly doings at
Gwen's — and by Dolly's moving in and out of the house — greatly contributed to Dolly's destabilisation. Natalie Barney blamed Gwen for
this, and continued to do so long after Dolly's death. But Gwen Farrar
had nothing to do with Dolly's drug habits and Natalie knew it.

The Flowers of Evil

*Not the opium-eater, but the opium, is the true hero of the
tale . . .*

Thomas De Quincey

In 1936 Cole Porter's cleverly written song, 'I've Got You Under My
Skin' was a big success in New York and London. A few of Porter's
friends insisted that the title was a *double entendre*; that it referred not
only to the kind of love that burrowed 'into the heart of me' but also
to the hypodermic needle that was slipped under the skin and delivered a substance just as addicting as love. By the time Porter's song
was being danced to in nightclubs in Paris and London, Dolly had

been hooked on what went under her skin for perhaps eight years. But this cannibal part of Dolly's life – the urgent, addictive beast that ended by making a meal of much of the rest of her – was almost never conveyed in what she said or wrote.

According to the (sometimes less than accurate) memoirs of Mercedes de Acosta,[39] Dolly Wilde was a fully-fledged morphine addict by 1928. Victor Cunard, Dolly's closest male friend and, Berthe Cleyrergue said, yet another homosexual man who proposed to her, hinted in Dolly's memorial book who it was that gave Dolly her first serious drugs. 'I remember so vividly her bringing J. R. to dinner on the quai de Conti soon after she had found her way into the false paradise of which he held the key.'[40]

'J. R.' was Jacques Rigaut, an admirer of Dolly's cousin Arthur Cravan, a great friend of Dolly herself, and the creator of the Surrealist catchphrase: *'Je serais sérieux comme le plaisir.'* When he was twenty years old, in 1919, he announced that he would kill himself at the age of thirty.[41] In 1929, at the age of thirty, he did so, shooting himself in the head and inspiring a sad letter from Dolly to Honey Harris.[42]

Rigaut's life was the basis for central characters in two of his friend Pierre Drieu La Rochelle's novels: *Plainte contre un inconnu* and *Le Feu follet. Feu follet* was made into a film by Louis Malle, and one scene, shot on location, features the spoiled and unhappy young protagonist (who keeps sheaves of good shirts in his *maison de santé* in Versailles) walking in the garden of Natalie Barney's *pavillon* with a young woman played by Jeanne Moreau. The back of Natalie's salon room is perfectly visible in the film and books are piled high against the windows. Berthe Cleyrergue, who helped a bit with the production, said that a character in the film was based on Dolly[43] – probably the young woman played by Jeanne Moreau, who appears first in an art gallery, then in Natalie's garden, then in a milieu where drugs are the centre of the conversation and where she exhibits deep sympathy with the unhappy protagonist.

Jacques Rigaut was a friend of Jean Cocteau and also of Jean Bourgoint, Dolly's other great friend in 'the Cocteau set', and Dolly was taken with the writer René Crevel, whose highly coloured stories fascinated her. But it was Jean Bourgoint who was her particular friend. Ten years younger than Dolly, he was beautiful, artistic, lithe as a cat, and consistently drugged, thanks to Cocteau, who had blown a puff of opium into his mouth in 1925 and taken him for a lover. Jean was completely obsessed by his beautiful older sister, Jeanne, who shared a fetishistically decorated room with him and killed herself with barbiturates in 1929.[44]

When Cocteau made his film, *Les Enfants Terribles*, rifled from the lives of the Bourgoint siblings, could he have been thinking of Dolly's travesties of Oscar? He made the oddly inappropriate selection of a woman to play the boy-fascinator Dargelos in the film, a selection which is inconsistent with his stricter aesthetic formalities. Cocteau would certainly have heard the story of Dolly dressed as Oscar at the duchesse de Clermont-Tonnerre's *bal masqué*, possibly from Dolly herself, and he may even have been present to see it. And he was fascinated enough with Oscar to have sent a highly decorative letter to his surviving son Vyvyan, after meeting Vyvyan in Venice in 1908.[45]

Both Berthe Cleyrergue and Natalie Barney blamed Dolly's drug use on members of the 'Cocteau set'. Certainly Dolly circulated through all their favourite *boîtes*, like *Le Boeuf sur le Toit*, and continued to spend time with Cocteau regulars like Bébé Berard and Jean Bourgoint – whom Natalie finally banned from her house. In January 1935, when Bourgoint had been appearing in Paris regularly from his refuge on Jean Hugo's farm, Una Troubridge noted in her journal that she saw Dolly at the rue Jacob and that Dolly was 'haggard & much aged by her career of dope'.[46]

When Berthe Cleyrergue said at the end of her life that Natalie enjoyed watching her lovers suffer, she may have been thinking of the situation that confronted Dolly at 20 rue Jacob in the mid-1930s.

Sometime in 1934 Natalie Barney came across Nadine Hwang, a highly intelligent, licensed lawyer, who had fought in the Chinese wars for independence dressed as a man, and who was to become a bitter rival of Dolly. Nadine's appearance in male attire was so convincing that Natalie's friend, the novelist André Germain, was completely smitten by what he thought was this very attractive, young Chinese male. Nadine was in France on a mission for the Chinese government – or so Nadine said. Berthe Cleyrergue thought Nadine Hwang was a very accomplished 'intriguer' and Nadine never missed an opportunity to intrigue against Dolly.

Never one to pass up a good bargain, Natalie took Nadine on as lover, chauffeur (a position Dolly loved to fill informally), and substitute secretary. Nadine ran errands, answered correspondence, and, according to Dolly, took dictation for letters to *other* lovers of Natalie. Natalie began to make public appearances with Nadine in places such as Mme Fauchier Magnan's house in Neuilly, places where Dolly had been invited for years.

Dolly corresponded sympathetically with Romaine Brooks about the effects of 'that HORRIBLE Chineeese' on Natalie's life[47] and she wrote, pathetically and rather insultingly, to Natalie in New York in April 1935: 'Darling *don't* have N[adine] back again. Nothing to do with me as I shan't be in your house but for *yourself*. She is *so* shallow. Has been in high spirits after two days from your departure – boasting of her many conquests & her power over you! . . .'[48]

On 9 March 1935, just after Natalie had sailed on a trip to New York (a trip Dolly was supposed to take with her), Nadine betrayed the extent of her jealousy of Dolly by sending Natalie a slanderous letter:

> Darlingest Own,
>
> It is absolutely imperative that D.[Dolly] leaves the house at once . . . Apart from daily drugging and small packets of stuff being found in D's hand-bag, a letter from M.F.D. who had gone to Fontainbleau at D's instigation to fetch *150 kilogrammes of opium*, was also found in same hand-bag . . . The proof of the abominable traffic in which these two are indulging is enough, it seems, for you to act *immediately* . . .
>
> . . . My ultimatum is: either you make D. evacuate your

house *at once* or I will do it myself, and my arguments will be persuasive you can be assured of that . . .

. . . Taking drugs is already a crime but 150 kilos of opium? What do you think that could do to humanity? And your ring . . . the blue sapphire – *quel doigt orne-t-il?*

Do not mention anything to D. or her friend I beg you. The consequences are that I might be killed by one of their milieu.[49]

This *Grand Guignol* indictment of both Dolly and, apparently, of the highly repectable Marcelle Fauchier Delavigne for running an opium ring out of Fontainebleau(!) is part of the long history of extreme cross-charges levelled by most of Natalie's lovers at one another.

Marcelle Fauchier Delavigne had long been very taken with Dolly. She gave her money, she supplied her with places to stay, she provided her with sympathetic companionship, and she would, by some accounts, have liked to offer her more. The frustrations of her position intermittently hampered her friendship for Dolly and Natalie wrote that Marcelle was 'impeded by love'. Since Dolly's and Natalie's letters to Marcelle have not been found, there is nothing but hinting to hang theories on.

Although Dolly complained about Marcelle's fits of 'hysteria' to Natalie, was occasionally bored by the simplicity of Marcelle's delights, and felt compelled to say that it wasn't *she* who was running after Marcelle, Dolly also came to appreciate Marcelle Fauchier Delavigne's sterling qualities and faithful, loving support. She considered her, along with Natalie, one of her '*deux amies incomparables*' in Paris and she wrote to Natalie about Marcelle in 1939: 'Once again one realizes that people *don't* know how to love & only think of themselves. Marcelle – in her patient suffering & unselfishness – compels my admiration & in consequence I write to her with real sincerity & affection.'[50]

Marcelle, along with Natalie and Honey, paid for many of Dolly's disintoxications and must have seen her in some awful states. It is unthinkable that Marcelle would go to Fontainebleau to fetch 150 kilos of opium for a close friend whose disintoxications she was paying for. And Dolly would have been far more likely to inveigle a less concerned friend into bankrolling the drug, then convince that friend to throw a party in celebration of the acquisition.

Still, Dolly was a serious drug-user for many years. She had been strung out enough times to know the value of having drugs close at hand, and a letter, now lost, written to Natalie after this incident included apologies as well as 'confessions' from Dolly. The real frustration here is not whether Nadine Hwang is right or wrong – she obviously knew that Dolly was addicted to drugs and rifled her handbag to confirm it – the real frustration is that Dolly was so successful in keeping this part of her life severely partitioned off that it is impossible to judge whether Nadine's accusations are documentary or merely dramatic.

Nadine Hwang never produced the letter from 'M.F.D.' which she said she found in Dolly's handbag. It is possible that Dolly's friends in the 'Cocteau set' had something very concrete to do with those putative 150 kilos of opium. Doubtless Nadine did find packets of drugs in Dolly's purse, although it was the loss of Natalie's blue sapphire ring (which Nadine appears to be accusing Dolly of disposing of, since Dolly never ornamented her hands) that seemed to give Nadine the most pain.

Natalie's response to Nadine's accusatory letter was to send a note from America dismissing Dolly from her home, followed by ameliorations: 'for you mustn't stay in rue Jacob in your present state – with your present group of fiend-friends surrounding you . . .'[51] Dolly's reply to Natalie's note of dismissal was a combination of those painful excuses and evasions characteristic of someone whose life, through the distortions of drug-use, has come to resemble a Surrealist nightmare: there was the business of the 'man who fell in front of the car', Natalie's car, while Dolly was driving it; there was an error at her bank; there was trouble at her London flat and with an identity card; and Schiaparelli insisted that she hadn't received the money that Dolly insisted she'd sent.[52] Dolly's response to this accumulation of woes was characteristic: she went straight to bed to recover – and then was rousted out by Natalie's letter ordering her out of the house.

On 6 April (always her worst month) 1935, Dolly wrote to Natalie insisting she hadn't 'compromised your house'. *'Please* don't think that I criticize your action which I think *more* than justified but I do think I might have been given my congé [leave] a little less unkindly . . .'[53]

Natalie was already irritated with Dolly because Dolly had failed to join her on her trip to New York in the early part of 1935. Tergiversating as usual, Dolly missed the boat and had been planning – or said she had been planning – to 'follow' Natalie to New York when this latest series of disasters struck.[54] Only a small part of Dolly's seemingly insoluble troubles were catalogued in her letter to Natalie.

The confusions of Dolly's domestic arrangements were often repeated in her medical ones. In her 'revolving-door' relations with the many nursing homes where she went for her drug 'cures', Dolly's hidden addictions were sometimes ignored in favour of the ones she flaunted. She was occasionally treated for one addiction, such as heroin, while enterprisingly and secretly developing another, such as paraldehyde or alcohol. And her cancer treatments and mistreatments created a rotation of turmoils that Dolly blithely contributed to.

Of course Dolly was never 'treated' for the most profound addiction from which she suffered: the *chagrins d'amour* that kept sending her back to the liquids, the pills, and the powders. Nor were there any procedures available to analyse her magnetic attraction to all forms of unconsciousness up to and including death. The cyclic nature of her obvious manic-depressive behaviour went wholly, criminally unnoticed. And nowhere in her medical records is there mentioned a very obvious and important impediment to all her 'cures': that the woman who was underwriting so many of them — Natalie Clifford Barney — was also providing some of the turbulent circumstances which kept Dolly returning to the drugs — and thence to the nursing homes — in the first place.

After Dolly's death, Victor Cunard wrote sentimentally about 'the fantasia of her last years' saying he sometimes thought 'we were wrong in trying, even as much as we did to stop her seeking tranquility in the only place she had learned to find it'. 'Some palliative she had to have . . . but it was a tragedy that circumstances should have put in Dolly's way the most insidious and remorseless. And yet, perhaps, she enjoyed her shortened years more than she would have a longer period with a less potent ally.'[55]

Honey Harris, closer to Dolly's heart, saw things differently:

. . . if I think of faults it is only my own I can remember; that when the time came for her to have real troubles, such great unhappiness and suffering as in the last few years of her life, I allowed myself to feel hopeless and only made ordinary efforts to help her, not the superhuman ones which she deserved.[56]

1 6

Dolly in Bed

I don't see why people sing 'there's no place like home.' Every place is like home, what I should sing is 'there's no place like bed.'

Dolly Wilde

When happiness is definitely out of sight I shall retire like Emily Dickinson into just such a bedroom – the last refuge.

Dolly Wilde

When Dolly was staying in London at the Royal Court Hotel in Sloane Square in one of those single-rooms-with-a-bed to which she was so attached, she wrote a letter to Berthe Cleyergue in Paris. It is a lovely letter in French in Dolly's best imitation-convent-school hand, sending Berthe a long-owed 100 francs and thanking her for her '*charmante carte postale de Noël que j'ai beaucoup appreciée*'.[1] The letter has everything in it to make one aware of the sweetness of character of which Dolly was capable and – no other words for it – her loving kindness to people who did little things for her. All Dolly's maids were profoundly loyal to her, as she was to them, and Nora O'Shaughnessy, one of the last maids she employed, the one who saved her life in London when she took an overdose and slashed her wrists, once actually paid the rent on Dolly's service flat when a sublessee defaulted on the lease and Dolly was left without funds.[2]

Nora O'Shaughnessy did this secretly, without telling Dolly, and Dolly didn't come to know of it until after the fact. Loyalty of this kind can only be purchased with the currency of love, and not with the kind of careless behaviour often attributed to the impertinent Miss Wilde. Dolly liked Berthe's *carte de Noël* so much that she referred to it in a later letter to Natalie Barney, remarking a little snobbishly that it was 'unconsciously extremely *poetical*'.[3]

In the letter to Berthe, Dolly went on to say: '*Je regrette la Rue Jacob tellement et j'ai beaucoup de difficultés ici . . .*'[4] The letter is undated and, of course, that phrase — 'I regret the rue Jacob so much and I have many difficulties here' — would have been appropriate at almost any time during her long relationship with 'Mademoiselle Barney'. Dolly also asked Berthe for Dr Mahoney's address, a man who was not a doctor at all but a *faiseur des anges* who had also probably been one of Dolly's drug suppliers and who was certainly a fellow drinker. Dolly wrote that '*l'adresse du Docteur Mahoney est dans le livre de Mademoiselle. Miss Barnes en tout cas la saura.*'[5]

Since '*le livre de Mademoiselle*', Natalie Barney's address book, does not contain either Dan Mahoney's name or his particulars,[6] Berthe must have applied to Djuna Barnes for his address. What was it that Dolly in London might have wanted from Dan Mahoney in Paris? And how did Djuna Barnes, who had complicated feelings about Dolly, respond to Berthe's request? Suddenly, a casual recommendation to me from Sybille Bedford to stay at the Wilbraham Hotel in Sloane Square — near the hotel where Dolly had written the letter — took on an added significance.

The name 'Wilbraham' had a faintly familiar ring. Hadn't one of Dolly's expensive nursing homes been called the Wilbraham? Could the Wilbraham Hotel and the Wilbraham Nursing Home have been owned by the same person? Perhaps it was a Miss Wilbraham —

perhaps, even better, the Misses Wilbraham: a set of charitably inclined sisters with a private income from their father, the Major, a generous sampling of suffragette genes from their mother, the . . . um . . . the suppressed bluestocking, and an unwavering determination to provide a refuge for distressed gentlewomen. Dolly would have loved to pose — momentarily — as a distressed gentlewoman, and it was only too easy to imagine her trooping back and forth from one Wilbraham establishment to the other, with the Nursing Home mopping up her excesses at the Hotel and the indulgent hotel management perpetually reserving a favourite room for her.

But there was no trace of a Wilbraham Hotel on Dolly's writing paper, while sheaves of it bore the Hôtel Montalembert letterhead. At the Montalembert in Paris, Dolly's favourite room was Room 65, and she always requested it. In Natalie Barney's *pavillon*, Dolly usually made do with much less: a blue sofa she referred to as '*mon divan*'.

As it turned out, my little biographical fantasy of two Wilbraham establishments was not so fantastical after all, for the Wilbraham Hotel had been, before the Second World War, the Wilbraham Nursing Home, where Dolly Wilde, along with other sufferers, was disintoxicated for alcohol and heroin and treated for breast cancer at a cost of about eight pounds a week.[7]

In a telegram sent to Natalie Barney on 16 October 1939 telling her that the boils which had caused such a flapping amongst her friends did not mean a metastasising cancer, Dolly said she found the Wilbraham a 'charming nursing home'.[8] And she had written Natalie a painfully earnest and touchingly disjointed letter from a second *séjour* there on 22 January 1940.[9]

When Dolly died, Natalie Barney wrote: 'Just as no one's presence could be as present as hers, so no one's absence could be so absent.'[10] During my sojourn at the Wilbraham Hotel, it was impossible not to imagine traces of Dolly lingering inside that high narrow frontage of rust-coloured bricks near a charming casement window; or loitering on the velvety red carpets of a stair landing, where she had to go to make the telephone calls she could not live without, averaging about twenty-seven calls a week by the time she left the nursing home;[11] or wafting around the recesses of one of the flocked and flowered bed-chambers. For by now it was obvious just how important bedrooms had always been to Dolly, and how difficult they were for her to abandon.

Dolly Wilde conducted most of the business she considered important — i.e. the workings of her splendid, sympathetic, and *malicieuse* imagination on the large subjects of love and literature — from the many bedrooms in which she slept. It is remarkable that none of these bedrooms belonged to her. In borrowed flats and rented rooms, in luxury hotels and *maisons de santé*, in Venetian palazzi, French and English country houses, 'garden rooms' on the Isle of Wight, and in a variety of other *chambres à coucher* spanning a vast social and economic scale, Dolly made her bed (metaphorically of course; housework was not one of Dolly's talents) and lay down on it.

> Wherever [Dolly] lived, her room was always a headquarter of amorous intrigue, and she was busily involved knotting and unknotting her friends' liaisons. If she was in, her telephone was never free: people all over Europe were pouring out their passionate problems, or those of their acquaintances, over her line. And as she lay in bed, laughing and advising, or just exclaiming 'Oh' or 'Really, darling' she was also reading a love story about her friends. Perhaps it was Michael Arlen's 'Green Hat' or the more complicated adventures of Nancy [Cunard] by Aldous Huxley. Perhaps it was Evelyn Waugh or she might have been looking through a book of Benson again . . . the story coming over the wire she already knew much better than the excited person that was telling it to her, so she could quite well renew her acquaintance with Compton Mackenzie as she listened . . .[12]

There, besides the obvious uses beds are put to, Dolly yearned passionately, fantasised heavily, suffered from her melancholy nature, was badly ill from her *mauvaises affaires*, read voraciously, wrote especially beautiful letters, and made translations for Nancy Cunard, Natalie Barney, and the duchesse de Clermont-Tonnerre, among others. All the while dispensing crucial advice to lovesick friends, then heartlessly retailing their secrets to her large and very interested telephone audience. The bedrooms in which she could dream and read and write her letters, lie down on a bed or a divan (a couch or a hammock would do), and broadcast the news from her 'love's intelligence service',[13] were a wide world to Dolly. They allowed her both scope and protection, and the days and nights during which her life was confined to the dimensions of a duvet were among her happiest. 'Your letter arrived with my breakfast tray and a beam of sunlight cuts the pages like a golden paper knife. I lit a voluptuous cigarette and in the fresh morning solitude – before the incidents of the day have broken me into segments – I read your lovely words.'[14]

'. . . before the incidents of the day have broken me into segments . . .' What could be plainer? In bed, in her bedroom, Dolly was whole, inviolable, safe from the assailing day. The confidential integrity of her 'bedroom style' (Dolly had a 'bedroom style' for writing as other people develop 'bedroom eyes' for seduction), taken up again and again when she is corresponding from a nest of satin sheets and high-banked pillows and having her meals, her letters, and a silver vase holding a dewy morning rose brought to her on a lacquered breakfast tray, is as clear as Dolly's clever avoidance of a 'lasting' love affair or of the possible career she might have had as a writer.

One of the reasons Dolly spent so many of her daylight hours in beds and bedrooms is that she was a lazy, luxurious creature (in both the economic and sexual senses) who loved lounging, felt safer enwombed, and asserted over and over in one way or another the pertinence of the anthemic sentence she wrote to Natalie Barney: 'In bed I feel alright.' In this predilection, Dolly followed her paternal grandmother, Lady Jane Wilde, who was plain on the subject while still an unmarried woman: 'In fact I never have the slightest inclination to lie down at night or to rise in the morning.' Jane Wilde's own bedroom in Dublin's Merrion Square never saw daylight before one or two in the afternoon and her agoraphobic retreats to her chambers after the death of her daughter Isola, during the worst of Dolly's father Willie's wayward behaviour, and again after Oscar's unfortunate fall, were the sad, genetic scaffoldings for Dolly's later attempts at self-immurement.

Another, more practical, reason for Dolly's confinement to bed-rooms was that Dolly usually stayed in luxury hotels (the Montalembert and the Ritz in Paris, the Royal Court and the Berkeley in London) where her mysterious budget was inadequate for a suite, and her friends, often stuck with her hotel bills, were probably too canny and/or exasperated to pay for one. In 1935 Honey Harris wrote resignedly on this subject:

> Why go & stay for weeks at such an expensive hotel if you know quite well that you won't be able to pay the bill? Because you know that someone else will *have* to — is the answer I suppose — but still it is no use complaining. One can never change people an atom can one & there are so many nice things that make up for the disadvantages![15]

Then, too, Dolly seemed to prefer the contraction of responsibilities which is one of the best features of single room occupancy. One of her *séjours* in Paris during the course of her relationship with Natalie Barney (in 1936) was at the exquisite but tiny borrowed home of the American heiress and small-press publisher of Harrison of Paris, Barbara Harrison, at 32 rue de Vaugirard.[16] Another one was at

> . . . an elaborate establishment with illuminated fishbowls and panelled oak rooms — one of which Dolly named 'Breakfast-room at Balmoral.' Here she had a staff of servants, and was

forced not only to entertain but be on time. Soon tiring of a
hostess's obligations and all that 'faux luxe', she resorted to a
single hotel room, and relaxed there quite happily in a large
bed, surrounded by books. (Books borrowed from Sylvia
Beach's circulating library nearby and which I regret to report
were never returned.) At this, her favorite Hôtel Montalembert,
she would 'lay low', calling on none of us to interrupt her
solitary well-being.[17]

Although Dolly was attracted by the cachet of good addresses, and
shared with her uncle Oscar the quality of being modern in her
artistic as well as her architectural tastes (the Hôtel Montalembert
opened in 1926 as the *dernier cri* of Parisian swank), she usually occupied those good addresses and exercised her predilection for
contemporary luxuries from the vantage point of rather modest quarters; and she seemed to be perfectly comfortable doing so. Her widely
lamented prodigality, though undeniable and offensive to all her
wealthy friends, was of a modest order: even Dolly's most 'extravagant' demands were rather circumscribed. Not, of course, according
to *her* prospects, but certainly according to the standards of the titled
social circles in which she continued to circulate in London and
Paris — the Carnarvons, the Harrises, and the Fabre-Luces, and the
haute bourgeoisie circles in Paris — the Fauchier Delavignes and the
Fauchier Magnans. Dolly's real economic extravagance was the expensive company she kept, who tended to treat her like a poor relation
and expected her to behave that way.

What Dolly really wanted out of all those first-class hotels, lovely
town houses, shaded *pavillons*, and *hôtels particuliers* (where she was so
welcome that 'After her capricious visits, a letter of thanks would
seem more appropriate from her hosts than from so entertaining a
guest')[18] was just One Good Room. And when she had anything
more, as with the borrowed house and staff of servants, or with the
rich accommodations rented for her at the Paris Ritz by an infatuated
married woman, Dolly was uncomfortable: she made fun of the

borrowed house, satirised her Ritz benefactor ('the pocket Napoleon')[19] and eventually quit the premises for something smaller.

Crowded into one room, Dolly's talents seemed to concentrate and collect and the centre of her power radiated out from her bed and its inevitable, accompanying telephone in powerful and seductive waveforms. Rather like the *grandes horizontales* of two generations ago – except that she was neither political nor *horizontale* in the conventional sense – Dolly turned her bedrooms into a kind of social salon-cum-psychological theatre-cum-emotional dressing station. As with her ambulance driving work during the First War, Dolly used the bedroom as a kind of Vehicle of Urgence. 'She had no use for anything but the immediate and answered our emergency calls as a sort of first aid to the injured – even when she was the injurer!'[20]

Still, a woman who makes *bedrooms* her principal place of residence has to have a fairly serious attitude towards what is commonly supposed to take place in them. Dolly considered love-making 'the logical conclusion to admiration',[21] and felt that 'it was often underrated'.[22] She frequently indulged in acts of love – or in what she called 'emergency seductions' – in the same, urgent way that she used drugs: to dissolve that pain for which there was no solution, her life on earth.

In many of Dolly's letters to Natalie Barney, and in many communications to Barney *about* Dolly, there are reports of the dark side of Dolly's sense of *bien-être* in bedrooms: those bouts of serious self-confinement when she barricaded herself in hotel rooms or flats or private bedrooms in an expense of spirit and a waste of shame. Here she is writing on 1 April 1934 from her flat in Queen Street in London:

> Darling
>   If I haven't written it's because I feel so ashamed of every-thing. I have been really frightfully ill. I thought I would disintoxicate myself without a doctor as over here they insist on one going into a nursing home – or having nurses. I bought a sleeping draught & took the normal dose & then, *unconsciously*, in my sleep, I took the whole bottle. I couldn't

imagine I should do this, especially as they are tablets rather difficult to swallow without water, & the thought never even crossed my mind. However, I did do it . . .[23]

There was a multiplication of similar instances in both London and Paris over the next eight years. Bettina Bergery thought these sad episodes all came about because of Dolly's failure to replenish herself. After Dolly had offered up her abundant talents at a thousand smart dinner parties and 'shared her highly coloured visions with her so often colourless and visionless acquaintances', she found herself – like so many performers – a beggar at her own banquet.

. . . one was shocked by the apathetic look that so recalled the hopeless apathy of the broken poet Oscar, just before his end. Dolly soon felt as she looked, so she stayed more and more in her hotel bedroom . . .[24] [where] all the bottles in the closet couldn't fill her inner void. Then did she think with fright of her future and of Oscar's past?'[25]

Dolly's misery in her self-enforced isolations is so palpable that it seems to leak out of her letter-writing pen, seep under her bedroom door, trickle down the corridor and pool up in front of her frightened neighbours' thresholds. Her sorrows in sequestration were more serious than the sorrows signalled by the histrionics of her scenes in hotel corridors. Those were merely the sounds of a frustrated woman on the assailing swell of a bad binge. What Dolly locked her door on when she withdrew from the world was something far more profound: a deep and unmistakable stream of anguish, as dark and as definite as blood.

Even barricaded in her bedroom, Dolly's wit was literary. When Dan Mahoney reproved her for staying alone in her bedroom for days, saying the isolation was 'killing her', Dolly retorted: 'Yes, I do prove Pascal wrong, don't I?'[26] Pascal thought that all unhappiness came from the inability to stay alone in one's room.

One afternoon in Paris, Dolly was wandering through the Louvre with her friend George Beckwith, the man who later went up in flames in his yellow sports car. Dolly stopped, suddenly mesmerised, before a painting by Delacroix, 'The Death of Sardanapolus'.

> 'Oh' cried Dolly, 'Darling look! that bed! and the city burning behind! and the horses having their throats cut! and the lovely pearly nakedness of those slaves being strangled! and he, so comfortable on all his pillows! That's how I should like to die.' Dolly said 'I don't see why people sing "there's no place like home." Every place is like home, what I should sing is "there's no place like bed."'[27]

'The Death of Sardanapolus' is an enormous, spatially violent work in oil paint, depicting the Emperor Sardanapolus reclining comfortably, as the painter Delacroix wrote, on his 'superb bed at the summit of an immense funeral pyre' just before he commits suicide.[28] Sardanapolus's city is being burned to the ground in rebellion against his sybaritic ways and he has just commanded the slaughter of 'his women, his pages — even his horses and his favourite dogs, so that nothing that had served his pleasure might survive him . . .'[29] Among the images in the painting are six murdered and dying concubines (with whom Dolly apparently did *not* identify) and a horse having its throat cut. The foreground is dominated by a slave woman 'having a knife slotted into her clavicle'.[30] The source of the painting is usually assumed to be a poem by Dolly's beloved Byron about the suicide of the Assyrian King of Nineveh.

This turbulent painting, which gave Dolly such a comfortable view of her own end, is one of the most sexually tempestuous and erotically anxious works hanging in the Louvre. Its scene is set in a bedroom.

Before the coroner's report on Dolly's inquest was available in all its mysteries and contradictions, I spent a long time trying to understand how and of what Dolly Wilde died. Did she die of the breast cancer?

dead, if indeed it be true that there is no rest and no respite for the scarred soul of the suicide.'[33]

For 12 April, Holland wrote: 'The papers today are full of "Oscar Wilde's Niece found Dead" "Drug Bottles in Flat".'[34]

For 16 April, he noted:

> There has been a hitch in Dolly's funeral, as the inquest, fixed for tomorrow, has been put off for further examination of the deceased: how sordid it all is! Her friends are expecting a verdict of anything up to felo de se, though, as she apparently died of simple parahaldehyde poisoning, there might quite easily be a verdict of accidental death.[35]

Despite the report of Natalie Barney's friend, Dr LeMasle, that he had found Dolly in late March of 1941 (a fortnight before her death) on a park bench in Westminster drunk and unconconscious, and the report of her personal physician, Dr Cregan, that Dolly was always asking him for more heroin, Dolly, during the last month of her life, was certainly giving the appearance of wan sobriety. Her last meal, described by the waiter Harold West, was a sad model of abstinence and good intentions and it is another argument against suicide. A Dolly intent on self-extinction would surely have ordered an extravagantly calorific final banquet.

Victor Cunard told Nancy Mitford that Dolly was quite jolly and 'like herself' to the end; and she was apparently determined to hang on to her dignity. For although Dr LeMasle discovered Dolly 'sleeping it off' on a park bench, she had not chosen to collapse supine on a sidewalk or to fall prone on a piece of park grass. She had managed to pass out – perhaps in her role as a distressed gentlewoman – on a park bench, something that must have looked to her rather like a divan. Given her lifelong affinity for beds and lounging, the choice she made was an appropriate one.

Dolly's death – this conclusion was slow to develop for me – happened at the end of a lengthy, difficult, and early menopause, which

But the medical reports given by Honey Harris, Marcel
Delavigne, Natalie Barney, Gwen Farrar, and Barbara Grah
letters – and the conclusions of the doctors themselves – d
many inconsistencies. In her 2 March 1939 letter to Nat
London, Honey says:

> I wish I knew what to think about her illness. I never heaı
> anything except second hand versions of her London doct
> reports, and she is so dead against all ideas of operations –
> . . . She had no faith in [Dr Hughes's] diagnosis although s
> was upset and scared by his report . . . the only comforting
> thing is that as far as one can tell from outward appearances
> she doesn't seem to be getting any worse . . . and whenever oı
> sees her she is her usual charming, gay self.[31]

The lumps in Dolly's breast and under her arm seemed to gı
and shrink with the metaphors used by her worried invigilatc
And her awful scare about her lymph nodes was a product of ł
own fastidiousness. In a decade where the use of deodorant was
novelty in both London and Paris – a short ride on the tube or th
métro in London or Paris in July can convince one that it still is –
Dolly powdered herself with too much Odorono,[32] probably after
shaving her underarms – an activity she had stopped when first
sleeping with Natalie Barney because Natalie found her sexier
unshaven. Reacting against the powder, Dolly's sensitive skin broke
out in bumps, and raised a rippling scare amongst all her friends that
the cancer had spread. Dolly, of course – how typical of her – never
used the word 'cancer'. 'Cyst', she would write. 'The cysts are smaller.'
But she spelled it (was this another of her orthographical jokes?)
'kyst'. Like 'kissed'.

Oscar's son Vyvyan Holland's diary entries give the impression
that he regarded Dolly's death as a suicide. The day after Dolly's
death, 11 April 1941, he wrote: 'Yes I am afraid I rather quarrelled
with Dolly eventually . . . Ah! Well! She is dead now, and unhappily

probably started in late 1939. The early menopause would have been partially masked by one of the discoveries of her autopsy: a fibroid tumour in her uterus which could have mimicked her menses. It was still bleeding slightly at the time of her death.[36]

In this early, unrecognised menopause, Dolly's body began to empty itself of oestrogen the way a broken bottle drains its contents — in sudden, surprising floods — and she found it harder and harder to dissolve her many worries — breast cancer (the word she *never* used), drug addiction, and bad finances were only three of them — in the luxurious oblivion of deep-drowning sleep, the only physical state besides sexual ecstasy that she pursued like a lover. Increasingly desperate for what the night should have brought her, Dolly sought it out in doses of paraldehyde.

Of the panoply of difficult symptoms that escort a woman down the dark passage out of her menses, sleep deprivation is perhaps the hardest one to bear. It howls through every corridor of a woman's life and multiplies the terrors of perceived unattractiveness that always accompany a cessation of fertility. For Dolly — a woman who lived very much in and for her body, a woman who manipulated her love-making rendezvous according to her menstrual cycles, and a woman who had the acutest perception of every square inch of her skin — that early and mostly unidentified menopause must have felt like a season in hell. The parching, shirring, and ruching of her creamy complexion is evident in late photographs; and the loss of lubricious moisture, the desiccation of her lovely *bleu marin* eyes (in earlier portraits they seem to be swimming in individual, crystalline ponds), the bad depressions that accompanied the withdrawal of essential oestrogen, were all suffered by Dolly without the knowledge that this was the next, natural cycle of her life. She confused her symptoms with her hangovers, her drug withdrawals, and the general malaise that followed her around like a bad fate. She was 'drying out' all right, and the irony of a phrase which is ordinarily applied to a voluntary withdrawal from alcohol or drugs would not have been lost on her.

By 1940 Dolly was back in the Wilbraham Nursing Home and beginning to understand what had happened to her.

> . . . the disastrous original 'cure' which left me a wreck through insane treatment, followed by what I now know (& from doctors) to have been the change of life, real insomnia, depression & melancholia leading to my doing self-destructive things in order to sleep *anyhow* & later to shut out that despair — a nervous breakdown, compusory sleeping draughts etc leaves me without the will to do anything except get through the moment . . .[37]

For Dolly, menopause *was* the ultimate drug withdrawal — a withdrawal from vital oestrogen — and it culminated, dramatically, in her final drive to unconsciousness, to the hunt for that last bed in which she could rest. She began, increasingly, to use the paraldehyde to induce a peaceful sleep. Who was it who first supplied Honey Harris with the adjective 'peaceful' to describe Dolly's death? It had to have been a doctor making a remark meant to take the edge off the awful appropriateness of Dolly's demise.

Dolly began ingesting 'compulsory sleeping draughts' in the form of paraldehyde in late 1939 at the Wilbraham Nursing Home.[38] Paraldehyde was partially responsible for her sleep of 10 April 1941, the one from which she did not wake, and it was a poor trade-off for her heroin addiction: she never completely threw off the heroin.

In its instability, inconclusivity, and illegibility, the coroner's report on Dolly's death does not provide proofs which would bolster Vyvyan Holland's and Janet Flanner's judgement of suicide, or Victor Cunard's and Nancy Mitford's conclusion of accidental overdose; but suicide and/or accidental overdose are certainly two of the three conclusions — the other one is murder — that can be drawn from what HM Coroner wrote.

Dolly's 'suicides' were rarely acts that she took credit for; they were rarely acts that she *could* take credit for. Two of her recorded attempts were performed in a kind of blackout, a somnambulistic state brought on by too much of the sleep-inducing drugs she took to get back to . . . what? Death, it always seemed, which is often the only end that romantics like Dolly can imagine.

Time spent in bed was Dolly's remedy for everything, and she did an enormous amount of day-dreaming. Since Dolly almost never wrote about her night- or day-dreams — and she was a very dreamy sort of person — she must have slept, when she slept, very heavily: the knocked-out sleep of the almost-dead, the sleep that drugs provided her with. She usually slept very late, and late, heavy sleeping often indicates a serious resistance to consciousness.

There is only one night-dream described in all of Dolly's letters. It was such a painful one that it woke her up. She wrote about it to Natalie: 'A horrid dream of desolation & you trying to rescue me has filled me with desire to be near you.' Dolly dreamed this dream in Alice DeLamar's house on the rue Gît-le-Coeur, a place where, she said, she had been 'happy'.

If on the night of 9 April 1941 — or sometime early the next morning — Dolly, seeking sleep, had drunk more paraldehyde than showed up in her autopsy, she might have lapsed into the kind of unconsciousness that at least two times before had caused her to swallow a whole bottle of pills without knowing it. She called the instinct that made her do it 'that strange impulse [that] makes me head for destruction, so that even my subconscious dictates death to me . . .'[39]

But if this were one of her 'unconscious' suicide attempts, it lacked the crucial feature of wrist-slitting. Her only fully conscious attempt at suicide — the one in the Hôtel Astoria in 1931 — had begun with wrist-slitting; one other serious, drugged try had also ended in Dolly cutting an artery. But at her last residence, Twenty Chesham Place, Dolly made no attempt to slit her wrists; and the lack of a viable syringe to deliver heroin and the absence of a killing amount of paraldehyde in her organs made even the diagnosis of accidental death impossible.

There is only one explanation for Dolly's death that fits the 'facts' of her autopsy report – assuming that the 'facts' (the time of death, the findings in the tissues) are accurate, a large assumption in itself. This explanation rests on the incident of another person being in the room with Dolly at the time of her death. It is an implausible explanation at best, but perhaps no more implausible than the confusions presented by the autopsy report itself. This explanation is worth entertaining, if only for a paragraph or two.

Suppose Dolly had an undetected visitor in her room at Twenty Chesham Place on the last evening of her life. In any rental establishment there are always one or two ways to slip people past the management. Dolly, who spent her life in rented rooms doing things she didn't want people to know about, would have understood very well how to get by a front desk – if, indeed, there even were a front desk at Twenty Chesham Place. Suppose, too, that this hypothetical visitor brought Dolly the extra dose of heroin she had been trying unsuccessfully to extract from Dr Cregan that week. This heroin would not have been cut or weighed with the same accuracy available in a medical office – the dependability of the dosage is probably why Dolly liked to get her drugs from doctors. Perhaps there was something wrong with the mixture Dolly's hypothetical visitor brought; perhaps the heroin had not been cut enough.

Suppose, again, that Dolly's visitor was someone (a woman presumably) who spent the night or part of the night with Dolly – all the more reason for concealing the visit. Suppose that there was enough heroin left over for Dolly to do up a morning injection. If the heroin, undetectable in the blood of an addict, combined in a reactive way with the small amount of paraldehyde that Dolly had apparently taken at the beginning of yet another sleepless dawn, it might have caused the slam-down death described in her autopsy report: the bruised and abraded cheek, the suddenly stopped heart. The visitor, in a panic, picks up the syringe and leaves the room, again undetected.

Of course this scenario for Dolly's death is an improbable one. The undetected entrance and exit of a visitor at Twenty Chesham

Place leaves almost too much to coincidence and Dolly doesn't seem to have had a known lover at this time. Moreover, this visitor would almost certainly have had to be someone who knew Dolly – and all Dolly's friends always tried to keep drugs *away* from her.

Dolly's days of one-night stands and 'emergency seductions' were over – for now at least; for always, as it turned out. Someone she didn't know well would hardly have spent the night in her room. But would someone she *did* know well have left her so disrepectfully in death? Half in, half out of her bed, if one witness is correct; sprawled and bruised on the floor, if the other witness is accurate. And yet, if this visitor were an addict herself, badly disoriented by drugs . . . and in a room with a convulsing, then a suddenly dead, lover? Dolly had so many secrets.

And what was in that postmarked bottle the chambermaid said she did not deliver to Dolly on the morning of her death? Could it have been a vial of paraldehyde sent from the chemists, ordered the day before to replace the almost empty paraldehyde bottles in Dolly's room? Proof that those bottles had been already drained and that Dolly couldn't have died of the sleeping draught? Dr Roche Lynch said that he could find only 'a small quantity' of paraldehyde in Dolly's organs. Dr Simpson, however, noticed a 'distinct smell of paraldehyde' about her more than thirty hours after she died. (The image of an intent Dr Simpson bending his head down to Dolly's lips and sniffing sharply for the odour of paraldehyde before cutting into her body, is a disturbing one.) So maybe it *was* the paraldehyde after all, just one small dose too many and Dolly died as she had been living – alone – then sliding partially and heavily on to the floor.

Dr Simpson had also noted a 'marked dilation of the R side of the heart, with a deeply cyanotic blood-clot'. Was it possible – how like her if it were true – that Dolly died of a broken heart? The one conclusion that coroners can never come to.

Dr Josephine Day, the chirologist who read Dolly's hand for this book, said she thought Dolly had died with a terrible pressure on her chest, 'like a tombstone over her heart'.[40] (See Appendix 3).

Dolly's funeral was as strangely put together as any explanation of her death, and it remains just as resistant to interpretation. She was buried on 15 April in the Catholic section of Kensal Green Cemetery, St Mary's, in a grave with her mother Lily.[41] Like Oscar, Dolly had a priest presiding at her service, for she had worn 'a small gold cross chained around her neck, and at odd times entered churches, and went through all due signs and genuflections of worship' at the end of her life. Natalie Barney said that Dolly's 'faith in God grew with her need of God'![42]

The day of her interment was the day after the worst air-raid London had yet experienced, and so Dolly was put to rest in her final bed against the backdrop of a brilliantly stained and smoky sky. The clouds had all been coloured by the fires started by German bombs falling on London, and the effect must have been rather like the violence and beauty of Delacroix's 'Death of Sardanapolus', the painting that had given Dolly such a lovely idea for her own death in a bed.

Cara and Honey Harris came up from the country for Dolly's funeral, and they brought Viva King with them. Victor Cunard appeared from Liverpool Street Station, 'bad-tempered and cursing the havoc in the City', which had caused him to be late. Viva King said there were about eight other people at the funeral, Gwen Farrar among them 'on crutches, the result of bumping into something in the blackout'.[43] That makes twelve or thirteen people at Dolly's burial, counting the priest. André Gide said there had been seven people at Oscar Wilde's interment, but Miriam Aldrich, who was there, said Oscar had fourteen people to attend him.[44]

Later on, Viva King's husband Willie got a very odd letter from Lady Waverly, the former Ava Bodley, Dolly's old companion on that motor trip around Morocco in 1922, the trip Dolly tried to record in her travel journal. Lady Waverly wrote that she had been to Dolly's funeral (it is unclear whether or not she actually was in attendance) and found it disgraceful 'that she was the only person present'. She and the priest had been quite confused, she said, when he turned and said 'we will now form a procession' – a thing impossible to do with so few mourners.

'Thus does history sometimes come down to us,' Viva King wrote enigmatically about Ava's remark.[45] And whether she meant that Dolly's funeral was historic or whether she meant that Ava Bodley had taken leave of her senses and therefore the story of Dolly's funeral was now in Viva's own hands, is yet another of the interesting questions that continues to surround the life and death of Dolly Wilde.

7

The
Letters

Love Me: the Letters of Dolly Wilde

As for Dolly's letters they are to me the richest and most civilized in their interests and comments that I have ever read. They are her anthology . . .

Janet Flanner

*H*undreds of Dolly's letters sallied forth from her temporary boudoirs into the wide world of her correspondence. Her favourite place from which to write them continued to be her bedroom of the moment, wherever that bedroom was. Many of her letters were written when she lay in these rooms ill or slightly stunned by life, and it is too easy to assemble an image of a Dolly Wilde for whom a bed and four walls were the world. Nothing could be further from the truth. Still, if Dolly had taken the trouble to design a letterhead — but that would have been too decisive a gesture for her — a bed, couchant, would have been the perfect emblem.

Every letter Dolly wrote left her pen under the assurance that it was being mailed into a letter-writing world: a world where correspondents knew that mail could be sent and received twice a day, or sent as often as they liked by 'the little boys' or the *chasseurs* who served as private couriers. Dolly's letters ring with this comfortable knowledge.

Even the *look* of Dolly's letters mattered to her. Some of them are illustrated with drawings of objects she bought or wanted to buy or with sketches of dresses she was having made. She put spaces between her sentences where a breath would be appropriate. She used the dash as liberally as did her writing grandmother. The full stop of her paragraphs is sometimes honoured with a gap. She underlined constantly to indicate the pressure of her ideas — and the exclamation point was her favourite orchestrating tool.

> My amusement — my gaiety — even my hostess instinct have all left me. I am in a trance & reality is only you & love. What a world I am heir to now — what miraculous rights I possess — what secret bread is mine.

> Your letters are love-making — continue to assuage me! . . .[1]

> I come to you thrilled & full of love — meet me how you like! Oh! but love me, *love* me, darling.[2]

Dolly once regretted that her momentarily ragged handwriting (she was being disintoxicated at the time) was unlike that of Mary Queen of Scots, whose execution-eve letter she had taken the trouble to look at; *anything* to do with hands or handwriting interested Dolly. '. . . the [Mary Queen of Scots']letter exists & I have seen it — not a tremor, not a correction, not even a blot from one over-flowing tear!'[3]

More than a little lax as to appointments and hotel bills, Dolly was scrupulous with the imagined sound of her sentences, which follow theatrical speech in emphasising the stress and juncture of vocal line. Dolly's intimate and accosting speaking voice saturates her letters as if she is calling out from them to us.

Darling

I had a lovely sleep, a lovely tea & now I am off to the uncom-
prehending world, powdered, painted & armed with wit. I
miss you & would much rather stay with you in cosy inter-
change of thought. Yes, old cigarettes *do* smell *horrid* – I have
flung them in disgrace in the most disgraceful of places.

Your loving

Dolly[4]

Dolly was also careful about her writing paper – she used letter-
heads (other people's, of course) – and she was choosy about her pen
nibs. So attached was she to the 'voice' of her letters that she sometimes characterised her pen in speaking terms: 'This thin-lipped pen,
too, & the almost invisible ink no ally either to my laziness!'[5] When
she was very ill in Venice she wrote to Natalie shakily and fadedly
only in pencil, as though to illustrate her faintly recuperative, revenant
self. Using pencil again, and writing again to Natalie (who was just in
the next room at 20 rue Jacob), she blamed the pencil's failure to
incarnate her favourite greeting: 'Darling – (how I wish the pencil
blushed its leaden heart red whenever one wanted that tired old word
"darling" to mean something for *once!*)'[6]

Dolly often apologised in the middle of a letter for possible
spelling errors – usually excusing herself for the word correctly
spelled and missing the mistake – and her grammatical manners were
grand, if not entirely *comme il faut*. The word was, she said, 'the only
thing I understand and feel at home in' and the idea of 'home' to this
perpetually homeless woman was a potent one.

Janet Flanner, who studied Dolly carefully, said that she was 'very
particular' about her friends having a 'full vocabulary' and that 'she
loved narrative'; and Dolly herself repeated this. Yet Dolly sent out
her letters as carelessly as the autumn wind scoops up and hurls a

volley of leaves into the air, insisting that she wrote them for herself.

'Shall I post this letter?' she wrote to Natalie. 'If the first person I meet leaving is a woman I shall – if a man into the waste paper basket!'[7] As in her life, Dolly's instinct for self-preservation in letter-writing was muted. Only three or four different sets of Dolly's letters have survived her refusal to keep track of her life.

Perhaps for the same reasons that she could not bear to engrave the address of her London service flat on a ream of good writing paper, Dolly could not put herself into any of the literary forms the world acknowledges or rewards. The brilliant bits of her imagination that remain are embedded most fully in those letters of love, longing, and evasion which she addressed to Natalie Barney between 1927 and 1941.

Written by a woman thrust suddenly into solitude or loneliness or despair, Dolly's letters were delivered to Natalie's sometimes wandering attentions from venues as wildly varied as a borrowed bedroom on a grand Polish estate, the house of another lover in London, any number of de luxe hotels in London and Paris and Venice, a breakfast tray in an English country home, or the dark at the top of Barney's own bedroom stairs, where Dolly sat writing through a long afternoon while Natalie had her bath.

Though she persistently described herself as 'logical' – by which she meant that she could reason her way into and out of any situation – Dolly's letters to Natalie are the apotheosis of romance. They feed greedily on indefinite separations and the high delights of literature, float gauzily on sensual promise, pursue every possible illusion (the worst of them being that Dolly thought herself incapable of sexual jealousy) and sink under the weight of bitter knowledge. They also go in for long bouts of emotional blackmail and poisoned suspicions of infidelity – all the more hurtful for involving women Dolly knew, women she had perhaps slept with herself.

And always, in every one of her later letters to Natalie Barney, is the anti-romantic, the *Wildean* note: the requests, the bargains, and the sometimes manipulative pleas for that commodity which is love's most uncomfortable escort: money. Oscar had written: 'I am always worried by that mosquito, money . . . my soul is made mean by sordid anxieties.' In Dolly's case the 'mosquito' bit often, but the requests she made were for rather small amounts of money. Still, she made them steadily and the money was rather steadily distributed. Over the years, the debts to Natalie, to everybody, piled up considerably. Natalie, hard-headed and hard-boiled when it came to finances, always required receipts and Dolly sometimes even paid her back. But the economics of their desire was badly unbalanced and this imbalance, naturally, hardened into attitude. Once again, Oscar sums up this attitude very nicely: 'The only thing that can console one for being poor is extravagance. The only thing that can console one for being rich is economy.'

At their best, Dolly's letters to Natalie, and her surviving letters to other friends, are filled with long passages that are limitlessly imaginative, insistently voluptuous, and obsessively conversational – much like the best descriptions of Dolly herself. And since the bulk of Dolly's letters was written to a woman famous for her seductions of other women, Dolly's correspondence gives the old subject of love (and love's old subjects) a new – sometimes a *very* new – look.

A Note-paper Lover: Letters to Natalie

But how derive satisfaction from a note-paper lover – how conduct love with words? And yet that's all I understand & feel at home in – & the intimacy of thoughts, words is jarred by reality.

Dolly Wilde, letter to Natalie Barney

Do you leave my letters on your desk – I fear so. Burn them now. Silly to gather them up eventually & pop them in a clerk's folder under the letter 'W'.

Dolly Wilde, letter to Natalie Barney

It wasn't exactly a 'clerk's folder' that Natalie Barney saved Dolly's letters in. There were too many of them for that. It was a large orange box, the largest of all the boxes in which Natalie preserved the more than 40,000 letters she received in her lifetime; and it and its contents went to a small, private library in Paris after Natalie's death. There, all of Dolly's letters were catalogued and placed, two or three at a time, in ordinary paper covers that appear to imitate the shape and size of . . . clerks' folders. Dolly was nothing if not prescient.

She was prescient – and she was also mildly felonious. Every one of her letters is written on purloined – Dolly would have said 'borrowed' – writing paper. Of course the writing paper had been made available for Dolly's personal use. What is the point of having charming guests staying at your lovely country house or happy customers residing in your elegant hotel if they cannot practise the mutually advertising art of sending out letters engraved with your coronated initials or your raised address?

But Dolly, as usual, went very far with her borrowing; went, in fact, to the limit with it. She took to using Lady Cara Harris's seal on Lady Harris's sealing wax. She 'borrowed' black-bordered stationery for a joke from an exclusive 'bath club' when she was missing Natalie. She used paper from the Berkeley Hotel because it had a bishop's mitre on it and because she was thinking of Natalie as 'a cold bishop preoccupied with her Diocesan affairs'. Over the years, she removed what must have been thousands of sheaves of stationery from any number of private houses, exclusive clubs, hotels, castles, and fashionable spas, using them grandly wherever she went.

And so the seductive headings – Highclere Castle, 10 Catherine's Gate, Hotel Ritz, Hôtel Montalembert, Hôtel Metropolitain, 20 rue Jacob – reassuringly graven across the top of Dolly's letters, are quite often a diversion from where Dolly really was; perhaps they were merely expressions of where Dolly really wanted to be. The 'reality' of her current address is best determined by looking at the postmark on the envelope.

Most of Dolly's letters to Natalie – more than two hundred of them are preserved — are love letters to their last syllable, although Dolly was perfectly aware that 'Love, like inspiration, can really only be a matter of twenty minutes in the 24 hours!'[8] Each subject is wrapped in her grand passion and takes on an added lustre from being treated with a lover's pen for presentation to a lover's eyes.

Dolly's feelings always fled towards — and away from — the larger emotions and, like anyone who locates her greatest pleasure in human intercourse, she was doomed to disappointment and knew it. She used her letters to parse her love affair with Natalie like a favourite novel, signalling to Natalie that she was on to the story, that she knew where the plot was headed, and that she had already guessed the ending. Dolly tried to translate the book of love she and Natalie were writing with their lives into a narrative she could live with, finding that it was easier to let her imagination leap to the dénouement of their romance at the moment of commitment, rather than to dwell on its weekly, sometimes daily, difficulties.

I have put a match to a perfectly laid fire & sit contentedly in this mysterious world of fire-light & lamp-light at a strange, enchanted hour. Free from pain I have stretched luxuriously & savoured quiet thoughts in my charming room. You walk down the avenues of my mind, peacefully, wonderfully . . .

Do you love me? I wonder. Not that it matters at all. Perhaps I shan't even mind when you leave me — only then there could be no love-making — *impossible* thought . . . I give you eternity as a (terrifying!) guarantee . . . of *my* love, while you beg for favours because the end is so near! Who will flee first? Just now I am too in love with you to dream of change, & grant you precedence darling.[9]

Dolly used the occasions of these letters to Natalie to write out everything she knew about love relations, but never to examine *how* she knew what she knew. She wrote, for the most part, with an admirable and often uncomfortable emotional honesty. The frankness and acute analysis that Dolly was capable of were fatal to the operating methods of someone like Natalie Barney and Natalie's response to them was often less than sympathetic. 'Keep your thoughts – I don't want them – I want *you* – your body!' Natalie responded cruelly after one such conversation; but Dolly's letters to Natalie Barney were her graduate course in love.

Here is Dolly's urgent, insolent, sexually inviting voice, calling out from what are perhaps some of the first *petits bleus*[10] she sent to Natalie Barney at the beginning of their long affair.

> Darling
> Did you know there was a *law* in France forbidding people to put flower vases on the window ledge? The femme de chambre has just told me. My room is full of flowers – all anonymous – so I prefer to think of them as from you (as they ought to be) & that tonight I must die … of your fragrant attentions! Come fold my shrouds tomorrow.
> Love <u>D</u>[11]

> Mon petit homme!
> A lazy morning given up to dreaming with Lily's [de Clermont Tonnerre] translation untouched by my side. Mais à toi la faute!

> Stay in your cool, dusty house all this afternon and I'll leave *as soon as possible*. Is the émail bleu* of your eyes purely intellectual to-day? Say no, darling.
> Love me, Dolly[12]
> *Liane [de Pougy]

> Forgive me darling if I don't come to dinner tonight & call me

an aesthete rather than a mondaine when I tell you that I am seeing a ballet given for the first time in Paris written by a friend of mine Sachie Sitwell. Friendship & enthousiasm prompt my choice & this is no idle indifferent 'placquage' (spell it for me darling, please). Such a busy day one way & another. One returns home these gentle, dusty evenings like warriors home from the wars!

What has been your mood lately? Too tired & busy even to be unfaithful to me? I am a darting trout; shifting, glancing & flashing my iridescent tail in a hundred pleasant pools!

What a horrid pen so thick & insensitive it's taking away even the frivolity of this handwriting! Dearest, all serious thoughts lie under this layer of white, lacy paper!
    D.[13]

Dearest
    An importunate car is at the door & I am off on the loose with Nature! Such a lovely day & the air as soft as powder puffs.

Now sweetness, frivolity apart let it be *quite* clear that I am going to … the *environs of Paris*, a matter of 80 kilometres or so, that I shall be back just when the afternoon becomes early evening. Let it also be clear dear grumbling darling that I love you & that I shall be so anxious to prove it to you that I shall probably dash into the rue Jacob just as I am from the country, making any necessary ablutions in that absurdly small wash basin in your bathroom. Feel me with open arms & love your faithful
    <u>Dolly</u>[14]

Natalie dearest, Natalie darling

I'm going to spend the day in the country – take lunch at a farm house & drink the 'unquenchable milky streams' of Madame Madrus' [Lucie Delarue-Mardrus] Arcadian cows!

When you come to write 'The Life & Letters' (if I should acheive [sic] fame two salient qualities I hope you'll stress – that I'm une grande amoureuse & a lover of Nature!!

Was it today we lunched with that delicate blonde? Say I'm souffrante & make a hundred *sincere* excuses. I like her so much & would liked to have lunched. Think of me as you sit at the table with your indifferent head & smile at secret thoughts with your brutal *but subtle* mouth! I'll pass by on my return – & fly across the bridge of a distance I have constructed during the day. One should always step back from one's happiness the better to contemplate it.

What an excellent, flattering mood I'm in darling. I look 20 & feel 16 too. But I'm treading gently lest the desert stretch before me at crossing. My love to Mimi(?) & tell her I haven't forgotten her present. Be clever & knit up our tattered friendship. Love, D.[15]

Dearest of all Professors

Did you know that it was nearly four o'clock when I left you last night? And the coiffeur was insistent at 9:30 this morning.

I am lying down in my room with drawn curtains after a long stupid luncheon & I am going to renounce the visit [Saloman

Rienach] & his cool garden. I ache with tiredness & darling, I am *bruised!*

Toujours, D.[16]

All of these *petits bleus* were written from the Hôtel Metropolitain, a small hotel just off the place de la Concorde on the rue Cambon, the street made famous by Coco Chanel — and all of them were written in the anticipatory mode: Dolly was expecting to see Natalie within hours of her writing. A repeated theme is Dolly's perpetual postponing of her pleasurable meetings with Natalie.

When Dolly first began her affair with Natalie, the little mahogany telephone box on the ground floor of Natalie's *pavillon* had not yet been installed (it was put in sometime in 1935) and so these intimate communications have the confidentiality of a telephone call whose messages are being delivered directly into the lover's ear; Dolly writes them as though they were meant to be spoken. None of the notes is dated (the only dates Dolly paid attention to were her birthday and her menses), but one or two of them are marked with an hour well into the afternoon, the hour, presumably, when Dolly was rising or resting after lunch. All the *petits bleus* have been delivered by messenger, the hand-delivery emphasising their intimacy.

Every public pose Dolly adopted in her short life is contained or suggested in these early notes to Natalie — and in the iridescent and offhand manner in which Dolly styles herself. The retreats and the advances, the overthrowing of expectations and cancelling of appointments, the aesthetic pique at a too-broad pen nib, the sly reference to Natalie's ex-lover Liane de Pougy's memoirs (Dolly *footnotes* Liane), the suggestively gendered sexuality of 'mon petit homme', the implied curtsy in 'Dearest of all Professors', and the deliberate, erotically tantalizing use of 'darling, I am *bruised!*' all present a floating, shimmering, socially and sexually provocative Dolly, cutting a wide swath through Paris and a deep furrow at 20 rue Jacob.

Her piquant references to a life of infinite alternatives show how well Dolly's instinctive style suited the woman to whom these notes are addressed. Dolly's airy intimations to other possibilities, as well as her last-minute cancellations, could only have helped to focus Natalie Barney's famously wandering attentions.

Two weeks after she began her affair with Natalie, Dolly was already back in London, writing to Natalie on 14 July 1927 with obvious pleasure in her perverse delight in physical distance and secrecy. Dolly liked secrets, she liked thinking about them, and she liked — perhaps even more than keeping them — to flaunt her secrets before her friends.

> Osbert Sitwell was at lunch & I brought you into the conversation — at the risk of compromise — with devilish cunning. My secret excitement is becoming a definite hunger now, & less pleasant in consequence. Why do I linger here? In augmenting my own love I shall probably lose yours . . . Am I right? How lightly I like you — how terrifyingly lightly when you consider what I might be losing.[17]

The next day, the force of her feeling has caught her by surprise.

> I've been asleep all this golden afternoon & now it's tea-time & life is a dreamy, yawning affair full of stillness & quiet. I am all alone in an enchanting room with yesterday's flowers like elegant fountains subtly playing . . . I confidently thought content would begin to set in after a week — & here I am still madly in love with you![18]

Separation from Natalie, even in the beginning of their affair, seemed almost a relief from all their initial, blazing emotion and Dolly wrote to Natalie from London:

> Fidelity stores up passion like honey & I am filled with all its sweets.

Why do I linger here? I try to understand my own perversity.
Is it a slight sense of relief at shifting the burden of my emotion? Away from you I have no pain only divine desire, which
is exquisite torture I admit but thrilling & wonderful. I dislike
the fret of incident with you . . .[19]

The 'fret of incident', by which Dolly meant Natalie's several other
lovers, must have been very fretful indeed, and Dolly loved to roll her
possibilities around in her mind when she was alone. Delaying her
pleasures was a real pleasure for her and any decision was always a
painful one. The Natalie she imagined was so much easier to treat
with than the Natalie she was beginning to know. '*What are* you
Natalie darling? I have created you so firmly in my head – or in my
heart – that reality is shocking & lacks conviction.'[20]

A week later Dolly writes from Bembridge, the summer home of
Sir Austin and Lady Cara Harris, Honey Harris's parents, on the Isle
of Wight, in much the same vein.

Always-wonderful Natalie!
 . . . I am so lazily happy – horribly brown & freckled & you
won't love me as a blonde with dark hair anymore – until perhaps a soft light shines down on my body – 'pasture to your
eyes . . .' I miss you every night with fierce discomfort &
wonder at my voluntary estrangement.

Then the day slips & slides into kaleidoscopic patterns & I
feel outrageously content, outrageously well: stabbed with
thoughts of you it is true – but wrapped in the petals of this
gigantic flower – summer.
 Your paradoxical Dolly.[21]

Dolly, whose favourite valedictory in these letters was 'Love me',
continued to write to Natalie paragraphs like this one:

Darling, darling Natalie don't shake me off – don't stop
loving me . . . yet! Explain my own foolishness to me. Bring
me to reason . . . I love you & am sad, & feel full of presentiment & foreboding: & angry, too, at your intolerant
acceptance of anything but classified emotions.[22]

And this one:

Why do I linger? Because I have no news of my house;
because Dorothy *will* not let me go & because the days slip by
as in a lotus-eating land, pleasantly, swiftly; because tho' tired
(unutterably tired) I . . . enjoy the respite & fear to break the
calm; because I am lazy, weak & prevaricating.[23]

And, in one way or another, in almost every letter she wrote to
Natalie for the rest of her life, Dolly kept repeating this plea: 'Don't
leave me darling, ever. Reassure me, draw up a contract to that
effect – sign it & seal it & lock it in the strongest safe![24]

Dolly's love for Natalie was enormous – a 'turmoil of love' she
came to call it – and she wrote that it 'shatters the fortress of my self-
sufficiency to a terrifying degree'. Perhaps Dolly's love seemed larger
to her because she saw herself as smaller in comparison to Natalie.
'How like me to underrate Natalie, I thought, by endowing her with
my own reactions & words! Why do you *like* someone so inferior to
yourself? I can understand your loving me, but not liking me!'[25]

Dolly was perhaps six inches taller than Natalie's five feet two
inches and built on longer lines, but she continued, between bouts of
sore-hearted and sometimes bitter analysis, to 'look up to' Natalie
Barney with something like the wide eyes of a child until she died.
'You are the only serious thing in my life emotionally. I remember in
those days feeling as if you over-shadowed me like a great mountain –
that at once uplifted me & awed me.'[26]

When Dolly wrote to Natalie, even in her more disillusioned,
later letters, she never failed to include the kind of praise that

amounts to homage. No one was more talented, more perfected in her intellect, no one was wiser than Natalie – although Dolly's unswerving fidelity to aesthetics did force her to slip in the fact that Natalie was '*much* too fat, darling, but you are such an exceptional person that the more of you, the better I suppose!' Dolly seemed to *need* to write the fulsome language – and Natalie was quite used to receiving this kind of homage from everyone.

Dolly refused to tolerate criticism of Natalie, at least from anyone else. Marcelle Fauchier Delavigne wrote to Dolly that Natalie, for her own convenience, had thrown Dolly into the arms of someone else, thus making a fool of Marcelle, and then she wrote to Natalie saying that Dolly was taking money from her (Marcelle) while disliking her. 'I accept *all* from people I like – but *nothing* from people I don't like,' Dolly wrote to Natalie in a rage and, '*poisoned* with anger' on account, she said, of Marcelle's criticisms of Natalie, Dolly tore up letters and papers from Marcelle in the presence of Jean Bourgoint.[27]

'Dearest,' Dolly wrote to Natalie on 28 July 1927, 'So you lie like a disappointed bridegroom in the cascade of your mosquito netting – while outside your windows roses & gardenias open to the night in wasted decor!'[28] Dolly had a way – subtle but insinuating – of sketching Natalie as mildly male. 'My little man', 'my blockhead bridegroom', 'my little Jew boy', 'mon petit homme', 'mon-beau', and 'Why didn't you give me the key so that I could be Cinderella & be with you for *one* minute before mid-night? I thought of it in the taxi, & frowned darling.'[29]

Although Dolly often served as chauffeur when she and Natalie went out driving together, and although Natalie herself was quite determinedly 'feminine' in dress and deportment, it was clearly Natalie – '*la seule, l'unique* Natalie' – whose imagined hands were on the steering wheel of their relationship.

How you inhabit my thoughts – how easily you take possession of my mind, subjugating me. Why do I wait? Yet the waiting is sweet & in no way lessens my desire. Will your love

outlast this delay? . . . But you give me glib assurances in your
letter & I am comforted, altho' I sense a certain tired aptitude
of phrase . . . You have held so many hands . . . so many
waists . . . written so many love letters . . . [30]

Dolly's frequent separations from Natalie – because of Natalie's
other lovers and because of Dolly's own complicated life – forced
Dolly's sexual feelings into her language; and so Dolly was always
offering up her body to Natalie in the letters she wrote. ('My darling,
both bifsteaks are yours to bite *off!*')[31] Short of describing herself in
the arms of another lover, which she always stopped herself – just in
time – from doing, these offerings took the form of sexual fantasies
and sensuous self-descriptions.

From Bembridge, again, the week before she called Natalie a 'disappointed bridegroom', Dolly sent a delicately veiled little piece of
auto-erotic writing. Plainly designed to arouse Natalie sexually, it
actually (and touchingly) owes something to the formal conventions
of Victorian fiction and it is as prim as a perambulator. Dolly marked
it *Please Tear Up* and, apart from whatever else it conveys, it makes clear
that Dolly's sexual life was a perfectly satisfying one; she knew how to
give pleasure and she knew how to take it.

Oh! Darling I am fallen from grace, sadly! Last night a starry
night outside my windows and the exciting darkness full of
your presence. I was assailed by the most furious desires . . .
No listless surrender this to your memory, Natalie – but irresistible, tremulous ecstatic passion lifting one high on the
crest of imagination of love, leaving one finally shaken and
exhausted with one's heart furiously beating against one's
side . . . and with all my knowledge I possessed you as deeply
and as actually as if you had been there . . . that blinding
lightening – like possession too swift, too acutely felt . . . I
sought quick comfort in excess [and] it was *you* who soothed
me with your own desire this time and filled me with that

well-remembered delight. Oh! The *force* of your love as you
gave it; making me cry out; darling . . .[32]

And she follows this up with another view of her body, clothed this
time, but still avid.

> I've bathed and played tennis and walked with an encircling
> arm around Honey down leafy lanes – and talked and read
> and danced. And now fresh from a bath, irreproachable in a
> Chanel frock and pearls, I wait for dinner this exquisite
> evening – with a delicious evening sun slipping up the legs of
> the chairs and splintering through the windows in final golden
> rays. The cook must be putting the last touches to her dishes
> and I am hungry for food. I am hungry for *everything*.[33]

Besides the anatomy of a turbulent love affair, Dolly's letters deliver
up a sensual, literary, *housekeeping* world; a world observed from the
bedroom, the salon, the dining room, and the garden. It is a world
where Gertrude Stein comes for a visit '. . . showing her preference by
only staying ten minutes, nibbling a few candies – dont le choix lui
semblait lamentable à juger par ses grimaces – & stealing the
two 'New Yorkers'![34] And where Gertrude's real interest is in Dolly's
'enthusiasm over her [new] book. Except for the irritation of childish, unmusical style, I think it *excellent* and *extremely* witty and amusing.
Her ideas are always *new* and mostly wise and go off like Christmas
crackers in a blaze of fiery sparks, coloured paper, tinsel and all!'[35]

It is a world where 'Elsie' Arden (the future cosmetics queen)
brings Dolly's coat across the Channel to save her the customs tax.
Where Osbert Sitwell proposes marriage and is palpably relieved
when Dolly refuses him. Where Dolly catches Virginia Woolf yawn-
ing during a Shakespeare play 'as if I had caught God in a domestic
moment of relaxation' – and turns her head quickly away so as not to
observe such a natural act from such a divine being. Where the
banned-from-rue-Jacob Jean Bourgoint comes to pick Dolly up for

dinner but doesn't dare set foot inside Natalie Barney's house. Where Dolly dances all night at a ball in London which 'provides a strange whiff of Paris' because 'everyone came dressed as a sailor'. Where Dolly and Romaine Brooks finally sit down to lunch and try to sort out the problems created by the fact that they are both in love with Natalie and sleeping with her. And where Natalie's famous indiscretions (many of Dolly's letters are helplessly marked '*Please don't repeat this darling!*') — matched only by Dolly's own — make infinite trouble for Dolly amongst her friends.

Dolly's letters also depict the kind of social relations which permit close friends like Janet Flanner to spread stories about a 'break-up' between Dolly and Natalie, and which allow Djuna Barnes to create awkward situations with her bluntness and her queries. The letters are pervaded by the assumption that a remittance relative like Dolly should expend her tiny capital on four-star luxuries like the Hôtel Montalembert, and then have to accept, second-hand, her ball-gowns from Lady Carnarvon, whose social secretary she sometimes seems to be. And Dolly continues, faithfully, to record her infidelities and to send them on to her lover Natalie as proof, by comparison, of her lasting passion and profound love.

Dolly liked to augment her 'upstairs' view of Paris and London life in her letters with 'downstairs' talk from 'the servants hall' — where her identification with people who led 'satellite lives' kept her hard at work on the archaeology of kitchen gossip. Dolly's inherent tendency — rather like her uncle Oscar's — to treat people democratically, is one of her more attractive traits and it was rare enough in the circles she frequented. It consistently moved her to console and defend a legion of Natalie's much-maltreated maids. As late as 1936 Dolly was still regaling Natalie with a list of virtues possessed by an unjustly fired servant named Mary who came to Dolly for comfort; and Dolly ended the list resolutely with: 'I do think you were unnecessarily cruel to her & she is completely broken up *in spirit* . . . & there is no one more willing & gay.'[36]

Dolly hated the workaday world and spent her life — *gave* her life, really – to avoid its manifestations. In her letters to Natalie, she seems never to have cooked a meal, cleaned a bathroom, laid a fire, or purchased her own writing paper. She did once mend a good coat when she found that the repair bill at Bradley's would have been too high. (With her acute performer's sense, Dolly, like the music-hall actors in Colette's *The Vagabond*, knew very well the value of 'one good coat' which 'covers everything'.) And she did once whitewash her service flat in London, and enjoyed the job immensely.[37] This was during a brief period of domestication when she also enjoyed choosing some curtains. She had her hair cut in her hotel rooms in Paris when she could afford it and she had her nails manicured at home – wherever home was – when she was in London and in funds. And since Berthe Cleyrergue ran her up copies of designer dresses – Dolly found fashion talk neither 'dull' nor irritatingly 'real', it was part of the art of living for her and her letters are filled with careful descriptions of dresses and coats – she must have stood on a chair in Berthe's tiny flat at 20 rue Jacob (the top of Dolly's head would just have brushed the low ceiling) while Berthe, with a mouthful of pins and a store of good gossip, draped material on her.

The things that Dolly noticed had more to do with the beauty of immediate surroundings. Her descriptions of the rooms where she reclined on divans, sat in front of flickering fires, prepared for dinner parties, or simply lay in bed writing, are precise and beautifully turned. For the entertainment of her friends, Dolly wrote many sharply observed portraits of the interesting women she was always meeting. The best of them is the one Dolly sent to her mysterious friend 'Emily'. Dolly so profoundly admired the 'sitter' for this portrait – 'she will never know what marginal notes of understanding mark every page of her books in my library' – that she dreaded a prospective dinner with the woman as 'an ordeal'. Nonetheless, she still managed to set down this likeness of Virginia Woolf, surely one of the subtlest ever written. Natalie published it in *Oscaria*.

Cambridge on a frosty night. The Dean's room in King's

College, fire-light, books, sober colours, elegance, and a group
of charming people holding conversation. We are waiting for
dinner when someone says 'Leonard and Virginia are very late.'
The smooth waters of my mind ruffled by this unexpected
remark and my heart beats perceptibly quicker. The chief
Lama of Thibet will be here any moment — easy manners
must give place to decorum, familiar friendship be brought
stiffly to attention. Then the door opens and a tall, gaunt
figure, grey-haired, floats into the room. Her age struck me
first, and then her prettiness — shock and delight hand in
hand. How explain? There is something of the witch in her —
as in Edith Sitwell — with the rather curved back and sharp
features. She is dressed in black, old fashioned, elderly clothes
that make me feel second-rate in my smart clothes. All is
faded and grey about her, like her iron grey hair parted in the
middle and dragged into a 'bun' in back. And yet immediately
one sees her *prettiness* and a lovely washed away ethereal look
making all of us look so gross and sensual. The eyes are deep-
sunk and small, the nose fine and pointed, a little *too* pointed
by curiosity, but the feature that strikes one is the mouth — a
full round mouth, a pretty girl's mouth in that spinster face. It
is so young, young like her skin that is smooth and soft. She
greets Honey and me without looking at us and at dinner
never once makes us the target of her eyes — there is embarrassment around the table and she only talks to her intimates.
She is witty and kindly malicious. Then suddenly I say something that makes her laugh and we talk together flippantly,
delightfully. I had once been told one must never mention her
books and as we threaded byeways of humour I thought of
your letters about her so much. I saw her, too, all the time as
such a pretty little girl in a big hat, and Kew Gardens with the
governess planting a kiss on the back of her neck — do you
remember? — which was the parent of all the kisses of her
life . . .

She has nothing to do with maternal life – is supposed to be a virgin, to have experienced no physical contact even with Orlando [Vita Sackville West]. She says she has no need of experience – knows everything without it: and this impression she gives as one meets her. I felt cruelty in her, born of humour – tiredness, great tiredness and her eyes *veiled* with visions rather than brightened by them.[38]

But Dolly applied none of this precision of description to how she got through her own days. Her uncle Oscar had written: 'Nothing that actually occurs is of the smallest importance . . .' and Dolly seemed to agree; action – 'realistic' action – simply didn't interest her. When she talks about playing tennis, it is always just that – no details of the game, no winning or losing; and swimming is just swimming and rowing a boat is always just a way to get from the luxurious houseboat where she is quartered to Mantes-la-Jolie for the afternoon. But the *pleasure* she takes in the appointments of that houseboat, or the *feelings* evoked by a much-missed Natalie – *those* conditions always inspire Dolly to densely, deeply detailed description.

Does one fall into one delight after another? Does this midsummer madness never cease? The house-boat is a floating dream (a floating debt – I also call it!) white and cool and festooned with flowers. The rooms are spacious retreats with wide deep sofas, while the decks are those of an ocean liner with hammocks swung under striped awnings. My bedroom is made for two and the little white boat lies moored beneath my three windows so that any lover could just step into my room any of these moon-light nights. Last night we sat on deck after dinner with a moon high in the sky – so steadfast in the sky but in the shifting water tossed like juggler's plates in the air – and, as always, under the moon I thought of you, and Emily says I was suddenly very silent for half an hour.[39]

Dolly's most civilised emotions were reserved for these movements of her mind over beautiful, stationary surfaces and for her copious and passionate reading. Except for those brief, flaming moments of sexual love, social success, or natural beauty, or for the rare and perfect conversational duets she created with people like Edmond Jaloux, the life that really marked Dolly was lived in and through the books she read and the letters she wrote. She came to fear that 'meetings are disappointing, almost distasteful'. She describes too well the anaesthesia of emotion that can blight a lovers' tryst.

> That strange ending of all intimacy at the very moment of re-forming – that suspicious getting-acquainted-again with the beloved – that horrible shyness & small talk – that sudden cessation of emotion – the dead level of reality, flat & terrifying. Is that a provision of Nature to prevent spontaneous combustion?[40]

In a letter to Natalie sent to Algeria after the first gauzy clouds of their love had been dispelled, Dolly spoke flippantly – she always spoke flippantly when most affected – about what the absence of reading and writing meant to her:

> What a dull letter you wrote me – ni l'amour ni de la littérature – il me faut ou l'un ou l'autre! [neither love nor literature – and either one or the other is necessary to me!] Tu m'as jeter un froid et j'étais infidèle – je te raconterai l'histoire à ton retour. [You chilled me to the bone and I was unfaithful – I will tell you the story when you return.] A charming, silly *beautiful* woman – but it was done so stupidly & I was so shocked by my own indifference, so coldly displeased within myself, that I cried unseen penitent tears & carried a heavy, contrite heart indeed. I missed you with terrific force.[41]

Literary talk and its by-product, beautiful sentences, were so important to Dolly that she could use the excuse of their absence to fall into bed with another woman. Natalie must have sent off one of her impersonal 'business-man's letters' and Dolly, deprived of both a romantic letter *and* a literary discussion, turned to the temporary fix of an 'emergency seduction' — which made her instantly miserable. (It would *never* have had that effect on Natalie.) Even Dolly's very favourite song — 'Parlez-moi d'amour', the *succès fou* sung by Lucienne Boyer in 1928 (so successful that every Parisian *still* knows the words) and requested by Dolly from Berthe Cleyrergue over and over again as she lay in bed recovering from a suicide attempt — is much more about the language of love than about love itself. '*Parlez-mois d'amour/Redites-moi des choses tendres/ . . . Je veux écouter encore les mots que j'adore,*' Lucienne sings. 'Speak to me of love/Say again some tender things/ . . . I want to hear once more the words that I adore.'

Dolly's passion for reading — for *living* through her reading — was a passion that absolutely equalled her other emotions. It is a testimony to the secrecy and separateness with which Dolly conducted all her relations that all we know about 'Emily,' the mysterious friend to whom she conveyed much of this passion, is that she was an intensely musical Englishwoman living in France who shared many friends with Dolly (Natalie Barney, Honey Harris and Elmer Harden of the headless brioches among them). Dolly has had, perhaps, a sexual relationship with Emily and now has a romantic, letter-writing one. She calls her 'dear, chaste nacreous Emily', speaks of a time 'when I was allowed to see you', refers to Emily's 'petal hands' as opposed to Dolly's own 'valentine' ones, and writes: 'I wish we [Honey and Dolly] could see you — but that's impossible I suppose. The impossible gets easier and easier to accept in every situation.' In her best, respectful, bejewelled, flirtatious manner, Dolly wrote some of her most vivid descriptions of literature to 'Emily'.

We have discovered Henry James! I ADORE him. *What* phrases if only I wasn't too lazy to copy them out. A gifted

pig I find out all the succulent truffles and pop them in S.'s
[her designation for NCB] mouth! . . .

And-oh-dearest Emily – I have stumbled on a wonderful classic. Staying with the Herons I was rummaging in the shelves
and Madame Bovary in her tattered yellow-back cover kept
glancing at me, I took her up and put her down and passed
her by and slighted her – and pouted and sulked at her. I took
her to bed and was so *entertained*, so amused, so delighted with
the *beauty* of it – the exquisite delicate thought – the brilliant
delicate analyses . . . Do you remember how as a girl she was
so entranced with the satin valentines and their pictures of
love that she drew in her breath with delight and made the
thin silk paper gently lift from the pictures and fall gently
back again! Dear, worldly dreaming Emma Bovary, how wonderful to have found you at last.[42]

A persistent problem for both Dolly and Natalie (and surely a new
convention for the love letter genre) were the attempts they regularly
made to coordinate their meetings with their menstrual cycles. Both
Dolly and Natalie cared terribly about lovemaking; neither of them –
out of delicacy – wanted to make love with the other while 'unwell'.
Unlike the situations of women who actually lived together, where
the biological clocks would ordinarily adjust to each other and the
menses would usually arrive on the same day, Dolly and Natalie
spent enough time apart so that this timing of monthly cycles was a
continual worry for them. Dolly was particularly anxious to mediate
each meeting with lovemaking and there are whole paragraphs in her
letters to Natalie – and in Natalie's letters to her – trying to arrange
a date when neither of them was, as the perhaps too-practical Natalie
put it, 'inutilisable'.

When are you ill? I don't want to meet you before you are well,
so *do* let me know the moment you are. I should be awkward

with you for days unless I could rush into your arms & be made whole. I seem to remember the 18th — in which case no good my arriving before the 16th. But give orders, darling, give orders & curtail the waiting. I *want* to meet you the 15th . . .[43]

Despite Natalie's complaints that Dolly preferred the *mot à mot* to the *corps à corps*, Dolly was adamant about lovemaking — especially at a distance. 'No dearest Nat-Nat I have neither seduced the pretty piano-playing child nor tightened my encircling arms around Honey in too amorous a manner! I am as chaste as Diana & hot on the pursuit of my blonde love . . .'[44]

She wrote to Natalie with a fine disregard for her own behaviour in staying away so much: 'Quarrel with your lover if needs be — be cross, disaggreable [sic], indifferent or cold but *always* be within lovemaking distance! Surely this is a lesson never to be un-learnt.'[45]

And when Dolly's period comes a week late it brings black moods, literary frustrations, sexual jealousy (prescience, really, since Natalie ended up in bed with the 'brilliant, didactic' Esther Murphy) and another delicate reference to masturbation.

Oh! darling I am in bed, unwell, with a devilish pain and wrapped in black melancholy. Even Honey cannot cheer me up & I have wept mollifying tears — the easiest way out of a difficulty. A letter from you by my tray sent a beam of hope through me — but alas! it was as cold & empty as a circular & I could find no word of comfort in it — not even a Natalie epigram spluttered over the page . . .

Fancy Esther [Murphy] being with you . . . Does she sleep in my bed? I don't like that. Have you made listless love to her — out of charitable curiosity? *Tell* me if you have. Last night I was gloriously unfaithful again . . . swimming out into — it seemed to me — an *eternity* of delight — so that fairly I broke the shelves with a cry.[46]

There were countless instances of Dolly having to accommodate the comings and goings of Natalie's other lovers, scheduled to arrive and depart Natalie's two houses like the changing of so many de luxe trains in a railyard:

What a cold draught blows through your letters to me. I don't mean because you have fallen in love — you know how absolutely free I think everyone should be & I am only pleased that you should be happy. But having all along arranged that I should come to you (in fact, I remember you making *me* promise) when R.B. left for Italy I do feel hurt that this plan should be swept aside so easily . . .[47]

You don't say (and I felt you *dared* not say!) what is going to happen after the 7th? . . . but if I come back to you for a week what happens after? If Lily [de Clermont Tonnerre] comes to Rome couldn't I stay on with C. ['Corydon,' Natalie's new lover] & Germaine [Beaumont]? Or have you other plans?[48]

It was awful for Dolly, the constant adjusting of Natalie's schedule and the constant need for Dolly to readjust hers in reaction — often just to have a place to stay. Sometimes Dolly wasn't even Natalie's second-best lover, but her third- or fourth-best. Who could have borne it for so long? And who could have borne it without taking something to kill the feelings — or to help express them? Natalie was not responsible for Dolly's addictions — there was something hypnotised and inevitable in Dolly's make-up that led her to that 'poisoned and perfect' place — but Dolly was transfixed by Natalie and the tumultuousness of their love affair splashed fuel of a very high octane over the bonfire Dolly was making of her life.

To relieve the pressures — and because it was her style to satirise — Dolly used to complain to Berthe Cleyrergue and mock Natalie's vagaries terribly. Berthe said: 'You don't have to indulge her every caprice.'[49] In fact, Natalie herself had patiently put up with much bad behaviour from Dolly, but Dolly did regularly bow to Natalie's exigencies — *everyone* bowed to Natalie. In this way, Dolly in love was reminiscent of her uncle Oscar, whose great, post-prison regret was the submission he exhibited in the face of Alfred Douglas's implacable will.

Nonetheless, Dolly was capable of getting her own back, often through patently self-destructive behaviour. One time, perhaps in exchange for drugs, Dolly took a dressing gown and a beautiful Vionnet coat from 20 rue Jacob and when she returned at three in the morning, she didn't bring them back. Natalie was very angry at Berthe for giving them, but Berthe, always capable of meeting Natalie squarely, said: 'I repeat, mademoiselle, you told me to give Dolly anything she wanted, you were very specific in your instructions and when you give them, mademoiselle, I execute them'.[50]

This fragment of a letter from Natalie to Dolly shows how Dolly could play fast and loose with lovers herself — and how she could set the magisterial and demanding Natalie back:

> . . . but as you have many friends far more wealthy and older than I, I naturally feel that it is now up to them . . . Though I would still go on doing everything if I did not feel that it's their turn as I see that my role is so little appreciated that I am sent to get 'calves for the mares' and laughed at . . . Do put the saddle on the right horse and save me from these corvées for better things.[51]

> Dolly, no longer my Dolly,

> . . . and so as you first declared and have since proved 'you

have Natalies in every quarter' (I didn't realize this extended so close to St. Germain) . . .

Words were blurted out again by Djuna [Barnes] of a sudden — '*who* now is Dolly in love with' — . . . and, again as last summer, Djuna is the messenger of ill omen . . .

Don't keep me guessing Dolly, let me just keep loving, which is disquieting and absorbing enough.[52]

One way to keep Natalie 'loving' was to help with her desire to be published in England. Natalie, who never scrupled to make use of the women she also loved and was generous with, sent Dolly to try to find a London editor for her novel, *The One Who Was Legion.* Dolly worked hard and long for Natalie's manuscript, researching whom she should see and networking with style. It was during this time — early December 1927 — that 'Vyvyan Holland (Oscar's son) gave a delicious dinner for me: only bachelors know how to be really comfortable. He remarked on my new thinness saying "Darling what has made you so thin?" — to which I *could* only reply "Requited love I suppose'!"[53]

Vyvyan gave her a letter recommending her to the publisher Duckworth, and some good advice about book pricings; and she continued to use her extended circle of friends to make the proper contacts, deploying her considerable store of charm to get the right appointments. She saw Grant Richards and found him unreliable. When Duckworth returned Natalie's manuscript, Dolly resolutely visited the 'Bloomsburys' (at Hogarth Press), journeyed to Reading to speak with Richard Aldington, went to Chatto & Windus; made, in short, every effort to circulate Natalie's manuscript properly and to reassure Natalie that she was doing so.

I know all the reservations of your mind with regard to my methods — which, of course, darling, you dare *not* tell me because I'm tiresomely sensitive etc etc!! But you can tell me, Natalie — *anything!* I am shedding that perishable skin of sensitiveness & growing a thick one of wise indifference instead. (Indifference *without* wisdom is bitterness.)[54]

Withal, Natalie was nervously criticising her from Paris, threatening to send Djuna Barnes into the breach (Djuna, blunt and incapable of telling a falsehood, proved herself a terrible emissary to publishers) and irritating and undermining Dolly no end. And, careful as Dolly was of Natalie's literary feelings, she was too uncompromising a reader to withhold the important criticisms. The letter that contained this paragraph could not have added to Natalie's sense of *bonheur:*

> . . . so often I didn't know what you meant: the depth of your
> ideas is made clear — it is simply the meaning of phrases
> etc . . . You *know* what I think of [the book] — but a certain
> incoherence has worried me — & as I am your perhaps more
> than average reader it is important.[55]

In March 1929, Dolly was still trying to peddle Natalie's manuscripts in London, still being criticised for her efforts, and still being threatened with an intervention by Djuna Barnes. Dolly ended the matter with a paragraph as plain as a punch, turning down yet another one of Natalie's complicated invitations.

> In future you must do all your own arrangements as you misunderstand & mistrust others — the former being the most
> exasperating . . .

> I have the impression that with all of you I am the performing
> animal — eternally criticized, alternatively approved & disapproved according to the temper of the audience. . . . I don't
> know what day I return to Paris — probably the 10th or 11th:

at the moment I don't feel that our plans depend on each other.[56]

Many of Dolly's letters, while seeming to be part of an extended conversation, are in fact monologues constructed to deliver a complete 'character'; a character that kept Dolly's correspondents right where she wanted them: engaged, ensnared, and at a distance from what she was often up to. When Dolly 'breaks' her usual letter-writing character, it is sometimes to defend herself against an accusation — and then rage strips her prose of metaphor. Dolly sent a furious, undated letter to Natalie sometime in the early 1930s after Dolly's addiction to heroin was well established, and after an afternoon during which Lily de Gramont had seen her spending 'too much time' in the lavatory. Lily imagined the worst and reported to Natalie that Dolly was 'killing herself' with drugs again. Natalie, with her 'usual indiscretion', reported the incident to Germaine Beaumont and to 'Corydon' — a new lover of Natalie who was a painful rival for Dolly.

I make no defence of my life — but I *do* rebel *against* the *ludicrous caricature* of that life! . . . To be the subject of light gossiping amongst people who are not in my intimacy is *very* unpleasant — especially when their sense of drama leads them to wild exaggeration. [Dolly is so incensed that, for once, she doesn't make a play on the word 'wild'.]

Don't worry about me. Look after Romaine & yourself — & all your little crowd of second rate beings unworthy of *your* superiority . . . you have *nothing* to consider in my regard, as far as material things are concerned. I owe *you* all too much, but I think in return for past stoicism on my part and elegance of conduct, besides present help, you owe *me real* discretion & loyalty, however harshly you judge me yourself. D.[57]

What is missing from Dolly's letters is often as important as what is in them: her motives (particularly in relation to drug matters), certain actual events as they happen, the true state of her finances (which she was often too over-extended to determine), and, regularly, whom she was sleeping with – or not. She writes from an epistolary 'I' who is, with some notable exceptions, almost never too sad to turn a graceful phrase, or follow a lovely comparison to its root, or provide descriptions – both fulsome and lissome – of whatever luscious countryside or wonderful woman or brilliant book she is looking at during this very moment. Nor does she shy away from mentioning the disgraceful state of her personal economy or delicately or overtly suggesting a loan.

So serious a concern was money for her – and so frequently was it a subject of her sentences – that it seemed, as money worries can do, to cancel her joy, paralyse her hopes, and annul her sleep. Dolly 'worked' as a translator – she did more than a few translations – but often did not sign her name to them and just as often she was left unpaid. She circled around great hostesses – that 'satellite' life again – sometimes assisting women like Lady Carnarvon or Elsa Maxwell, and was lightly remunerated for the work, occasionally with cast-off clothes. She flirted with getting a job, but the flirtation was never a serious one and she seems to have applied too late – or not at all – for the one job that might have suited her best: fashion correspondent in Paris for British *Vogue*.

Although she died with '500 disregarded pounds to her credit', the margins of her love letters are sometimes filled with feverish calculations of debts, and many letters often include mentions of money requested or thanks for money received. Her worst 'worries', the ones that kept her howling down the long corridors of insomnia by night, or doing furtive drug transactions by day, were often financial ones. Like every person living beyond her means and paralysed by the thought of an impoverished future, Dolly sometimes deluded herself with the idea that lack of money was the root of all her evil.

Natalie Barney was in her fifties – almost two decades older than

Dolly when they first met, loved, and began their correspondence – and Dolly had an unusually and carelessly youthful cast of mind until she entered her forties. The heartbreak Dolly found in her fully requited love for Natalie Barney perfectly fitted her romantic sense of doomed passion; it also fitted her doomed sense of herself as a Wilde and as the much younger lover of an older woman. Dolly's letters often show her striving – unsuccessfully – for a dignified maturity of response to Natalie's long-settled habits of multiple relations and open (though not always philosophic) acceptance and encouragement of the same habits in Dolly. On the other hand (there is always an 'other hand' with Dolly) Dolly could present herself as the scapegrace, irresponsible 'Puppy Wilde', breaking engagements, flaunting her rude-nesses and her intimacies, making off with Natalie's much-discussed Buick (the ultimate in teenage rebellion), and generally playing up to Natalie's late-middle-aged disapproval. But Natalie's feelings for Dolly over the years continued unquelled and unequalled – even if Natalie presented them with the kind of classical detachment which drove Dolly wild – and kept her coming back for more.

> The divine part of us loves and understands but the human part suffers and complains! . . . My puppy, may the melancholy . . . joys of [a new love] save you from that drugged state of indifference which was death in life . . .[58]

> Here in the gentle light of this tapestried room (I'm having it well-beaten and cleaned also bath etc) your pallour will regain its lustre, and your lips their smile and your feet bring you as far as the white room with you by open window on the fall of leaves – I wait! Darling, the world looks like a musical instrument, and vibrates at your approach. Yet do not fear. I shall know how to seem distant enough.[59]

It is said that Dolly was the only woman who could make Natalie Barney cry and Natalie's friend Jenny Bradley recounted one instance of this phenomenon. Natalie and Dolly had broken up – once again – and Natalie bought Dolly a plane ticket to London and packed her off to the airport. Once there, Dolly saw no good reason to step on the plane and so she turned right around and taxied back to the rue Jacob, where she found Natalie weeping and eating a consolatory dessert, 'her tears running onto the cake and discoloring the chocolate.'[60]

It was only in the letters Dolly wrote towards the end of her life, when she was in her early forties, that the phrase Lily Wilde had written to Oscar all those years ago – 'After 40 one loses someway the power of being happy' – seemed to drop down on Dolly's life like the portcullis of a confining castle, permanently closing off her drawbridge to joy. These last letters are much like her grandmother Jane Wilde's desperate, dunning letters to Oscar written before Dolly was born; they represent the shutting down of every open passage in Dolly's imagination. How she must have felt the iron bars descend as she approached the fatal Wilde age of forty-six – the death age of both Willie and Oscar – burdened by a self-consuming disease and an unshakable addiction.

Here is another letter from Dolly in which she 'breaks' her usual letter-writing character. It is a short letter and Natalie's response to it has been lost. Like most of Dolly's letters – like Dolly herself, really – the letter never had a date or a definite address. It contains no superlatives, theatrics, rich metaphors, or calculations in the economics of desire along the lines of Dolly's 'why don't you advance me my legacy before you die?' propositions to Natalie – propositions which, anyway, came to seem painfully ironic when Dolly died so young and it was the elderly multi-millionaire Natalie Barney who inherited a little something from the impoverished Dolly Wilde.

Dolly's writing voice in this letter is hushed and low, as simple as a monosyllable and as unadornedly sad. Her 'fine' writing is gone here but her finest feeling, finer than the situation which has released it, opens its arms – 'true lover's arms' – and embraces both Natalie and herself.

Darling Natalie

Your distress distressed me on the telephone & if I seemed
hard it was because a period of sadness makes one anaesthetised — arms all too ready to stretch out become paralysed
by a certain shock of suffering. Last night I had to go to the
pitch of acceptance which has despair always hot on its
heels — because thought no longer weaves hopes, plans, illu-
sions . . .

Don't be sad — especially when you are in love. I have come to
terms with myself . . . & realize one must stand alone & not —
like a beggar — ask for tenderness. My letters have insinuated
that you are under obligations which is *all wrong* — sentimental
blackmail in fact! Honey & I will be delighted to come — we
have both got very thin & very ugly!

I shall always love you so there shall be no more bargaining of
affection. D.[61]

8

Afterword

Afterword: Truly Wilde

*D*olly's uncle is supposed to have said that one of the world's great tragedies is that one usually ends by getting what one wants. Dolly quoted that remark, saying it was the only tragedy she looked forward to with pleasure. It turned out to be almost the only tragedy she didn't experience.

Formed for the most delicious farce, perhaps formed to *write* the most delicious farce, Dolly played out the last part of her life in a succession of domestic tragedies and hotel melodramas. She loved love, but she fled from it when she found it – and she found it with the one woman who could not give her love's full attention. Death, first in the form of sleep, then in its final form, had the greatest attraction for her, but it is quite likely that her own death was some kind of accident. She had immense spiritual yearnings, imagining a world beyond the world that so frequently disappointed her – but the only way she could get to it was by obliterating herself.

Dolly's drug-taking was only ever meant to imitate or assuage the two deeper imperatives which directed her behaviour: death and love. Oscar had similar interests: 'Death and Love seem to walk on either hand as I go through life: they are the only things I think of . . .' Though Dolly came up short, finally, in the latter condition and fell, mostly through trial and error, into the former one, there was never anything superficial in her relationship to either state. Dolly's lifelong lover's quarrel with love and death was always a profound one.

When she failed to establish her authority over her material (which is what a creative talker does when she refuses to write something down), Dolly allowed her life to pick up the rhythm of the lovers she lived with and of the stimulants she used. She suffered the profound boredom of a 'born' writer who can feel her talent but who cannot find her form. Thomas De Quincey said it was this 'taedium vitae' for which the opium poppy was created. James Joyce could have been describing Dolly when he identified the 'Irish disease' as 'paralysis'.

'Writing', wrote her grandmother Jane Wilde before Dolly's birth, 'is a fatal gift for a woman.' But it was *not* writing that was perhaps the fatality for Dolly. Still, she maintained her original, unclassifiable hold on the writer's life by turning writers' materials – thought and language – into performance. She entertained as a prodigal talker in the most important salon of her century; she discoursed as an avid reader to her many admiring friends; she enchanted as a 'personality' in more public (and more social) circles; and she let slip, carelessly, her beautifully turned letters to her intimates, drawing back (with hesitations like the syncopations of a minuet) from all possibility of commitment. She seemed always to be in rehearsal for a final work whose contract she could not bring herself to sign. Perhaps, as Janet Flanner thought, she belonged in a romantic, unwritten 'intranational' novel by Stendhal – 'who could also have equipped her with resolute action'.

Dolly's letters to Natalie Barney are shirred with her craving for the lost paradise of the rue Jacob (lost to her, really, from the moment she found it), ruched with requests for love and money, and pitted by a risky emotional honesty and the occasionally interesting lie. They are full of what lovers say to each other when there is an imbalance in bank accounts, an opposition in temperaments, a disagreement on fidelities, and when a sexually exclusive coupling cannot be formed, the kind of coupling only Dolly – and then only sometimes – seemed to want. They show the writer Dolly was as well as the writer she might have been. They are, as Janet Flanner said, her anthology.

The 'character' that Dolly assembled for the world, the character that suited her swift wit and electric repartee, could not have made use of her childhood years as they occurred. Those years were too orphaned, too poor, and, by anyone's calculation, too abandoned. Sorrow and anger were most likely the motives for her brilliant, self-deprecating, and sometimes cruel comedy; but they were never the subject. That subject – the deeply destabilising sadness of her life – she kept to herself, and it became the silent partner in the emotional drama of approach and withdrawal that characterised all of Dolly's adult relations.

After she died, a casual acquaintance said to one of Dolly's friends that of course Miss Wilde had once been delightful, but that in her last years she had only been like herself for half an hour every six months. Dolly's friend flared up in anger, retorting: 'Half an hour of Dolly was worth six months of anyone else.' Dolly's linguistic charm was more than just etymologically linked to enchantment. When it worked positively, it was like enchantment's older sister: it spun straw into gold. It kept, as Victor Cunard said, 'so many of [her friends] perpetually telephoning to the Hôtel Montalembert, or wherever else she happened, for the moment, to be living'.

Her effect was akin to the *ambiance* of a perfume, or a newly mixed colour, or a line of good poetry: she lingered on the ends of the nerves, was taken up by the senses, and recreated herself as a category just beyond the borders of descriptions. That so essentially original a woman remained a subordinate clause in her uncle's more significant sentence, was just one of the many ironies that pervaded Dolly's life.

A scrap of vignette, recounted by Bettina Bergery long after Dolly's death, conveys something of Dolly's uncanny persistence in memory.

The last person I asked about Miss Wilde was an English girl who I believed had known her before any of us heard of her.

She answered: It's such a long time ago, so much has happened since then. All I can remember is that my sister who loved Dolly used to drive us mad by singing over and over mournfully, in the tune of that time which she'd changed the words to:

> *Good-bye Dolly, I must leave you*
> *Though it break my heart to go.*

and my sisters and brothers and I used to join heartily in the refrain which was:

> *Good-bye Dolly Wilde.*

Dolly's cousin Vyvyan Holland, who had slight and uneasy relations with her, recollected her asking him why he didn't love her more. Shadowed by Oscar, haunted by Natalie, it was the question Dolly put, in one form or another, to almost everyone. A Romantic in all things, a Modernist – if Modernism means a constant quarrel with the enveloping past, and Attic, too, in her love of beauty and tragic assumption of the sins of her fathers, Dolly's self-presentation crossed all categories: here, but never quite 'all there'; true, but never entirely 'real'. She was the Beautiful Loser of the Wilde Family and, written out of the Wilde history, she repeated that history too well, very badly, and over and over again.

None of the French or English authors of the twenties or thirties – and Dolly was acquainted with most of them – wrote about Dolly in their published novels. 'This omission is probably a good thing,' Janet Flanner said, 'as they wrote about other women of her many circles and theirs, whom she knew, whom many of us knew' and, in those novels, the women were 'nothing like what we all remember'.

Janet Flanner was right about Dolly; it would have been impossible for contemporaries to sketch her in a novel. There was something too evocative about her, *too* artistic. The 'work' was already there and Dolly had done it; there was nothing left for the writer to transform. Dolly already was, as Janet had written, 'like a character out of a book, even if it was never written'. She seemed 'like someone one had become familiar with by reading, rather than by knowing. She was made for adjectives such as writers use, in long novels, where the description of characterizations becomes intense, intelligent, elaborate, fanciful and repeated with variations . . .'

Those who remembered Dolly fondly were, Janet Flanner thought, like Stendhal's 'happy few'.

Notes and Sources

Besides the quoted and consulted works listed in the Bibliography, sources for *Truly Wilde* came from numerous interviews, private archives and collections, and public and university libraries cited in the Notes. Important unpublished materials were in the archives of Cara Lancaster and Berthe Cleyrergue. Natalie Clifford Barney's own voluminous archives, including all of Dolly Wilde's letters to her, are at the Fonds Littéraire Jacques Doucet under the executorship of François Chapon. The William Andrews Clark Library in Los Angeles holds the largest collection of Wildeana in the United States. Somerset House in London stores useful public documents, and important information is on file at the Westminster Coroner's Office.

For simplicity's sake, the letters from Dolly Wilde, Tancred Borenius and Pamela 'Honey' Harris *to* Natalie Barney are preceded by their date of composition (when discernible), cited as 'Letter' and followed by their number in the file; the letters *from* Natalie Barney to Dolly Wilde, Tancred Borenius, and Pamela 'Honey' Harris are preceded by their date of composition (when discernible), cited as 'Letter' and followed by their number in the file and the abbreviation, 'Lets and Docs'. Letters from Lily Wilde and Jane Wilde are cited by their dates and provenance. Interviews are indicated by the abbreviation CWA – Conversation With the Author – and, except in the case of Berthe Cleyrergue with whom I talked so long and so often that date notation seemed irrelevant, are followed by the date of the interview. Translations from the French are my own unless otherwise noted.

Abbreviations used in the Notes:

More Adey:	MA
Berthe Cleyrergue:	BC
Natalie Clifford Barney:	NCB
Bettina Bergery:	BB
Tancred Borenius:	TB
Dorothy Ierne Wilde:	DIW
Victor Cunard:	VC
Janet Flanner:	JF
Allanah Harper:	AH
Fonds Jacques Doucet:	JD
Pamela 'Honey' Harris:	PH
In Memory of Dorothy Ierne Wilde:	IMDIW
Dorothy Ierne Wilde:	DIW
Jane Wilde:	JW
Lily Wilde:	LW
Oscar Wilde:	OW

Chapter 1, Atlantis Rising: an Introduction

1 JF, *IMDIW*, pp. 25–6.
2 BB, ibid., pp. 42–58.
3 VC, ibid., p. 18.
4 JF, ibid., p. 25.
5 BB, ibid., p. 56.
6 DIW to NCB, 9 December 1927, Letter 47.
7 As his friend Ada Leverson said.
8 Hesketh Pearson.
9 DIW to NCB, 26 October 1931, Letter 86.
10 Ibid., 27 January 1937, Letter 126.
11 Vyvyan Holland, unpublished journal entry, 17 April 1941, collection of Merlin Holland.
12 VC, *IMDIW*, p. 18.

13 BC, CWA.

14 Ibid.

15 Ibid.

16 Ibid.

17 JF, *IMDIW*, p. 23.

18 BC, CWA.

19 JF, *IMDIW*, p. 21.

20 Eyre de Lanux. See Appendix 2: 'I Don't Remember Dolly Wilde.'

21 Heilbrun, p. 48.

Chapter 2, Stormy Weather

1 Bulletin Quotidien de Renseignements de l'Office National Météorologique, mardi, 28 juin 1927.

2 BC, CWA.

3 Relevés Météorologiques, Paris, 28 April 1927.

4 NCB to DIW, undated, Lets and Docs.

5 Relevés Météorologiques, Paris, 28 April 1927.

6 Ibid.

7 Rosamond Harcourt-Smith, *IMDIW*, p. 28.

8 NCB, *IMDIW*, p. 11.

9 PH, *IMDIW*, p. 37.

10 NCB, *IMDIW*, p. 8.

11 BC, CWA.

12 BB, *IMDIW*, p. 47.

13 BC, CWA.

14 BB, *IMDIW*, p. 44.

15 BC, CWA.

16 DIW to NCB, 4:30 p.m., Letter 11.

17 Ibid., undated, Letter 176.

18 DIW to NCB, 10 March 1932. DIW writes: 'I have been here just a week but this is the first time I have felt equal to writing. My time in Paris was a nightmare . . .'

19 NCB, *IMDIW*, p. 7.

20 BC, CWA.

21 BB, *IMDIW*, p. 53.

22 NCB, *IMDIW*, p. 135.

23 Ibid., p. 15.

24 Secrest, p. 348.

25 BC, CWA.

26 Ibid.

27 NCB, MS 104 (list of items served in the salon), JD.

28 Wickes, p. 28.

29 BB, *IMDIW*, p. 46.

30 JF, quoted by Wickes, *Amazon of Letters, p.266*.

31 Putnam, p. 75.

32 NCB, *IMDIW*, p. 15.

33 BB, quoted by Wickes, *Amazon of Letters*, p. 253.

34 NCB, *IMDIW*, p. 10.

Chapter 3, Dead Again

1 Unless otherwise indicated, all information in this chapter comes from reports on file in the Westminster Coroner's Office (London) under the administration of HM Coroner, Dr Paul Knapman. These detailed documents include the 'Coroner's Inquiry into the Death of Dorothy Ierne Wilde', reports from the Department of Chemical Pathology, St Mary's Hospital (10 May 1941), P. C. MacDonald's report of the witnesses' statements, (filed 10 April 1941), the coroner's office's report concerning death (11 April 1941), the burial order issued to Miss Willes, the post-mortem examination (11 April 1941), letters from Holmes, Son, & Pott to the coroner's office, 'Certified Copy of Death' certificate, the 'Last Will and Testament of DIW', and the coroner's report from the inquest itself.

2 Mosley, *Love From Nancy*, pp. 90–91.

3 JF/Solita Solano papers, Library of Congress.

4 NCB, *IMDIW*, p. 145.

5 Schmidgall, p. 408.

Chapter 4, Fathers Are Depressing

1 J. E. Holroyd, p. 230, and Melville, pp. 148–50.

2 See accounts of Willie by L. Purser, Frank Boyd, A. M. Binstead, and Leonard Cresswell Inglesby.

3 Letters of LW , Florence Leslie, and Max Beerbohm.

4 In *Victorian Doctor* (Wilson, p. 324), T. G. Wilson remarks, with the kind of forthrightness that only the gap of a century can convert to humour, that 'Speranza, some say, was a repressed homosexualist. If this is true, all the more credit to her, for unlike her son she had the pluck to suppress it.'

5 Henriette Corkran, *Celebrities and I*, quoted by Melville in *Mother of Oscar*, p. 14.

6 Robert Harborough Sherard, *The Real Oscar Wilde*, and Harold Hartley, *Eighty-eight Not Out*, quoted in ibid., p. 157.

7 Letter from JW to an unknown correspodent, University of Reading, quoted in ibid., pp. 52–3.

8 'Dark', 'oily', 'ugly', 'dirty', 'pithecoid', suffering from 'gigantism', 'ungainly', 'awkward', 'lurching', 'oversize', 'clumsy' are only a few of the adjectives affixed to the Wilde father and sons.

9 JW to an unknown correspondent, University of Reading, quoted in *Mother of Oscar*, p. 47.

10 Max Beerbohm, Letters to Reggie Turner, ed. R. Hart-Davis (1964), p. 63.

11 L. Purser to A. J. A. Symons, 28 January 1932, William Andrews Clark Library.

12 Hesketh Pearson, *The Pilgrim Daughters* (1961), pp. 177–8.

13 Sterne, p. 161. Three weeks after her marriage to Willie, 'Mrs. Florence M. Wilde received permission once again to change her name officially to "Frank Leslie".'(p. 156).

14 'Mr. William Wilde Forgot a Little Matter of $14,' *New York Times*, 17 September 1892.

15 Sterne, pp. 160, 162.

16 Ibid., p. 162. Because of his marriage to Mrs Leslie, Willie Wilde can be said to have made a considerable, though involuntary, contribution to North American feminism. At the end of her life Florence Leslie was so disillusioned with her marital experiences that she left her entire fortune to Suffragette causes.

17 Entries for William Armit Lees, *Thom's Directory*: 1859–1882, National Library of Ireland, Dublin.

18 Will of William Armit Lees, Somerset House, London. Probate granted at London, 16 November 1885.

19 JW to OW, 8 October, 1893, William Andrews Clark Library.

20 A. Mynors to Constance Wilde, 30 October 1893, William Andrews Clark Library.

21 NCB, *IMDIW*, p. 8.

22 JW to OW, 4 February 1894, William Andrews Clark Library.

23 JW to OW, 27 February 1894, William Andrews Clark Library.

24 A. Mynors to Constance Wilde, 30 October 1893, William Andrews Clark Library.

25 Beerbohm, p. 63.

26 Ethel Smyth, *Impressions That Remained*: vol.I, (London, Longmans Green, 1919). pp. 100–3.

27 Behrman, p. 239.

28 LW, quoted by H. Montgomery Hyde, *Oscar Wilde* (London: Methuen, 1976), p. 301.

29 LW to MA, 18 October 1895, William Andrews Clark Library.

30 LW to OW, date unknown, William Andrews Clark Library.

31 LW to MA, 9 November 1896, William Andrews Clark Library.

32 LW to 'Dear Heart', ca. 1899, William Andrews Clark Library.

33 BB, *IMDIW*, p. 51.

34 LW to OW, October 1900, William Andrews Clark Library.

35 Translation by Kevin O'Brien, 'Lily Wilde and Oscar's Fur Coat', *Journal of the Eighteen Nineties*, p. 18.

36 LW to OW, 7 May 1899, William Andrews Clark Library.

37 Birth Certificate for DIW, Somerset House, London.

38 LW to MA, 13 March 1896, William Andrews Clark Library.

39 LW to OW, 7 May 1899, William Andrews Clark Library.

40 Gertrude Atherton, *Adventures of a Novelist*, quoted by Joy Melville in *Mother of Oscar*, p. 247.

41 Holroyd, p. 237.

42 LW to MA, 7 May 1897, Bodleian Library, Oxford, cited by Kevin O'Brien.

43 Ibid.

44 NCB, *IMDIW*, p. 8.

45 Kevin O'Brien, CWA, 1 January 1997.

46 McKenna, pp. 1–34.

47 Ibid., p. 85.

48 Will of Sophia Lily Wilde Teixeira de Mattos, Somerset House, London.

Chapter 5, Mädchen in Uniform

1 NCB, Letter 10, Lets and Docs.

2 BB, *IMDIW*, p. 55.

3 NCB, *IMDIW*, p. 9.

4 Two examples of Dolly's telegrams: VIENS D'ARRIVER AMUSEE ETONEE (9 December 1927). DARLING DISTRESSED DELAYED DEPRESSED (27 June 1928).

5 DIW to NCB, undated, Letter 171.

6 Stressed by Stephen MacKenna throughout his biography of Teixeira de Mattos.

7 Much of Dolly's later conduct in public gives the tranced, blank, isolated, and spellbound impression of deposits left in an adult woman's psychological life by a sexually abused and/or incestuous childhood. But there is no scrap of evidence from Dolly's early years to support this or any other conjecture; just

a whiff of brimstone about her behaviour – and the slow, crumbling wreck her life became. Biographers, as Lord Peter Wimsey's creator said of detectives, must never reason ahead of their evidence.

8 BB, *IMDIW*, p. 56.

9 See Appendix 3, 'Dolly's Left Hand', for a chirologist's reading of what might have happened to Dolly during this time.

10 NCB, *IMDIW*, p. 9.

11 Ziegler, p. 22.

12 Scharff, p. 97.

13 JF, Introduction, p. xiii.

14 Louÿs, pp. 19–20.

15 Barney, *Souvenirs indiscrets*, p. 21.

16 Monroe Wheeler, while living with both novelist Glenway Wescott and photographer George Platt Lynes, had a lengthily ambiguous romance with publisher Barbara Harrison, the woman who loaned Dolly her house on the rue Vaugirard; Elizabeth Eyre de Lanux married, and then had affairs with NCB, Louis Aragon, Drieu La Rochelle, and Evelyn Wyld. The list goes on and on.

17 See Shari Benstock, *Women of the Left Bank*, for a discussion of the creative responses by the 'City of Women' residing in Paris to the Modernism practised by male artists there. And for a full exposition of Parisian salon life as it was conducted in the first forty years of the twentieth century.

18 Ibid., p. 51.

19 DIW , *IMDIW*, Letter to 'Emily', p. 89.

20 JF/Solano Papers, Library of Congress.

21 According to Berthe Cleyrergue, when NCB once reproved Dolly for a desire to marry her friend Victor Cunard with, 'But Dolly, you're a lesbian,' Dolly retorted, 'You're dreaming.'

22 DIW to NCB, 3 January 1928, Letter 54, Lets and Docs.

23 DIW to NCB, 14 July 1927, Letter 22.

24 DIW to NCB, undated, Letter 197.

25 DIW to NCB, undated, Letter 171.

26 Bronia Clair (Mme René Clair), CWA, 24 July 1997. Bettina Bergery said that NCB and Bronia Clair had startlingly similar eyes; an unlikely cornflower blue with a star-iris marking in the pupil.

27 Summerscale, p. 25.

28 Ibid., pp. 25–6.

29 Ibid., p. 26.

30 Ibid., p. 28.

31 For the wonderfully 'eccentric story of Joe Carstairs', see *The Queen of Whale Kay* by Kate Summerscale. Joe Carstairs lent Dolly her flat in Mulberry Walk, not, as the book suggests, for Dolly to convalesce from a suicide attempt but because Dolly had separated from her lover Gwen Farrar. For an account of Dolly staying in Joe Carstairs's flat in 1939 see DIW to NCB, 25 February 1939, Letter 144.

32 DIW to NCB, 7 December 1927, Letter 44.

33 Baker, p. 125.

34 Ibid., p. 126.

35 Mercedes de Acosta once referred to Dorothy Todd, editor of British *Vogue*, as 'the bucket in the well of loneliness'.

36 Thurman, p. 386.

37 Lambert, pp. 224–5.

38 Another of these war-working women was the American financier J. P. Morgan's daughter, Anne Morgan. She became the treasurer for the American Fund for French Wounded, known, somewhat smartly, as the 'heiress corps' for the wealth and social position of its founders. Anne Morgan lived for years in a kind of *ménage à trois* with the interior decorator Elsie de Wolfe (later Lady Mendl) and her lover, the international theatrical manager Bessie Marbury. Bessie Marbury had represented Oscar Wilde's plays in the United States when he was still alive, hid his American royalties for him when he was in prison, and was able to sell subsidiary rights to 'The Ballad of Reading Gaol' when no British publisher would touch them. Anne Morgan would have been fascinated to hear - as she must certainly have done - that Oscar Wilde's niece Dolly was driving an ambulance in France.

39 Meade, p. 48.

40 BB, *IMDIW*, p. 43.

41 NCB, *IMDIW*, p. 15.

42 BB, *IMDIW*, p. 45.

43 Jamison, p. 6. Dr Jamison goes on to quote Hippocrates who said that 'mania and melancholy' were more likely to occur in the spring and autumn. Many of Dolly's serious attempts at self-immolation occurred in September and, most often, in April. Dr Jamison's full and convincing exposition of manic-depressive illness as it affects and is expressed by the psychology of creative people leaves little doubt that Dolly herself was so afflicted.

44 DIW to NCB, 3 December 1932, Letter 106.

45 DIW to NCB, 5 August 1927, Letter 36.

46 BB, *IMDIW*, pp. 45–46.

47 Quoted by BB, *IMDIW*, p. 51.

48 Ibid.

49 DIW to NCB, 30 July 1936, Letter 123.

50 DIW to NCB, 27 July 1927, Letter 32.

51 See Elyse Blankley's essay, 'Return to Mytilene', in *Women Writers and the City* for an interesting discussion of Renée Vivien's recreation of Lesbos in her Paris poetry.

52 NCB, *IMDIW*, p. 14.

53 About ten years after the end of the Great War, Laura Dreyfus-Barney wrote an infuriated letter to her sister Natalie Clifford Barney on the always touchy subject of Dolly Wilde's rude behaviour with Buicks and the beau monde.

> ... I am afraid that Miss W. still made trouble, as [the chauffeur] has already been forced to chauffeur her 3 times in less than a week. Too bad Miss W. has been rude often to Lily [duchess of Clermont-Tonnerre, another long-time lover of Natalie Barney] – they had a tea arranged to Tuesday & two hours before Miss W. [announced] that she preferred going to the country – Now Lily will not give her work to translate & is furious, *she* thinks you are mad to let her take out the Buick without your chauffeur ...

NCB marked this letter with an arrow and had obviously shown it to Dolly – for on the bottom of the page is this pencilled, exasperated, good-natured notation in NCB's hand: 'Why must history & 'histoires' so repeat themselves & you resort to rudeness?? And waste your best chance (the only best chance) of work? My puppy are you incorrigible?'

Well, yes, Dolly *was* incorrigible, as NCB must have known very well by the time this letter was written. But Dolly's future lover had her own brand of incorrigibility: a positive talent for sitting serenely in the centre of a serpent's tangle of tales while listening with obvious enjoyment to the endlessly counter-referenced accusations and grievances brought by her intimates against each other. All NCB's friends and lovers seemed to decry each other to her as she hovered, goddess-like and unusually bemused, over the fray. In this case her sister is the plaintiff but there is no doubt that NCB enjoyed her position as Juno the Adjudicator and that she showed to Dolly both this letter from Laura and her own gentle, written reproach – thus practically guaranteeing a future fracas. This would not be the last time Dolly's penchant for driving (and for breaking appointments) was to get her into trouble.

54 BB, *IMDIW*, p.47.

Chapter 6, The Friends of Dorothy
NOTE: Much of the information in this chapter is drawn from the archives of the
Harris family and from interviews with Cara Lancaster, who is Pamela
Harris's niece, Lady Cara Harris's granddaughter, and Osbert Lancaster's
daughter.

1 DIW to Sacheverell Sitwell, 12 May 1937, Sitwell Papers, Harry Ransome
Humanities Research Center, University of Texas, Austin.
2 Dolly is listed in the London postal directories at the Queen Street address
from 1922–33, but she wrote to NCB as late as April 1934 on stationery
which she marked '14 Queen Street'.
3 'Truth' was the parlour game of the twenties – and its guiding requirement
was candid answers to any questions. Djuna Barnes played it at Peggy
Guggenheim's English country house Hayford Hall (dubbed Hangover Hall
for the number of alcoholics summering there) and Tallulah Bankhead played
it in her Mayfair living room. Dolly played it with an interesting twist in the
parental homes of her friend Honey Harris.
4 Scott Fitzgerald was to delete before publication the episode in *Tender Is the
Night* which featured Dolly as a 'tall, rich American girl' named Vivian Taube.
5 Cara Lancaster, 14 December 1996, CWA.
6 Michael Parkin, ed. *Exhibition Catalogue for 'Rognon de la Flèche'* (1989) unpaginated.
7 Ibid.
8 Ibid.
9 DIW to NCB, 2 December 1927, Letter 42.
10 Cara Lancaster, 14 December 1996, CWA.
11 Ibid.
12 Ibid.
13 VC, *IMDIW*, p. 19.
14 Cara Lancaster, 15 October 1997, CWA.
15 DIW, *IMDIW*, p. 118.
16 DIW to NCB, 22 July 1927, Letter 26.
17 Charles Henri Ford, 4 September 1998, CWA.
18 Cara Lancaster, 14 December 1996, CWA.
19 PH, *IMDIW*, p. 37.
20 Cara Lancaster, 14 December 1996, CWA.
21 DIW to PH, undated, private collection.
22 Ibid.
23 PH to DIW, date illegible, private collection.

24 DIW to PH, undated, private collection.

25 Ibid.

26 PH to DIW, 21 April 1929, private collection.

27 PH to NCB, 24 November 1939, Letter 262.

28 DIW to NCB, 28 July 1927, Letter 30.

29 Cara Lancaster, 7 November 1997, CWA.

30 PH to NCB, 24 November 1939, Letter 262.

31 DIW to NCB, 11 July 1932, Letter 100.

32 PH, *IMDIW*, p. 39.

33 PH to NCB, 27 April 1951, Letter 277 and 30 May 1951, Letter 278.

34 Schenkar, pp. 68–9.

Chapter 7, Behaving in Public

1 BB, *IMDIW*, pp. 53–4.

2 This account of Dolly at a country dance is taken from Rosamond Harcourt-Smith, *IMDIW*, pp. 28–9.

3 BB, *IMDIW*, p. 51.

4 Ibid., p. 47.

5 Souhami, p. 230.

6 VC, *IMDIW*, p. 19.

7 Ibid.

8 Quoted by Milford, *Zelda*, p. 153.

9 Quoted by BB, *IMDIW*, p. 48.

10 Ibid.

11 Ibid., p. 49.

12 Ibid., p. 47.

13 DIW to NCB, undated, Letter 12.

14 JF, *IMDIW*, pp. 25–6.

15 DIW to NCB, undated, Letter 12.

16 AH, *IMDIW*, p. 33.

17 Toklas, *What Is Remembered*, pp. 118–19.

18 DIW to NCB, undated, Letter 197.

19 DIW to NCB. undated, Letter 5.

20 Nancy Mitford to Jessica (Mitford) Treuhauft. Quoted in Mitford, p. 397.

21 DIW, *IMDIW*, pp. 104–5.

22 Vyvyan Holland, 11 April 1941, unpublished journal entry, collection of Merlin Holland.

23 Princesse Violet Murat – famously decadent and with 'a strange lack of visible proportions' as she had virtually no neck – eventually went down to

Toulon and lived in an abandoned submarine where she smoked opium intemperately. Marcel Proust said she looked more like a truffle than a violet.

24   DIW, *IMDIW*, 'Rencontre', pp. 128–9.

25   In his biography of Diana Cooper, Philip Ziegler describes the studio on Fitzroy Street kept by Nancy Cunard, Iris Tree and other young decadents for their debauches with alcohol and drugs. He quotes Diana Cooper's description of the night she and Katherine Asquith had reclined 'in ecstatic stillness . . . drugged in very deed by my hand with morphia. Oh the grave difficulty of the actual injection . . . the conflict of my hand and wish when it came to piercing our flesh . . .' Ziegler, pp. 54–5.

26   Toklas, *What Is Remembered*, pp. 106, 118.

27   Lorna Lindsley, *IMDIW*, pp. 40–1.

28   BC, CWA.

29   Edith Wharton, p. 406.

30   Summerscale, p. 152.

31   Zita Jungmann James, 23 December 1996, CWA.

32   TB to NCB, 17 September 1934, Letter 240.

33   Secrest, p. 345.

34   DIW, *IMDIW*, p. 96.

Chapter 8, Smart Society

1   'Lady C is giving a big ball tonight & I must go to help her with the tables,' DIW to NCB, 14 July 1927, Letter 22.

2   British *Vogue*, 21 February 1934, p. 89.

3   Daintrey, p. 121.

4   Lauretta Hugo, 22 February 1999, CWA.

5   Zita Jungman James, 22 December 1996, CWA.

6   Ibid.

7   DIW to NCB, 3 December 1932, Letter 106.

8   Zita Jungman James, 22 December 1996, CWA.

9   Hoare, p. 68. Also, Vickers, p. 90.

10   Cecil Beaton, *Self Portrait With Friends: The Selected Diaries of Cecil Beaton, 1926–1974*, edited by Richard Buckle (Weidenfeld & Nicolson, 1979), pp. 4–5.

11   NCB, *IMDIW*, p. 130.

12   Beaton, p. 5.

13   See *Serious Pleasures* by Philip Hoare for the full history of Stephen Tennant and his circle.

14   Quoted by Vickers, p. 90.

15 Hoare, p. 72.

16 Ibid.

17 Fallowell and Ashley, p. 27.

18 King, p. 171.

19 Ibid., p. 144.

20 Daintrey, pp. 121–2.

21 Clarissa (Borenius) Lada-Grozicka, 12 June 1996, CWA.

22 Vickers, p. xxvii.

23 Clarissa (Borenius) Lada-Grozicka, 22 June 1996, CWA.

24 Ibid.

25 Marcelle Fauchier Delavigne to NCB, 8 April 1951.

26 Ibid.

27 Ibid., 27 January 1940.

28 Guest books of Valentine Fauchier Magnan, 1925–1936, archives of the Fauchier Delavigne family.

29 Quoted and translated by Wickes, *The Amazon of Letters*, p. 91.

30 For the characterisation of Nazimova, I have drawn upon both Lambert's biography, *Nazimova*, and DeWitt Bodeen's article, 'Nazimova', in *Films in Review*, December 1972.

31 DeWitt Bodeen, 'Nazimova,' *Films in Review*, December 1972, p. 577.

32 Gavin Lambert also suggested in a conversation (3 April 1997) that George Cukor told him off the record that Dolly's affair with Nazimova began some-time around 1923.

33 Lambert, p. 224.

34 Barnes, 'Alla Nazimova'.

Chapter 9, Natalie Clifford Barney

1 NCB printed the anecdote one way, and told it another; this version is a medi-ation between the two.

2 NCB, *Aventures de l'esprit*.

3 For accounts of NCB'S life, I have drawn on books by and interviews with George Wickes, Jean Chalon, and Berthe Cleyrergue, as well as on four books of memoirs by NCB: *Aventures de l'esprit*, *Pensées d'une Amazone*, *Nouvelles pensées de l'Amazone*, and *Souvenirs indiscrets*. The Barney Archives at the Fonds Bibliothèques Jacques Doucet holds a wealth of primary material from the life of NCB, much of it listed in the catalogue, *Autour de Natalie Clifford Barney* (Paris: Université de Paris,1976), by François Chapon, Nicole Prévot, and Richard Sieburth.

4   NCB to DIW, undated, Letter 41, Lets and Docs.

5   The list, drawn up by NCB in very late life, is in a private collection.

6   DIW to NCB, undated, Letter 181.

7   DIW to NCB, undated, Letter 179.

8   Sybille Bedford, 12 November 1996, CWA.

9   Ibid.

10 NCB to Eyre de Lanux, 14 May 1965, private collection.

11 See Liane de Pougy, *My Blue Notebooks* and *Idylle sapphique*. Also Jean Chalon's biography, *Liane de Pougy*.

12 NCB, *Les Amants feminins*, unpublished, JD.

13 NCB, *Éparpillements*.

14 Sybille Bedford, 12 November 1996, CWA.

15 NCB to PH, 21 August 1937, private collection.

16 NCB, MS 81, 'Jews', JD.

17 Wickes, Interview with Louis N. Moulton, unpublished.

18 Chalon, *Chère Natalie Barney*, p. 232.

19 NCB to PH, 11 April 1944, private collection.

Chapter 10, The Knights of Natalie's Round Table

1   Wickes, pp. 256–9.

2   Sybille Bedford, 12 November 1996, CWA.

3   Truman Capote, interviewed by George Plimpton, *The Paris Review* (1975), quoted by Wickes, pp. 255–9.

4   Ibid.

5   Ibid.

6   DIW's sole extant telegram to Acosta, sent at the beginning of DIW's affair with NCB, consists of a charming excuse: 'Just summer laziness darling/ love and thoughts Dolly,' MDC papers, Rosenbach Library.

7   In a letter to Anita Loos in 1960, Toklas wrote of Mercedes de Acosta that 'She has had the two most important women in the United States – Garbo and Dietrich.'

8   Mercedes de Acosta is a minor – and very interesting – figure in many memoirs of the period. Her autobiography, *Here Lies the Heart*, is an occasionally unreliable source of her involvements – professional, emotional, and spiritual – on several continents.

9   DIW to NCB, 28 February 1927, Letter 51.

10 In *The Pure and the Impure*, Colette wrote that Renée Vivien betrayed her foreignness, 'by exuding Baudelairism in the years 1900–9, which was rather late for us.'

11 JF, Introduction, pp. xii–xiv.

12 JF, Interview with Wickes, in *The Amazon of Letters*.

13 Jean Chalon, 1 August 1998, CWA.

14 NCB, *carnet d'adresse*, private collection. NCB MS 155; NCB MS 166; NCB MS 81, JD. NCB's diagram of her salon, published in *Aventures de l'esprit*.

15 Ibid.

16 Benstock, pp. 39–48.

17 See Secrest, *Between Me and Life: A biography of Romaine Brooks*, for a partial account of Brooks's very interesting life and career.

18 DIW to NCB, undated, Letter 197.

19 Ibid., undated, Letter 197.

20 Ibid., 10 August 1927, Letter 39.

21 Secrest, p. 348.

22 JF, Interview with Wickes, *The Amazon of Letters*, p. 263. Also JF, *Paris Was Yesterday*.

23 DIW , *IMDIW*, pp. 115–16.

24 The two most current biographies of Djuna Barnes – each problematic in its own way – are: Philip Herring, *Djuna: The Life and Work of Djuna Barnes* (New York: Viking, 1995), and Andrew Field, *Djuna: The Life and Times of Djuna Barnes*. There is also a memoir by Hank O'Neal, *Life is painful, nasty and short*.

25 Berthe Cleyrergue said there was great rivalry and jealousy between Dolly and Djuna; she thought it was because they were both so beautiful, 2 June 1996, CWA.

26 Chester Page, 'Memories of Djuna Barnes', quoted by Herring in his biography of Djuna Barnes.

27 Mrs Eliot wrote to me that she had 'no recollection of what [Djuna] said about Dolly Wilde' because she was 'concerned that Ezra and Olga [Pound] were waiting for us at James Laughlin's flat' and that 'Djuna was spinning out the evening . . .' 12 March 1960.

28 Quoted and translated by Wickes, p. 86.

29 Ibid., pp. 86–7.

30 *IMDIW*, insert to 2nd edition, 1952.

31 DIW to NCB, 4 April 1929, Letter 75.

32 Ibid., 26 January 1937, Letter 125.

33 Barnes, p. 45.

34 Barnes, *Ladies Almanack*, p. 12.

35 Ibid., p. 31.

36 NCB, 31 October 1928, Letter 29, Lets and Docs.

37 It would be interesting to know if Virginia Woolf, who met and was amused by Dolly, might have had Dolly in mind while she was writing *A Room of One's Own*. The parallels are disconcerting.

38 Acton, pp. 183–4.

Chapter 11, Oscaria

1 DIW , *IMDIW*, p. 92.

2 NCB, *IMDIW*, p. 16.

3 Quoted by NCB, *IMDIW*, p. 15.

4 Ibid.

5 Rosamond Harcourt-Smith, *IMDIW*, pp. 29–30.

6 PH, *IMDIW*, pp. 36–7.

7 Ibid., p. 38.

8 JF, *IMDIW*, pp. 21–6.

9 Germaine Beaumont, *IMDIW*, pp. 59–62.

10 Élisabeth de Gramont, *IMDIW*, pp. 63–4.

11 Marcelle Fauchier Delavigne, *IMDIW*, pp. 65–6.

12 Guillot de Saix, *IMDIW*, pp. 72–3.

13 NCB to PH, 23 July 1951, private collection.

14 NCB to PH, undated, private collection.

15 BB, *IMDIW*, pp. 42–58.

16 Ibid.

17 NCB to PH, undated, private collection.

18 PH, *IMDIW*, p. 38.

19 See Helen Potter, *Impersonations* (New York: Edgar S. Werner, 1895), in which she transcribes Oscar's speech patterns precisely.

20 NCB to PH, 11 April 1945, private collection.

21 NCB to PH, 11 April 1951, private collection.

22 Honey Harris later relented: 'I think to make them *public privately* is alright perhaps,' PH to NCB, 17 August 1951, Letter 281.

23 PH to NCB, 29 July 1951, Letter 280.

24 PH to NCB, 4 April 1951, Letter 277, and 30 May 1951, Letter 278.

25 NCB to PH, 11 April 1951, private collection.

26 Sybille Bedford, 12 November 1996, CWA.

Chapter 12, Living up to Oscar

1 BB, *IMDIW*, pp. 45–6.

2 DIW to 'Emily', *IMDIW*, p. 95.
3 DIW to PH, undated, private collection.
4 Rosamond Harcourt-Smith, *IMDIW*, p. 28.
5 King, p. 147.
6 DIW to NCB, 2 February 1937, Letter 127.
7 DIW to 'Emily', *IMDIW*, p. 93.
8 DIW to NCB, 18 February 1932, Letter 94.
9 AH, *IMDIW*, p. 34.
10 BB, *IMDIW*, p. 57.
11 AH, *IMDIW*, pp. 31–2.
12 Ibid., p. 32.
13 Rosamond Harcourt-Smith, *IMDIW*, p. 27.
14 Ibid., p. 29.
15 Vyvyan Holland, 4 April 1941, unpublished journal entry, collection of Merlin Holland.
16 King, p. 177.
17 AH, *IMDIW*, p. 31.
18 Antoine Gentien, *IMDIW*, pp. 70–71.
19 DIW to 'Emily', *IMDIW*, p. 93.
20 Ibid., p. 97.
21 DIW to NCB, 3 December 1932, Letter 106.
22 AH, *IMDIW*, p. 34.
23 BB, *IMDIW*, p. 57.
24 DIW to NCB, 28 February 1928, Letter 51.
25 JF, *IMDIW*, p. 22.
26 Steegmuller, pp. 33–4.
27 Burke, pp. 234–65.
28 Antoine Gentien, *IMDIW*, p. 70.
29 DIW to NCB, undated, Letter 201.
30 NCB, *IMDIW*, p. 9.
31 DIW , 'Morocco', private collection.
32 DIW to NCB, undated, Letter 224.
33 JF, *Paris Was Yesterday*, p. 67.
34 DIW to NCB, undated, Letter 227.
35 Ibid., 25 February 1939, Letter 144.
36 NCB, *IMDIW*, p. 141.
37 Quoted by NCB, *IMDIW*, p. 135.
38 JF, IMDIW, p. 23.
39 Ibid., pp. 23–4.

40 DIW to 'Emily', IMDIW , pp. 93–4.
41 Ibid., p. 99.

Chapter 13, La Main Heureuse
 1 NCB, *carnet d'adresse*, private collection.
 2 JF, *IMDIW*, pp. 21–2.
 3 TB to NCB, 12 September 1934, Letter 238.
 4 BB, *IMDIW*, p. 46.
 5 NCB, *IMDIW*, p. 8.
 6 Rosamond Harcourt-Smith, *IMDIW*, p. 28.
 7 JF, *IMDIW*, p. 24.
 8 NCB, *IMDIW*, p. 7.
 9 DIW to NCB, undated, Letter 5.
10 Ibid., 14 July 1927, Letter 21.
11 Ibid., 14 July 1927, Letter 22.
12 Ibid., 22 July 1927, Letter 26.
13 Ibid., 28 July 1927, Letter 30.
14 Ibid., undated, Letter 181.
15 Ibid., 4 January 1928, Letter 55.
16 DIW , *IMDIW*, p. 130.
17 Ibid., undated, Letter 230.
18 DIW to NCB, 9 August 1931, Letter 82.
19 DIW , *IMDIW*, pp. 99–101, reprinted in Chapter 17.
20 DIW to NCB, 11 July 1937, Letter 128.
21 Cheiro, p. 57.
22 Information about the life and work of Dr Charlotte Wolff is drawn from interviews with Audrey Wood, A. L. Barker, and Sybille Bedford, as well as from Dr Wolff's own works and the following texts: Gershom Scholem, *Walter Benjamin: The Story of a Friendship* (London: Faber & Faber, 1982); Erika Duncan, 'Portrait of Charlotte Wolff', (Bookforum); Interview With Charlotte Wolff (BBC German Language Service, 27 August 1986); Heidi Geisengauer, 'A Strong Spirit is Ageless' (*Die Tageszeitung*, 27 October 1986).
23 Aldous Huxley, Introduction to Charlotte Wolff's *Studies in Human Hand-Reading* (London: Chatto & Windus, 1936).
24 Sybille Bedford, 12 June 1996, CWA. Mrs Bedford urged me to 'write a lot about Charlotte. She loved publicity and would have loved to be written about.'
25 DIW to NCB, 30 July 1936, Letter 123.
26 Ibid.

27 DIW to NCB, 13 October 1936, Letter 124.
28 Secrest, p. 342. Attempts to have Secrest confirm her interview with Dr Charlotte Wolff went unanswered.

Chapter 14, Dolly and the Doctors

1 BC, CWA.
2 DIW to NCB, 18 February 1932, Letter 94.
3 Ibid., 3 December 1932, Letter 106.
4 BB, *IMDIW*, p. 49.
5 LW to MA, 14 March 1896.
6 Quoted by JF, *IMDIW*, p. 22.
7 Dr Douglas Macauley to NCB, 5 September 1939, Letter 293.
8 DIW to NCB, 30 July 1936, Letter 123.
9 Ibid.
10 Ibid.
11 Ibid.
12 DIW to NCB, 9 February 1939, Letter 142.
13 Ibid.
14 DIW to NCB, 3 March 1939, Letter 145.
15 Dr Douglas Macauley to NCB, 19 April 1940, Letter 294.
16 DIW to NCB, 7 May 1940, Letter 157.
17 PH to NCB, 1 January 1940, Letter 267.
18 Ibid., 2 January 1940, Letter 268.
19 DIW to NCB, 4 January 1940, Letter 150.
20 PH to NCB, 16 January 1940, Letter 269.
21 Ibid., 4 April 1940, Letter 270.
22 Ibid., 24 January 1940, Letter 271.
23 Quoted by Allanah Harper, *IMDIW*, p. 33.
24 Vyvyan Holland, 10 April 1941, unpublished journal entry, collection of Merlin Holland.
25 DIW to NCB, 3 September 1932, Letter 104.
26 BB, *IMDIW*, p. 46.
27 DIW to NCB, undated, Letter 3.
28 Ibid., 27 July 1927, Letter 31.
29 BB, *IMDIW*, p. 46.
30 DIW to NCB, 9 February 1939, Letter 142.
31 DIW to NCB, 26 October 1931, Letter 86.
32 AH, *IMDIW*, p. 34.
33 DIW to NCB, 13 November 1936, Letter 124.

34 Ibid., 19 July 1927, Letter 27.

35 NCB to DIW , 14 October Letter 16.

36 DIW to NCB, 18 March 1932, Letter 98.

37 PH to NCB, 29 November 1939, Letter 264, Receipts and Requisitions from the Wilbraham Nursing Home.

38 In a letter to NCB on 25 July 1939, Honey Harris wrote: 'It is so dismaying & sad that there are now 3 nightmares to combat, drugs-cancer-&-drink — instead of the original one which was bad enough heaven knows!'

39 Mosley, *Love from Nancy*; pp. 90–1.

40 BC, CWA.

Chapter 15, *Dolly's Addictions*

1 DIW to NCB, 28 February 1928, Letter 51.

2 Ibid., undated, Letter 61.

3 R. Toulouse to NCB, 20 July 1939, Letter 295.

4 DIW to NCB, 23 July 1939, Letter 146.

5 Ibid., 4 August 1939, Letter 147.

6 Jessie Wadsworth to NCB, 15 August 1939, Letter 296.

7 TB to NCB, 13 September 1934, Letter 238.

8 NCB to TB, undated, Letter 242, *brouillon*.

9 DIW to NCB, 31 March 1934, Letter 112.

10 Ibid.

11 Ibid.

12 Ibid.

13 Ibid.

14 TB to NCB, 17 September 1934, Letter 240.

15 NCB to TB, undated, Letter 243, *brouillon*.

16 DIW to NCB, undated, Letter 179.

17 DIW to NCB, 30 July 1936, Letter 123.

18 Cocteau, *Opium*, pp. 44–5.

19 Quoted by Steegmuller, p. 398.

20 Her uncle Oscar exhibited just such indecision when, before his first trial, he failed to board the waiting yacht that would have taken him beyond the jurisdiction of English Law.

21 PH to NCB, 16 October 1939, Letter 261.

22 Ibid.

23 Ibid., 24 October 1939, Letter 262.

24 Ibid., 1 December 1939, Letter 264.

25 Berthe Cleyrergue said that she took every opportunity to throw what she

assumed were Dolly's supplies of cocaine into the Seine – apparently, without fear for the fishes. CWA.

26 PH to NCB, 17 April 1940, Letter 272.

27 Ibid.

28 Ibid.

29 Ibid.

30 Ibid.

31 Information about Gwen Farrar is drawn from *Who's Who in Theatre*, 5th, 8th and 9th editions (1925, 1936 & 1937), and from Gwen Farrar's London *Times* obituary, 27 December 1944.

32 Gwen Farrar to NCB, 12 February 1938, Letter 244.

33 DIW to NCB, 25 February 1939, Letter 144.

34 Lauretta Hugo, 22 February 1999, CWA.

35 DIW to NCB, 6 November 1938, Letter 137.

36 Ibid., 25 February 1939, Letter 144.

37 Ibid., undated, Letter 228.

38 Ibid., August 1938, Letter 132.

39 Acosta, *Here Lies the Heart*.

40 VC, *IMDIW*, p. 19.

41 Information about the life of Jacques Rigaut is drawn from Pierre Billard's biography of René Clair, *Le mystère de René Clair*, pp. 24–6.

42 DIW to PH, private collection.

43 BC, CWA.

44 Information about Jean Bourgoint is drawn from Georges Lauris's Catholic biography, *Itineraire d'un infant terrible: de Cocteau à Citeaux*.

45 Steegmuller, p. 34.

46 Souhami, p. 276.

47 DIW to Romaine Brooks, 1935, Letter 234.

48 DIW to NCB, 6 April 1935, Letter 119.

49 Nadine Hwang to NCB, 9 March, Letter 287.

50 DIW to NCB, 25 February 1939, Letter 144.

51 NCB to DIW, undated, Letter 57, Lets and Docs.

52 DIW to NCB, 6 April 1935, Letter 117.

53 Ibid.

54 Ibid.

55 VC, *IMDIW*, p. 19.

56 PH, *IMDIW*, p. 39.

Chapter 16, Dolly in Bed

1 DIW to BC, undated, private collection.
2 DIW to NCB, 18 February 1932, Letter 34.
3 Ibid., 28 January 1939, Letter 140.
4 DIW to BC, undated, private collection.
5 Ibid.
6 NCB, *carnet d'adresse*, private collection.
7 PH, to NCB, 29 November 1939, Letter 264.
8 DIW to NCB, 16 October 1939, Letter 148.
9 Ibid., 22 January 1940, Letter 151.
10 NCB, *IMDIW*, p. 11.
11 PH, to NCB, 29 November 1939, Letter 264.
12 BB, *IMDIW*, pp. 43–4.
13 Ibid., p. 43.
14 DIW, Letter to 'Emily', *IMDIW*, pp. 95–6.
15 PH, to NCB, 24 October 1939, Letter 262.
16 NCB to DIW, undated, Letter 1, Lets and Docs; Barbara Harrison to DIW, Letter 2, Lets and Docs; DIW to NCB, 4 January 1928, Letter 55.
17 NCB, *IMDIW*, p. 11.
18 Ibid., p. 10.
19 DIW to NCB, 28 April 1928, Letter 62.
20 NCB, *IMDIW*, p. 12.
21 DIW to NCB, 3 January 1928, Letter 54.
22 Quoted by NCB, *IMDIW*, p. 13.
23 DIW to NCB, 31 March 1934, Letter 55.
24 BB, *IMDIW*, p. 54.
25 Ibid., p. 53.
26 Quoted by BB, *IMDIW*, p. 54.
27 Ibid.
28 Quoted by Osborne, p. 168.
29 Ibid.
30 Ibid, p. 169.
31 PH, to NCB, 2 March 1939, Letter 255.
32 Ibid., 16 October 1939, Letter 148.
33 Vyvyan Holland, unpublished journal entry, collection Merlin Holland.
34 Ibid.
35 Ibid.
36 See Chapter 3, 'Dead Again', for notations and sources of all autopsy findings.
37 DIW to NCB, 21 January 1940, Letter 151.

38 See Chapter 15, 'Dolly's Addictions'.

39 DIW to NCB, 31 March 1934, Letter 112.

40 Dr Josephine Day, CWA.

41 In November, 1997, following information found in the letters of Pamela Harris, I discovered the double grave in Kensal Green where Lily and Dolly were interred together. See Schenkar, pp. 68–9.

42 NCB, *IMDIW*, p. 14.

43 King, p. 187.

44 Richard Ellman, p. 585.

45 King, p. 187.

Chapter 17, Love Me: the Letters of Dolly Wilde

1 DIW to NCB, 15 July 1927, Letter 24.

2 Ibid., 10 August 1927, Letter 40.

3 Ibid., 30 July 1936, Letter 123.

4 Ibid., undated, Letter 183.

5 Ibid., August 1938, Letter 132.

6 Ibid., undated, Letter 204.

7 Ibid., 14 July 1927, Letter 22.

8 Ibid., 4 November 1928, Letter 64.

9 Ibid., Tuesday, 2:30 a.m., Letter 25.

10 Blue notepaper that can be folded to make its own envelope.

11 DIW to NCB, undated, Letter 1.

12 Ibid., undated, Letter 2.

13 Ibid., 6:00 p.m., Letter 3.

14 Ibid., undated, Letter 4.

15 Ibid., undated, Letter 5.

16 Ibid., 3:15 p.m., Letter 6.

17 Ibid., 14 July 1927, Letter 22.

18 Ibid., 15 July 1927, Letter 24.

19 Ibid., 14 July 1927, Letter 21.

20 Ibid., 2:30 a.m., Letter 25.

21 Ibid., 23 July 1927, Letter 29.

22 Ibid., 14 July 1927, Letter 22.

23 Ibid., undated, Letter 176.

24 Ibid., Friday evening, Letter 71.

25 Ibid., 18 February 1932, Letter 94.

26 Ibid., undated, Letter 196.

27 Ibid., Monday, Letter 198.

28 Ibid., 28 July 1927, Letter 30.

29 Ibid., undated, Letter 7.

30 Ibid., 28 July 1927, Letter 30.

31 Ibid., undated, Letter 187.

32 Ibid., 20 July 1927, Letter 28.

33 Ibid.

34 Ibid., undated, Letter 232.

35 Ibid,

36 Ibid., 13 October 1936, Letter 124.

37 Ibid., 19 October 1932, Letter 105.

38 DIW , *IMDIW*, pp. 99–101.

39 DIW to NCB, 10 August 1927, Letter 40.

40 Ibid., 27 July 1927, Letter 31.

41 Ibid., undated, Letter 61.

42 DIW , *IMDIW*, p. 90.

43 DIW to NCB, 27 July 1927, Letter 31.

44 Ibid., 7 August 1927, Letter 37.

45 Ibid., 11 July 1927, Letter 17.

46 Ibid., 27 July 1927, Letter 31.

47 Ibid., 18 March 1932, Letter 98.

48 Ibid., 26 January 1937, Letter 125.

49 BC, CWA.

50 Ibid.

51 NCB, 2 January 1929, Letter 30.

52 Ibid., Letter 89.

53 DIW to NCB, 7 December 1927, Letter 44.

54 Ibid., 9 December 1927, Letter 47.

55 Ibid., 2 December 1927, Letter 42.

56 Ibid, 4 April 1929, Letter 75.

57 Ibid., undated, Letter 221.

58 NCB, 18 October, Letters 34 and 35.

59 Ibid., undated, Letter 10.

60 Wickes, p.182.

61 DIW to NCB, undated, Letter 195.

APPENDIX I:

Poulet Maryland

Thanks to Berthe Cleyrergue, and to Marie, her predecessor in the kitchen of 20 rue Jacob, Natalie Barney's salon was justly famed for its handsome, even luxurious, table. Everyone who visited the rue Jacob remembers Berthe's chocolate cakes and cucumber sandwiches on salon Fridays. With Berthe's help, Natalie also entertained extensively around a dinner table or a table set for lunch with three or four intimate friends.

Natalie's favourite dish, one she obviously remembered from her youth as a semi-southern belle in Washington DC, was called 'Chicken Maryland' and Berthe developed a gallicised version of it – Poulet Maryland – to please her.

Transcribed from Berthe Cleyrergue's words and translated, here is the recipe for Poulet Maryland as Berthe cooked it and served it at 20 rue Jacob for more than forty years.

Poulet Maryland

Buy a hen.

Bring water, lightly salted, to a boil and put the hen to boil in a broth made with carrots, leeks and onions.

Let it simmer for an hour or so, until tender.

When the hen is cooked, sauté mushrooms in a skillet in butter, with parsley, a little salt, a touch of pepper. When the mushrooms are done, add a tablespoon and a half of flour. Mix well, add some broth and stir well.

After that, cut the head off the hen, remove the skin, and mix the morsels in the sauce blanche.

Let it cook slowly a while longer.

Meanwhile, keep ready an egg yolk and some fresh cream. When it is time to serve, stir the egg yolk in the cream and mix with the sauce. Be careful not to let it get too thick or too thin.

Make some rice and eat the hen with rice.

And it is good.

APPENDIX 2:

I Don't Remember Dolly Wilde

'Get hold of Eyre de Lanux, because she's the best person. Eyre knows more than anyone else knows because of her intimacy with Natalie and the flexibility of their friendship . . .'

Janet Flanner to George Wickes

'Why don't you look her up?' said George Wickes, Natalie Barney's American biographer, over lunch. 'Look her up in the telephone directory. After all, she was still alive in 1974. You never know.'

I forgot all about this practical injunction until I saw Eyre de Lanux's name once again in the carbons of some notes the good professor had given me. The name was certainly an intriguing one. It managed to convey both an air of luxury *and* mystical association (the 'lux' in that surname and the 'airiness' of the first) and the little scrap of her writing about Natalie Barney that I'd read seemed to carry these qualities with panache. For seven years in the 1920s Eyre de Lanux was, as they used to say, a close friend of Natalie Clifford Barney; if she were still here, she would be the last woman artist alive who had fully participated in Barney's Parisian salon.

The telephone book proved as useful as it always does. 'Look,' I said to the housekeeper who answered. 'Won't you please just ask Miss de Lanux if she'll speak with me? Tell her I've come' – and I thought quickly – 'directly from Paris, from *Paris* with photographs of all her friends.'

'Why yes I can do that. I'll ask her if she'd like to talk on the telephone right now.'

'Miss Eyre,' I heard, and then a patient, utterly garbled explanation of who I was.

Then suddenly a marvellous, cultivated, confused voice on the telephone. 'From where, darling? You're from *where?*'

I had an inspiration.

'Ah rue Jacob. Where I used to live.'

After trying several names she should have known but did not remember, I had another inspiration.

'How marvellous, darling. Natalie Barney.'

That name she recognised immediately and I felt the fog of decades lift and all her attention crystallise for a moment. 'Is the book finished? How far have you got with it?' The voice was invigorated. 'Of *course* you'll call, darling,' she said. 'Of *course* you will. And you must come to my birthday party.'

Eyre de Lanux's birthday celebration on the first afternoon of spring 1996 began quietly enough. It was, after all, her 102nd birthday – though she remarked that it was the first birthday that had interested her – and she had to be got up out of bed and brought to the table in a wheelchair to attend it.

Eyre lived in a large, bohemianly cluttered and shuttered studio apartment in a building named, appropriately enough, after Pablo Picasso, a man she had known. Eyre herself was a remarkable artist in the Modernist tradition and her career had spanned almost the entire century. She had been variously and at the same time, poet, fiction writer, painter, photographer, sculptor, and furniture designer; and she was surely the oldest living contributor to both the *New Yorker*, which published her stories in the sixties and seventies, and the Smithsonian, where her drawing of Natalie Clifford Barney still hangs. Her art deco furniture is collected in European museums, her paintings and frescoes have been exhibited in the US, France, and England, and her poetry was vetted by Ezra Pound and published by Ford Madox Ford. Famously beautiful and 'artistic' even as a teenager, she married a French diplomat and publisher, and went to live in Paris at exactly the right time – just after the First War. There, she had a daughter, studied with Brancusi, was photographed by Man Ray, Berenice Abbott, and Brassai and painted by Romaine Brooks, became a lover of Natalie Clifford Barney, and frequented Barney's literary salon. She is sometimes rumoured to be the One Who is Legion in Natalie Barney's *roman-à-clef* of that name.

Eyre was still extremely beautiful, though more in the Modigliani/Giacometti mode now, with ivory skin, long artist's hands which she used almost as eyes, and a decidedly emaciated elegance. She was attired for her party in a crimson silk brocade bedjacket and a jaunty camel-coloured cap, and said 'hurrah' several times when I pointed out that it was both the first day of spring *and* her birthday. She was brilliantly witty when her failing memory allowed her to be and exquisitely polite when her poor sight and hearing absented her from conversation. When I made a remark that particularly pleased her, she leaned over the armrest of her wheelchair and stole a swift, delicate, and far-from-innocent kiss.

Eyre preferred to see people one at a time, though she did make an exception for her party where there were two of us: Lillian Morrison, a poet, former librarian, and an old friend whose book of poetry Eyre had illustrated with beautifully surreal photographs in 1981. After she had conducted the singing of her birthday anthem and blown out the three candles on her cake with a single breath, Eyre said she felt that perhaps something further should be done to mark the occasion. A toast was tentatively proposed. 'Too ordinary,' she declared. She thought it would be amusing to be written about, but observed: 'You've come so late, darling. I believe that's the term, late. Think of how much earlier you might have come.' She wasn't referring to the time of day.

The party went bubbling on for almost two hours until Eyre suddenly displayed her Surrealist sympathies and indicated her fatigued neck by remarking that she wished someone would cut off her head and put it on a plate. Settled carefully back in her bed, she was very particular about not being too near the edge — the place where she had spent most of her artistic career.

Eyre de Lanux lived surrounded by portfolios of handsome portraits she drew of her personal friends — Lytton Strachey, Eva Le Gallienne, Romaine Brooks, Liane de Pougy, Natalie Barney, etc. — by stunning photographs renowned photographers made of her; and by books of the beautiful furniture she designed and built herself out of an apparently inexhaustible creativity. At the end of the party I wished her, from the bottom of my heart, a thousand more happy birthdays. She smiled her enchanting smile, murmured, 'Now wouldn't *that* be interesting' — and waved me out of the room.

I visited Eyre de Lanux many more times in the year or so before she died, and each time, no matter how well or how really bad she was feeling, she provided an astonishing discovery of language and witty comment. Her *jeux de mots* — she was serious about them — were always elegant and experimental and even on the days when she had no memory a remembered phrase could set her on the straight path in a moment. Dolly had called her that 'vague "joueur de tennis"' and said she wasn't particularly threatened by Eyre's association with Natalie; but Dolly had also intensely appreciated Lanux's beauty, which was vivid and unusual and remained so until she died.

When I asked Eyre about Dolly, she fixed me with a glance and said: 'I don't remember Dolly Wilde and I don't *want* to remember Dolly Wilde.' Natalie Barney's infatuation with Dolly had coincided with the trailing off of her relationship with Eyre.

The last time I saw Eyre de Lanux, a few days before she died, was terribly fraught. I was trying very hard to persuade a hospital to keep her in the luxury room to which she had inadvertently been assigned, rather than return her to the shabby nursing home to which she had been brought when the last of her inheritance from Alice DeLamar had run out. Her memory had deteriorated considerably, but she remembered me and, unconcerned about the nightmare of bureaucracy and misdiagnosis surrounding her temporary lodgings, wondered if I couldn't perhaps bring Natalie Barney to her bedside. She knew, she told me, that it would cause an upset in her life, but she really felt strongly that she wanted to see her. Natalie Barney was the only name she mentioned.

Eyre de Lanux died just a few days after our last encounter in the city-run nursing home to which she had been returned. I'd heard that she'd bitten and scratched one of the attendants who frightened her; that she'd died fighting. It was a terribly sad — and somehow appropriate — finish for the oldest surviving member of Natalie Barney's celebrated salon.

APPENDIX 3:

Dolly's Right Hand

Dr Josephine Day, a present-day palmist who practices in the Chelsea district of London where Dolly was born, did the following reading from a photograph of Dolly's handprint in 1999. She notes that 'a black and white print cannot give an in-depth analysis as examining two *real life* hands would show colour, texture, flexibility, consistency, plus other essential clues of character. Even the temperature of the hands tells much about the person.' Dr Day was given only the hand-print, Dolly's name (which she did not recognise) and the years of Dolly's birth and death. And she was asked to analyse the handprint only after this book was completed.

What Josephine Day found in Dolly's palm supports with uncanny accuracy many of the conclusions I came to in *Truly Wilde*. If Dr Day's suggestions about the 'severe emotional upset' Dolly suffered at the age of eleven and the 'stress and anxiety' she under-went 'throughout her early teens' could be confirmed by other means, they would go a long way towards explaining the mysteries of Dolly's childhood, her impulsive flight to France, and, quite likely, some other of the conditions that prohibited her from becoming a 'successful and famous' writer – a destiny that should have been (a destiny that *was*, in the most literal sense) in the palm of Dolly's hand.

Analysis of Dorothy Wilde's Handprint, by Dr Josephine Day

The handprint shows a charismatic woman. The Jupiter mount, below the Jupiter (index) finger has both a well-defined star depicted as well as a definite line across the mount. This is only ever found on the hands of those who become distinguished and famous . . . From this handprint I am able to deduce that Dorothy Wilde had a beautiful smile. She disarmed those around her.

The shape of Ms Wilde's hand tells she was an analytical thinker. She was blessed with an uncommonly active mentality. A highly intuitive person, she was often critical of others. She had a childlike curiosity about life and the world around her in all its aspects.

The thumb shows strength and obstinacy. It is the thumb of a fighter. She battled her way through much of her life . . .

Her thumb is unusually high set and long. The first, or nail, phalanx shows enormous strength of will and a hard brittle obstinacy.

The second section of her thumb shows how she used logic and reasoning in her thinking, yet at times would purposely, knowingly close her mind to a particular situation in order to manipulate.

The third phalanx of her thumb is huge in relation to the rest showing how deeply, strongly and completely she was able to love.

This woman had an inherited strength, which enabled her to withstand whatever life threw at her.

It is an unusual hand in many respects. Independent, strong and unconventional.

She didn't suffer fools gladly.

She was restless, always seeking change.

There is laughter, humour and a sense of fun in the palm lines. She was a lively personality.

The shape of her Jupiter and Saturn fingers indicates creativity. From the head and heart lines I see that she suffered an inner emotional poverty which did not match her outer material reality. This inner barrenness of the soul sometimes led to deep feelings of depression, desperation, and free-floating anxiety. I believe such feelings lie at the core of those people who are termed 'manic depressive'.

She was self-critical and demanded a lot of herself as well as from those around her.

The tiny fine line slightly above the heart line suggests she enjoyed aesthetic objects in her surroundings.

The heart line itself is broken up into small-chained sections, indicating small heartbreaks and hurts. Ms Wilde was compassionate; she showed kindness toward people who often let her down.

The extensive marks set in the Venus mount show someone who had overcome hurt and sadness, not just once, but several times.

Dorothy Wilde was open and extrovert by nature, but early on learned to hide her feelings. She knew how to be secretive when necessary.

On examining the finger phalanges, I found that the third, lowest section of each finger was the longest of the three. This denotes that Ms Wilde had an ability to find whatever she needed materially, if not emotionally . . . She was often 'in the right place at the right time'. Her type of hand could easily have led her toward solvency and wealth . . .

The health line shows an inclination to 'chestiness', either asthma or a similar condition which caused intermittent breathing difficulties.

The other health dysfunction I detect in the fate line is a tendency toward a rheumatoid condition.

The line of life shows she was not 'meant' to die so early. This causes me to conjecture on whether her death was unnatural, rather than normal.

The breaks in certain lines, such as head, life and heart depict stress and anxiety throughout her early teens.

She had problems of life between the ages of thirty-eight and forty-one. Some three years previous to the death of Dorothy, she had major changes in her life.

This woman was 'highly strung' and moody. At the age of eleven she had severe emotional upset.

She had a quick clear constructive way of thinking, was highly intelligent but her personality was anything but serene.

She was a hoarder, possessive, and possibly collected things, art objects or paintings.

Her personality was obsessive, once she set her mind on something; like a bulldog, she wouldn't let go until her objective was reached.

During the two years before she was deceased she had an anxiety which led to conflicting emotions and loyalties. She found it difficult to make decisions, even small ones.

A mentally agile woman, whose life line shows that physically, she tired easily. She built up energies like a volcano, then quickly became almost unbearably exhausted.

Marks in her heart line and in the Venus mount of the hand show that her emotions surfaced in dreams in which she was struggling up a mountain or in similar difficulties.

Those who knew her closely would tell you she suffered nightmares . . .

The unusually high mounts of her hand, both Venus and Luna mounts, show that she was possessive in relationships. She was difficult to live with and be with.

She was often misunderstood, and as well as being magnetic, she created a certain type of hostility toward her. Many people were envious of her.

The more I analyse the palm lines, measure and examine them microscopically, I perceive how tough and strong a woman she was. That toughness and steely strength was inherited like the colour of her eyes or hair. It was part of her essential self, in her genes. She was a fighter in all she attempted in life.

Finally as I look at the hand without analysing each part separately:

She suffered from some sort of arthritic condition. The spaces between Apollo and Mercury fingers show her life was divided into three parts, maybe three careers or three partners, I am not sure. She had trouble with eye or face on the right-hand side, which might have been tooth or jaw trouble.

She was inhibited in some aspects of her personality. She had not reached the full potential of her talents by the time she died . . . She was meant to live more years than she did.

APPENDIX 4:

The Lesbian in
Louise Brooks's Life

*Poor Dolly! A thorough-going Lesbian and an intimate
of Gwen Farrar, Natalie Barney, Joe Carstairs and all
those deadly people.*

Vyvyan Holland

*Yes Paris still harbours many an old mistress of Miss
Wilde – most Lesbians seem to live forever – oh why did
she have to go?*

Nancy Mitford

In her penetrating collection of essays, *Lulu in Hollywood*, Louise
Brooks, that luminous film actress and lucid critic of the Seventh Art,
devotes an entire chapter to her brilliant, witty friend Pepi Lederer,
dead for more than forty years when *Lulu in Hollywood* was published
in 1977. 'Nobody can know for certain why anyone commits suicide,
but it seems likely that being Marion Davies' niece was one of the reasons for my friend Pepi Lederer killing herself in 1935. And Marion's
being the mistress of William Randolph Hearst was probably
another.'

Newspaper magnate Hearst and his film-star mistress Davies treated Louise Brooks's friend Pepi like a 'naughty, entertaining child, incapable of any serious endeavor', in contrast to their 'serious treatment' of her brother Charlie Lederer, whom they helped to a career as a prominent screenwriter. Pepi Lederer responded accordingly and

> in all her twenty-five years (the last twelve of them spent with Marion) she had acquired no discipline of any sort. She could not discipline her gluttony . . . although she had a beautiful face and fine bone structure . . . and she could not discipline her consumption of alcohol, which led to her addiction to cocaine, which, in turn, led to her death. And if she could not do this, then certainly she could not learn to write, for writing is perhaps the most disciplined of all the arts . . . (p. 34)

Although Pepi had a quality of 'seeing and paying attention' from 'a uniquely witty point of view' – 'a combination that might have made her a great writer' – she was dismissed by her famous relations because she was both a young woman and a lesbian.

Of course, said Louise Brooks, Pepi's fatal taste in girlfriends did not help her case. Brooks herself was particularly pained to discover that Pepi had taken up with 'a scruffy little blond blues singer' and then with the dreaded 'Stage-Door Ferret', Monica Morris, 'the most predatory among the mob of girls who had fought over Tallulah Bankhead when she became the darling of the London Theatre in 1923'.

Pepi's addictions to cocaine and alcohol got worse and worse until finally, at the age of twenty-five, committed by Davies and Hearst to the Good Samaritan Hospital in Los Angeles for a drug cure, she took a running dive at a mesh-covered window and hit the ground with enough force – said her autopsy report – to fracture almost every bone in her body.

Louise Brooks recounts the history of Pepi Lederer to make a very specific point: that her brilliant, witty, and imaginative friend was caught up in a web of stupid circumstances (Hollywood), bad values (Hollywood again) and dreadful psychological choices (her own), exacerbated by her rich and famous relatives and by the use her so-called friends made of her in trying to get to those relatives.

Certainly, there is nothing in the lives of Marion Davies and William Randolph Hearst that could be compared to the grand, self-appreciating, literary monument that was Oscar Wilde. But in what passes for culture in Hollywood, and in the influence Hearst and Davies wielded over public opinion and private desire in America, they became, like Oscar himself, arbiters of public thought and far more powerful dispensers of destiny than Oscar ever was.

Pepi Lederer, on the other hand, seems to have been quite a bit like Dolly: shadowed by prominent relatives; brilliantly witty and frustrated in her creativity; addicted to drugs and imaginative fun; a pushover for actresses and a writer manqué. Although Dolly's adult prospects were much more promising than Pepi's — and the props of her private drama were very different ones — Pepi's brief life and painful death add a new terror to Dolly's history: they make it appear a little less singular.

Time and again, tucked in the waistcoat pockets of the stories of their (for the most part) male relatives, 'hidden' female relations like Pepi Lederer and — in a more significant way — like Dolly Wilde can be found. The histories of these women have to be hunted resolutely down, for they have almost always been concealed, dispersed, or 'lost'.

Although young women like Pepi Lederer do not always make their sexual identities obvious, what they are is almost always apparent: women who prefer women in a way that can be called lesbian. Frequently endowed with wit and abundant talent, these women, lost to history, shine with an original brilliance and darken with a well-developed self-destructive streak. They are usually the improvident relatives of rich and/or famous people and there is no place for them to put their brains or their ambitions but in the shadow of where their money lies, or — as in Dolly's case — in the shadow of where their publicity comes from. They are often remittance relatives living on a grudgingly bestowed income. Their brothers or their heterosexual sisters generally fare better than they do, making good marriages or establishing successful careers. Because of their sexuality, their lack of purposeful direction, or both, these women are always an embarrassment to their families and are frequently written out of family histories.

The brilliant American intellectual, literary scholar, and talker, Esther Murphy, sister of Gerald Murphy and daughter of the family that owned the Mark Cross Company in New York City, is one of these 'lost' relations. Her book on Mme de Maintenon, notated for years, was never finished, and she died, alcoholic, in Paris in her sixties. The diarist Alice James, Henry and William James's intellectually formidable sister, who used to dream of knocking off the head of her 'benignant pater', was another; when she succumbed to breast cancer, her brother Henry burned his copy of her journal. Despite being 'the most famous unknown in the world', Djuna Barnes was an embarrassment to her family for the latter half of her life: poor and alcoholic, she published very little for almost fifty years, and her wealthy brothers wished only for her silence on their family subject — which was the substance of her art. Tylia Perlmutter, lover of Berenice Abbott, model for a story by Djuna Barnes and for paintings by Marie Laurencin, first translator of Ann Frank's diaries (under the name of Tylia Caren), and sister to the wife of French film *auteur* René Clair, is another of these forgotten relations of the famous. And Henrietta Bingham, of the North American newspaper family, is yet another. Henrietta looked like a 'Giotto Madonna' and cut a wide, sexual swath through London. She was Dora Carrington's only woman lover and she ended her life as a Park Avenue alcoholic, living on a small remittance from her family. The list goes on and on.

Pepi Lederer spent five years in London during the time that Dolly would have been in and out of that city. It is quite likely that she spent those years in the company of some of the women in the *demi-monde* of show business and café society who knew Dolly. Certainly her association with Monica Morris, the 'Stage-Door Ferret', would have introduced her to the Variety actress Gwen Farrar, who was a friend of Tallulah Bankhead (whose 'ferret' Monica initially was), an ex-love of Dolly's early friend, Joe Carstairs, and a future lover of Dolly herself. And she would have known the actress Teddie Gerrard, whom Dolly used to see in Paris. Dolly and Pepi might easily have met.

Pepi died twenty years younger than Dolly did, but she was already famous for the patterns that came to blight Dolly's later life – and the similarities in some of their circumstances are disquieting. Both Dolly and Pepi were related (in different ways) to Great Accomplishers; both had brilliant and inventive minds that never found their final expression; both seemed incapable of developing the habits that would release their full talents; and both habitually dissolved their disappointments in acid baths of chemicals and liquids.

Although Dolly had the advantage of Pepi in literacy, demonstrated talent, and in an association with a salon that honoured women, celebrated lesbians, and raised the value of women's art to a virtue, her dead uncle's artistic shadow was so long – and her resemblance to him was so pronounced – that it is impossible to avoid the conclusion that this relationship contributed in many minor ways – and in perhaps one major one – to the devastation of her natural assets. Like Pepi Lederer, Dolly was often thought of as much in terms of her 'uncle' as she was spoken of in terms of herself. She was in the odd position of a woman who loved women – but whose name would always be linked with a man.

There can be few conditions more difficult for an aspiring woman writer than that of having to live up to a celebrated male relative. The ways in which Dolly did and did not do so raise all the soaring, social questions about how what you are and whom you sleep with can be misinterpreted both by the small circle in which you entertain and by the larger world in which you live.

Dolly, however, never showed the slightest interest in *any* of the soaring, social questions. She refused theoretical interpretations of her life as she refused all interpretations outside her senses and beyond her inclinations — even the useful ones. She preferred to confine herself to what her friend Nancy Mitford said was the 'receipt for being missed': exercising her talents in a 'small society' of which she was 'the life and soul', and taking care not to 'die too old'. In this circumstance, at least, she seems to have had a great deal of interesting company.

Acknowledgements

Sometime in 1937, Dolly Wilde consulted a psychic who told her that a 'new life' was waiting for her in America. Although Dolly never made it to the New World, she did acquire an American for a biographer. Perhaps this book about her will become, in some settling way, the 'new life' that was promised to her all those years ago.

Acknowledgements for *Truly Wilde* could be twice as long and four times as grateful: the book has been helped along – literally and figuratively – by hundreds of heads, hands, and hearts. The many kindnesses of strangers in North America, Western Europe, and the United Kingdom who turned themselves into Friends of Dorothy have put me in danger of believing, as Dolly herself did, that 'life *could* be one delightful sensation after another . . .'

I owe deep debts for scholarship, provocative discussions, sources, research, references, the lending of archives, hospitality, and profound support of many different kinds to: Merlin Holland, Joy Melville, M. J. Lancaster, Cara Lancaster, Hervé and Claudie Fauchier Delavigne, and especially to Laurence Parade, whose imaginative explorations have enhanced every aspect of this work. I thank George Wickes, Jean Chalon, Lillian Morrison, Fanny Myers Brennan, Paul Eyre, Bikou Strong, and the late Audrey Wood for generously sharing their reminiscences and private collections with me. I am grateful to Linda Gaboriau and Ruth Warner for scrupulously notated readings of various versions of the manuscript, and I thank Linda Gaboriau for her considered opinions on French language usage.

For invaluable interviews I am grateful to: Sybille Bedford, the late Eyre de Lanux, Mme René (Bronia) Clair, Buffie Johnson, Cara Lancaster, the late Audrey Wood, Charles Henri Ford, Derek Hill, Jean Chalon, Clarissa Borenius Lada-Grozicka, Honoria Murphy Donnelly, Ivan Nabokov, George Wickes, Judith Karolyi, A. L. Barker, Kevin O'Brien, Lauretta Hugo, M. J. Lancaster, Mary Thacher and the late Peter Thacher, Joy Melville, Robert Maguire, Zita Jungman James.

Thanks also to the late Faith Gillespie, Bernard Minoret, Ginette Billard, Hugo Vickers, Marina Warner, Valerie Eliot, Davis Coakley, Ann Scott-James, Edmund White, Kate Summerscale, David Rose, The Hon Mrs. Desmond Guinness, Odile Hellier and Michael Neal of the Village Voice (bookstore, Paris), Yanic Mercier of the Hôtel Montalembert, Liz Nagle (Basic Books), Jean-François Questiaux (for videography and photography), the Wilbraham Hotel, and the Cornelia Street Café.

I thank my charming and eagle-eyed editor, Lennie Goodings of Virago, for her inspirational courtesies and serious literary support. I thank my equally charming New York editor, John Donatich of Basic Books, for his helpful critiques and excellent conversation. I thank Russell Galen of Scovil Chichak Galen and Derek Johns of A. P. Watt for their elegant agenting and sound advice.

I am grateful to the following institutions and people attached to them: **London:** Principal Registry of the Family Division Somerset House; Guildhall Library; British Museum Library; Theatre Museum Library; Colindale Newspaper Archives; HM Coroner Dr Paul Knapman and Coroner's Officer Geoffrey C. Kirby at the Westminister Coroner's Court Archives; Lydia Cresswell-Jones and the Beaton Archives of Sotheby's; Emma Floyd at The National Portrait Gallery. **Liverpool:** A. D. Lovie of the Archives of the British Psychological Society. **Paris:** François Chapon, Nicole Prévot, and

Paul Cougnard at Fonds Littéraire Jacques Doucet; Bibliothèque Nationale; Ariane de Billy at Bibliothèque de Méteo. **Dublin:** National Library of Ireland; the National Archives; the Genealogical Office. **Philadelphia:** The Rosenbach Museum & Library. **New York:** The Public Library of the City of New York and Julia Van Haaften, in her double capacity as curator and fellow biographer; John McCue at the House of Guerlain. **Los Angeles:** Academy of Motion Picture Arts & Sciences; William Andrews Clark Library. **Austin:** Tara Wenger of the Harry Ransome Center for Humanities Research at the University of Texas.

I am grateful for permissions to quote from manuscripts and documents and/or reproduce from images to: François Chapon, George Plimpton, Eugene and Angela Power, the William Andrews Clark Library, the Cecil Beaton Archives at Sotheby's London, George Wickes, Merlin Holland, Hervé Fauchier Delavigne, Cara Lancaster, Mary Thacher, Sybille Bedford, the late Berthe Cleyrergue, The Authors League Fund (literary executor of the Estate of Djuna Barnes) and Alfred A. Knopf, a Division of Random House, Inc.

And I thank everyone who has ever saved a scrap of handwriting, an old love letter, or a fragment of photograph from the half-forgotten life of an unusual woman in the hope that it might be important; in the hope that *she* might be important.

JOAN SCHENKAR
Paris, New York, Vermont
2000

Selected Bibliography

Acosta, Mercedes de, *Here Lies the Heart* (New York: Reynal, 1960)

Acton, Harold, *Nancy Mitford, a memoir* (London: Hamish Hamilton, 1975)

———, *Memoirs of an Aesthete* (London: Methuen & Co., 1948)

Amor, Anne Clark, *Mrs. Oscar Wilde* (London: Jackson, 1983)

Amory, Mark, *Lord Berners* (London: Chatto & Windus, 1998)

Anonymous, 'Our Lives From Day to Day' *Vogue* (London: 21/2/1934)

Baker, Michael, *Our Three Selves* (New York: William Morrow, 1985)

Barnes, Djuna, *Nightwood* (New York: New Directions, 1961)

———, *Ladies Almanack* (New York: Harper Row, 1972)

———, 'Interview with Alla Nazimova', *Theater Guild* (New York: June 1930)

Barney, Natalie Clifford, *Aventures de l'esprit* (Paris: Emile-Paul, 1929)

———, *Éparpillements*. Présentation Jean Chalon (Paris: Persona, 1982)

———, *Nouvelles pensées de l'Amazone* (Paris: Mercure de France, 1939)

———, *Pensées d'une Amazone* (Paris: Emile-Paule, 1921)

———, *Souvenirs indiscrets* (Paris: Flammarion, 1960)

———, ed. *In Memory of Dorothy Ierne Wilde: Oscaria* (Dijon: Darentière, 1951)

Beach, Sylvia, *Shakespeare and Company* (1956. Reprint, Lincoln: University of Nebraska Press, 1980)

Beckson, Karl, 'The Importance of Being Angry: the mutual antagonism of Oscar and Willie Wilde.' ed. Norman Kiell,. *Blood Brothers: Siblings as Writers* (Int'l Universities Press, 1984)

Beerbohm, M., *Letters to Reggie Turner*, ed. R. Hart-Davis (Philadelphia: Lippincott, 1964)

Behrman, S. N., *Portrait of Max* (New York: Random House, 1960)

Belford, Barbara, *Bram Stoker* (New York: Alfred A. Knopf, 1996)

Bell, Quentin, *Virginia Woolf* (New York: Harcourt Brace, 1972)

Benstock, Shari, *Women of the Left Bank* (Austin: University of Texas Press, 1986)

Billard, Pierre, *Le mystère René Clair* (Paris: Plon, 1998)

Brillat-Savarin, Jean Anthelme, *The Physiology of Taste*, annotated and translated by M. F. K. Fisher (San Francisco: North Point Press, 1986)

Brooks, Louise, *Lulu in Hollywood* (New York: Alfred A. Knopf, 1983)

Burke, Carolyn, *Becoming Modern: The Life of Mina Loy* (New York: Farrar, Straus & Giroux, 1996)

Caracalla, J-P., *Saint-Germain-des-Prés* (Paris: Flammarion, 1996)

Cecil, David, *Max* (New York: Atheneum, 1985)

Chalon, Jean, *Chère Natalie Barney: Portrait d'une séductrice* (Paris: Flammarion, 1992)

————, *Liane de Pougy* (Paris: Livres de Poche, 1994)

Chapon, François and Prévot, Nicole, *Autour de Natalie Clifford Barney* (Paris: Bibliothèque littéraire Jacques Doucet, 1976)

Cheiro, *Cheiro's Memoirs: reminiscences of a society palmist by Cheiro* (London: Ballantyne and Company, 1912)

Cioran, E. M., *A Short History of Decay*, translated by Richard Howard (New York: Quartet Encounters, 1990)

Cleyrergue, Berthe, *Berthe: ou un demi-siècle auprès de l'Amazone* (Paris: Éditions Tierce, 1980)

Cocteau, Jean, *En Verve* (Paris: Pierre Horay, 1973)

————, *Les Enfants Terribles* (Paris: Grasset, 1947)

————, *Opium* (Paris: Stock, 1930)

Colette, Gabrielle, *The Collected Stories of Colette* ed. Robert Phelps (New York: Farrar, Straus & Giroux, 1983)

————, *The Pure and the Impure*, translated by Herma Briffault, Introduction by Janet Flanner (New York: Farrar, Straus & Giroux, 1967)

————, *Chéri and The Last of Chéri* (London: Penguin, 1954)

————, *The Vagabond* (New York: Wings Books, 1995)

Cunard, Victor and Thompson, Sylvia, *Golden Arrow* (London: Heinemann, 1935)

Daintrey, Adrian, *I Must Say* (London: Chatto and Windus, 1963)

Dearborn, Mary V., *Queen of Bohemia: Life of Louise Bryant* (Boston: Houghton Mifflin, 1996)

Donnelly, Honoria Murphy, *Sara and Gerald* (New York: Holt, Rinehart and Winston, 1984)

Donoghue, Denis, *Walter Pater* (New York: Alfred A. Knopf, 1995)

Dormann, Geneviève, *Colette: A Passion For Life*, translated by David Macey and Jane Brenton (New York: Abbeville Press, 1985) Originally published as *Amoureuse Colette* (Paris: Éditions Herscher, 1984)

Douglas, Lord Alfred, *Oscar Wilde: A Summing Up* (London: Duckworth, 1940)

Ellman, Mary, *Thinking About Women* (New York: Harcourt Brace, 1968)

Ellman, Richard, *Oscar Wilde* (New York: Alfred A. Knopf, 1984)

Eyre de Lanux, Elizabeth, 'Letters of Elizabeth', *Town and Country* (1922–4)

Faderman, Lillian, *Surpassing the Love of Men* (New York: William Morrow, 1981)

Fallowell, Duncan and Ashley, April, *April Ashley's Odyssey* (London: Jonathan Cape, 1982)

Field, Andrew, *Djuna: The Life and Times of Djuna Barnes* (New York: G.P. Putnam's Sons, 1983)

Fitch, Noel Riley, *Sylvia Beach and the Lost Generation* (New York: W. W. Norton, 1983)

Flanner, Janet, *Paris Was Yesterday* ed. Irving Drutman (New York: Popular Library, 1972)

Ford, Hugh, ed., *Nancy Cunard: Brave Poet, Indomitable Rebel, 1896–1965* (Philadelphia: Chilton, 1968)

Foster, Jeannette, *Sex Variant Women in Literature* (Baltimore: Diana Press, 1975)

Garber, Marjorie, *Vested Interests* (New York, London: Routledge, 1992)

Gilbert, Sandra M. and Gubar, Susan, *The Madwoman in the Attic* (New Haven: Yale University Press, 1979)

Gilman, Richard, *Decadence* (New York: Farrar, Straus & Giroux, 1979)

Glendinning, Victoria, *Vita* (London: Penguin Books, 1983)

———, *Edith Sitwell: A Unicorn Among Lions* (London: Phoenix, 1988)

Gourmont, Rémy de, *Histoires magiques et autres récits* (Paris: 1918, 1982)

Gramont, Élisabeth de, *Mémoires* 4 vols (Paris: Grasset, 1928)

Grindea, Miron, ed., 'The Amazon of Letters: A World Tribute to Natalie Clifford Barney' (*ADAM International Review* 299, 1962)

Guggenheim, Peggy, *Out of this Century* (New York: Universe Books, 1987)

Hall, Delight, *Catalogue of The Alice Pike Barney Memorial Lending Collection* (Washington, DC: Smithsonian Institution, 1965)

Hall, Radclyffe, *The Well of Loneliness* (London: Jonathan Cape, 1928)

Hamnet, Nina, *Laughing Torso* (London: Constable & Co., 1932)

Hardwick, Elizabeth, *Seduction and Betrayal* (New York: Vintage Books, 1975)

Harris, Frank, *Oscar Wilde*, (London: Constable & Co., 1938)

Hart-Davis, Rupert, ed., *The Letters of Oscar Wilde*, (London: Hart-Davis, 1962)

Heilbrun, Carolyn G., *Writing A Woman's Life* (New York: Ballantine Books, 1988)

Herring, Philip, *Djuna: The Life and Work of Djuna Barnes* (New York: Viking, 1995)

Hichens, Robert, *The Green Carnation* (London: Robin Clark, 1992)

Hoare, Philip, *Serious Pleasures: The Life of Stephen Tennant* (New York: Penguin, 1990)

Hodgson, Simon, 'Sublime Governess' (*New Statesman* 65, 22 February 1963): 268.

Holland, Merlin, *The Wilde Album* (London: Fourth Estate, 1997)

Holland, Vyvyan, *Son of Oscar Wilde* (London: R. Hart-Davis, 1954)

Holroyd, James Edward, 'Brother of Oscar' (*Blackwood's Magazine*, March 1974)

Hyde, H. Montgomery, ed., *The Trials of Oscar Wilde* (London: William Hodge, 1948)

Israel, Lee, *Miss Tallulah Bankhead* (New York: G.P. Putnam's Sons, 1972)

Jamison, Kay Redfield, *Touched With Fire: Manic-Depressive Illness and the Artistic Temperament* (New York: The Free Press, 1993)

Jullian, Philippe and Phillips, John, *Violet Trefusis* (New York: Harcourt Brace 1976)

Kaplan, Louise, *Female Perversions: The Temptations of Emma Bovary* (New York: Doubleday, 1991)

Kasl, Charlotte D., *Women, Sex and Addiction* (New York: Harper & Row, 1990)

Katz, Jonathan Ned, *The Invention of Heterosexuality* (New York: Dutton, 1995)

Kelley's Post Office Directories; Kelley's Street Directories (1927–1936) entries for Miss D. Wilde (Guildhall Library)

King, Viva, *The Weeping and the Laughter* (London: Macdonald and Jane, 1976)

Lambert, Gavin, *Nazimova* (New York: Alfred A. Knopf, 1997)

Lauris, Georges, *Itinéraire d'un enfant terrible: de Cocteau à Cîteaux* (Paris: Presses de la Renaissance, 1998)

Louÿs, Pierre, *The Songs of Bilitis*, translated by M. S. Buck (New York: Capricorn Books, 1966)

McKenna, Stephen, *Tex* (New York: Dodd, Mead & Co, 1922)

Meade, Marion, *Dorothy Parker: What Fresh Hell Is This?* (New York: Penguin, 1989)

Mellow, James R., *Charmed Circle* (New York: Praeger, 1974)

Melville, Joy, *Mother of Oscar* (London: John Murray, 1994)

Milford, Nancy, *Zelda* (New York: Harper & Row, 1970)

Mitford, Nancy, *The Nancy Mitford Omnibus* (London: Penguin, 1974)

Mosley, Charlotte, ed., *A Talent to Annoy: Nancy Mitford's Essays, Journalism and Reviews 1929–1968* (London: Sceptre, 1996)

————, *Love From Nancy: the Letters of Nancy Mitford* (London: Hodder & Stoughton, 1993)

————, *The Letters of Nancy Mitford and Evelyn Waugh* (London: Hodder & Stoughton, 1997)

Mugnier, Arthur, *Journal de l'Abbé Mugnier (1879–1939)* (Paris: Mercure de France, 1985)

Murphy, Esther, Unpublished letters and documents to and from Esther Murphy, including drafts of 'The Sublime Governess' and 'A Marriage of Conscience'. (Collection of Honoria Murphy Donnelly)

O'Neal, Hank, *Life is painful, nasty and short . . .* (New York: Paragon House, 1990)

Osborne, Laurence, *The Poisoned Embrace: A Brief History of Sexual Pessimism* (New York: Vintage, 1994)

Parkin, Michael, ed., *Exhibition Catalogue for 'Rognon de la Flèche'* (1989)

Pearson, Hesketh, *The Life of Oscar Wilde* (London: Methuen, 1948)

Phelps, Robert, ed., *Belles Saisons: A Colette Scrapbook* (New York: Farrar, Strauss & Giroux, 1978)

Pohorilenko, Anatole, *The Travel Albums of George Platt Lynes, Monroe Wheeler, and Glenway Wescott: 1925–1935* (Arena Editions, 1998)

Pougy, Liane de, *My Blue Notebooks*, trans. by Diana Athill (London: André Deutsch, 1979)

Putnam, Samuel, *Paris Was Our Mistress* (New York: Viking Press, 1947)

Quincey, Thos. De, *Confessions of An English Opium-Eater* (New York: Hurst and Company, 1822)

Rodker, John, *The Future of Futurism* (London: Paul, Trench, Trubman, 1926)

Root, Waverly, *The Paris Edition* (Berkeley: North Point Press, 1987)

Scharff, Virginia, *Taking the Wheel* (New York: The Free Press, 1991)

Schenkar, Joan, 'The Last of the Wildes' (*The Wildean* 10, 1997): 68–69.

Schmidgall, Gary, *The Stranger Wilde* (New York: Dutton, 1994)

Secrest, Meryle *Between Me and Life: A Biography of Romaine Brooks* (Garden City, NY: Doubleday, 1974)

Smith, Jane S., *Elsie de Wolfe* (New York: Atheneum, 1982)

Souhami, Diana, *The Trials of Radclyffe Hall* (London: Weidenfeld & Nicolson, 1998)

Steegmuller, Francis, *Jean Cocteau* (Boston: Little, Brown, 1970)

Stein, Gertrude, *Lectures in America* (Boston: Beacon Press, 1985)

———, *Paris France* (New York: Liveright, 1970)

Sterne, Madeleine B., *Purple Passage: The Life of Mrs. Frank Leslie* (Tulsa: University of Oklahoma Press, 1953)

Suleiman, Susan Rubin, ed., *The Female Body in Western Culture* (Cambridge: Harvard University Press, 1986)

Summerscale, Kate, *The Queen of Whale Cay* (London: Fourth Estate, 1997)

Thurman, Judith, *Secrets of the Flesh: A Life of Colette* (New York: Alfred A. Knopf, 1999)

Toklas, Alice B., *The Alice B. Toklas Cook Book* Foreword by M. F. K. Fisher (New York: Harper & Row, 1986)

———, *What Is Remembered* (San Francisco: North Point Press, 1985)

Troubridge, Laura, *Life Amongst the Troubridges*, ed. Jaqueline Hope-Nicholson (London: Tite Street Press, 1999)

Valery-Radot, Pasteur, *Mémoires d'un non-conformiste (1896–1966)* (Paris: Grasset, 1966)

Vickers, Hugo, *Cecil Beaton* (New York: Primus, Donald I. Fine, 1985)

Wharton, Edith, *The House of Mirth* (New York: Collier Books, 1987)

White, Terence De Vere, *The Parents of Oscar Wilde* (London: Hodder & Stoughton, 1967)

Who's Who (London) 1956. Entries for Sir Austin Edward Harris, Osbert Lancaster, C.B.E.

Wickes, George, *The Amazon of Letters* (New York: G.P. Putnam's Sons, 1976)

Wilde, Oscar, *The Complete Works of Oscar Wilde*, introd. by Vyvyan Holland (London, Glasgow: Collins, 1990)

Wilson, T. G. *Victorian Doctor* (London: EP Publishing, 1974. pp. 306–8, 315–325)

Wineapple, Brenda, *Gênet* (New York: Ticknor and Fields, 1980)

————, *Sister Brother: Gertrude and Leo Stein. New York* (New York: G.P. Putnam's Sons, 1996)

Wolff, Charlotte, M. D., *Love Between Women* (New York: Harper Colophon, 1971)

————, *On The Way To Myself* (London: Methuen, 1967)

————, *The Hand in Psychological Diagnosis* (New York: Philosophical Library, 1952)

————, *The Human Hand* (London: Methuen, 1942)

Woolf, Virginia, *A Room of One's Own* (New York: Harcourt Brace, 1989)

Ziegler, Philip, *Osbert Sitwell* (New York: Alfred A. Knopf, 1999)

Index